THE LEGACY OF APOLLO: ANTIQUITY, AUTHORITY,
AND CHAUCERIAN POETICS

JAMIE C. FUMO

The Legacy of Apollo

Antiquity, Authority, and Chaucerian Poetics

UNIVERSITY OF TORONTO PRESS
Toronto Buffalo London

ISBN 978-1-4426-4170-9

Printed on acid-free, 100 per cent post-consumer recycled paper with
vegetable-based inks.

Library and Archives Canada Cataloguing in Publication

Fumo, Jamie Claire, 1976–
The legacy of Apollo : antiquity, authority and Chaucerian poetics /
Jamie C. Fumo.

Includes bibliographical references and index.
ISBN 978-1-4426-4170-9

1. Chaucer, Geoffrey, d. 1400 – Criticism and interpretation.   2. Apollo (Greek
deity) in literature.   3. English poetry – Middle English, 1100–1500 – History
and criticism.   4. England – Intellectual life – 1066–1485.   I. Title.

PR1924.F86 2010   821'.1   C2010-901237-2

This book has been published with the help of a grant from the Humanities
and Social Sciences Federation of Canada, through the Aid to Scholarly
Publications Program, using funds provided by the Social Sciences and
Humanities Research Council of Canada.

University of Toronto Press acknowledges the financial assistance to its
publishing program of the Canada Council for the Arts and the Ontario Arts
Council.

University of Toronto Press acknowledges the financial support of the
Government of Canada through the Canada Book Fund for its publishing
activities.

For Vincent and Rocco
Al this mene I by Love

Contents

Illustrations

Acknowledgments

If, as Ovid claims at the end of the *Metamorphoses*, the 'better part' of an author is her book, the best of all surely is the intellectual generosity and goodwill of friends and colleagues which have improved both book and author. I want first to thank John V. Fleming, who supervised the Princeton University doctoral dissertation out of which this book developed, and whose penetrating scholarship, rare wit, and personal integrity set a standard to which I have long aspired as a scholar. From John I learned the importance of reading *all* available criticism on a given topic, or at least trying one's best; the thrill of watching sparks fly between medieval and ancient poets (and modern critics); the value of eschewing critical fads and alluring gimmicks; and the felicity of regarding Chaucer as a poet among poets. Vance Smith, second reader of my doctoral dissertation, provided crucial input that challenged me to reconceptualize many aspects of the work and to nuance my theoretical assumptions as I transformed the project from dissertation to book.

That metamorphosis, as dramatic – and at times gruesome – as most of those Ovid describes, formed the major enterprise of the first period of my professional career, initially in a visiting appointment at Mount Holyoke College, where Carolyn Collette was a most generous and supportive senior colleague, and then at McGill University, where I am fortunate to be part of a vibrant community of medievalists and scholars in other fields whose interests happily intersect with my own. Dorothy Bray and Sebastian Sobecki, fellow medievalists in the English Department at McGill while I was at work on this book, both read sections in draft and offered valuable feedback and warm encouragement. Faith Wallis in the History Department, with characteristic intellectual enthusiasm, directed me toward fundamental primary and secondary materials in the history of medicine that facilitated my study of Apollo Medicus. Faith, together with Carlos Fraenkel, Jamil Ragep, and Robert Wisnovsky, collaborators in a McGill-based research group on medieval textual transmission, challenged me to consider how the phenomena explored in this book partake of a cross-disciplinary and cross-cultural matrix of learning. My greatest scholarly debt at McGill has been to Maggie Kilgour, whose work on Ovidian intertextuality in the Renaissance helped me immeasurably to situate Chaucer's responses to classical antiquity and trace Ovidian chains of association. In addition to reading substantial portions of the manuscript, Maggie prompted me over the course of numerous conversations to think broadly through the ideas in it, always believing resolutely in the project's value. My chairman Paul Yachnin has been an unflagging supporter of my scholarship; his leadership and good counsel have made the English Department at McGill a most fulfilling place in which to complete this book. Finally, two McGill doctoral candidates deserve warm thanks: Rory Critten, for assisting with Old French and Anglo-Norman translations; and Jake Walsh Morrissey, for providing heroic research and editorial assistance as this book neared completion.

My scholarly debts, to be sure, reach beyond my home institution. Frank Coulson has been a greatly valued mentor and friend whose unparalleled knowledge of the medieval Ovidian commentary tradition has enriched this study in vital ways. Significant portions of the research pertaining to medieval commentaries on Ovid included in the first two chapters of this book were undertaken in June 2004 when I held a Virginia Brown Postdoctoral Fellowship in Palaeography at the Center for Epigraphical and Palaeographical Studies at Ohio State University, where I worked with the splendid microfilm archive of Ovid manuscripts under Frank's supervision and benefited greatly from his expertise. Donald Maddox and Sara Sturm-Maddox generously provided research materials assembled by the late Judson Boyce Allen which guided me to lesser-known Ovid commentaries. Stephanie Kamath drew my attention to the relevance of Guillaume de Deguileville's *Pèlerinage de vie humaine* and offered timely insight into its points of intersection with the *Manciple's Tale*. C. David Benson and James Simpson graciously read this book in manuscript and supported its journey into print with an enthusiasm and conviction for which I am deeply appreciative. The two anonymous readers of the manuscript for University of Toronto Press offered many valuable observations that helped me improve the book's stylistic presentation and clarify particular junctures of its argument. Suzanne Rancourt and Barb Porter were responsive and discerning editors whose professionalism made the complexities of the publication process far less daunting to navigate. My most profound gratitude is to my husband Vincent, who accompanied this project throughout its entire life cycle, abided its many intrusions on civilized existence, and improved every page of it through countless painstaking readings. I am lucky for, and endlessly inspired by, the 'joie and bisy-nesse' (*Tr* 3.1413) of sharing Chaucer with him for so long.

This book was completed with the support of a Programme d'établissement de nouveaux professeurs-chercheurs grant from the government of Quebec's Fonds de recherche sur la société et la culture (FQRSC). Research for this project was conducted at Princeton University's Firestone Library, McGill University's McLennan-Redpath Library and Osler Library of the History of Medicine, the Warburg Institute of the University of London, and the British Library. I am grateful to the staff of all of these libraries for their unfailing assistance. Portions of this book were presented in earlier forms as invited lectures and conference papers at Carleton University, Fordham University, Harvard University, McGill University, Ohio State University, Sewanee (University of the South), University of Connecticut-Storrs, University of Leeds, University of Toronto, and University of Wisconsin-Madison. The feedback offered by audience members at these scholarly venues helped greatly in this book's completion, and I warmly thank the organizers of these events and all those who offered input. What faults remain in the book are, of course, my own. Drunken mice and sober scholars alike 'seken faste after felicitee, / But we goon wrong ful often, trewely' (*KnT* 1266–7).

Portions of this book appeared previously in journal articles and chapters of edited collections. An earlier version of a brief section of chapter 1 formed part of '"Little *Troilus*": *Heroides* 5 and Its Ovidian Contexts in Chaucer's *Troilus and Criseyde*' in *Studies in Philology* 100.3 (2003): 278–314. A segment of the fourth chapter was originally included, in different form, in 'Aurelius' Prayer, *Franklin's Tale* 1031–79: Sources and Analogues,' *Neophilologus* 88 (2004): 623–35, incorporated here with kind permission of Springer Science and Business Media. Finally, parts of the Introduction and fourth chapter reframe a short section of 'Chaucer as *Vates*? Reading Ovid through Dante in the *House of Fame*, Book 3,' in *Writers Reading Writers: Intertextual Studies in Medieval and Early Modern Literature in Honor of Robert Hollander*, ed. Janet Levarie Smarr (Newark: University of Delaware Press, 2007),

89–108. I am grateful to Oxbow Books for permission to quote from D.E. Hill's four-volume edition and translation of Ovid's *Metamorphoses*, published by Aris & Phillips.

Abbreviations

Periodicals and Reference Works

AJP	*American Journal of Philology*
BHM	*Bulletin of the History of Medicine*
CCSL	*Corpus Christianorum Series Latina*
ChR	*The Chaucer Review*
CJ	*The Classical Journal*
CP	*Classical Philology*
CQ	*Classical Quarterly*
ELH	*English Literary History*
ES	*English Studies*
IJCT	*International Journal of the Classical Tradition*
JEGP	*Journal of English and Germanic Philology*
MAe	*Medium Aevum*
MED	*Middle English Dictionary*
MP	*Modern Philology*
OED	*Oxford English Dictionary*
OLD	*Oxford Latin Dictionary*
PL	*Patrologia Latina*
RES	*Review of English Studies*
SAC	*Studies in the Age of Chaucer*
SP	*Studies in Philology*
TPAPA	*Transactions and Proceedings of the American Philological Association*
UTQ	*University of Toronto Quarterly*
VC	*Vigiliae Christianae*

Mythographers

VM I	First Vatican Mythographer
VM II	Second Vatican Mythographer
VM III	Third Vatican Mythographer
Remi-CMC	Remigius Autissiodorensis, *Commentum in Martianum Capellam*
Bern-CMC	Bernardus Silvestris, *Commentary on Martianus Capella's* De Nuptiis Philologiae et Mercurii

Abbreviations of titles of Chaucer's works follow the *Riverside Chaucer*, p. 779.

THE LEGACY OF APOLLO: ANTIQUITY, AUTHORITY,
AND CHAUCERIAN POETICS

Introduction

A young Apollo, golden-haired,
  Stands dreaming on the verge of strife,
Magnificently unprepared
  For the long littleness of life.

Frances Cornford, 'Youth' (1910)

The classical god Apollo, like his young protégé in Cornford's verses, may have been unprepared for the melodrama of the quotidian in which he frequently found himself a luckless player. Celebrated prophet and god of eternal youth that he was, however, Apollo assuredly took solace in the rich and extensive afterlife that would be his. Apollo's legacy in post-classical culture is indeed illustrious, embodied in the numerous Renaissance paintings and engravings portraying the god as leader of the Muses, the Arts, or the Graces; the long-lived cult of fascination with the Apollo Belvedere upon its rediscovery in the late fifteenth century; the celebration of Apollo as the quintessence of Doric art in all its rational majesty in Nietzsche's *Birth of Tragedy*; and, even, closer to our own day, the aspirations of modern science to defy human limitations in the Apollo Program space missions. Apollo's substantial and complex afterlife in the Middle Ages, however, has yet to be acknowledged, much less critically defined or theorized. The many medieval intellectuals and creative artists who appropriated and struggled with Apollo and his legacy were every bit as acquainted with Apollo's celebrity: for them, Apollo was the quintessential emblem – the truth-bearing yet necessarily contested voice – of pagan antiquity. To engage with Apollo was therefore to engage with a perpetually reinvented tradition of thought, expression, and worship. It was to engage with the idea of tradition itself.

This book explores the imaginative status of Apollo, god of poetry and truth, in the literary and mythographic discourses of late medieval England. It excavates Apollo's rich position in the reconceptualization of authorship, authority, and the capacities of the vernacular at a time when the precedent of classical antiquity was appropriated in increasingly complex ways – in England as on the Continent – to serve new forms of cultural expression. It is no coincidence that Apollo looms large in the works of the medieval English poet most consciously and creatively to engage with classical tradition: Geoffrey Chaucer.[1] From the early dream-visions to the last notes of the *Canterbury Tales*, Apollo is a central and intricately wrought presence in Chaucer's imaginative encounters with the Latin classics, at once guiding and haunting the poet's construction – tentative and self-reflexive as it was – of a cult of authority in English poetry. Because Apollo is not merely a pagan god but a focal point of shifting attitudes regarding inspiration, eloquence, and authority, he functions, in effect, as a nerve centre in the still-uncharted anatomy of Chaucer's self-fashioning as inheritor and transmitter of the classical tradition in English. Chaucer's vernacular experimentation with antique form and subject matter together with classical vocabularies of poetic vocation and ambition led, in the century after his death, to the (in many ways unlikely) reinvention of Chaucer himself as a kind of Apollo figure: a semi-mythic icon of literary *auctoritas*.[2] To trace the mythic history of Apollo in the Middle Ages, then, is to restore to our understanding of medieval English intellectual culture an intriguing chapter in the history of literary authority and its anxieties. Adopting medieval England as a geographic focus of Apollo's afterlife and the poetry of Chaucer and his most immediate followers as field of study, this book redresses the lack of critical attention to Apollo's literary and mythographic transmission in the Middle Ages, at the same time that it situates Chaucer as an active collaborator in the remythologization of classical conceptions of authority and poetic inspiration by which Apollo was translated from Ovid's Rome to 'Brutes Albyon,'[3] and by which Chaucer himself, in the years after his death, would be metamorphosed from maker to *vates*.

Ruptures of Authority: Apollo on the Edge of Text

We begin in 1819, at a moment seemingly far removed from Chaucer's enterprising, late medieval negotiations with his recalcitrant muse. In

April of that year, a distant literary descendant of Chaucer, John Keats, abandoned his mythological epic *Hyperion* partway through its third book, in the midst of the metamorphosis of its hero, Apollo, into an immortal Olympian fated to supplant the dethroned Titan Hyperion. In a letter to John Hamilton Reynolds dated 21 September 1819, Keats attributes *Hyperion*'s incompletion to his dissatisfaction with its Miltonic character.[4] But it is equally true that the poem collapses under the physical stress of Apollo's traumatic apotheosis, which seems to be more than the final lines can sustain: 'At length / Apollo shrieked – and lo! from all his limbs / Celestial ...' (*Hyperion* 3.135–6).[5] With these words the poem ends abruptly. What simultaneously overwhelms and deifies Apollo is the force of 'knowledge enormous' (3.113) of a specifically textual sort, reflected in the face of Mnemosyne (traditionally, mother of the Muses):

Names, deeds, grey legends, dire events, rebellions,
Majesties, sovran voices, agonies,
Creations and destroyings, all at once
Pour into the wide hollows of my brain[.]   (3.114–17)

Just as Keats elsewhere observes of the poet 'an[ni]hilated' by the identity of those he encounters, so is Apollo, as universal poet, at once overcome and transformed by the weight of literary history.[6] As Carol L. Bernstein aptly puts it, Apollo's 'immortality emerges as the afterlife of old texts, as the creation of divine and poetic catastrophe.'[7]

The extent to which the not-yet-divine Apollo stands for the human poet, who can similarly transcend human limitations through imaginative vision, is confirmed by Keats's reworking of this poem later the same year in the *Fall of Hyperion*. Here, the poet-narrator himself replaces Apollo as the central transformed consciousness of the poem, and 'faded, far-flown Apollo' (*Fall* 204) is but an absent presence in a dream-world. Keats's association of Apollo in the earlier *Hyperion* with the overwhelming force of literary tradition – the very stuff by which human authors court immortality – epitomizes Apollo's enduring identification with textual authority as a Foucauldian complex of power, knowledge, and truth. Apollo's question to Mnemosyne just before his metamorphosis – 'Where is power?' (*Hyperion* 3.103) – reveals that what is at stake here, in Foucault's terms, is a contestation within a geneaology of power legitimized by an apparatus of knowledge (literary tradition) from which issues the poetic commodity of 'truth.' Such authoritative power, however, betrays its human origins by destabilizing the very artistic structures that would sustain it, resulting in textual fragmentation. If progress, in *Hyperion*, is possible only through a catastrophic break with the past,[8] the Apolline mythology of literary history in which the poet seeks to enrol himself – just as Keats struggles in the poem to follow the titanic Milton, Shakespeare, and Dante – is itself a deeply vulnerable one, in which the poet's 'limbs celestial' may well be left half-formed at the limen of the fallible text.

With this paradox we find ourselves in the same conceptual neighbourhood as Chaucer's own 'chamber of maiden thought,' the House of Fame, in which the exuberant force of literary history and the reality of communicative rupture similarly interpenetrate. In a celebrated Ovidio-Dantean apostrophe, Chaucer invokes Apollo at the beginning of Book Three of the *House of Fame* for poetic guidance in his versification of the climactic scenes of his dream: his tour of the houses of Fame and Rumour. But Apollo – invoked here for the first time in English – proves to be a most unhelpful authorial guide. By the end of the third book, the monologic authority of the 'God of science and of lyght' (*HF* 1091) has been substantially depreciated as the scene shifts from the absolute pronouncements of Fame's court to the dialogic barter of rumour among shipmen, pilgrims, and pardoners (no doubt slouching toward the Tabard to be born). Finally, a mysterious 'man of gret auctorite' – so he 'semed' – is peremptorily defaced, like Keats's reborn Apollo, by the abrupt termination of the text (*HF* 2157–8). While it is doubtless coincidental that both Keats's *Hyperion* and Chaucer's *House of Fame* are fragmentary 'epics' that break off in mid-sentence in their respective third books, the two poems' analogous association of Apollo, font of literary tradition, with the dissolution of the text in the face of authority is hardly casual: it indicates a deep-seated ambivalence surrounding Apollo as epitome and medium of textual authority. As we shall see, this is a specifically English form of ambivalence, although one shaped by a broadly European fascination with Apollo, and it takes its origins in Chaucer's distillation of vernacular eloquence from classical and medieval conceptions of Apollo as a hermeneutic force in cultural expression.

Apollo and the Critics

Apollo is the most complex and elusive of the Olympian gods, following closely upon Jupiter in importance. As such, he has generated a considerable body of scholarship in the fields of classical studies, religious history, and comparative anthropology, much of which aims to penetrate the 'essence' of Apollo or elucidate the historical features of Apollo and Apolline cults.[9] Two important book-length studies of the Greco-Roman Apollo have been published in the last decade and a half, indicating renewed interest in the god among classicists as well as heightened attention to Apollo's ideological function as a mythic figure associated with both religious ritual and political propaganda. The first, Jon Solomon's collection of diversely authored essays, *Apollo: Origins and Influences* (1994), fruitfully offers 'a fresh attempt to understand not only the original essence of Apollo but his multiple variations, hybrids, and influences' from the archaic period through the Silver Age.[10] The second, Marcel Detienne's suggestively titled *Apollon le couteau à la main* (1998), explores the ambivalent nature of Greek cultic treatments of Apollo, particularly his association with oracles, colonization and foundation legends, purification, and sacrifice. Detienne's study is especially important for calling attention to the darker aspects of Apollo, such as his frequently impetuous and punitive behaviour, that have been obscured by the canonical idealization of the god as a serenely rational and intellectually luminous figure.[11] Rounding out this recent renewal of attention to Apollo's cult is the provocative reexamination of his cohorts, the Muses, in Efrossini Spentzou's and Don Fowler's *Cultivating the Muse: Struggles for Power and Inspiration in Classical Literature* (2002), which views power dynamics and contests of authority within discourses of classical inspiration as related broadly to poetic practice, a matter treated only indirectly by the volume's contributors in relation to Apollo as inspiring agent.[12]

None of these wide-ranging studies devotes attention to Apollo's mythic legacy in the Middle Ages. Mary E. Barnard's *The Myth of Apollo and Daphne from Ovid to Quevedo: Love, Agon, and the Grotesque* (1987), by contrast, is substantially concerned with Apollo's medieval development. Her valuable analysis is confined, however, to the transmission of a single Apolline myth which, though probably the most popular, provides only a partial picture of Apollo's significance to medieval mythographers and poets. Furthermore, Barnard's focus on the literary appropriation of the Ovidian Apollo and his later allegorizations in the medieval and Renaissance literature and art of the Mediterranean leaves unexplored classical traditions of Apollo beyond Ovid as well as the god's reception in the British Isles. At the same time, Barnard's structuring concern with imagery of conflict and hybridity in Apollo's erotic pursuit of Daphne, while rewarding, somewhat limits her treatment – and, indeed, her selection – of the literary evidence. Because it is focused in these ways, Barnard's study, while it enriches our understanding of the narratological power of one particular Apolline melodrama, does not approach the larger, metapoetic issue of what it means for a medieval vernacular poet to frame his own poetic activity, and indeed his conception of antiquity, in relation to the classical Apollo.

Although questions such as those posed here regarding the medieval Apollo have not yet attracted the attention they deserve, scholarship on medieval literary encounters with classical antiquity has made vigorous advancements in recent years. Increasingly, older, positivistic models of source analysis and mythic evolution have been enriched by critical interest in the implications of literary appropriations of pagan mythology for medieval poetics more generally, and resituated within a new recognition of the dynamic forms of exchange between Latin and vernacular modes of discourse.[13] Thus defined, medieval English poetic attitudes toward antiquity are manifested in a range of forms: in the direct, humanistic encounters between medieval and ancient authors described by Winthrop Wetherbee and John V. Fleming in their respective studies of Chaucer's *Troilus and Criseyde*; in the profound creative influence of Ovidianism upon Chaucer's narrative procedures and writerly identity variously documented by John M. Fyler, Helen Cooper, and Michael Calabrese; in the shaping force of scholastic exegesis and mythographic commentary upon medieval conceptions of antiquity illuminated by A.J. Minnis in *Chaucer and Pagan Antiquity* and by Jane Chance in a series of encyclopedic studies and collections of essays; and in the mutually implicated operations of gender, subjectivity, and mythography identified by Theresa Tinkle, Kathryn L. McKinley, and Suzanne Hagedorn. Implicit, in varying degrees, in all of these studies is a heightened sensitivity to the ways in which medieval poets' appropriations of classical myth draw attention to the process and status of poetic creation itself. As Renate Blumenfeld-Kosinski observes of medieval French literature, 'rather than being folded directly into the story, myths tend to be integrated into the new texts in self-consciously "artistic" ways,' thus defying 'complete fusion with the text that receives them.'[14] In the poetry of Chaucer and his followers, poetic allusions to Apollo confirm the essential intertextuality and artificial quality of myth at the same time that they extend dramatically the implications of such artistic self-consciousness into these poets' own construction of themselves as vernacular heirs – albeit problematically belated ones – of classical *auctoritas*.

Apollo and Vernacular Poetic Identity

Although the medieval English Apollo remains an obscure figure,[15] the god of poetry's escapades in the literature of medieval Italy and France have not gone unobserved, even if they have not resulted in a synthetic book-length study. Petrarch's creative dialogue with the Apollo and Daphne myth in the *Canzoniere* – which Chaucer, who translates one of its sonnets in the 'Canticus Troili,' knew at least in part[16] – has been studied extensively as an evocation of the 'interiorized complexity of the poetic self' and the act of poetic memorialization.[17] Sylvia Huot draws attention to the comparable, if less frequently noted, significance of Apollo as a substantiating force in the new claims to authority for vernacular poetry by fourteenth-century French poets such as Machaut, Froissart, and Deschamps.[18] In the *dits amoureux*, a rich crucible of mythographic invention for medieval French poets, Apollo is on several occasions identified provocatively or otherwise associated with the God of Love, his traditional antagonist.[19] For example, in a central scene of Froissart's *La prison amoureuse* modelled upon Ovid's story of Pygmalion, it is Phebus, rather than Venus, who brings to life a lover's statue of his beloved, in response to a prayer that acts as a kind of *summa* of Apolline myth. In the *Prison amoureuse*'s internal series of epistolary exchanges, Apollo is hermeneutically equated with the God of Love himself.[20] Huot accounts for this trend of association between Love and Apollo, which also informs a late thirteenth-century interpolation in the *Roman de la rose* in which the God of Love rhetorically allies himself with Apollo as enemy of Marsyas, as a conscious move in French poets' establishment of the 'newly emerging figure of the learned author of love poetry.'[21] By conflating the territories of Love and Apollo, that is, French poets legitimize and lend authority of a classicizing variety to vernacular erotic poetry. At the same time, they expose (in an essentially Ovidian way) the subterfuge of a literary sensibility in which the Venerean sentimental reality of love is subsumed by Apolline poetic artifice and the lover 'becomes an instrument of himself as poet.'[22] Ultimately, for Huot, the French association of Apollo, himself both a poet and a lover, with the production of love poetry licenses a vernacular *auctoritas* with roots in Petrarchan paradox, in which Apollo acts as 'a figure for the poet who creates a monument at once enduring and beautiful, commemorative of love, yet at the same time embodying the eternal prolongation of desire, the absence of the beloved, the experience of loss.'[23]

The medieval poet's pose as lover, which Petrarch and medieval French poets refined using Apollo as a mythographic point of reference, was a fertile and contentious field of experimentation in the development of vernacular *auctoritas* in England as well. In his elegant 1991 essay 'De Vulgari Auctoritate: Chaucer, Gower and the Men of Great Authority,' A.J. Minnis contends that Chaucer's and Gower's divergent approaches to the pose of the lover-poet illuminate their essentially opposing attitudes toward the prospect of self-enrolment within an authoritative lineage of poetry based upon an 'allegorical rationalization of fiction' in service to the absolute truths of philosophy. In Minnis's reading, Chaucer's self-imposed distance from the lover-poet pose reveals his conscious rejection of the narrative conventions of the *dits amoureux* and thus functions as a de-authorizing strategy by which Chaucer styles himself a reporter or compiler, as opposed to an *auctor*.[24] In Gower's poetry, on the other hand, attraction to the erotic ideology of the *dits amoureux* creates tensions within a broader adoption of authorizing strategies associated with the scholastic commentary tradition on ancient *auctores*, by which Gower strives to carve out a space of vernacular *auctoritas* for himself as philosophical poet.[25] In both cases, the Continental notion of authority as an empowering, if inexact, textualization of desire is treated critically, even to some extent deconstructed, by medieval English poets.

Theresa Tinkle's 1996 book on the gods of love in medieval English poetry reorients the terms of Minnis's inquiry, in directions germane to the present study, by exploring the mythographic dimensions of the lover-poet pose in relation to vernacular *auctoritas*. Arguing that the medieval Venus and Cupid are multitudinous figures that function as potently contrasting 'symbols of poetic influences' for English vernacular poets, Tinkle identifies Cupid with the tyrannical artificiality of French making that Chaucer rejects, along with the conventionality of the lover-poet pose, in favour of the cosmological, humanist poetics of Venus, whose sponsorship of a 'classicizing dream of vernacular sensuousness and eloquence' distinctly informs Chaucer's poetry.[26] Chaucer thus emerges, in Tinkle's reading, as the 'poet of Venus and Cupid': these deities centrally impel Chaucer's classicizing poetics and legacy as 'the Ovid of English poetry.'[27] As Tinkle herself acknowledges, however, medieval poets' appropriations of these protean classical figures often defy such neat classification. Gower's *Confessio amantis*, for example, conflates the cosmological Venus with the 'narrow amatory conventions' of the makers' Cupid,[28] and these figures are, in any case,

hardly unique as poetic influences in Chaucer's mythographic universe. Although Chaucer invokes Venus as a partner of the Muses in
Book Two of the *House of Fame* after having toured her Virgilian temple,
the goddess of love is crucially displaced in the invocation of the final
book of the poem by Apollo, who (as god of poetry) figuratively presides over the House of Fame. As Tinkle observes, 'just as Venus supplants Morpheus [invoked in Book One of the *House of Fame*], so Apollo
takes her place.'[29] My contention is that Venus and Cupid, for all their
poetic allure, are rivalled in importance by Apollo as agents, inspirers,
and arbiters of the poetry of Chaucer and his followers. By attending
to Apollo's deeply ambivalent function in the construction of classical
models of authority, and the reinforcement and transmutation of this
ambivalence by medieval hermeneutic practices, we can more fully apprehend the complexity of Chaucer's attitude toward vernacular *auctoritas*, a structure of power that Chaucer both cultivated and denied.[30]
The key to understanding this paradox of artistic identity lies in the
ever-volatile amalgamation of love, truth, and *ars* embodied by Apollo,
mythographic icon of the classicizing poet's self-image.

From *Auctor* to *Vates*: Chaucer's Poetics of Authorship

To claim that Chaucer fundamentally envisions himself as a poet engaged in textual communion with Apollo, locus of the self-authorizing
aspirations of the late medieval love poet as well as of the classical convention of the truth-telling *vates*, is to depart from received critical
opinion regarding Chaucer's constitutional suspicion of the 'false absolute of *auctoritas*.'[31] One of the leitmotifs of Chaucer scholarship in
recent decades is the paradox of 'an author who is extremely reluctant
to make authoritative claims,' one whose 'de-authorized stance' on
poetic production has variously been understood as a reflex of the
conditional textuality that destabilizes truth-claims,[32] an outgrowth of
nominalist scepticism toward the attainability of absolute knowledge,[33]
an expression of a self-consciously troubled 'relationship with origins,'[34] and a semi-covert attempt to forge a discursive space for 'new
structures of non-clerical, non-aristocratic narrative authority.'[35] All of
these views assume Chaucer's rejection of a model of the poet as privileged conduit of *auctoritas*: if Chaucer's Franklin alleges to 'sleep
nevere on the Mount of Pernaso,' most critics believe the same of
Chaucer himself (*FranProl* 721).[36] Indeed, for a poet as sceptical of ultimate truths as Chaucer is often made out to be, the essence of poetry

would seem less an effervescent draft of ambrosia from the Castalian fount than the dregs at the bottom of the barrel – hardly a far-fetched metaphor for a vintner's son. Indeed, in a neat bit of wordplay at the end of the *House of Fame*, Chaucer performs this very riff on classical imagery of inspiration when he compares the 'lyes' (lees) caking the bottom of a wine bottle with the freight of 'lyes' (lies) dispersed around the world by merchants and shipmen, thereafter reconstituted as poetry (*HF* 2129–30). Chaucer, doubtless in counterpoint to his French and Italian contemporaries, cultivates throughout his works a (largely comic) self-image as a non-poet/non-lover: a failed suitor or mere voyeur whose literary productions, far from sublimating erotic loss as poetic success, insulate their framer from the responsibilities, and self-consuming desires, of authorship. My claim is that Chaucer's hesitance to embrace what appears in retrospect to be his rightful place in literary history as a vernacular *auctor* can no longer credibly be accounted for as idiosyncrasy, scepticism, flippancy, or a comic allergy to authority. Instead, Chaucer's ambivalent stance toward the powers of his own fiction reflects concerns deeply rooted in classical tradition itself, in which the position of the *vates* is ever-precarious and the construction of authority inherently contested. This book explores the poetic mythology behind this narrative stance, and how it in turn engendered a mythology of poetry by means of which the early English author, conceived in the shadow of Chaucer, wrote himself into existence.

Toward this end, some adjustment of current paradigms of Chaucerian poetics is necessary before proceeding. Of particular point is Chaucer's relationship to scholasticism, a dominant intellectual mechanism by which medieval culture 'processed' classical antiquity. Medieval scholastic study of authoritative texts, the dimensions of which have been masterfully elucidated by A.J. Minnis, Rita Copeland, and Suzanne Reynolds in relation to medieval vernacularity,[37] amounts to a set of discursive strategies by which classical poetry was authenticated and interpreted in ways that rendered it consistent with medieval principles of ethics. The scholastic commentary tradition, with its reliance on the Aristotelian interpretive mechanism of the 'four causes' of literary production and its emphasis on the ethical function of poetry, provided a readily available institutionalized vocabulary for medieval poets to draw upon in conceptualizing their responses to ancient authors. Scholastic idiom and convention also offered medieval vernacular authors a context in which to claim for their own writing a potentially authoritative place in intellectual tradition. As Minnis has shown,

Chaucer makes extensive use of the conventions of medieval scholastic theory ostensibly to distance himself from the role of *auctor* and to dilute, through what seems at times an uncanny modernity, the capacity of poetry to morally instruct.[38] Copeland has identified a more affirmative Chaucerian claim to *auctoritas* in the 'auto-exegesis' of the *Legend of Good Women*, through which Chaucer redirects exegetical strategies reserved for *auctores* toward the articulation and defence of his own intentions as vernacular translator.[39] This embrace of *auctoritas*, however, is both embryonic and incomplete in the *Legend of Good Women*, centred upon 'disclaimers of [Chaucer's] authorial control which inscribe him in the supplementary role of the translator, a role that is clearly related to the self-effacing posture of the exegete or compiler.'[40] Although the revisions of the G-*Prologue*, as Copeland argues, subtly move away from the translator's pose toward a more independent attitude of authorship, Chaucer is still far from presenting himself unambiguously or un-selfcritically as an *auctor*.

If Chaucer professes merely to skirt the outer margins of authorship, however, his palinodic self-review at the end of the *Troilus*, in the Prologue of the *Legend of Good Women*, and in the *Retraction* complicates what seems at first to be a thoroughgoing scepticism or conceptual ambivalence toward *auctoritas*. As I have argued elsewhere, Chaucer's palinodes respond coherently to scholastic theories of authorship that posit the human author as an agent of the divine by bringing into problematic focus both the reality of authorial responsibility and the creative texture of *auctoritas*. In these moments, Chaucer does not so much revoke his works as affirm the complex reality by which moral responsibility necessarily implies a domain of literary authority, even paternity, for the producer of texts – something that Chaucer may elsewhere occlude, but not deny.[41]

I argue in this book that beneath Chaucer's coy, even ludic, self-fashioning as a poet lies a legible theoretical fascination with the deep construction – not merely causes, prevention, and cures – of authority. By recognizing this intellectual investment on Chaucer's part, and its mythological focus in Apollo, we are in a position to define Chaucerian literary practice as something other than a poetics of contradiction. The 'scholastic' Chaucer who both absorbs and denies or subverts the authorizing strategies of the medieval commentary tradition is a case in point. In the conclusion of Minnis's study of medieval authorship roles, he suggests that Chaucer ultimately acts as a 'self-conscious author' precisely by exploiting the role of compiler – that is, non-author – so ingeniously: 'If Gower was a compiler who tried to present himself as an author, Chaucer was an author who hid behind the "shield and defence" of the compiler.'[42] Appealing as this paradox is, it invites an image of an ambidextrous Chaucer for whom authorship is less a coherent literary attitude than a covert and perhaps not fully conscious instinct. Chaucer's pose as compiler or recorder is thus implicitly valued in the spirit in which he (no doubt teasingly) presents it to us: as a cherished 'mask' let drop, by way of afterthought or accident, in his palinodes.[43] The conclusion – that Chaucer is an author in spite of himself – finally satisfies less than the paradox because it leaves unarticulated what it *means* for Chaucer to 'be' an author. Indeed, to answer this question, we need a more sharply conceived model of what 'being an author' meant to Chaucer, if he could 'be' one in the very act of denying it.

Another kind of internal division is frequently held to inform Chaucer's relationship to his own legacy, which scholars have increasingly evaluated in political rather than merely aesthetic terms – thus rejecting an older, more deeply embedded paradox, by which the poet Chaucer disappointingly fathered a vast generation of poetasters. Recent studies of the process of Chaucer's canonization in the first half of the fifteenth century by David Lawton, John Fisher, and others have emphasized the differences in outlook toward the notion of English authorship held by Chaucer and his early emulators. Nicholas Watson, for example, contends that 'what made Chaucer so important to English literary history may have had less to do with any belief he had in himself as the founder of a self-conscious vernacular poetic tradition than with his *invention* as a founding figure, shortly after his death, by poets such as Hoccleve and Lydgate.'[44] In its most extreme form, this school of thought regards the literary tradition that issues from Chaucer's works as a purely political fabrication designed to insulate the conservative interests of the crown by naturalizing them as 'culture.' By this argument, epitomized by the recent work of David R. Carlson, the Chaucerian tradition markets 'an English literature which … knew its place, which was to serve and to protect (not to subvert) the dominance of the ruling class. In the circumstance, had Chaucer not existed, it would have been exigent to invent him.'[45] This politicized, servile Chaucer – who, it should be noted, in turn serves the interests of twenty-first century Marxist argument – is thus a thing 'invented' rather than an inventor, and his poetic boldness in engaging with literary tradition and the imaginative fabric of authorship is consigned, in quite a different spirit from that of Minnis, to the realm of accident and rhetorical circularity. As Carlson asserts, 'Chaucer was made 'the father of English poetry' *not because he was a good poet, though he was* ... Chaucer was made the father of English poetry because he was servile, doing useful work serving dominant social interests, materially and ideologically, in both his poetic and other employments' (emphasis added).[46]

The alternative to this poetics of contradiction – in which Chaucer, unlike the more assertive Gower, declines to exploit the scholastic apparatus or self-promoting torque of authorship at the same time that he *writes*, ahistorically, like an author – lies in the simple fact that Chaucer, perhaps more out of private experimentation than public vision, mythologized a new idea of authorship in English.[47] This new mode of authorship, after Chaucer's death, would be both more accessible and more resilient than the devices of medieval authentication that Chaucer ultimately found inadequate to his expression of textual authority (and thus used in the self-diminishing or counterproductive ways outlined by Minnis). Chaucer's imaginative construction of the author as an Apolline crucible of literary tradition and locus of artistic self-reflection links him, in a way that Gower could never be linked, with the 'greats' of classical tradition and with a line of poetic descendants including Skelton, Spenser, Milton, and Keats. It is not surprising, then, that Chaucer's modus operandi was fundamentally different from that of Gower, whose more rigid adherence to the authoritative structures of scholasticism produced what is perhaps the greatest contradiction: a 'medieval vernacular author, his hour come at last,' whose claims to vernacular authority are not founded upon the grandeur of his English poetry but upon the moralizing Latin commentary and encomia with which it is encrusted.[48] Perhaps because Chaucer was finally an outsider to the formalities of the university,[49] he enjoyed the freedom to shape a position of authorship, and to engage creatively with classical models of authority, without relying narrowly or exclusively upon scholastic commentary traditions for conceptual guidance.[50]

A missing piece in current accounts of Chaucer's poetics and the nature of their influence is his structuring interest in the poet's role as *vates*, inspired vessel of truth. Ancient Greek in origin, this role came to be identified with Virgil and (in a newly Christianized form) Dante, and was closely associated with Apollo as god of poetry and prophecy.[51] Not surprisingly, the sceptical, impish Chaucer of modern criticism is widely thought to treat ironically or comically subvert the classical notion of the poet as *vates*. Fyler, for example, identifies an Ovidian spirit in what he calls the 'comic irony' of Chaucer's flirtations with the vatic pose, opposing this 'comic indirection' to the high seriousness of Virgil and Dante. The key difference between these two poetic stances, for Fyler, lies in the potential of vatic inspiration to transcend the fragile structures of human artifice: 'the *vates* can present truths he could not normally discern, because he is speaking for a numinous power that allows him to escape human limitations; the *poeta*, on the other hand, is self-consciously trapped by those limitations.'[52] In a similar spirit, Spearing draws attention to Chaucer's 'unease in the sublime mode' in engaging with Dante's 'excessively arrogant claims for the poet' in the *House of Fame*. This discomfort with 'a Renaissance sense of the poet's calling,' Spearing suggests, may well account for Chaucer's abandonment of the poem.[53] Finally, Lois A. Ebin goes so far as to claim that fifteenth- and early sixteenth-century 'Chaucerian' poetry invents for itself a vatic prerogative – visible in an increasing confidence, of a secular and humanist variety, regarding the illuminative power of vernacular poetry – that had been absent in the more cautiously medieval Chaucer.[54] When early modern poets, in Ebin's reading, do respond to Chaucerian precedent in their development of a humanist poetic, they do so by reformulating in positive terms what in Chaucer had been merely 'parodic,' for example when Stephen Hawes, in the *Pastime of Pleasure* (1506–7), recasts the ambivalence of Chaucer's *House of Fame* as an affirmation of the power of poetry to sustain fame.[55] Ebin's analysis, however, relies on the awkward logic that the parody – Chaucer's sceptical vision of the poet's role – precedes the 'straight,' and therefore more meaningful, treatment. Moreover, it implies that Chaucer's ironic procedure cannot at the same time be serious, and so must be bracketed as a separate, unrelated, or undigested poetic approach with no direct link to the newly forceful claims of poetic authority by early modern poets influenced and, in their own way, authorized by Chaucer.

Claims such as these risk oversimplifying both Chaucer's earnest interest in structures of authority and inspiration and the problematic fluidity and contested basis of the ostensibly transcendent poetics of the Apolline *vates* as imagined by classical poets. In defining the tradition of the *vates* as it reached Chaucer, we must recognize that the 'arrogant claims' of poetic authority that Spearing associates with the *vates* are only one relatively unrepresentative part of a larger picture. No reader of Virgil and Dante can fail to notice how painfully aware these poets are of their inadequacies as vessels of truth; this awareness, surely more than merely rhetorical, makes the grace of divine inspiration all the more wonderful. In a darker vein, the humanity of the *vates* sharpens the threat of the vatic project from within by frustration, loss, and failure. Milton registers this point in a memorable intimation of the *vates*'s native weakness, and the danger of adulterated inspiration, at the beginning of the book of *Paradise Lost* that most centrally concerns the collapse of human resolve:

> ... unless an age too late, or cold
> Climate, or Years damp my intended wing
> Deprest; and much they may, if all be mine,
> Not Hers who brings it nightly to my Ear.[56]

Not only the integrity of the poet as truth-bearer but the intactness of the poetic artefact itself is at stake in such a poetics of inspiration, as is evident from the fragmentary status of Chaucer's *House of Fame* and Keats's *Hyperion*, both of which, as we have seen, are centrally concerned with the poet's role as *vates*. Far from being alien to vatic poetics, the perverse energies of fragmentation and ironic self-reflexivity are fundamental to this poetic mythology. As we shall see, these issues accrete around Apollo as an all-too-human figurehead of authority; in turn, they impel the transmission and reinvention of that authority by means of a continuous, if irregularly shaped, literary tradition. The poetics of the *vates*, as defined here, takes two essential forms. On the one hand, vatic poetics can enact a kind of art that is transformative and consolatory: the triumph of poetry that renders loss beautiful (the loss of Daphne, the loss of control over the self) and grants the illusion of eternal possession. On the other, however, such art *is* an illusion, an attractive exterior that conceals, and potentially is compromised by, a core of failure, imperfection, and loss. Chaucer, intrigued by the friction between these two poetic possibilities, provides a poetic record of something closer to the second model of vatic art. My contention, accordingly, is that a deconstructive approach to poetic inspiration centrally informs Chaucer's treatment of Apollo and his classicizing poetics more generally. At the same time, it opens a space of inscription for the many forms of early English poetry that self-consciously take inspiration from Chaucer's precedent.

If Chaucer's interest in the poet's role as *vates* has been incompletely understood, his various treatments of Apollo have attracted little attention, with the exception of the god's appearance as protagonist in the

Manciple's Tale. Two articles on the *Manciple's Tale*, both from the last twenty years, have begun the work of situating Apollo's problematic role in this penultimate tale in relation to his treatment in medieval mythographic and literary texts as well as, to a lesser extent, his significance elsewhere in Chaucer's poetry.[57] The first, Brian Striar's 'The "Manciple's Tale" and Chaucer's Apolline Poetics,' which also draws attention to Apollo's role in the *House of Fame* and *Legend of Good Women*, rightly recognizes that Apollo signals a concern with narrative authority in both Chaucer and Ovid. Striar's application of this insight to a reading of the *Manciple's Tale*, however, presses the tale rather too ponderously and abstractly into a self-conscious allegory of poetic composition, by which, it is argued, Chaucer validates rather than (as most critics suppose) renounces poetic fiction. Striar's expansion of this metapoetic reading as a paradigm for Chaucer's poetics, particularly as expressed in the *Retraction* – in which he detects the mythic influence of Apollo as 'a figure invested with the power to give and to reclaim speech and signification' – raises important questions about the mythographic basis of narrative authority but does not, in my view, convincingly situate Apollo in the context of Chaucer's poetics or medieval literary ideas of authority more generally.[58]

Whereas Striar discerns in the *Manciple's Tale* a latently humanist affirmation of poetic voice, Michael Kensak, in 'Apollo *exterminans*: The God of Poetry in Chaucer's *Manciple's Tale*,' argues the opposite point: that the silencing of poetry in the *Manciple's Tale*, which follows from the repression of the crow's speech and the breaking of Apollo's instruments, is a metonym for Chaucer's essentially Christian renunciation of a poetic journey inspired by Apollo rather than the Christian God. The movement in the final two fragments of the *Canterbury Tales* from pragmatic silence to penitential speech, and from pagan myth to Christian truth, derives, argues Kensak, from medieval pilgrimage narratives such as Dante's *Commedia* and Alain de Lille's *Anticlaudianus*; it is to this Christian genre, then, as well as to certain moralistic strands of mythographic exegesis, that the insufficiency of Apollo's inspiration should be referred. The defeat of Apollo, according to Kensak, 'represents the inability of classical wisdom to comprehend Christian mystery and the incapacity of human language to represent the divine.' The debacle of the *Manciple's Tale* thus necessitates the corrective intervention of the Parson's 'new Christian poetics.'[59]

Kensak's important insight into the generic affinity of the *Canterbury Tales* to other medieval travel narratives that frame a Christian pilgrimage against a counter-journey through literary paganism leaves little doubt that Christian moralism informs Chaucer's disquieting rejection of Apollo as poetic avatar in the final narrative sequence of the *Canterbury Tales*. What Kensak's reading overlooks, however, is the striking, and thus far unexplained, congruity between the breakdown of Apolline poetics in the *Manciple's Tale* and the various crises, anticlimaxes, and unfulfilled promises associated with Apollo as inspirer or creative principle elsewhere in Chaucer's poetry, outside of the framework of pilgrimage narrative. This book aims to explore this congruity, demonstrating its basis in classical tradition – principally Ovidian, but to a lesser extent Virgilian – and its perpetuation in medieval hermeneutic attempts to interpret and legislate this tradition. Indeed, if Chaucer's ultimate intent in dramatizing Apollo's defeat at the end of the *Canterbury Tales* is to usher in a new Christian, anti-poetic model of inspiration, his *method* of repudiating classically inspired poetics is paradoxically – even mischievously – *classical* in inspiration.

Because my focus is the poetry of Chaucer as well as what will be referred to more broadly as 'Chaucerian poetics' or the 'Chaucerian tradition,' a brief definition of these terms and the assumptions that inform them is necessary at this juncture. A methodological principle of this study is that in a period in which literary creativity was defined by a dynamic approach to authoritative tradition, the cultural significance of Chaucer's works must be viewed in a multilateral textual setting that looks backward to the influence of ancient precedent and forward to the momentum of literary effect. This book's procedure is in some respects unusual in placing Chaucer's poetry in a densely intertextual matrix consisting both of pertinent classical texts, with their accumulated medieval interpretations, and the rich stock of vernacular works that follow in Chaucer's imaginative tradition (courtly-mythological, classicizing, aureate) in the late Middle Ages and at the cusp of the Renaissance. This latter body of writing, which I make no claim to examine comprehensively but nonetheless treat as a tradition with coherent features and a common Chaucerian point of origin, is important for bearing witness to the gradual development of a new mode of English poetry beginning to seek a changed historical vocabulary for its own position as inheritor of an ancient poetic legacy. That it does so while cautiously, self-reflexively, and at times awkwardly questioning its own capacity to sustain (and reclaim) that tradition helps us appreciate a particularly telling point of connection with the poetic practice of Chaucer. In order to capture the complex energies of the overlapping and competing voices that constitute this tradition, this study often foregoes straightforward chronology and refrains from lengthy treatment of the more commonly studied exemplars of the Chaucerian tradition in favour of less predictable focal points of textual commerce. My broadest aim, then, is to shed new light on Chaucer's position in the development of what might be called a proto-humanist – and yet still firmly medieval – way of viewing the past and the role of the (literary) present within it, one that several of his most immediate followers thought important enough to perpetuate in ways that advanced their own interests.[60]

The Ovidian tradition runs in tandem with the development of Chaucerian poetics and is crucial to an understanding of these concerns surrounding poetic inheritance and their relation to Apollo. Indeed, more than any other single tradition, Ovid's pivotal and widely influential treatments of Apollo inform Chaucer's assimilation of the god into his poetics and his evolving vision of authorship. The first chapter, therefore, establishes the poetic framework and ideological dimensions of Apollo with reference to the competing forces of textual authority, art, and love in Ovid's poetry. It furthermore traces a line of continuity from Ovid's sceptical, amoral vision of Apollo as inspirer, lover, and healer to the ethical appropriation of Ovidian material by medieval commentators and poets. Because Ovid's shaping of Apollo has largely been treated unsubstantially, and never synthetically, in classical scholarship, it is necessary here to advance a sustained reading of several key narrative strands involving Apollo across a range of Ovidian works, focusing on problems that arise in Apollo's transmission of authority and his authorization of *ars*. In his amatory works, *Metamorphoses*, and exile poetry, Ovid's complex and self-aware treatment of Apollo as a spectacle of authority and an emblem of the self-consuming properties of art fundamentally shapes the god's medieval legacy in ways that influence Chaucer's vision of the poet's role, as well as the interests of late medieval classicizing love-visions fashioned in the Chaucerian tradition.

The strikingly ambivalent image of Apollo as icon of authority that emerges from Ovidian tradition was culturally malleable, and thus was moulded by broader mythographic trends in the Middle Ages that evince a problematic ideological position for the god of Truth at the juncture of pagan and Christian systems of reference. Looking at the multivalent treatments of Apollo in medieval mythographic handbooks intended for pedagogical and homiletic use, as well as his function in popular (non-Chaucerian) vernacular genres dealing with pagan subject matter, chapter 2 draws attention to ways in which Apollo functioned as an iconic focus of medieval anxieties surrounding literary paganism. Apollo emerges in these medieval texts as a type of Christ or image of wisdom but also as the quintessential pagan idol; just as frequently, he represents an ambiguous stage of transition between the two that uneasily balances enlightenment with stagnation. Of particular importance is the medieval reimagination of Apollo's classical function as *interpres* (as inspirer, prophet, and healer). As the solar god whose rays penetrate obscurity, Apollo offered medieval commentators a mythographic image of their task as exegetes, and supplied late medieval English poets with a model of poetic creation as aureation. At the same time, however, the Latin commentary tradition emphasizes Apollo's own multiplicity as a subject of interpretation and his intensely overdetermined status as signifier. Insofar as he features both as linchpin of competing religious ideologies and rhetorical agent in the project of exegesis, Apollo exposes many of the problems inherent in the processes of interpretation and representation of antiquity encountered by Latin and vernacular mythographers of the Middle Ages.

Chapter 3 considers the impact of the Virgilian tradition of Apollo upon the legacy of artistic ambivalence and contested notions of authority that the first two chapters charted in the Ovidian and medieval mythographic spheres. In the *Aeneid* Apollo embodies a distinct trajectory, closely associated with Augustan propaganda, as a stabilizing force in the founding of Rome and its consolidation of power. In light of this, I reassess Chaucer's *Troilus and Criseyde* as a poem in imaginative friction with Virgil's *Aeneid*, functioning both as belated retrospective and conceptual pre-history of the matter of Rome. One way that Chaucer mediates the cultural difference presented by his Trojan material is by reading Virgil's epic – and particularly his portrayal of Apollo – through an Augustinian lens. Specifically, Chaucer exposes Apollo's status as a *destabilizing* force in Troy in order to evoke tensions within the process of nation-building – and poetic construction – that Virgil too summarily resolved. In the *Troilus* Chaucer deploys Apollo, mythic builder of the walls of Troy but (untraditionally) enemy of Troy, as a reference point for Troilus's and Criseyde's experiences of love and its circumscription by the rhythms of nature and history, as well as its eventual entrapment by tragedy. In medieval adaptations of the chronicles of Dares and Dictys, particularly that of the ostentatiously classicizing Joseph of Exeter, Apollo acts as a kind of totem figure around which the ambivalent loyalties and cultural tensions of the Trojan War circulate. While Virgil largely defers these tensions in the *Aeneid* by reworking them into an epideictic of the founding of Rome, Chaucer's

Ovidian concern with the erotic biographies that underlie the impulse of *translatio imperii* activates them anew, ultimately placing them in a Christian context in which Apollo's *ars* is displaced by Christ's *remedium*.

Turning from the collapse of an Apolline ethic in the *Troilus* to Apollo's association with narrative discontinuity and rupture elsewhere in Chaucer's poetry, chapter 4 focuses on Fragment V of the *Canterbury Tales*, which features the Squire's and the Franklin's successive imaginings of the pagan world and the artist's role within it, as well as a series of dramatic failures on the part of Apollo in connection with textual processes. I argue that Fragment V centrally examines conceptions of poetic inspiration and defines a cult of artistic identity allied with Apollo as a figure of poetic authority. Here Chaucer resituates his encounter with the legacy of antiquity in 'modern' terms, presenting differing social visions of literary privilege and eloquence on the part of his Squire and Franklin. Apollo's role in the astrological machinery and pagan texture of the storytelling contest staged in Fragment V also impels fifteenth- and early sixteenth-century appropriations of Chaucer as a figure of inspiration – and even, in some cases, an Apollo-figure – in his own right. The chapter thus contextualizes Apollo's function in the poetic discourses of this central fragment in relation to their reinscription in works by Lydgate, Bokenham, Skelton, and others, all of which invoke the dynamics of the Franklin's and the Squire's textual competition as a means of negotiating their own relationship to Chaucerian authority.

The final chapter considers how Apollo's Ovidian association with the deconstructive aspects of poetic art and authority produces the narrative debacle of the *Manciple's Tale*, in which Apollo features as homicidal protagonist and silencer of poetic discourse within the tale and beyond. Specifically, the *Manciple's Tale* offers a problematic meditation on issues of prophecy, speech, and interpretation centring upon augury (avian counsel); for this reason, the troubled relationship between Phebus and his informing crow must be understood in light of oracular discourses, and the ambiguity surrounding them, with which Apollo is associated in the classical and medieval traditions charted in previous chapters. These concerns with pagan ritual reinforce and complement the tale's engagement with problems of political counsel, while the matter of language and its relation to truth, centred urgently upon the figure of Apollo in this last and bleakest poetic contribution of the *Canterbury Tales*, allows us to understand in new ways Chaucer's formation of a voice of poetic authority and the pressure that he puts on readers to interpret that stance.

1 Apollo as Human God: Ovid and Medieval Ovidianism

The three gifts of Apollo, celebrated by Horace in a central articulation of the poetic vocation in his *Odes* (4.6), are inspiration (*spiritum*), the art of song (*artem carminis*), and the name of poet (*nomen poetae*). In ancient literary tradition, these blessings do not come cheaply for the poet who writes in the name of Apollo. By the time that the young Ovid began the first of his amatory works in the last quarter of the first century BCE, Apollo carried with him considerable literary-historical baggage as a deity whose powers had been exercised in countless real and literary battlefields, revered and appropriated by archaic, Alexandrian, and Augustan poets alike. Through a body of work encompassing, most notably, erotic elegy, epistolary discourse, erotodidacticism, epic, and tragic autobiography, Ovid so fully exploited the traditions surrounding the Apollo from whom he frequently claimed (and disclaimed) inspiration that he effectively redrew the map of Apolline mythology for his own generation as well as the numerous medieval poets and scholars who would take the Roman poet as their master. The Virgilian Apollo, with his Trojan associations, would also substantially inform the complex program of authority associated with the god in the Middle Ages, as this book's third chapter will demonstrate. But because of the seminal importance of Ovidianism to the development of Chaucerian discourses of authority, for the purposes of this study the story begins – and must begin – with Ovid. Ovid's creative interest, this chapter argues, centred most generatively upon Apollo's recurrent fallibility, his self-reflexive status as a poetic proxy, and his image as authority figure and agent of inspiration. These motifs together shape an Ovidian Apollo whose traces pervade Chaucerian tradition as it channels the textual authority of the *auctores* into the turbulent stream of the vernacular. In order to elucidate the distinctive mythic idiom that made the classical Apollo ripe for cultural appropriation in later periods, this chapter focuses primarily on Ovid's works in their own literary context, and secondarily – through targeted illustration and a coda – to points of contact between Ovid's vision of Apollo and medieval moralizing commentaries, learned tracts, and poetic love-visions that engage substantively with the Ovidian Apollo. The relatively direct lines drawn here between the Ovidian Apollo and key texts in his medieval reception frame later chapters' treatment of the various permutations of Apollo's medieval legacy that emerge from competing poetic traditions, distinctly medieval cultural preoccupations, and renewed energies of myth-making circulating within the works of Chaucer and his followers.

Ovid's contribution to the literary history of Apollo as it was transmitted to the Middle Ages was in the first instance a purely functional one, supplying what would become by Chaucer's time the canonical versions of major mythological episodes including Apollo's defeat of the Python, pursuit of the virginal Daphne, responsibility for Phaethon's fiery demise, murder of the adulteress Coronis, punishment of the impious Niobe, flaying of the musician Marsyas, homosexual love for the youths Cyparissus and Hyacinthus, fatherly protection of the bard Orpheus, endowment of Midas with ass's ears, and servitude as shepherd and lover of King Admetus (or in medieval versions, his daughter). Ovid's oeuvre was also a repository of more obscure Apolline narratives, many of them duly puzzled over by medieval commentators, including various rapes and seductions[1] as well as an array of enigmatic metamorphoses.[2]

Whether critics have found Apollo to be 'the most sympathetic ... of all the gods' in Ovid's mythic cosmos or a typically 'impious, subhuman deity,'[3] they have not failed to acknowledge his prominence in Ovid's poetic vision. Ovid playfully associates Apollo with his self-defence as an elegiac poet in his amatory works and, furthermore, designates him the star of the first, most memorable of the litany of stories of gods denatured by carnal passion in the *Metamorphoses*. Nonetheless, few critics have attempted a broad examination of the particular forms and significance of Ovid's treatment of Apollo, and none has considered this significance with respect to the entire range of Ovid's output or its medieval afterlives. Instead, interest has centred almost exclusively upon Ovid's engagement with Apollo's conventional status as a poetic inspirer and, still more prominently, upon the political dimension of Apollo as a mythic surrogate of Augustus, who strove to glorify himself and his cultural program by means of Apolline propaganda.[4] Ovid's treatment of Apollo on both fronts is widely held to be parodic, intent upon undermining Apollo's poetic and Augustus's political authority in one fell swoop by revealing the man truly in charge of Roman artistic production and the cult of taste to be the libidinous Cupid or, more accurately, Ovid himself. A recent review of this issue by Rebecca Armstrong asserts that Ovid in fact 'sidelin[es]' Apollo throughout his amatory poetry by means of anticlimax and intentional elision, revealing him to be 'at best peripheral and at worst redundant' while 'rarely, if ever, 'tak[ing] the god's input and authority seriously.'[5] The conclusion drawn by Armstrong and others that Ovid's peculiar scepticism toward Apollo's authority can be satisfactorily attributed to an anti-Augustan stance has, however, been unduly emphasized and incompletely contextualized. In the case of Apollo, the widespread critical tendency toward topical interpretation has had the unfortunate effect of closing down what seems to be 'a far larger concern with *auctoritas* – with authority and the author's relationship to it' in Ovid's works,[6] within which the political import of a devalued Apollo discloses only one layer of the god's complex association with artistic authority, one that is by no means the most meaningful for Ovid's medieval readers and adapters.

At least as important for Ovid as Apollo's status as facilitator of political critique was his unique ability to serve as a reflection, with all the narcissistic registers of the word intact, of the poet himself as a cultivator of *ars*. Not merely an inspirer or patron figure but a mythic projection of poetic praxis itself, Apollo could not simply be dismissed as irrelevant, as Armstrong contends, or manoeuvred as a political whipping boy for anti-authoritarian dissension. Instead, Apollo opened to Ovid a field of almost unlimited possibilities in which to stage an ongoing critical examination of the power of artifice and its connection to (self-)deception and illusion. As literary patron, archetypal lover, and healer of bodily ills, Apollo was a complex fulcrum of authority for Ovid, encompassing Augustus's power as authorizer of political and poetic mores as well as Ovid's self-image of the poet in love (and poetry *as* love). When Ovid undermines Apollo's authority, therefore, he undermines his own as well, quietly framing beneath the comedy of Apollo's errors and misfortunes a sustained vision of art's hidden origins – and, in turn, its destination – in emotional defeat, imaginative compromise, and corporeal suffering (concerns implied as early as the erotic works but only fully realized in the exile poetry).

This chapter examines the conceptual means by which the tradition of Apollo as 'human' god reached Ovid, tracing the permutations of this theme across Ovid's oeuvre in connection with recurrent concerns with textual authority, the role of the poet as *vates*, and the mutual implication of poetic and medical arts. In so doing, it assumes the methodological importance of interpreting Apollo's appearances in Ovid's works, particularly the *Metamorphoses*, with a view to narratological patterns of development and their repercussions in the developing expectations of the reader.[7] Treating the *Metamorphoses* as a heuristic and centre of gravity, this chapter links Apollo's pivotal appearances in the epic with his creative deployment in Ovid's erotodidactic works, *Heroides*, and exile poetry, all of which variously exerted influence in the school curriculum and vernacular poetic practice in the Middle Ages. Lastly, this chapter explores the transmission of these concerns in one portion of the circuit of Ovid's direct literary influence, highlighting principles of difference as well as consistency between Ovid's poetic self-examination and medieval views of the liabilities of poetic discourse – and of Apollo – as inexact agents of truth.

'Un Olympien de ce monde': The Birth of Apollo

For modern readers, the mythologer of Apollo par excellence is Friedrich Nietzsche, whose *Birth of Tragedy* (1872) continues to shape, directly and indirectly, most scholarly and popular treatments of the god, including criticism on Chaucer's Apollo.[8] Associated with oneiric image-making, the power of contemplation, and the 'magnificent illusion' of culture, Nietzsche's Apollo represents the sublimation of the *principium individuationis* through the disciplining force of art, which exists in perpetual tension with the collective intoxication and intimacy engendered by Dionysus.[9] This view, granted elegant canonicity for twentieth-century mainstream classical criticism by Walter F. Otto, regards Apollo as 'what is loftiest, most eminent, and at the same time brightest,' and identifies him with an essential sense of distance that rejects the Dionysian 'entanglement in things' by virtue of an 'attitude of cognition' associated with the Delphic principle of self-knowledge.[10] At once a suppression of and alternative to Dionysian regress, Nietzsche's vision of the Apolline emphasizes the recuperative function of artistic illusion, which provides access, in the words of one modern commentator, to 'a perfection, a truth, whose shining provides a certain release from the negativity of the everyday, a certain relief from that fragmentariness, a healing.'[11] Nietzsche's Apollo is, in short, a god in control, one who asserts the potential of humanity to rise above the limitations of passion and to access (if only temporarily) the tranquility of the divine. This Nietzschean view of Apollo is memorably anticipated by Percy Bysshe Shelley's 'Hymn of Apollo' (1820), which culminates in Apollo's confident assertion of the artistic principle itself in its most sublimated and self-reflective form:

> I am the eye with which the Universe
>> Beholds itself and knows itself divine;
> All harmony of instrument or verse,
>> All prophecy, all medicine is mine,
> All light of art or nature; – to my song
> Victory and praise in its own right belong.[12]

In ideological terms, the Nietzschean Apollo epitomizes the imperial impulse of Western culture, an impulse self-consciously allied with Apolline myth from Augustan Rome to the Space Age. Claiming Apollo's supervision in his victory over Sextus Pompey (36 BCE) and, more famously, over the Dionysian Antony at Actium (31 BCE), Augustus orchestrated a Golden Age of peace and moral revival by means of a 'visual language,' in Paul Zanker's characterization, centred upon Apollo. By merging the aesthetic with the political, Augustus developed an Apolline propaganda – galvanized by Virgil and burlesqued by Ovid – that would be sustained by literary patronage, architectural planning, and religious reform; indeed, as Zanker illustrates, Augustus's 'sense of mission and his entire program for healing Rome's wounds bore the stamp of Apollo.'[13] Discipline, morality, purity, and moderation thus formed the cultural and imagistic Apolline climate of a newly defined Roman *virtus*. Denis Cosgrove has argued that the 'Apollonian perspective' refined by Augustus, which 'seizes divine authority for itself, radiating power across the global surface from a sacred centre, locating and projecting human authority imperially toward the ends of the earth,' remains active in modern discourses of globalism and globalization.[14] In Cosgrove's view, these discourses evolve out of imperialist ideology and culminate in the rhetoric and photographic legacy of the Apollo space missions of the 1960s and 1970s. Such globalist discourse, for Cosgrove, is predicated upon a tacitly Nietzschean understanding of Apollo through which the 'synoptic vision' identified with globalism in its Apollonian sense 'implies rising above the mundane; thus it is a mark of the exceptional being, the call to heroic destiny of the paradigmatic human.'[15]

The civilizing power of Apollo's panoptic vision has often been regarded as coterminous with 'truth.' Shelley's Apollo, for example, lyricizing a medieval mythographic commonplace, boasts that 'The sunbeams are my shafts, with which I kill / Deceit, that loves the night and fears the day' ('Hymn of Apollo' 13–14). Apollo's circumscription by imperialist ideology substantiates, in mythological terms, Foucault's insistence upon the cultural construction of truth through the operation of political power, to which this book's introduction alluded. According to Foucault, every society is defined by a '"régime" of truth,' that is, a structure of power that authorizes specific expressions of what is and is not true. 'Truth' is thus a political construction rather than a value-free absolute, one linked integrally 'in a circular relation with systems of power which produce and sustain it, and to effects of power which it induces and which extend it.'[16] The Apollo of imperialist rhetoric, then, is empowered by an apparatus of veracity that carries profound cultural authority. Marked by a Nietzschean identification with illusion and discipline, this Apollo disseminates 'truth' – and contributes to its mythologization – by affirming, governing, and universalizing a given culture's formations of power.

Turning to classical and medieval literary representations of Apollo, however, we encounter a very different god from Nietzsche's sublime individualist. Recent scholarship on Greek cultic traditions and tragic conceptions of Apollo, for example, has stressed his startling obliquity, violence, and lack of temperance. Writing of Apollo's role in Greek tragedy, Anton Bierl attributes Apollo's problematic association with human suffering to his function as the god who oversees the initiation of youths into civic adulthood, a process problematized by tragedy, and to his unresolved tension with respect to the female principle.[17] Marcel Detienne's study of the Apollo of Greek cult and epic goes further, recuperating a proud and irascible Apollo – a deeply ambivalent, if not hypocritical, god who cures the diseases he himself causes, who propounds morality but is himself the most 'elegantly immoral' of gods, and whose immoderate cultic appetite for bloody sacrifice stands in awkward juxtaposition with the blood-crimes for which those supplicatory sacrifices are meant to atone.[18] Detienne's Apollo, far from sublimating human instinct into an austere realm of spirit and moral equilibrium, extracts purity from the dross of impurity, emerging as *more* human – because more invested in the imperfect reality of the individual – than Dionysus. Apollo, in Detienne's view, is a veritable 'Olympien de ce monde' [Olympian of this world] who 'semble privilégier le champ de l'action humaine' [appears to privilege the field of human action] in all of its failings.[19]

As we shall see, the human bias – and liability – Detienne underscores in his account of Apollo's cultic roles as god of colonization and oracular guidance becomes, for Ovid and his medieval poetic followers, an artistic principle. The Apolline artist, as imagined in Ovidian tradition, is poised between mastery of the energy of creation (in Detienne's terms, self-authorization and the durable construction of cultural artefacts) and the gravitational pull of defeat. A complex poetics of authority, the following pages argue, results from this tension, permeating a range of ancient and medieval confrontations with Apollo as a model of the poetic self.

Apollo's problematic amalgamation of a divine prerogative with human vulnerability is a central feature of some of his earliest and most influential literary treatments. The trend toward 'humanization' in Apollo's character is therefore considerably more ancient, and profoundly situated, than the 'novel mortality' recently observed in Ovid's flippantly portrayed Muses.[20] This point is illustrated particularly well by the story of Apollo's birth on the island of Delos in the first part of the Homeric Hymn to Apollo (eighth century BCE?),[21] versions of which were known to the Middle Ages through Ovid's allusions to Apollo's nativity in Book Six of the Metamorphoses, Hyginus's Fabulae 53 and 140, and Servius's gloss on Aeneid 3.73, as well as numerous later mythographies that transmit these materials.[22] In the Homeric Hymn to Apollo, Leto (Latona) is repeatedly frustrated in her search for a land that will shelter her while giving birth to Apollo, her child (along with Diana) by Zeus, because of widespread fears of Hera's jealous wrath and troubling, albeit false, rumours of Apollo's future arrogance. Finally, Leto is welcomed apprehensively by the personified Delos, a rocky and barren island scorned by all, and Apollo eventually is born, but only after a long and painful delivery. The second part of the hymn presents the young Apollo's complementary quest for a land in which to build his great oracle. He finally settles upon the rugged, inhospitable terrain of Delphi on Mount Parnassus, but is first rebuffed and tricked by the envious Telphusa and must rid Delphi of the scourge of a resident shedragon known in later versions of the myth as Python. The Homeric Hymn to Apollo notably risks undercutting the subject of its own cultic praise in so strongly emphasizing the contingency and undignified status of Apollo's birth and establishment of his worship, not to mention in associating him with the *hubris* that his future Delphic precepts of self-knowledge and moderation are ostensibly intended to thwart.[23] Although the *Hymn*, representing an essentially religious genre, ultimately redirects such concerns regarding Apollo's 'humanity' into a celebration of the god's Olympian heroism and sanctioned mediation of Zeus's will, it nonetheless also transmits to more cynical future mythologers a rationale for conceptualizing a dubious beginning for an all-powerful god.

One such mythologer is Ovid's impious Niobe, who decries Latona's humble godhead as an embarrassment to the pantheon: 'nec caelo nec humo nec aquis dea uestra recepta est; / exsul erat mundi, donec miserata uagantem / "hospita tu terris erras, ego" dixit "in undis" / instabilemque locum Delos dedit' [Your goddess was accepted neither by sky nor earth nor waters; / she was an exile from the world till, pitying her as she roamed, / 'You are wandering, a stranger, on the lands, but I,' said Delos, 'on the waves,' / and she gave her an unstable place'] (*Met.* 6.188–91).[24] Niobe is no more impressed by Latona's two divine children. Apollo's and Diana's ruthless punishment of the would-be Theban goddess, of course, serves to condemn Niobe's impiety – and it is noteworthy that Ovid emphasizes Apollo's agency in this scene of torture, almost to the exclusion of Diana. Just as importantly, however, this cruel retaliation functions to prove, indeed to establish, the divinity of Latona and her family, which had been in sufficient doubt for Niobe's scandalmongering to have had some influence: the townspeople had stopped worshiping Latona with full rites (6.202–3). Whereas the hymnic tradition upon which Ovid draws invokes the experience of Niobe as unambiguous evidence of Apollo's omnipotence in all aspects of his cult,[25] Ovid's use of the example of Niobe in *Met.* 6 limns the equivocal process by which the divine powers of Apollo and his family are manufactured and marketed to a sceptical public.

The two stories that follow, of Latona's punishment of the Lycian peasants (*Met.* 6.317–81) and Marsyas's ill-advised challenge of Apollo to a musical contest (6.383–400) – both told by way of awed flashback – serve, after Niobe's debacle, to magnify the Latona clan's reputation of power in the public mind. In the former, Ovid presents a sympathetic, long-suffering Latona in part 'to correct the negative impression that we may have developed concerning Latona as a cruel deity';[26] at the same time, he continues to reinforce Latona's association with human weakness. Ovid emphasizes the apparent vulnerability of Latona as divine vagabond and single mother ('cui quondam regia coniunx / orbem interdixit, quam uix erratica Delos / orantem accepit') [whom the king's wife (i.e., Juno) / debarred from the world, whom, though she begged, wandering Delos / scarcely accepted] suffering a most human thirst and lack of breast milk for her nursing twins on a hot day (6.332–4).[27] Ovid's efforts to arouse our sympathy for Latona as a pathetic victim of random human spite, however, have the paradoxical effect of rekindling Niobe's ill-fated scepticism about the quality of her divinity: why, we may well wonder, should a bona fide goddess find herself thus discomfited in the first place? The twins' requirement for Latona's breast milk raises similar questions, since in the Homeric Hymn the newborn Apollo is explicitly said to have fed on nectar and ambrosia instead of his mother's breast.[28] Apollo's acceptance of this superior sustenance in the hymn in fact marks his conversion (in a moment that would influence Keats's Hyperion) from human-like infancy to divine immortality.[29] Ovid's conscious rejection of this tradition of Apollo's nourishment in Met. 6, then, serves further to problematize the strength of both Latona's and Apollo's divinity in the context of their more immediate, vulnerable circumstances. Indeed, Latona's angry transformation of the Lycian peasants into hoarse frogs for scornfully refusing her water is cast as much as her own momentous recovery (or discovery) of her divine powers as an assertion of them (6.366–8). In the very motion of confirming the power of Latona's divinity, then, it would appear that Ovid also associates her, in a potentially equivocal way, with the human weakness of her victims.

It is more difficult to sympathize with Latona's son Apollo in the next story, the flaying of Marsyas, which must nonetheless be understood in the context of the Latona clan's early struggles, as Apollo's sole designation as 'Latous' [son of Latona] in this episode implies (6.384). Although some critics would downplay the shock-value of the satyr's gruesome flaying by moralizing it as 'a graphic metaphor for stripping the artist of his pretensions' or a stylistic exercise in clinical detachment,[30] Ovid takes pains to present Apollo's punishment of his musical challenger as cruel and unusual in the extreme. In essence, Ovid reinvents the punishment of Marsyas as a narrative of human sacrifice, causing nearly every line to spill over with palpitating entrails and the surge of blood and tears – all the more overwhelming for the episode's brevity, not to mention its position in a book of the Metamorphoses that thereafter turns to the even more notorious cases of the cannibals Tantalus and Tereus. Meanwhile, the musical competition that occasioned this grisly event is only fleetingly alluded to, in the space of half a line, as a past victory of Apollo's, conspicuously without mention of Marsyas's imprudent challenge of the god. Indeed, Marsyas's presumption, for which he compellingly repents ('"a! non est ... tibia tanti"' [ah! the flute ... it is not worth so much]), is acknowledged only briefly and in the vaguest of terms (*Met.* 6.386).[31] We must conclude that Ovid has subtly turned his attention in this episode from the 'official' matter of righteous divine offence at human transgression, a structuring theme of Books Five and Six, to a more fractious exposure of the transparent fictions of a divine authority overcompensating for what is otherwise a visible absence of real power. Apollo emerges in the story of Marsyas as too defensive about his own divinity, too intent upon proving those powers which have been (perhaps justifiably) open to question. Far from redeeming Apollo as a god, this sequence of episodes concerning Apollo and his family prepares us conceptually for another outrageous family history, this time human: that of Tereus, Procne, and Philomela (6.412–674).[32]

If blood must flow in order to confirm the divinity of Apollo and his family in Ovid's *Metamorphoses*, the Apollo of the *Homeric Hymn* takes a more affirmative approach to his lowly origins. As Andrew M. Miller has insightfully argued, the hymnist's emphasis on Apollo's proximity to mortal weakness in the *Hymn* validates rather than undermines the god's divinity by presenting him as an apt model of *human* self-knowledge: 'for all his greatness and his glory, Apollo will henceforward remain cognizant of the metaphysical and ethical implications of his natality ... thereby acknowledging the elements of contingency and dependence that limit divine existence at its origin.'[33] Precisely because Apollo shares a personal history of sorts with the tribes of men who 'live an unresourceful and thoughtless life, unable / to find a cure for death and a charm to repel old age' (*To Apollon* 192–3), Apollo serves as an oracular resource and mediator of the gods' will for humanity. The contrast with Latin treatments of Apollo, however, could not be starker, and Ovidian tradition capitalizes upon these obscurities in Apollo's characterization to engage a broader and more pressing set of concerns surrounding the poet's authority and identity.

The Unharmonized Subject: Apollo in Exile

In Latin tradition, Apollo is never entirely at home in the Olympian order. Partly because of his natal association with human weakness and his role as interpreter of the divine will for humanity, Apollo both facilitates and participates in familiar sublunary rhythms of aspiration, error, and achievement. Accordingly, Apollo's roles as a god are multifarious; most notably, he presides over the realms of prophecy, urban planning and colonization, the solar cycle, youth, medicine, music, and poetic expression. Medieval iconographic tradition accentuates the multiplicity of Apollo's attributes. A synthetic late medieval mythographic manual such as De deorum imaginibus libellus (c. 1400), which draws from a number of earlier medieval accounts of the pagan gods and in turn influences their depictions in visual art, associates Apollo with no fewer than twelve key features: the sun, youth, the tripod, bow and arrows, the cithara, the three-headed griffin, a jewelled crown, the laurel, the raven, the Muses, Python, and Parnassus.[34] In some texts, e.g., Servius's gloss on Eclogue 5.66, the compendia of the second and third Vatican Mythographers, and Boccaccio's Genealogie deorum gentilium libri, the potentially conflicting nature of Apollo's attributes – which pertain to peace and beauty as well as violence – generates the topos of the triplex Apollo: the same deity apprehended as Sol in the upper regions, where he bears the lyre as image of celestial harmony, is known as Liber Pater on earth, where his attribute is the three-headed griffin,[35] and as Apollo in the underworld, where his destructive powers are represented by his arrows.[36] To his ancient worshippers and literary expositors, Apollo is less a stable ontological signifier than an expression of the force of transition: from childhood to adulthood, impurity to purity, exile to colonization, disease to health, darkness to light. Yet, because Apollo's various functions, allegiances, and attributes are dynamic in these ways, they tend in literary accounts to work against or compete with one another instead of cohering in a global image of power. What emerges is a god who straddles precariously, rather than confidently mediates, the divine and human realms.

   This tension in Apollo's identity is notably rendered in ancient tradition – and, we shall see, perceived in the Middle Ages – through the motifs of self-displacement and exile. In contrast to the choral ode or hymn (e.g., the Homeric Hymn to Apollo, Callimachus's Hymn 2 [to Apollo], and Horace's Carmen saeculare), whose purpose is to celebrate the harmonious plurality of a god's cultic powers and functions, Ovidian tradition capitalized upon Apollo's potential for fragmentation, incongruence, and dispersion. When Ovid does define Apollo's 'composite' identity in the Metamorphoses, he does so strictly by means of ironic negation, evoking those attributes that have been compromised or neglected by Apollo in his infelicitous and ultimately thwarted desire to share in the human condition. Ovid's representation of Apollo's sudden infatuation with the mortal Daphne in *Metamorphoses* 1, for instance, hardly encourages us to ignore the god's divine functions and instead imagine him simply in his human-lover aspect. Rather, it plays off the obsessive futility of Apollo's erotic desire against his prophetic powers, here ignorant that Daphne's reciprocation of his love is not fated to be. Similarly undercut is Apollo's divine archery, which pales before the arrow that has pierced his own heart, and his art of medicine, with which he cannot heal his own lovesickness. In a related story later in the *Metamorphoses*, Apollo programmatically rejects his own divine privileges and wilfully relocates to the mortal world of sport, hunt, and chance inhabited by the boy Hyacinthus, with whom he falls desperately in love. With nary a second thought, Apollo disowns his Delphic duties, his lyre, and his bow in order to emulate Hyacinthus's carefree life as a hunter in Sparta (10.168–70). Because Ovid draws such pointed attention to Apollo's rejection of his divine identity, he encourages an ironic response to his various failures in this episode, as, for instance, when Apollo as god of prophecy is caught unawares by Hyacinthus's accidental death, and later when his medical arts fall short of healing the boy's mortal wound. Even more ironic are the terms of Apollo's self-blame for the loss of Hyacinthus: in contrast to other gods who yearn to grant their earthly lovers either eternal youth or divine status,[37] Apollo's first reaction, fittingly, is to ignore his divine resources altogether. Instead, he revealingly (if finally unconvincingly) expresses a desire to be *human* so that he could either die with Hyacinthus or, like Alcestis, die for him.

Apollo's empathy for the human condition thus engenders in these narratives a compromising descent in the chain of being that eludes generative fulfilment, and stands in contrast to the more flippant (and successful) sexual intrigues of Jove and the other Olympians. Equally suggestive are the various narratives of enforced exile and compulsory servitude with which Apollo is identified in classical and medieval tradition. As Detienne observes, the frequency of Apollo's periods of confinement to the mortal world radically, if temporarily, dislocate Apollo's authority by suspending his claim to the 'toujours' of immortality.[38] Early versions of Apollo's slaying of Python, his vengeance upon the Cyclops after the execution of his son Aesculapius, and his involvement in the construction of Troy all portray Apollo, in varying degrees, as an exile or a transgressor against the divine order. Whereas Latin poets, including Tibullus and Ovid, develop the comic and erotodidactic implications of such episodes, philosophical and religious commentators in the classical, early Christian, and medieval periods recurrently exploit them as evidence of the misleading nature of fable or as moral exempla illustrating behaviour to be avoided. To demonstrate this point, three seminal representations of Apollo as exile will be considered in turn, in light of the philosophical and moral commentary that coloured their transmission in various periods.

Apollo's first kill, his victory over Python, is an exploit that ancient authors usually encourage us to regard as straightforwardly heroic, but in pre-Ovidian treatments of the story (e.g., in Callimachus, *Aetia* 4) it also carried an association with blood pollution requiring cleansing and expiation. According to this version of the legend, after killing Python Apollo wandered to the Tempe valley in Thessaly in order to purify himself of the deed, then returned to Delphi, carrying Thessalian laurel, and founded his oracle.[39] The notion that Apollo's brave feat necessitated a process of exile and purgation like that endured by his protégé Orestes elicited a cynical response from Ovid, who, as we shall see, commented obliquely on Apollo's cleansing in his very different revision of the story. Plutarch's 'Obsolescence of Oracles' directly remarks upon the problematic implications of the legend through the voice of Cleombrotus, who argues that it is 'utterly ridiculous' that Apollo, god of Delphi, 'should flee to the ends of Greece in quest of purification' so as to 'placate and mollify the wrath of spirits whom men call the "unforgetting avengers."' Rather, argues Cleombrotus, the legend must concern a demigod who has been conflated with the real Apollo.[40]

Apollo's association with transgression and punishment is developed more fully – and, for the Middle Ages, more influentially – in the story of his servitude as shepherd to the Thessalian king Admetus as punishment for murdering the Cyclops, whose thunderbolts, wielded by Jove, had taken the life of Aesculapius. Apollo is sentenced to spend a year 'spoliatus divinitate' [deprived of divinity] (Servius on *Aen.* 6.398), but enjoys the experience so much that he falls in love either with his master Admetus or with Admetus's daughter.[41] Apollo's servitude to Admetus furnished Tibullus and, after him, Ovid with an iconic vision of the imperative of debasing oneself in the pursuit of love. Tibullus renders Apollo's exile by means of a series of ironic inversions that directly anticipate Ovid's 'negative' approach to Apollo's composite nature in the episodes of Daphne and Hyacinthus discussed above. Tibullus 2.3 revels in the comic potential of Apollo's amorous frolics in a bucolic dreamscape: in the service of love, Apollo makes cheese like a country maiden;

cradles a calf in his arms, to the mortification of his sister Diana; sings lofty songs ('carmina docta') to the accompaniment of lowing cattle; neglects his oracle in troubled times; and causes his mother to grieve over his tousled hair (2.3.11–28; cf. 3.4.65–72). Ovid reworks this Tibullan set piece at *Ars amatoria* 2.239–41, where Apollo's example becomes a coy injunction to self-compromise and voluntary suffering on the part of all those who wish to succeed in the game of love.

Not surprisingly, the image of Apollo as sanguine exile provoked wide-ranging moral critique and interpretive calisthenics in later periods. In the course of discussing the deceptive effects of pagan fables in *De civitate Dei* 18.13, Augustine (adopting a strategy reminiscent of that of Plutarch's Cleombrotus) asserts that the Apollo of the Delphic oracle was a separate personage from the Apollo whose mother was Latona and who served Admetus, though, he notes, most people erroneously assume that the two are identical. In contrast, Arnulf of Orléans's twelfth-century commentary on the *Metamorphoses* confronts the problem of Apollo's loss of dignity by representing his labour as a shepherd as an actual metamorphosis from god to man, included along with Book Two's other 'mutationes': 'Apollo in pastorem. Batus in lapidem. Aglauros in lapidem. Iupiter in thaurum' [Apollo into a shepherd. Battus into a stone. Aglauros into a stone. Jupiter into a bull].[42] Giovanni del Virgilio's early fourteenth-century commentary on the *Metamorphoses*, substantially indebted to Arnulf, further expands this interpretation of Apollo's transformation into a human shepherd: 'Duodecima transmutatio est de Phebo. Nam per Phebum intelligitur homo sapiens, qui aliquando delirat a sapientia et dat se viciis terrestribus' [The twelfth metamorphosis is that of Phoebus. For Phoebus is understood as a wise man who at some point becomes deranged, leaves behind wisdom, and gives himself over to worldly vices].[43] These moral implications are fully developed in the discussion of Apollo and his deeds in the fifteenth-century Ovidian mythographic compendium preserved in Milan, MS Biblioteca Ambrosiana E 128 sup. (12v–13v). Commenting on the obscure references to Apollo 'agrestis imagine ... utque modo accipitris pennas, modo terga leonis / gesserit, ut pastor Macareida luserit Issen' [in the guise of a countryman, / and here how he was wearing a hawk's feathers, here a lion's / skin, how as a shepherd he tricked Macareus's daughter, Isse], among the various unsavoury divine metamorphoses portrayed on Arachne's tapestry at *Met.* 6.122–4, the commentator allegorizes Apollo's transformations into a hawk and a rustic as an exemplum of the dangers of pride. When the wise man, represented by Apollo, begins to grow proud in his wisdom ('incipit in sua sapientia superbire'), he becomes ensnared by worldly allurements ('mundanis illecebris irretitur'). Apollo's transformations into a shepherd – both when he loved Admetus's daughter and when he lingered with ('iacuit') Macareus's daughter – and his prideful murder of the Cyclops are cited as support for this moral interpretation. In his transgression and ensuing exile, then, as well as in his voluntary subjection to love, Apollo offered medieval commentators a fertile image of human sin, rendered through the implicit connection between wisdom compromised and divine status displaced.

Our final example of Apollo as exile – as a day-labourer, together with Neptune, for the ungrateful boss Laomedon, who refused to pay their wages – at first seems to present Apollo's involvement in mundane affairs in a more positive light. According to Ovid, Apollo 'mortalem induitur formam' [put on mortal form] and volunteered to construct the walls of Troy as a favour to Laomedon (*Met.* 11.203).[44] In Apollodorus's account, Apollo did it as a test of Laomedon's character.[45] In the Biblioteca Ambrosiana E 128 sup. commentary, the assistance that Apollo offers to Laomedon represents the counsel of wisdom ('sapienti consilio'), in contrast with the interpretation of his other exiles as the *loss* of wisdom. Even here, however, there is room for more sceptical readings: this is, after all, a story of servitude and perjury that features a mortal's humiliation of a deity, his later vengeance for that humiliation notwithstanding. An example is Augustine's discussion of the details of the gods' Trojan servitude in *De civitate Dei* 3.2: logical as always, Augustine deplores the foolishness of worshipping Apollo, god of prophecy, who could not *foresee* that Laomedon would fail to pay him. Further problematical is the fact that the walls built by two sets of divine hands – one pair of which belongs to the god of urban foundations himself – are doomed one day to fall, despite Apollo's loyal protection of the city of Troy (a problem to which chapter 3 will return). As Ovid's Neptune himself acknowledges to Apollo in the late days of the Trojan War, their construction of the walls was done 'inrita': vainly, uselessly, invalidly (*Met.* 12.587). In *Olympian Odes* 8, Pindar, a priest of Apollo, had attempted to evade this implication by relating that a human, Aecus – great-grandfather of the Trojan scourge Neoptolemus (Pyrrhus) – helped Apollo and Neptune build the doomed walls of Troy, and that the walls were vulnerable only in the mortal's section. In most versions of the story, however, the gods alone build the walls, and must themselves bear the responsibility for their ultimate unsoundness. Viewed in relation to treatments of Apollo's other exiles and displacements, the penetrability of Troy's divine fortifications could be said to encode Apollo's own 'humanity' as a god whose worldly priorities often compromise his integrity as a pillar of divine authority.

Defining Apollo: *Metamorphoses* 1–2

Earlier we saw in the sequence of narratives in Book Six of the *Metamorphoses*, centring upon Apollo's youth and the early establishment of his familial cult, Ovid's cynical recasting of the hymnic tradition of Apollo's inborn affiliation with the human condition. Books One and Two concern a different history of origins, distinct from Apollo's cultic introduction to the Thebans and Lycians later in the poem: Apollo's introduction to the world of Ovid's narrative. As has often been recognized, Apollo's escapades in these first two books establish a fertile tension, much exploited by Ovid, between elegiac and epic modes. In so doing, they infuse the poem with a 'comic anthropomorphism' that colours virtually all of its deities and facilitates its structuring concern with the 'universal contiguity' of creation.[46] Just as importantly, however, these first books – whose influence in the Middle Ages cannot be overstated – define Apollo in ways that recursively raise broader problems of identity crucial to Apollo's actions elsewhere in the *Metamorphoses*, as well as their exemplary effects in Ovid's self-fashioning as Apolline artist and doomed love doctor.

The first postdiluvian narrative in the *Metamorphoses* features Apollo's slaying of the Python, which constitutes the god's initial appearance in the poem. Like the story of his birth on the island of Delos, this tale of Apollo's youthful heroics is of venerable antiquity, with origins in archaic hymnic tradition.[47] Nonetheless, Ovid creates suspense as to Apollo's identity by withholding his proper name until the very end of the last line of the episode (*Met.* 1.451), referring to him up to that point only as 'deus arquitenens' [the archer-god] (1.441), one of Apollo's many cult epithets, and associating him with the Pythian games, which take their name from the slain serpent and in turn serve as another learned appellative of Apollo. The fact that Apollo's heroic attributes and cultic associations precede his actual naming serves to elevate his deeds and the range of his powers – a strategy reinforced in flashback several lines after the conclusion of the episode: 'Delius hunc, nuper uicto serpente superbus' [Recently the Delian, made haughty by his conquest of the serpent] (1.454). Apollo's identity is thus, in this first episode, based quite literally on the *fama* of his heroic deeds.

Cupid's appearance immediately following this scene of epic bravado instantly destabilizes the poet's stylized picture of Apollo's identity, even before his golden dart fatefully pierces Apollo's breast. Introduced by means of his awesome bow ('adducto flectentem cornua neruo' [bending his bow with string drawn tight] [1.455]), Cupid's very presence challenges Apollo's identity as *deus arquitenens* – the archergod, intrinsically and uniquely knowable through his actions. What Apollo does not yet realize – but would, if he had read Ovid's *Amores*, in which the poet himself failed a similar contest of wills with Cupid (*Am.* 1.1) – is that heroism (in this case archery) has already been redefined as erotic combat. Under the dispensation of love, even as distinctive a deity as Apollo becomes as utterly generic as any *amator* imbibing mass-market love advice from the *magister amoris*. Accordingly, Apollo is referred to only by his proper name (Phoebus or Apollo) throughout his encounter with Cupid, as if to puncture the god's inflated self-image as Panhellenic superpower. Cupid's verbal assertion of his superiority to the obstinate Apollo further undermines the god's conception of his identity by sanctioning a comparative formula by which Apollo's divinity is precariously partnered through analogy with the realms of the altogether undivine: 'quantoque animalia cedunt / cuncta deo, tanto minor est tua gloria nostra' [by how much all creatures / yield to god, by so much is your glory less than mine] (1.464–5). Ironically, if the divine Apollo is shown here – and later in his actions as a lover – to be no better than human, the mortal Daphne with whom he falls madly in love wishes to be *more* than human, emulating and measuring herself against the divine standards of Apollo's own sister Diana (1.476, 483–4).

In a comically intricate speech replete with (self-directed) hymnic features,[48] in which Apollo attempts to seduce the fleeing Daphne en route, Apollo disastrously appropriates Ovid's own strategy of introduction in the Python scene.[49] Working from the desperate assumption that Daphne flees because she does not know who he is, Apollo reveals his identity to her indirectly, as if to build suspense, first with reference to what he is *not* ('non incola montis, / non ego sum pastor, non hic armenta gregesque / horridus obseruo' [No mountain dweller I, / no shepherd; this is no uncouth fellow watching / the herds and flocks] [1.512–14]), then, by means of a circuitous list of epithets and attributes, to what he *is* (master of Delphi, Claros, Tenedos, and Patara; son of Jove; prophet; musician;

archer; healer), without ever actually naming himself. Even as Apollo's strategy predictably fails to seduce Daphne, for whom the only aspect of the god's identity that ever mattered was his maleness, it does appropriately result in his proud attainment of the boasting right of another attribute: the laurel (which both is and is not Daphne). Granted the ambiguous reward of escaping Apollo's embrace but becoming a symbol of *his* prowess and eternal youth (see 1.557–65) rather than her own vindicated virginity,[50] Daphne's metamorphosis paradoxically crystallizes the fictions of *Apollo's* identity. Not only does Apollo here '[betray] his own lack of insight into his own subjectivity,'[51] but his very attempt to reconstitute and communicate that subjectivity in his pursuit of Daphne pales in comparison to the coherence of her single-mindedly virginal selfhood, giving the strong impression that the real *agon* in this scene is not between the sexes but within Apollo himself.

Ovid caps the Daphne episode with an intentionally enigmatic 'nod' of consent on the part of the breeze-blown laurel, and a deeply ironic final epithet for Apollo: 'finierat Paean' [Paean had finished] (1.566). Ovid identifies Apollo here with the one divine function – healing – that the god himself had disclaimed while seducing Daphne as woefully ineffective:[52]

> inuentum medicina meum est, opiferque per orbem
> dicor, et herbarum subiecta potentia nobis.
> ei mihi, quod nullis amor est sanabilis herbis,
> nec prosunt domino quae prosunt omnibus artes!   (1.521–4)

> [Medicine is my invention and I am called throughout the world
> Bringer-of-help, and the power of herbs is subject to me.
> Ah me, that there are no herbs that can cure love,
> that the arts which help all men do not help their master!]

Apollo's identity, and by extension his potential to project authority and guide those who, like him, attempt to shape circumstances through poetic creation (in his hymn of seduction and his appropriation of the 'tenui ... libro' [thin bark/book; 1.549] of the laurel),[53] emerges as radically unstable in these first episodes. At the same time, Apollo's crisis of identity gives shape and momentum to the fluid possibilities of Ovid's narrative world, as the multitude of divine-human rape narratives that follow in the first two books of the poem attests. Unlike Jove, who reveals himself much more directly in the following episode of Io's rape, or Mercury, whose rhetorical adaptability ensures regular success, Apollo by no means shows himself able to master this metamorphic world – quite the contrary, he is a 'constant failure,' as B.R. Fredericks has observed, because he is unable to adapt his identity to circumstance.[54] Indeed, Apollo identifies himself with a mode of artistic creation that is self-defeating, founded upon an illusion of authority that conceals a fundamentally unformed sense of self.

This crisis of identity spills over onto Apollo's biological sons as well as his poetic descendants. Our next encounter with Apollo in the *Metamorphoses* concerns the perverse impotence of the god in his solar aspect: the story of Phaethon's demise.[55] Phaethon's encounter with his father Apollo and his failed attempt to guide the god's solar chariot is a tragic *Bildungsroman* impelled by Phaethon's quest to prove to himself and others his identity as son of the sun, without regard for the mortal half of that identity, which derives from his mother Clymene. As in his pursuit of Daphne, Apollo's rhetorical attempt to persuade Phaethon reveals the god of poetry's verbal powers as disturbingly ineffective, despite the length and formality of his speeches.[56] Once again, Apollo's authority fails in action: the exemplary artistic vision of cosmic harmony crafted on the doors of Apollo's solar palace (2.1–18) is cancelled out like an airy illusion by a madman's brush as his son, an artist overtaken by art, redraws the map of the universe in black smoke and flame.[57] What Phaethon's unchecked art produces, significantly, is the universe in which we now live (2.235–59), a universe in which Apollo's idyllic fictions are undermined by forces of reality against which even the god of poetry is powerless to provide a constructive alternative. Furthermore, the illusion of a stable, coherent identity implicit in the aesthetic of Apollo's solar palace is transformed, much as it was in the Python-Cupid-Daphne sequence, by a challenge to that identity: in this case, Phaethon's desire to share publicly in it. Phaethon's own crisis of identity as Apollo's son leads to a similar crisis for Apollo himself: 'genitor Phaethontis ... / ... lucemque odit seque ipse diemque / datque animum in luctus et luctibus adicit iram / officiumque negat mundo' [the father of Phaethon ... hated the light and himself and the day, / and gave his spirit up to grief, with anger added to his grief, / and refused to perform his duty to the world] (2.381, 383–5). Wishing no longer to be himself, as defined with compact irony through a brilliant zeugma (in hating himself, the mourning sun necessarily also hates *lux* and *dies*), Apollo attempts a self-cancellation that recalls Ovid's more overtly ironic naming of the unhealed Apollo as Paean at the end of the Daphne episode. This reversion to form in turn prepares us for the next Apolline drama of the *Metamorphoses* – the tale of Apollo and Coronis – which even more fully reprises the turbulent narrative experiences of Apollo as archer, lover, and healer.

The dark story of Apollo's murder of his mortal lover Coronis vied with the popularity of the Apollo and Daphne story in the Middle Ages: commented upon and illustrated regularly, it was disseminated in the vernacular by Machaut, Gower, and Chaucer, most prominently in its pivotal position near the end of the *Canterbury Tales*, to be considered in chapter 5. In the *Metamorphoses*, the Coronis melodrama immediately invites association with Apollo's first failed love affair through the fact of its setting in Thessaly (i.e., Haemonia, 2.543).[58] Apollo's Delphic status – evoked in the earlier episode by his defeat of Python, the references to prophecy at 1.491 and 1.517–18, and the mention of Delphi at 1.515 – is prominently heralded at the beginning of the Coronis story by means of Ovid's sarcastically hyperbolic vocative 'Delphice' ('placuit tibi, Delphice, certe, / dum uel casta fuit uel inobseruata' [she (Coronis) certainly gave pleasure to you, oh Delphic one, / while she was true, or unwatched] (2.543–4).[59] It is doubly ironic in the present context that the Delphic Apollo, ever complacent, cares only about the *appearance* of truth in his beloved's conduct – he would happily live in ignorance of the reality – and that one of Apollo's cult birds, the raven, trumping the god's own powers of prophecy and insight, must reveal to him the adultery taking place in his own bed.[60] As in the Python-Cupid-Daphne sequence, Apollo's status as 'Delphice' jars with his casting in the role of elegiac lover. As if to ensure that the reader registers the episode's intertextual affinity with the less tragic jealousies and squabbles that impel an elegiac poem such as the *Amores*,[61] Ovid conspicuously refers to Apollo simply as 'amans' for the bulk of the episode (2.600, 612). In a direct reminder of Apollo's first erotic defeat in Thessaly, the laurel wreath crowning his head (ever an unsteady consolation prize) slips to the ground upon Apollo's discovery of Coronis's infidelity (2.600).

Apollo in his seduction of Daphne proved an unconvincing imitator of Ovid's strategy of circumlocutionary introduction, and in the Phaethon episode emerged an ineffective artistic instructor, but in the story of Coronis he sinks to a new poetic low: this time, as a disastrous reader of his own *historia*. A review of the literal events of the narrative discloses the awkward reality that both the raven and

Coronis know more about the details of the story of which Apollo is a protagonist than does Apollo himself. The story may be summarized as follows: Apollo discovers Coronis's infidelity through his avian informant; Apollo shoots Coronis without first exchanging words with her; the dying Coronis reveals an important part of the story unknown to either Apollo or the raven (that she is pregnant); Apollo wishes to rewrite his own actions but cannot; and, finally, Apollo saves the unborn child from the funeral pyre. Poor as he is as an interpreter of the narrative in which he finds himself, Apollo, by trusting to rash action rather than verbal communication, makes matters yet worse by denying himself the very knowledge that would have allowed him to perpetuate the illusion of domestic happiness (i.e., the hope that the child was his). Indeed, Apollo proves himself an inefficient reader of poetic tradition, since it was a mythological commonplace well before Ovid's time that divine-mortal coitus is always fertile – thus making Apollo's ignorance of Coronis's pregnancy even more of an interpretive embarrassment. In rescuing the fetus (Aesculapius) from the pyre – an act that suggestively balances Apollo's inability to save his other son Phaethon from the flames earlier in Book Two – Apollo salvages the 'ending' of his story, as it were, by ensuring the survival of an artistic heir, albeit one associated with the healing rather than the poetic arts. It is no coincidence that the god of poetry's miraculous deliverance of his son echoes portions of Ovid's elegy of Tibullus in *Amores* 3.9, in which a sober vision of the flames consuming the poet's breast on his funeral pyre is tempered by the promise, repeated by Ovid elsewhere (most significantly in the final lines of the *Metamorphoses*), that 'defugiunt avidos carmina sola rogos' [song alone escapes the greedy pyre] (line 27).[62] Like the story of Apollo's doomed love of Daphne, the episode of Coronis is, on one level, a parable of the loss, fractured understanding, and waste of humanity implicit in the perpetuation of art.

These are not the only respects, however, in which Apollo in the Coronis episode is a tragically ineffectual reader of his own story. Most striking in this episode are the botched literary instincts with which Apollo seems intent upon reenacting, in ridiculously incongruous and banally domestic circumstances, his heroics and the thrill of first love as related in Book One. As if in a perverse attempt to relive his own story, Apollo as elegiac lover reverts to epic form, irrationally viewing his own beloved's breast as a field of victory for his second triumph as *arquitenens*:

   utque animus tumida feruebat ab ira,
arma adsueta capit flexumque a cornibus arcum
tendit et illa suo totiens cum pectore iuncta
indeuitato traiecit pectora telo.   (*Met.* 2.602–5)

   [and, as his spirit seethed with boiling anger,
he took his customary weapons and stretched his bow bent
from its horns and, with his ineludible arrow, pierced
that breast so often joined with his breast.]

Apollo's shooting of Coronis is remarkably similar in form and intensity to his slaying of the Python, evoked by 'arma adsueta' (2.603), which is still fresh in the reader's memory in Book Two:

hunc deus arquitenens, numquam letalibus armis
ante nisi in dammis capreisque fugacibus usus,
mille grauem telis, exhausta paene pharetra,
perdidit effuso per uulnera nigra ueneno.   (1.441–4)

[The archer-god, who had never before used his deadly
weapons except on fleeing red or yellow deer,
almost emptied his quiver to load him with a thousand arrows
and so destroyed him, as his venom flowed through his black wounds.]

The 'indeuitato' (unerring) shaft with which Apollo pierces Coronis, moreover, recalls the 'certa' arrow (1.519) of which Apollo boasts in wooing Daphne. This unsavoury parallel between Python and Coronis as quarry of the wrathful hunter Apollo is picked up provocatively in Chaucer's *Manciple's Tale*, in which an even darker rendition of the Apollo and Coronis story – to which this book's final chapter will return in depth – is prefaced by Apollo's famous first exploit 'heere in this erthe adoun': 'He slow Phitoun, the serpent, as he lay / Slepynge agayn the sonne upon a day' (*MancT* 105, 109–10). After a brief encomium of the god's 'mynstralcie' (113), which is of unique importance in Chaucer's version of the story, and a few rote comments on his 'worthynesse' (124), Apollo's bow is again emphasized in connection with his slaying of the Python: 'For his desport, in signe eek of victorie / Of Phitoun, so as telleth us the storie, / Was wont to beren in his hand a bowe' (127–9). Eliding the connected episode of Daphne altogether, Chaucer's Manciple then moves directly into the Coronis story ('Now hadde this Phebus in his hous a crowe' [130]), introducing a significant end rhyme on *bowe/crowe* that is repeated at the tale's climax (269–70). In these ways, Chaucer closely links the stories of Apollo's slaying of Python and his murder of Coronis, in effect reimagining them within a causative sequence that displaces the less savage, if equally unflattering, Ovidian narrative of Apollo's purely erotic 'hunt' of Daphne.[63]

At the same time that the homicidal Apollo's crime of passion in *Metamorphoses* 2 parodically revisits the establishment of his heroic identity in his victory over Python, it also reinforces the discolouring of that heroism by the usurper Cupid. If the reader is encouraged at the moment of Coronis's murder to recall in a tragic key the path of Apollo's *certa* arrow from the earlier scene, the recollection of a *certior* arrow is quick to follow, advanced by the rhetoric of Apollo's own admission to Daphne: 'certa quidem nostra est, nostra tamen una sagitta / certior, in uacuo quae uulnera pectora fecit' [My arrow is sure indeed, but there is one arrow / surer still which has made wounds in my empty heart] (*Met*. 1.519–20). With compact irony, the guilty Coronis's correspondence with the vicious Python gives way to an even more startling parallel: between the wounded breast of Coronis and that of the lovestruck Apollo. The fact that it is Coronis's *pectus* that is pierced by Apollo's *indeuitato* arrow receives notable emphasis. As a site of tenderness and vulnerability, the breast serves as a pathetic image of the mutual, equalizing passion that joined god and mortal: 'et illa suo totiens cum *pectore* iuncta / indeuitato traiecit *pectora* telo' [and, with his ineludible arrow, pierced / that breast so often joined with his breast] (2.604–5, emphasis added; Coronis's *pectora* is mentioned a third time at 2.626). Just as Apollo's *uacuo pectora* was, by his own admission, transfixed by Cupid's *certior* arrow, thus dulling Apollo's *certa* shaft and his epic pretensions, so does Apollo's supposed victory over the empty breast of his faithless lover reveal him to be no true conqueror, but rather the *victim* of a continued erotic disorder the effects of which are increasingly destructive.[64] This disorder manifests itself within both house and self, exposing Apollo to the deceit of mortals; furthermore, as Apollo's continued ineffectiveness attests, it alarmingly compromises his divine prerogative.

As William S. Anderson has noted, Apollo's repentant funeral rites for the slain Coronis – whom his healing powers fail to revive – disturbingly mock the ritual of divine sacrifice. Ironically, the deity who, in a rightly ordered world, ought to be the recipient of sacrifice is instead its performer; moreover, as the (unjust) murderer of the human victim, Apollo could himself be said to require ritual cleansing.[65] In fact, Apollo

identifies with his victim in this scene to such an extent that Ovid outrageously encourages us to imagine him not as archer-god or domestic
lover but heifer on the slaughter line:

> alto de corde petitos
> edidit, haud aliter quam cum, spectante iuuenca,
> lactentis uituli dextra libratus ab aure
> tempora discussit claro caua malleus ictu.   (2.622–5)

> [he uttered groans summoned up from the bottom
> of his heart, just as when, with the heifer looking on,
> a hammer, balanced by the right ear, smashes
> the hollow temples of a suckling calf with a resounding blow.]

As a god, however, Apollo cannot truly imagine the pain of death; if he
could, why should he have executed his beloved so unthinkingly in the
first place? Despite his charitable tending of Coronis's corpse, it comes
as no surprise that the only sacrifice performed in this dark story is that
of the ungrateful Coronis to Apollo's own egotism. Apollo has little difficulty quelling his momentary grief over the fallen Coronis and resum-
ing life as a blissfully unreflective *amator* – the state in which he
reappears fewer than fifty lines after his rescue of the fetus Aesculapius
from Coronis's womb.[66] At this point, the centaur Chiron, to whom
Apollo entrusted the care of his newborn son, is in desperate need of
Apollo's help, but 'Delphice' – again a comically unapt appellative – is
out of reach and in love again (*Met.* 2.677–83). The lovesick Apollo is
predictably oblivious to Chiron's loss of his own daughter Ocyroe,
who, as a prophetess, deserves Apollo's protection. Apollo is equally
heedless of his responsibilities as herdsman – the rustic role in which he
finds himself in serving his new, unnamed beloved (usually taken as
Admetus). This bucolic scene, which serves as a transition to Mercury's
erotic adventures, fittingly caps Ovid's extended introduction of Apollo
as a feckless 'human' lover, deceived as much by his fellow gods –
Mercury promptly absconds with Apollo's herd without obstruction –
as by mortals.[67] Here as throughout this series of first appearances,
Ovid studiously undermines and trivializes Apollo's actions, occluding
the traditions in which Apollo's service as a shepherd is explained as
punishment for a righteous offence (Jove's slaying of Aesculapius) or,
as in the *Homeric Hymn to Hermes*, assimilated into an etiology of divine
powers. Instead, Ovid privileges the elegiac celebration of Apollo's

servitude to Admetus, in the spirit of his treatment of the story in *Ars amatoria* 2, as a model for the human lover who must similarly endure the humiliations of '[n]ox et hiems longaeque viae saevique dolores' [night, storm, long journeys, cruel pains] (*Ars Am.* 2.235).[68] Even on this level, however, Apollo's artistic authority fails to sustain itself. Marred by their discouraging frequency and questionable success rate, Apollo's erotic efforts at this point in the *Metamorphoses* imply that his status as a valid exemplar within the elegiac tradition is as fragile as his eroding reputation as dragon-slayer.

Nomen Poetae: Ovid's Love of Art

'[A]rtificis status ipse fuit' [he was the very image of an artist] (*Met.* 11.169): with these words Apollo appears, nine books after his pro-longed introduction, in full, stylized possession of his divine attributes – Parnassian laurel garland, flowing robes, gem-studded lyre, elegant bearing – about to pluck the mellifluous string that will prove him, to the chagrin of the opinionated bystander Midas, the musical superior of the rustic Pan. This vision of Apollo, following closely upon the god's protection of his artistic heir Orpheus (named as Apollo's son at 10.167), offers a deliberate reminder of Apollo's mythic status as exem-plary artist, model and epitome of *ars* in its most ethereally perfected form. The reader does indeed require reminding of this fact after the preceding books' gradual devaluation and displacement of Apollo's powers and, by implication, the efficacy and relevance of his *ars*. To be sure, Midas's blunt scepticism regarding the superiority of Apollo's musical expression is deemed foolish and deserving of punishment, but his irreverence appears in some respects understandable: after the god's unbalanced and frequently debased appearances in Ovid's poem thus far, Apollo as an austere image of the sublimity of art cannot help but appear 'artificial.' That is to say, Apollo's is not an art that conceals art (like that of the Venerean Pygmalion) but an art that emphatically *calls attention to itself* as art – in a way that Midas's experience suggests may not be entirely convincing. In this light Ovid's sustained criticism of Apollo in the *Metamorphoses*, which the preceding analyses have shown ranges from the lighthearted to the scandalous, cannot be ex-plained as mere flippancy or rebellious 'disaffection' on the part of a poet intent upon asserting his own poetic independence from the god of poetry or, by cultural extension, Augustan propriety.[69] Instead, Ovid's preoccupation with Apollo as a frequently compromised agent of artistic authority serves the larger purpose of facilitating Ovid's exploration of the complex function of *ars* as a performance of (and surrogate for) love, and a tool for ordering experience in general.[70] The following discussion resituates the Apollo of the *Metamorphoses* within the context of his role as advisor and inspirer in Ovid's amatory poetry, with the aim of demonstrating that Ovid's critique of Apollo is founded upon a far-reaching program not of dismissal but of self-identification with the god as a locus and mirror-image of the artist engaged in an essentially narcissistic, and often self-defeating, activity. These broadly (meta-)poetic aspects of Apolline *ars*, treated here in isolation, will in the next section be reabsorbed into the richly medical dimensions of *ars* by which Ovid most fully expresses the significance of Apollo's erotic ethic to his own artistic legacy in the *Remedia amoris* and exile poetry. The intertwined aesthetic and medical dimensions of the Ovidian Apollo, later chapters will show, provided fertile ground for medieval Christian challenges to, and poetic appropriations of, the authority of pagan antiquity.

As is widely recognized, the *Amores* begins by supplying a kind of urbane prehistory in the poet's own experience for what in the *Metamorphoses* is the archetypal mythic narrative of love's sway over the gods: Cupid's defeat of Apollo. Both *Amores* 1.1 and *Metamorphoses* 1.441–567, as Alison Sharrock has aptly observed, stage Cupid's 'theft' of Apollo's poetic authority through an intricate play on ancient literary conventions and narrative expectations.[71] As W.S.M. Nicoll has influentially demonstrated, in *Amores* 1.1 Cupid usurps the role of the Callimachean Apollo (the god who interrupts and redirects the poet's erring ambitions in the *recusatio* tradition) while 'Ovid,' like Apollo in *Metamorphoses* 1, arrogantly taunts the interfering Cupid and asserts the prerogative of 'serious' poets, i.e., *vates* (*Amores* 1.1.6), proclaiming Cupid's mastery an affront to the lyre of Phoebus (1.1.16).[72] Just as will be the case with Apollo in *Met.* 1, Cupid's 'certas … sagittas' pierce 'Ovid''s 'vacuo pectore' by way of response (*Amores* 1.1.25–6). This most intentional of intertextual filiations between the opening scene of the *Amores* and the first postdiluvian love story of the *Metamorphoses* establishes an implicit level of identification between 'Ovid' and Apollo, elaborated elsewhere in Ovid's works, by means of which Apollo functions both as poetic alter-ego and role model. In the very motion of criticizing Apollo's insufficiencies as victim of Cupid, then, Ovid inevitably reflects upon his own activity as a *magister* and wielder of *ars*.

Far from being dismissed or displaced, the form of *ars* represented by Apollo in the *Amores* – as in the *Metamorphoses* – is recharged by, and absorbed into, a new world order radically defined by the necessity of love. Significantly, Cupid repeats rather than refutes Ovid's self-designation as *vates* when handing down his new poetic assignment (*Amores* 1.1.24), implying that vatic poetry now encompasses private amatory experience as serious and truth-bearing subject matter.[73] Fully alive to the paradox of a truthful medium communicating deceitful content (the turbulent rhythms of cultivated desire), Ovid is quick to appropriate the divinely inspired image of the *vates* in the service of incongruously erotic ends: the bawd Dipsas claims, for example, that poet-suitors should be prepared to give women material gifts because Apollo himself, 'deus vatum' [the god of poets], wears a golden robe and plays a gilded lyre (*Amores* 1.8.59–60) – advice precisely contradicted by Ovid's own more miserly counsel to women courted by bards at *Ars Am.* 3.533–52, which pleads that *vates* make better lovers because their trade ('commercia') is with heaven rather than merchants.[74]

If Apollo's lyre, together with Ovid's ostensible authorial identity, is displaced by Cupid's poetic direction in *Amores* 1.1, Apollo returns to affirm Ovid's authority as poet in the last poem of the first book of the *Amores*, which bears an important connection to Ovid's self-celebration in the last lines of the *Metamorphoses*. A meditation on poetic immortality, through which the 'pars ... mei multa' [great part of me (*Amores* 1.15.42); cf. 'parte ... meliore mei' (better part of me, *Met.* 15.875)] survives the flames of death, this last poem in the *Amores* features Apollo pouring full cups of ambrosia for the triumphant Ovid, who claims his place in a line of love poets including Tibullus and Gallus. The scene is partly comic, with its fantasy of an overdecadent Apollo ministering to a mortal poet,[75] but placed in the larger context of the *Amores* Ovid's point is not merely flippant self-assertion of his own poetic prowess. The poet's imaginative proximity to Apollo, first dramatized in his proto-Apolline branding by Cupid and reinforced through his self-conscious performance of the lover's life as truth-bearing *ars*, takes on a darker hue in the companion piece to *Amores* 1.15, the elegy of Tibullus in 3.9. Unlike the rosy-cheeked youth solicitously padding Ovid's ego in 1.15, the Apollo of this later poem is portrayed as the mournful father of a series of doomed *vates* (Orpheus, Linus, Homer) (*Amores* 3.9.19–27) – a series in which Ovid, again, claims his place ('at sacri vates et divum cura vocamur' [Yes, we bards are called sacred, and the care of the gods] [3.9.17]). Like the earlier poem, 3.9 celebrates the immortality of *ars*, but it also places much greater emphasis upon the mortality of the artist, vividly evoked in the flames that feed upon the unrecognizable corpse of Tibullus as his lovers fight over his memory. The elegy of Tibullus thus leaves us with an image of Apollo as god of poets overwhelmed by melancholy circumstance and, this time, largely unaffiliated with the promise of artistic transcendence. Ovid sets the stage in the *Amores*, then, for an ongoing imaginative association between himself as poet and Apollo as poetic avatar, at the same time linking Apollo's insufficiencies to a nascent mythology of poetry concerned with the construction of authority and the status of *ars* as its ambivalent expression.

In the *Ars amatoria* Ovid's self-identification with Apollo becomes rapidly more complex. Whereas the *Amores* presents Ovid as a poet who implicitly writes in the name of Apollo ('vix etiam Phoebo iam lyra tuta sua est?') and depends upon his approval (1.1.16), 'Ovid' in the *Ars amatoria* insistently denies inspiration by Apollo, asserting instead his own experiential authority over his erotic subject matter. Once again inhabiting a neo-vatic stance ('vera canam' [true will be my song] [*Ars Am.* 1.30]), 'Ovid' dismisses in the opening passage of the *Ars amatoria* the prospect of any direction whatsoever by the god of the *vates*, fortifying the truth-value of his amatory instruction with the claim that he cannot tell a lie regarding the source of his subject matter: 'Non ego, Phoebe, datas a te mihi mentiar artes' [I will not falsely claim that my art is thy gift, O Phoebus] (*Ars Am.* 1.25).[76] Again at the close of the *Ars amatoria* Ovid emphasizes the superiority of his empirical Muse to 'Phoebei tripodes' (Phoebus's tripods [3.789]).

This picture of Ovid's self-reliance and veracity as poet is, however, unsettled from an early point by the content and technique of his instruction, which relies consistently – and one might add, exuberantly – upon tactics of deceit, performative artificiality, and strategies of self-delusion both as tools for the prospective lover and leverage in Ovid's own manipulative intercourse with the reader.[77] The god of artifice may not inspire Ovid in *Ars amatoria*, if we can indeed take at face value Ovid's defence of his own authority, but Apollo is every bit a conspirer in the poet's game. This becomes clear when, in a much-analysed epiphany at the rough midpoint of the poem (*Ars Am.* 2.493–510), Apollo ostentatiously appears to Ovid and offers his own amatory counsel. This epiphany activates an intricate *mise en abysme* in which Apollo functions as mirror-image of Ovid while drawing attention to the essential narcissism of erotic poetry, and indeed the central 'gimmick' of the poem: love's intelligibility as *ars*. Like the stylized Apollo *artifex* of *Metamorphoses* 11, the laurel-crowned Apollo of *Ars amatoria* 2 is a visual spectacle of artistic authority: 'vates ille videndus adit' [he draws nigh, a poet worthy to behold] (*Ars Am.* 2.496). Significantly, Apollo's appearance as a *vates* echoes Ovid's self-declaration as such (1.29; cf. 3.547–50) – ironically, in the very passage in which he had brazenly disclaimed Apollo's inspiration. A puzzling redundancy characterizes Apollo's amatory counsel, which awkwardly repeats tips that Ovid has already given (e.g., 1.465, 1.595–6) – to the extent that the epiphany has been regarded as a 'miniature *Ars amatoria*' mischievously meant to highlight the superior currency of the larger poem in which it is embedded, in relation to which Apollo's advice is by now passé.[78]

Like the counsel of the 'vatic' Ovid, Apollo's speech espouses a vocabulary of *veritas* only to undermine it by endorsing an ethic of self-deception. The central moral of Apollo's counsel at first seems strikingly out of place in Ovid's world of erotic manipulation and expediency: if you wish to love 'sapienter' [wisely], commands Apollo, behold the Delphic injunction to know yourself, *nosce teipsum* (2.501). However, the expectations raised by the scene's dense allusions to Apollo's pedigree as disseminator of literary instruction and ritual wisdom are quickly shattered: as Apollo elaborates upon his Delphic precept, it becomes obvious that what he advises is not self-knowledge but its inverse – narcissistic self-regard. Reinforcing advice already well-rehearsed by Ovid on the importance of making the most of one's good qualities, Apollo counsels the lover to display himself if he is handsome, to bare his shoulder if his skin is fair, to sing loudly if he has an attractive voice, and so on, closing with a warning directed at rhetoricians and poets to maintain propriety of speech.

This passage is ironic on several levels. As a narrative device, it is not unlike a hall of mirrors opening outward onto the poem: trumpeting the virtues of physical self-reflection as a strategy of 'wise' seduction, Apollo necessarily 'mirrors' Ovid as narrator, as we have seen, and in so doing renders Ovid's own poetic self-image all the fairer. For this reason, Apollo's epiphany is generally understood to communicate a lesson on poetics through which Ovid (or the reader) is made aware of some aspect of the *Ars amatoria*'s literary motivation. However, it also requires placement within Ovid's larger vision of Apollo as inspiring force and elegiac lover. The reader moving backward through Ovid's oeuvre from the *Metamorphoses* to the *Ars amatoria* may well be surprised to find

Apollo, the most dismally unlucky of lovers, offering erotic counsel not only to Ovid's students, but (ostensibly) to the *magister* himself. The very strategies of self-celebration that Apollo advises in the *Ars*, after all, fail miserably to impress the fleeing Daphne – and at the same time reveal, as suggested earlier, that exultation in such physical charms does not facilitate a coherent or productive sense of identity, which must be achieved through *true* self-knowledge. If, as Sergio Casali has suggested, part of Apollo's point in the *Ars* is that Ovid (as narrator) should better 'know' his own poem,[79] Ovid (as author) also implicitly criticizes *Apollo* by putting these words in his mouth: having evacuated *nosce teipsum* of its traditional moral significance and reduced it to mere frivolity, Apollo proves that he does not know *himself* – the orientation of his own cult, even the details of his own erotic history.

Nor does Apollo 'know' his own *literary* history, as a comparison of his speech with one of its primary Latin influences, Cicero's *Tusculanes* 1.22.52, makes clear. In the course of defending the theory of the soul's immortality, Cicero observes that the Delphic injunction 'know thyself' signifies knowing one's soul, not one's body: 'Non enim, credo, id praecipit, ut membra nostra aut staturam figuramve noscamus; neque nos corpora sumus, nec ego tibi haec dicens corpori tuo dico' [For I do not suppose the meaning of the maxim is that we should know our limbs, our height or shape; our selves are not bodies, and in speaking as I do to you, I am not speaking to your body].[80] In Cicero's formulation, the soul defines the self, while the body merely shelters the soul. By privileging narcissistic (bodily) over ethical self-reflection, then, Apollo's counsel in *Ars* 2 inverts Cicero's moral-philosophical dictum precisely. At the same time, Ovid's Apollo implicitly endorses a didactic program based on *usus* (in its most superficial sense as bodily experience) rather than inspiration or inherited wisdom. In fact, Ovid cleverly underscores the narcissism of Apollo's counsel later in his career by deploying his narrative of Narcissus in *Metamorphoses* 3 as a retrospective gloss of sorts on the shallow Delphism of the *Ars* 2 epiphany. In the *Metamorphoses*, when the blind Tiresias, presented as a *vates* like Apollo in *Ars* 2, is asked by Narcissus's mother to predict her boy's future, he cryptically responds that Narcissus will live to a happy maturity only 'si se non nouerit' [if he does not get to know himself] (*Met.* 3.348). This fatal self-knowledge, of course, turns out to be the purely physical kind that entails revelling in one's own charms, and in this sense its achievement is wholly consistent with Apollo's advice to lovers in *Ars* 2. Ironically, in the case of Narcissus, this neo-Apolline self-knowledge not only fails to produce a successful erotic union, but leads to a total ethical collapse in which Narcissus finds himself unable to function in the social world – and hence unable to love 'sapienter' in its true sense. In Tiresias's vatic prediction as in Apollo's bathetic epiphany, the difference between superficial self-regard and true philosophical self-knowledge is a matter of sharp irony. Despite the differing tones of the two scenes, the implication is the same: if Narcissus, or any lover seeking amatory instruction, 'had arrived at Socratic self-knowledge ... [he] could have led a useful, significant existence, even one that brought him love.'[81] Instead he becomes a self-consuming artefact.

Elsewhere in the *Metamorphoses* Ovid further exposes the un-Delphic implications of the *Ars* 2 epiphany by associating Apolline art with indiscrimination, narcissism, and even, perhaps surprisingly, the erotic disorder of incest (narcissism taken to its perverse extreme). Apollo's unsuccessful love intrigues in the *Metamorphoses* frequently culminate in the production of an artistic substitute (whether a tree, a flower, or a text) for the lost beloved, exemplifying Philip Hardie's eloquent identification of Ovid as 'the great anatomist of unsatisfied desire, of desire founded on lack.'[82] We have already observed the narcissism inherent in Apollo's self-celebratory performance as seducer of Daphne as well as his appropriation of the laurel-text as a consolatory emblem of his own powers.[83] If Apollo loves Daphne only insofar as she functions – first imaginatively then physically – as an extension of himself, his affair with the boy Hyacinthus reveals that even a happily consummated love can prove one-dimensional. The story of Apollo's love of Hyacinthus is first of all embedded in another instance of a mortal *vates* finding his own experience 'mirrored' in that of Apollo. This time it is Apollo's son Orpheus who draws upon the mythic authority of his father, in an attempt to artistically assuage his guilt over the loss of Eurydice. Indeed, Apollo's amatory suffering has a special relevance to that of Orpheus in Book Ten, serving both as preface to and chapter within Orpheus's extended account of homosexual and forbidden loves. The anecdote of the ill-fated love of Apollo for the boy Cyparissus, who died of grief after mistakenly shooting a beloved stag (*Met.* 10.106–42), first constitutes a conspicuous digression in Ovid's description of the arboreal grove that surrounds the mourning Orpheus. Orpheus himself then relates, in the second tale of his sequence, Apollo's love for another boy, Hyacinthus, whom he killed accidentally (just as Cyparissus killed his stag, and Orpheus 'killed' his Eurydice – thus continuing the hall-of-mirrors effect). It is no coincidence that Orpheus, this most Apolline of poets – who not only inherited his poetic skills from his father but conceives of himself as heir to Apollo's erotic misfortunes – has been understood in this sequence of metamorphic narratives as a rival-poet to Ovid, pitting his *auctoritas* against that of his creator while subtly 'challeng[ing] Ovid's poetry and poetic career, up to and including the *Metamorphoses*.'[84] In adopting this role, Orpheus truly follows in his father's footsteps: Apollo too had appeared as a kind of 'embedded narrator' in *Ars amatoria*, rivalling the authority of Ovid as master of his own work while rubbing shoulders as a fellow *vates*. At the same time, Orpheus's (ultimately doomed) attempt to find a surrogate for a lost object of desire in artistic production exposes the illusion of controlled possession upon which the Ovidian Apollo's poetics of vatic inspiration rests.

Apollo's love for Hyacinthus, like Narcissus's love for his own reflection, exemplifies the god's perverse counsel in *Ars amatoria not* to (truly) know oneself. In loving Hyacinthus Apollo is 'immemor ipse sui' [unmindful of himself]: forgetful, unreflective, reduced to a state of purely physical self-awareness (*Met.* 10.171). Apollo willingly jettisons his various divine functions – significantly, Ovid calls attention to his desertion of his Delphic temple, where the true wisdom of *nosce teipsum* is disseminated – and instead 'mirrors' his beloved in dress, hobbies, and, of course, gender.[85] When Hyacinthus 'expalluit' [grew pale] from his mortal wound, Apollo's face simultaneously loses its colour from dread ('aeque / quam puer ipse deus' [*Met.* 10.185–6]). That such mirroring is less an image of true mutual understanding than further self-reflective desire on Apollo's part is underscored by the fact that we see nothing whatsoever of Hyacinthus's perspective on the affair, despite its status as Apollo's sole unobstructed romantic liaison in the *Metamorphoses*. Although it is implied that Hyacinthus willingly returns his love and they are separated only by his death, happiness is conceived only in terms of its erotic immediacy to Apollo, who 'longaque alit adsuetudine flammas' [fed the flames with long association] (*Met.* 10.173). As Hardie and Micaela Janan have ably demonstrated, the death of Hyacinthus, like the loss of Daphne, becomes an opportunity for Apollo to reassert his authority – his very sense of identity as a god – textually and prophetically over an erotic narrative over which he has otherwise lost control. Unable to heal Hyacinthus of his mortal wound, Apollo must settle for textual possession of the boy, whom he proclaims will always be with him ('semper eris mecum'), in the *carmina* of his *lyra* (*Met.* 10.204–5; cf. Apollo's promise to

Daphne-laurel that his hair, lyre, and quivers 'semper habebunt / te' [will always have you] (*Met.* 1.558–9; my translation). Reclaiming his identity as an artist and a prophet – an identity compromised by his own choice to 'mirror' his human lover – Apollo confronts his tragic role as *auctor* of Hyacinthus's death (*Met.* 10.199) not only by composing *carmina* but by transforming the corpse into a flower whose very design imagistically and textually preserves the god's grief. Unlike Cyparissus, who wastes away from grief over killing his beloved – a fate that Apollo momentarily envies at 10.202–3 – Apollo transforms his grief creatively by sublimating it as an artistic occasion.

As at earlier points of the *Metamorphoses*, Apollo's reaction to the loss of Hyacinthus draws attention to his peculiarly self-conscious textual participation in his own narrative. At the same time, it perpetuates the episode's concern with the dynamics of a narrowly mimetic relationship between subject and object, inspirer and receptacle. Apollo begins his lament over Hyacinthus's body by viewing himself, somewhat paradoxically, both as *auctor* and as text: he wishes that his right hand be 'leto / inscribenda tuo est' – that is, branded for your death, but also inscribed or titled with your death (*Met.* 10.198–9).[86] In a final, subtle instance of mirroring, however, it is not Apollo the *auctor* but Hyacinthus the flower who is inscribed like a book: Apollo 'inscribit' his groans on the hyacinth's 'foliis' (petals, but also pages) (10.215), so that the flower may 'scripto gemitus imitabere nostros' [imitate our groans in writing] (10.206) – the ambiguous 'scripto' refers either to the flower's markings as a kind of writing, or to Apollo's own poetic composition in his *carmina*. Similarly, Apollo predicts that the name of Ajax, also to be associated with the hyacinth, 'folioque legatur eodem' [will be read on the same petal/page] (10.208). As Janan has observed, Apollo's textual memorial of Hyacinthus – which we must remember is also an image of Orpheus's own *carmina* after Eurydice's death – is not truly charitable, but serves instead to recoup his own identity as an artist. Apollo relieves himself of guilt, while expanding his own artistic repertoire, by effectively 'erasing death in writing.'[87]

For Janan, Apollo's self-promoting artistic reinvention of a failed amorous experience functions primarily to limn Orpheus's subjectivity as an internal narrator attempting to cope with the implications of his own loss. Here and elsewhere, however, Apollo's actions as lover and artist also reflect upon Ovid's own self-critical vision of the fictions by which artistic authority is sustained and transmitted. In showing Apollo's poetic art to succeed where other aspects of his identity (amatory, athletic, medical) failed, Ovid's aim is not simply to vindicate poetic *ars* as a power that transcends death or compensates unproblematically for the loss of the desired object.[88] Instead, Ovid's repeated association of Apolline *ars* with deceit, self-deception, and self-love suggests the superficial nature of such compensation and the authority that it perpetuates. As long as art is a surrogate for (unfulfilled) love – and to 'learn' love is to master the art that shapes it – the artist essentially celebrates his own entrapment in a self-perpetuating program of illusion.

In the third book of *Ars amatoria*, the concern of which is female instruction, Ovid returns to Apollo's counsel of self-regard in a new set of erotic circumstances that further parody Apollo's already parodically devalued advice. Just as importantly, Ovid's application to *women* of Apollo's earlier counsel expands the implications of the dangers of narcissistic self-knowledge into the realm of serious erotic disorder.[89] As Apollo's authority continues to shift as an advisor of (self-)love, the god's gender becomes surprisingly fluid. In *Ars amatoria* 3 Ovid instructs women to look in the mirror to 'consulat' [take counsel] (3.136) – a word that often carries a moral sense and is sometimes used with reference to the consultation of a deity at his temple, as when Cadmus 'consulit' Apollo's oracle in *Met.* 3.9–10. What these women are told to meditate upon, however, is not a matter of ethics but of grooming: they are to closely regard the shape of their faces in order to make an informed decision concerning which hairstyle best suits them. Suppressing the 'source' of this kind of advice in Apollo's earlier counsel, Ovid instead imagines Apollo simply as the reflection of a pretty (female) face in the mirror. To each her own, says Ovid: if one woman models her hairstyle on Diana's modestly braided tresses, let another who is blessed with long flowing hair emulate the style of 'Phoebe canore' [tuneful Phoebus] when he plucks the lyre (*Ars Am.* 3.142) – significantly, the very pose that Apollo struck in his Book Two epiphany ('subito manifestus Apollo / Movit inauratae pollice fila lyrae' [Apollo suddenly appeared and moved with his thumb the strings of his golden lyre] [2.493–4]). Whereas in Apollo's epiphany to Ovid (and, by extension, its after-effects in Narcissus's and Apollo's homosexual desire in the *Metamorphoses*) narcissism was an artistic dynamic activated by and among males, in Book Three Apollo's own self-identity – what he sees when he looks in the mirror – morphs along the changed gender lines of Ovid's erotic instruction. Apollo is now the gender-indeterminate twin of the tomboy Diana, aided in his transformation into a model of female beauty by Ovid's first reference to Apollo in this section via the initially misleading vocative 'Phoebe' (for Phoebus) (3.142).[90]

As is the case with Apollo's epiphany, the *Metamorphoses* provides a narrative answer of sorts to questions regarding Apollo's identity raised here in the *Ars amatoria* – specifically, the connection between Apollo's association with narcissism and his pertinence to both genders' conceptions of physical beauty. Apollo figures provocatively as an exemplary figure within the narrative of Byblis's incestuous desire for her brother Caunus in *Metamorphoses* 9.[91] Byblis and Caunus are twin siblings and grandchildren of Apollo by the otherwise unknown mortal Deione (*Met.* 9.444, 453), and Byblis's forbidden love is capped by reminders of these two relationships, mortal and divine. In sexually desiring her twin brother, Byblis underscores the narcissism inherent in all Ovidian acts of incest, a theme advanced by Orpheus's narratives of misogyny, homosexuality, and incest in the next book. At the same time, Byblis's lust for her brother is explained – even, perhaps, half-justified – with reference to Caunus's status as descendant of Apollo, icon of male beauty: he is introduced, after all, irresistibly as 'Apollinei ... fratris' [her Apolline brother] (*Met.* 9.455). The tragic irony, of course, is that Byblis is descended from the same divine stock; Ovid reinforces this by naming the spurned girl as 'Phoebeïa Byblis' [Phoebean Byblis] at the moment when she is finally consumed by her own tears and metamorphosed into a spring (*Met.* 9.663). Byblis loves her own reflection – her twin brother – and that reflection *is* Apollo. In short, Byblis's experience suggests that, in the world of *real* (as opposed to textbook) erotics, Apollo's association with both male and female beauty as developed in the *Ars amatoria* leads not to equanimity but to moral disorientation and self-consumption.

At the end of his instruction of women in the closing passages of *Ars amatoria*, Ovid inflicts a final blow to Apollo's authority by scandalously re-interpreting his counsel of *nosce teipsum*, while explicitly rejecting Apollo's inspiration for the second time. Closely echoing the language of Apollo's earlier epiphany, Ovid advises, 'Nota sibi sint quaeque' [Let each woman know herself] (*Ars Am.* 3.771), this time explaining the maxim as an injunction for women to tailor their sexual positions in bed around the particular selling points of their bodies. As at the beginning of *Ars amatoria*, Ovid rejects Apollo by stressing the authority of his own *usus* (*Ars Am.* 3.791) over 'Phoebei tripodes' [Phoebus's tripods] (3.789), going so far as to dismiss the very aspect of Apollo – his prophetic authority – that supposedly informed his delivery of 'Delphic' advice in *Ars amatoria* 2. The sequence of revelations and concealments of Apollo's authority that ends here indicates that Apollo falls victim in the *Ars amatoria* to a kind of wasting disease, not unlike that of his own Cumaean Sibyl (*Met.* 14.130–53): diminished from god to man to woman to irrelevancy, associated with redundancy, self-doubling, hermaphroditism, and narcissism, Apollo is the mirror in which Ovid views the self-cancelling aspirations of his own poem as an itinerary for – and yet surrogate of – love.

Arts of Contagion

Apollo's *ars* in Ovid's works encompasses more than the aesthetic: equally important to Apollo's identity as his role as poet, musician, and inspirer is his function as healer. Apollo's powers over the health of the body – both beneficial and destructive – figure prominently in his literary history from his first appearance in Western literature as Homer's plague-god in the *Iliad* to his status in the Middle Ages as the legendary figure 'that first fond art of medicyne' (Chaucer, *Tr* 1.659), still deemed worthy of invocation as a medical authority in the technical writing of the period. Ovid recurrently emphasizes Apollo's medical abilities, particularly in association with the elegiac topos of the *medicina amoris* – the idea that love is a disease for which a cure must be sought. This topos, celebrated as the premise of the *Remedia amoris*, is underscored by a sense of futility encapsulated in the Propertian paradox that 'omnis humanos sanat medicina dolores: / solus amor morbi non amat artificem' [Medicine can cure all human pains: only love loves not a doctor of its disease].[92] For this and other reasons, Apollo is every bit as ineffective a doctor in Ovid's poetry as a lover; by extension, he serves as a reference point for Ovid's varied guises as social diagnostician, erotic healer, and ailing poet. Apollo's medical failures manifest themselves in a variety of forms, but all brutally stress the inefficacy of his *ars* (a suggestively broad word that Ovid often applies to medical skill) in his attempt to shape, or salvage, experience. For medieval writers, who instinctively viewed these failures in ethical terms, the record of Apollo Medicus testified powerfully to the insalubrious effects of pagan artistic principles and poetic presumption.

1. Corpus *and* Error: *Apolline Malpractice*

In the *Metamorphoses*, Apollo's dubious qualifications as god of medicine, in the first extended narrative in which he features, set the tone of his treatment in the remainder of the poem. 'Paean,' as Ovid facetiously calls Apollo at the end of the Daphne episode, defines his first love intrigue in specifically medical terms, diagnosing his condition as an affliction by wounds in the chest ('uulnera pectora' [*Met.* 1.520]). Apollo's self-diagnosis carries both figurative and medical connotations that correspond with Ovid's earlier, vividly physiological account of the source of Apollo's lovesickness in the arrow of desire that pierces his 'ossa' [bones] and penetrates to the 'medullas' [marrow] (*Met.* 1.473).[93] The ostensible point of this medically informed myth of love is the irony that despite Apollo's universal reputation as 'opifer' [Bringer-of-help], inventor of medical art, and master of healing herbs (*Met.* 1.521–2), his *artes* are insufficient to heal himself of love.[94] Only in the act of reinscribing his twin failures – to seduce Daphne and to heal himself – within the propagandist apparatus of 'Triumphum' that the laurel comes to serve (*Met.* 1.560) is Apollo able to achieve a superficially therapeutic resolution. Ironically, this 'cure,' which sees Apollo triumph only in the perpetual indulgence of his malady, is purchased at the cost of Daphne's own physical well-being, last seen halted in a death-like state of 'torpor grauis' [heavy numbness] (*Met.* 1.548).

Apollo's experience illustrates the Propertian truism that there is no cure, only palliatives, for the disease of love – at least within the realm of erotic discourse, in which cure and fulfilment are paradoxically intertwined.[95] Apollo's powerlessness over his own erotic malady also corresponds with his therapeutic failures within the purely medical sphere in Ovid's works, in which he is repeatedly hard-pressed to cure, or even comfort, those who are the objects of his love and pity.[96] In this respect, Ovid's handling of Apollo Medicus could be said to subvert the ancient folkloric motif known in Jungian discourse as the 'wounded healer': the physician whose 'own suffering and vulnerability … contribute crucially to the capacity to heal.'[97] Ovid's Apollo, in contrast, deploys his 'medicas … artes' vainly ('inaniter') upon all those unfortunate enough to be swept up in the wake of the misfortune, misprision, and sheer bad luck that surrounds him in the *Metamorphoses* (2.618): the lifeless Coronis, pregnant with Apollo's child, who does not respond to his attempts at resuscitation (2.617–18); the innocent Leucothoe smothered beyond revival beneath the earth (4.247–8); the fragile Hyacinthus, felled by an incurable wound ('immedicabile uulnus') that even the most tender ministrations cannot soothe (10.189). Similarly, when Ilioneus, the youngest of Niobe's sons, prays for mercy in the midst of his brothers' massacre, Apollo *arquitenens* is moved to pity, but without effect: his arrow, already in motion, inflicts the 'minimo … / uulnere' [smallest wound] in Ilioneus's chest but nonetheless proves deadly

(6.265–6). In each case, Apollo is too late, his medicines too weak, and the opposing power of *fatum* too overwhelming. Tardy or impotent in these circumstances, Apollo is neglectful or inefficient in others, like that of Phaethon's suicidal mission, that lack the medical specificity of his attempted healings but thematically echo them. Apollo's casual unavailability to protect the prophetess Ocyroe from deformation could also be regarded as a failure of healing (2.676–9), as could his frailty as guardian of his poet-sons Orpheus and Linus in *Amores* 3.9.21–4.

Apollo himself acknowledges his limitations as healer at the end of the *Metamorphoses* (15.634–40) when he redirects the plague-battered Romans, who seek his aid at Delphi, to his son Aesculapius, whose reintroduction in *Met.* 15.624 as 'Coroniden' [Coronis's son] recalls his origins in a scene of failed Apolline healing. The mood of this episode in Book Fifteen falls somewhere between the suspense of dynastic succession and the banality of medical referral; in this spirit Ovid deploys the Roman cult of Aesculapius as a final point of transition to the poem's destination in 'mea tempora' [my own times] (*Met.* 1.4). Structurally and thematically, Aesculapius's cultic debut in the last book of the *Metamorphoses*, imagistically centred upon the serpent as a healing emblem, correctively balances Apollo's narrative introduction in Book One as conquered victor (of Python) and unhealed healer (of himself) – a phenomenon revisited from the vantage point of Chaucer's *Manciple's Tale* in the coda of chapter 5. As the preceding story of Aesculapius's healing of Hippolytus indicates, the young physician is skilled in 'ualido medicamine' [powerful medicines] (*Met.* 15.533): unlike the profitless *artes* of his father, these have the power to cure death and legitimately earn him the title of Paean (attached to Aesculapius at *Met.* 15.535). Ovid's optimistic presentation of Aesculapius and his art in *Metamorphoses* 15 takes pains to portray him as an unambiguously potent, successful healer – and therefore studiously avoids mention of his punishment by Jove for the unnatural act of restoring Hippolytus to life (related in *Fasti* 6.746–62), which must logically precede his conversion into a deity, the form in which the Romans encounter him. Thus purged of its transgressive and blameworthy elements, Aesculapius's art triumphantly clears a path to the famous closing sequence of the *Metamorphoses* heralding an immortal destiny for Augustus, Rome, and Ovid's own poetry. By upstaging his own father in the art of healing, Aesculapius does not so much inherit Apollo's legacy as reverse his blemished record in the *Metamorphoses* as a practitioner of medical art. It is Aesculapius, not

Apollo, who propels into 'mea tempora' (and beyond) Ovid's vision of an art capable of sublimating and rendering eternal the 'parte ... meliore' [better part] of the self (*Met.* 15.875), promising to override the cycle of mortal corruption in which Apollo repeatedly proves conspirator as well as victim.

In light of this *entrelacement* of Ovid's poetic fate with the varied possibilities of the healing arts in the *Metamorphoses*, it is appropriate that Ovid's exile poetry presents the poet himself as the last and greatest of Apollo's therapeutic failures. In the *Tristia* and *Ex Ponto*, Ovid imagines himself a neglected patient of Apollo, one suffering gravely in body and spirit, 'aeger enim traxi contagia corpore mentis' [for being sick at heart I drew the contagion into my body] (*Tristia* 5.13.3).[98] Playing upon the correlation among his recurrent physical maladies in frigid Tomis, his mental suffering as an exile, and the *dolores* of lovesickness (in this case, for Rome),[99] Ovid complains that Apollo and the Muses have abandoned him (*Tristia* 3.2.3–4), that no practitioners of 'Apollinea ... arte' [Apollo's art] are available to attend him in his sickbed (*Tristia* 3.3.10), and that his illness is beyond healing because 'non est in medico semper relevetur ut aeger: / interdum docta plus valet arte malum' ['tis not always in a physician's power to cure the sick; at times the disease is stronger than trained art] (*Ex Ponto* 1.3.17–18). Indeed, Apollo's impotency in the exile poetry overwhelms its potential for correction: even the medicines of Aesculapius, which can bring the dead back to life, are unable to heal Ovid's 'vulnera cordis' [wounds in the heart] (*Ex Ponto* 1.3.22)[100] – an image that, significantly, recalls both Apollo's unhealed 'uulnera pectora' at *Met.* 1.520 and the fatal chest wound of Ilioneus, the son of Niobe whom Apollo had wished to spare (*Met.* 6.266).

2. *Apollo Medicus*, Aeneid 12, *and* Heroides 5

The extent of Apollo's failings in the two realms of *ars* with which Ovid specifically sought to identify his reputation, love and medicine, suggests that Ovid's elaboration of the elegiac traditions he inherited, particularly the topos of Apollo's inability to heal himself of love in Tibullus 2.3.13–14, is hardly casual. The medicinal urgency and specificity with which Apollo's *artes* are associated in the passages discussed above are not, however, solely elegiac in form. A rather unexpected source text, one that especially marks Oenone's self-presentation as failed Apolline healer in *Heroides* 5 – a text of importance to the medieval conception of Apollo and Chaucer's *Troilus* in particular[101] – also shapes Ovid's critique of Apollo Medicus: Book Twelve of Virgil's *Aeneid*. In many respects, the Apollo of the *Aeneid* could hardly be more remote from Ovid's feckless Apollo, as chapter 3 will illustrate in more detail. As a truthful prophet and guardian of Roman civilization, Virgil's Apollo stabilizes and authorizes the imperial project of the epic along with the credentials of its hero. In the Middle Ages, however, Ovidianism was assimilated quite naturally into the 'magnetic field' of the *Aeneid*, most notably in medieval vernacular adaptations of Virgil's epic such as the *Roman d'Eneas* and Chaucer's *House of Fame* and 'Legend of Dido,' which variously re-examine the *Aeneid* through a heightened focus on the feminine perspective and erotic ethics learned in substantial measure from Ovid's amatory works.[102] This twist of fate in the *Aeneid*'s reception is importantly anticipated, however, by Virgil's uncharacteristic inclusion (and apparent invention) of one jarring episode involving Apollo's erotic past in Book Twelve. Here, as in the Dido books, Ovid discovered, and henceforth exploited, an anticipation of his own concerns as a poetic diagnostician of *amor immedicabile*.

Ovid's reworking of this episode from the *Aeneid* in Oenone's letter, and its related contexts in Apollo's various Ovidian efforts as love doctor, may be approached in light of Stephen Hinds's provocative reading of the dynamics of Ovid's appropriation of Virgil in the mini-*Aeneid* of *Metamorphoses* 13–14. Rather than passively or unimaginatively recycling Virgilian material, Hinds argues, Ovid aggressively repossesses the *Aeneid* by 'constructing Virgil as a hesitant precursor of the *Metamorphoses*,' insinuating that, counterintuitively, 'there is a *Metamorphoses* latent in the *Aeneid*' which asserts Ovid's primacy as a poet despite his belatedness.[103] While Hinds's concern is with Ovid's programmatic expansion of Virgil's occasional references to metamorphosis in a poem that reconfigures the possibilities of epic, my interest here is with Ovid's attention to Virgil's manipulation of Apollo to expose the dangers of passion within an epic context.[104] In *Aeneid* 12, Virgil presents Apollo explicitly as erotic lover for the first time in the epic, in an episode, moreover, that links his expression of desire to the art of healing. Shortly after a broken truce, Aeneas is wounded by an arrow of unknown origin. Iapyx, a male doctor probably modelled on the *Iliad*'s Machaon (grandson of Apollo), tends to his wound but cannot extract the arrow; Turnus, meanwhile, continues to wreak havoc on the Trojan forces. Iapyx's medical skill is distinguished by an Apolline lineage and associated, paradoxically, with the god's own erotic suffering. Transfixed by piercing love ('acri ... captus amore') for Iapyx, Apollo had once offered his beloved all his *artes* and *munera*: augury, lyre, and swift arrows (*Aen.* 12.392–3).[105] Wishing to heal his sick father, Iapyx refused these and requested instead the 'mutas ... artis' of medicine. Virgil strongly emphasizes Apollo's legendary status as guarantor of Iapyx's medical techniques as he attempts to heal Aeneas by proceeding 'Paeonium in morem' [in Paeonian fashion] (12.401) and applying 'Phoebi ... potentibus herbis' [Phoebus's potent herbs] (12.402). However, Apollo's *artes* do not offer relief ('nihil auctor Apollo / subvenit' [12.405–6]) – the identification here of Apollo as 'auctor' accentuates his role as inventor and authorizer of medical art – despite Iapyx's best efforts. Finally, Venus intervenes, healing her son with a Cretan herb called *dictamnus* (dittany) which she hand-picks and steeps in ambrosia and panacea. Significantly, Venus succeeds in what is for her an unusual role as a healer through a combination of specialized medical knowledge (dittany's efficacy against arrow wounds is acknowledged by Pliny and Cicero and frequently observed in medieval encyclopedias) and a willingness to draw on resources restricted to the gods and associated with the mystery of immortality.[106] The awestruck Iapyx recognizes the superiority of such remedy to 'humanis opibus' [mortal aid] and 'arte magistra' [masterful art], which constitute his medical capacities under Apollo's jurisdiction, and subtly discredits Apollo in his conclusion that 'maior agit deus' [a greater god works here] (*Aen.* 12.427, 429; my translation).[107]

A primary reason for Ovid's creative interest in this scene is that Aeneas's stubborn wound is both real and metaphorical, a consequence of battle and a memorial of love's debilitating effects. The literary heritage of Virgil's scene is in the first instance Homeric, deriving from an episode in *Iliad* 5 in which Apollo intervenes to carry the wounded Aeneas from the battlefield when Aphrodite proves unable to protect him.[108] By inverting this scene to Apollo's detriment – since Venus succeeds where Apollo fails – Virgil associates this final image of Apollo with a later Homeric scene, in *Iliad* 20, in which Apollo abandons Aeneas to battle with Achilles in order to protect Hector. As John F. Miller has argued, Virgil's ultimate affirmation of the Homeric characterization of Apollo as a flawed protector of Aeneas reinforces the epic's recurrent warnings concerning the uncivic implications of sexual passion. These implications are dramatized here in the fervent extremity of Apollo's love for Iapyx which, Virgil implies, dilutes his medical arts and reduces them to fallible 'humanis opibus.'[109] Indeed, as Ovid seems to have recognized, both Apollo and Aeneas suffer from incurable conditions as battle rages around them. Just as Aeneas, memorably linked with Apollo through simile earlier in the epic (*Aen.* 4.143–9), is laid low by a festering battle wound, so has Apollo in desiring Iapyx been physically incapacitated, 'acri … captus amore.' The adjective *acer*'s primary sense of 'sharp, pointed' (*OLD* s.v. *acer*[2] adj. 1), not just the abstract 'passionate' (*OLD* s.v. *acer*[2] adj. 7), is appropriate here, likening Apollo's lovesickness to a quasi-somatic wound. In an elegiac renovation of a Virgilian moment that was itself at cross-purposes with epic values, then, Ovid developed this image into an *actual* arrow-wound in Apollo's side in *Met.* 1, another scene in which the god of healing is mastered by Love. In short, Apollo in *Aeneid* 12, as a lovesick instructor of a failed doctor, is but a few steps away from his tragicomic Ovidian role as the sick physician whose ministrations only make his patients sicker.

The dangers of unrestrained passion epitomized by Apollo in this scene are of course of utmost relevance to Aeneas, whose erotic self-abandonment in Carthage and tendency toward *furor* contribute to a 'sense of disquiet' surrounding the hero and his Roman legacy that correlates with the subtly cautionary tone of the Iapyx scene.[110] In fact, just as Apollo's erotic passion carries an association with physical trauma in this episode, so is Aeneas's battle-wound implicitly linked with the effects of disordered love.[111] The image of Aeneas pierced with a distant arrow, writhing in pain, evocatively recalls a cluster of imagery surrounding 'infelix Dido' in Book Four, at the point of her oppression by an agonizing *love*-wound: 'At regina gravi iamdudum saucia cura / volnus alit venis et caeco carpitur igni' [But the queen, long since smitten with a grievous love-pang, feeds the wound with her life-blood, and is wasted with fire unseen] (*Aen.* 4.68, 1–2). At 4.66–73 Dido the huntress is famously likened to a deer pierced with an arrow from afar (*procul*), the shaft sticking in her side as she rages in the agony of passion. Aeneas's wound, also inflicted by a distant arrow, carries an urgency that recalls Dido's: 'saevit et infracta luctatur harundine telum' [raging, he struggles to pluck out the head of the broken shaft] (*Aen.* 12.387). As Gareth Morgan has demonstrated, Virgil hints at an association between the deer with which Dido is figuratively equated – said to roam in a frenzy through the forests of *Dicte* ('Dictaeos,' *Aen.* 4.73, i.e., a region of Crete) – and the herb *dictamnus* (native to Crete and derived from *Dicte*), which Cicero indicates is sought by wild she-goats when wounded by hunters' arrows, and which Venus deploys in her cure of Aeneas in Book Twelve.[112] Support for the connection between Dido's love-wound and Aeneas's battle scar, then, is found in the correlation between the remedies of the Cretan deer and the sidelined Aeneas. Just as Dido's *tacitum volnus* (*Aen.* 4.67) festers and consumes her, so do the *mutas artis* of Iapyx fall short of healing Aeneas, whose past experiences in the battlefield of love mirror Apollo's own love-wound. In these ways, the slippage between medical and erotic disorders in the *Aeneid* reflects critically on Aeneas as well as the doctors who tend him.

The twelfth-century *Roman d'Eneas* helps situate the precociously 'Ovidian' character of Virgil's medical imagery in *Aeneid* 12, and thus prepares us to recognize the effects of the Iapyx scene and the related matter of Dido's love-wound in Ovid's conception of Apollo Medicus. In the *Roman d'Eneas*, the truce between the Latin and Trojan armies is not broken by an act of overt aggression but by the shot of an arrow bearing a love letter from Lavine to Eneas, the meaning of which only Eneas understands (8776–844).[113] Although Eneas is not pierced by the arrow, he is deeply affected by its message, which sends him into a fevered, sleepless state, familiar to medieval lovers, in which he complains to Love, 'Tu m'as de ton dart d'or navré, / mal m'a li briés anpoisoné / qu'entor la saiete trovai' [you have wounded me with your golden dart. The letter which I found around the arrow has poisoned me badly] (8953–5). When a fellow soldier observes that the arrow could not have wounded him because it did not physically touch him, Eneas replies, 'Ele aportot ma mort o soi, / angoisosemant me navra ... cop ne plaie n'i pert, / mais li brievez qui antor ert / m'a molt navré dedanz le cors' [it carried my death with it and wounded me painfully ... no blow or wound shows, but the letter which was around it has wounded my person sorely] (8968–9, 8971–3). The overwhelming erotic charge of this figurative arrow-wound, also associated with Lavine's glance at 9230–52, supplants the nearby episode from which it ultimately derives. Eneas's perilous wound by the arrow of unknown origin is treated with much less suspense than in the *Aeneid*, in part because the urgency of such a wound has already been fully developed with reference to emotional as well as physical distress in the earlier scene with Lavine. If, for Virgil, the most immediate figurative link to Aeneas's suffering in the Iapyx episode was Dido's love-wound in Book Four, the medieval poet instead presents the scene in relation to the optimistic thrust of Lavine's and Eneas's secret courtship. Unsurprisingly then, Eneas is swiftly healed, and Iapyx,. whose affair with Apollo is not mentioned at all, requires no divine assistance from Venus to salve his wound (9462–574). If, in the *Aeneid*, the physiology of love defined and delimited the experience of wartime trauma, the Ovidio-Virgilian *Roman d'Eneas* reverses direction to conceptualize love itself as a disease that strikes, and stubbornly persists, with all the compulsion of a military blow.

Ovid's *Heroides* 5 features a different cast of characters and is not generally regarded as Virgilian in conception; nevertheless, it plays a key role in the transformation of the Apollo of *Aeneid* 12 into the god whose inadequacies are explored in the bulk of Ovid's poetry. *Heroides* 5 concerns the prehistory of the *Aeneid* – the Trojan War – and, like *Aeneid* 12, subtly explores the matter of healing within a variegated context of love and combat involving Apollo Medicus. Oenone's letter to her lover Paris in *Heroides* 5 nostalgically recounts the earlier years of their relationship when Paris, unaware of his identity, lived as a shepherd on Mount Ida. Decrying his newfound love for Helen and wishing desperately for Paris to return to his former affections, the spurned Oenone finally attempts to capture Paris's attention by competing with Helen on her own promiscuous level. In the last twenty lines of the letter, Oenone boasts a bit too casually that she was formerly wooed by no less impressive a suitor than Apollo, who claimed her virginity and initiated her into the secrets of his medical arts as recompense.[114] Like Iapyx, Oenone in *Heroides* 5 refuses the first gifts that Apollo offers – in this case, gold and gems – and instead accepts the arts of healing. Again like Iapyx, she finds these treatments to fail in a time of need, for even with Apollo's full arsenal of herbs, Oenone cannot heal her own love-wound: 'deficior prudens artis ab arte mea' [Skilled in an art, I am left helpless by the very art I know] (*Her.* 5.150). Only Paris's love, she claims, can restore her health.

Ovid's reinscription of Virgil's Iapyx narrative within *Heroides* 5 as a vehicle for the expression of recalcitrant love and the limitations of Apollo's medical authority becomes clearer when we consider Ovid's broad adjustments to the shape of the Oenone story as then known. The earliest treatments of the Oenone story that survive, from the Hellenistic period, centre not upon the early days of Paris's and Oenone's romance but Paris's death in the Trojan War at the arrow of Philoctetes.[115] Apollo has no role in this alternate tradition, and Oenone's skill as a healer does not derive from his instruction. Unlike Ovid's Oenone, who though deeply hurt is prepared to forgive, her pre-Ovidian counterpart is so bitter toward Paris after his rejection of her that when his wounded body is carried to Mount Ida from the battlefield she at first refuses to heal him. However, she finally decides too late to help and, finding her lover dead, kills herself. Whereas in the earlier tradition it is said that only Oenone can heal the wounded Paris, in Ovid's version Oenone complains of a love-wound incurable by medical arts that only Paris can heal.[116]

The form of Oenone's story in which Ovid most likely knew it, then, was strongly reminiscent of the Iapyx scene of *Aeneid* 12: a warrior wounded in battle by an arrow is brought, on point of death, to a healer who is unable to heal him. In both cases, the warrior's erotic history adversely effects his capacity for recovery: in the *Aeneid*, through the poetic justice by which Dido's emotional suffering physically rebounds upon Aeneas; and, in the story of Oenone, through the vengeful jealousy of the spurned woman who wishes to see her betrayer suffer. Apollo's supporting role as lover and teacher of the physician in *Aeneid* 12 doubt-less gave Ovid the idea of incorporating the god in a similar capacity in *Heroides* 5. The association of Virgil's Apollo Medicus with the elegiac topos of Apollo as unhealed healer derived from Tibullus would then have been a natural one to make, as would the shift of the 'psychological moment' of the narrative from Paris's death back in time to the doctor's inability to heal herself of love. This medical paradox, presented almost as a point of lyric meditation in the poem's closing lines and associated both with Oenone (*Her.* 5.149–50) and Apollo (5.151–2, possibly spuri-ous),[117] serves as the thematic nucleus of the poem around which the portrait of Oenone's psychology – which effectively imprisons itself in a range of conflicting emotions and rhetorical strategies[118] – is given scope to develop. Hence, Ovid's creative reordering of the Virgilian and Tibullan material, together with his source materials concerning Oenone as physician of Paris, facilitates a newly supple focus for the matter of Apolline healing: in *Heroides* 5, instead of Love (Venus) stepping in for Apollo and curing the wound that is beyond the doctor's art to heal, Love *causes* the wound – and takes the doctor as its victim.

3. Apolline Pathologies from Thessaly to Tomis

Apollo's failure in self-healing in *Metamorphoses* 1, therefore, is shaped by a variegated tradition of association between the healing arts and the fragility of erotic love as crystallized in *Heroides* 5. Ovid's manipula-tion of other forms of source material in the Python-Daphne sequence likewise reveals his intention to emphasize the contaminating effect of desire upon Apollo as healer. *Metamorphoses* 1 is a particularly apt ex-ample of Ovid's scepticism toward Apollo Medicus, not only because it functions as a nerve-centre, as we have seen, of so many of Apollo's attempts to express authority in Ovid's works, but also because it provides a clear and deliberate image of Ovid's reappraisal of Apollo as a god weakened and defined by malady, in defiance of an earlier tradition that linked him with purification and social health. The surviving literary evidence suggests that Ovid was the first to link the Python and Daphne stories in causative sequence. Apollo's slaying of Python on Parnassus typically was linked with his foundation of the Delphic oracle, as in the *Homeric Hymn to Apollo*, and the Daphne story was set in either Arcadia or Laconia, as opposed to the Thessaly of Ovid's version.[119] As we observed earlier, however, pre-Ovidian versions of the Python story do include a journey to Thessaly: there, in the Tempe valley, Apollo purifies himself of blood pollution before returning to Delphi to institute his oracle. Notably, *Metamorphoses* 1 lacks any mention of Apollo's purification in Thessaly or the etiology of the Delphic oracle; as a result, Ovid's version of events produces a very different set of thematic implications. Instead of quelling the sensual, irrational forces represented by Python and then cleansing himself of their pollution, Apollo in his pursuit of Daphne is impelled by bestial ardour in his own right. Apollo's ontological degeneration from god to man to beast is epitomized by an epic simile, at the height of the chase (*Met.* 1.533–9), that imagines Apollo, in one critic's apt paraphrase, as 'a fierce, blood-thirsty hound eager to catch his succulent prey.'[120] Moreover, instead of purifying himself of Python's slaughter – a process closely linked with the notion of health in ancient custom – Ovid's Apollo succumbs to a new malady which his own medicines cannot heal. Ovid thus rewrites a foundation myth designed to celebrate Apollo's association with order and purification as an etiology of art's association with erotic dislocation and impaired remedy.[121]

The arts of contagion with which Apollo is so deeply associated, and in which Ovid finds the imaginative momentum for much of his poetic program, achieve their fullest expression in the *Remedia amoris*. Here, in what is less a palinode to than a reinforcement of the *Ars amatoria*,[122] we are encouraged to savour the heady irony of Ovid the physician's efforts to cure the patient he made ill in the first place. Fittingly, Apollo, in his capacities as patron of *carmina* (songs/spells) and of healing, acts as vatic inspirer and guide of the *Remedia*:

Te precor incipiens, adsit tua laurea nobis,
    Carminis et medicae, Phoebe, repertor opis.

Tu pariter vati, pariter succurre medenti:
    Utraque tutelae subdita cura tua est.   (75–8)

[Thee I beseech at the outset, let thy laurel be nigh to aid me, O Phoebus, inventor of song and of the healing art! Succour alike the poet and alike the healer; the labours of both are under thy patronage.]

Despite his invocations of Apollo Medicus, 'Ovid' retains his subject-position as a lover – hence Hardie's claim that the 'true presiding spirit' of the *Remedia* is more accurately Amor than Apollo – [123] and so preserves the stance of *vates* of experience delineated in *Ars amatoria*: 'ego semper amavi, / Et si, quid faciam, nunc quoque, quaeris, amo' [I have ever been a lover, and if thou askest what I am doing, I am a lover still] (*Rem. Am.* 7–8). Indeed, 'Ovid' admits that at times he has been 'medicus turpiter aeger' [a shamefully sick physician], one whose own 'herbis' struggled to counteract the powerful allure of love (313–14). Far from rhetorically increasing his authority as *magister* in any straightforward fashion,[124] such admissions on the part of 'Ovid' align him with a fully Apolline erotic ethic by which love is untreatable and convalescence possible only through the perpetuation of self-deception in poetic illusion. In this sense alone those who follow in the path of Apollo's (and 'Ovid''s) malady – as defined programmatically in the Daphne episode of the *Metamorphoses* – are, in the final words of the *Remedia*, '[c]armine sanati … meo' [made whole … by my song] (814).[125] Apolline – and hence Ovidian – poetry does not effect healing; it obscures failed healing. Viewed as an urbane literary game, the threat of such self-defeating therapy remains safely rhetorical. Viewed philosophically or morally, as it would increasingly be in the Middle Ages, it occasions the polemical position of Boethius's Lady Philosophy on the ministrations of the poetical Muses in the sick man's bedroom: 'quae dolores eius non modo nullis remediis foverent, verum dulcibus insuper alerent venenis' [Not only have they no cures for his pain, but with their sweet poison they make it worse] (*CP* 1 pr.1.30–2).[126] Much like Ovid's infectious remedies, which merely reinitiate the cycle of passion, the superficial therapies of Boethius's Muses 'hominumque mentes assuefaciunt morbo, non liberant' [accustom a man's mind to his ills, not rid him of them] (*CP* 1 pr.1.33–4).

It should not surprise us that Ovid, frequently regarded as an amoral writer whom only the most radical cultural reinscription could render consistent with medieval ethical mores,[127] anticipates the concerns of

Boethius's Lady Philosophy. As a boldly critical postscript to his earlier works,[128] Ovid's exile poetry, especially the *Tristia*, supplies a conceptual preface to the first book of the *Consolation of Philosophy*, with which it shares a concern with the sorrows of exile as manifested in the trauma of poetic composition.[129] Just as Ovid complains in exile that

> saepe etiam lacrimae me sunt scribente profusae,
> umidaque est fletu littera facta meo,
> corque vetusta meum, tamquam nova, vulnera novit,
> inque sinum maestae labitur imber aquae   (*Tristia* 4.1.95–8)

[often too my tears have flowed as I wrote, my writing has been moistened by my weeping, my heart feels the old wounds as if they were fresh, and sorrow's rain glides down upon my breast]

so does Boethius bemoan the ills of poetic self-indulgence:

> Carmina qui quondam studio florente peregi,
>   Flebilis heu maestos cogor inire modos.
> Ecce mihi lacerae dictant scribenda camenae
>   Et veris elegi fletibus ora rigant.   (*CP* 1 m.1.1–4)

[Verses I made once glowing with content;
Tearful, alas, sad songs must I begin.
See how the Muses grieftorn bid me write,
And with unfeigned tears these elegies drench my face.][130]

As Jeffrey Fish has argued, in Ovid's exilic self-presentation as an ailing poet lovesick for Rome we find that 'the shrewd physician has an illness which even he cannot heal,' and, further, that 'the poet himself is both patient and physician. He is the ailing patient looking at his own failed remedies and his failure as self-healer of *amor*.'[131] Poetic composition – the hair of the dog that bit him – does not provide meaningful remedy to Ovid in his exile; in a way, it shows him defying his own injunction in the *Remedia* to avoid reading erotic poetry, including 'mea … carmina' (*Rem. Am.* 766). The superficially palliative but more deeply self-evasive and narcissistic status of art has, of course, been the premise of Ovid's creative use of Apollo all along, and it reaches the breaking point in Ovid's self-presentation as exile. If, in the *Remedia*, Ovid poses gleefully as healer, like Achilles to Telephus, of the very wound that he caused (*Rem. Am.* 43–8), in *Tristia* the same paradox reemerges in a tragic key: 'et carmen demens carmine laesus amo' [madman that I am, though song has injured me, 'tis still song that I love] (*Tristia* 4.1.30; cf. 1.1.99–100, 2.19–21). In looking to *ars* for a *remedium*, Ovid consoles himself in one sense, but he also entraps himself in a circuit of self-cancellation that once again 'mirrors' that of the *magister*'s perpetual alter ego, Apollo.

Even as Ovid in the exile poetry confronts the power of reality over art, he reveals to what extent art has become for him the only reality. In these final writings Ovid imagines himself as a character in various Apolline melodramas. Like Phaethon, he has been struck down by Jove's (Augustus's) thunderbolt (*Tristia* 1.1.79–82); like Niobe, his tears are limitless (*Ex Ponto* 1.2.27–30); like Latona, he wanders as an exile from his native land (*Ex Ponto* 4.14.57–60). And in the last words of the last letter of the *Ex Ponto*, Ovid speaks, as if from beyond the grave, in the grotesque voice of the flayed Marsyas, who in the *Metamorphoses* was said to be nothing but wound ['nec quidquam nisi vulnus erat'] (*Met.* 6.388): 'omnia perdidimus' [I have lost all], laments Ovid, 'non habet in nobis iam nova plaga locum' [There is no space in me now for a new wound] (*Ex Ponto* 4.16.52). Like Marsyas, Ovid is torn from himself (cf. *Met.* 6.385), fragmented, self-divided, metamorphosed, and condemned to pay too high a price for his offending song. Yet Ovid does not speak in this last letter as Apollo's victim but as his vindicator: celebrating the ascendency of poetic fame over the forces of envy, Ovid places himself for the last time in an esteemed poetic lineage destined to preserve his *nomen* (4.16.3): 'claro mea nomine Musa / atque inter tantos quae legeretur erat' [my Muse was famed ... and she was one who was read among so many of the great] (4.16.45–6).

Coda: Medieval Afterlives

Ovid's shaping of Apollo as a lover with a seemingly inexhaustible set of 'human' liabilities – whether confronted directly or mediated by the moral and pragmatic concerns of medieval Ovidian commentary tradition – offered a great deal to medieval English poets who viewed the foibles of erotic love in an ethical context. Apollo's Ovidian legacy also provided a foundation on which late medieval English poets, particularly those who contributed to the mythologizing vein of courtly poetry in the learned idiom of the Chaucerian (and later Lydgatian) tradition, situated their own poetic claims to authority. The remainder of this book traces these phenomena in detail, but a sketch here of some of the more striking responses to Ovid's portrayals of Apollo as lover and healer within this learned English tradition sets into relief the problems of love, art, and illusion associated with the Ovidian Apollo with which this chapter has been concerned, and suggests some salient trends in medieval English poets' confrontation of these problems.

The first point of note is the strong tendency in medieval English poetry after Chaucer to highlight and, indeed, expand upon the 'negative' view embedded in Ovidian tradition of Apollo as a god – a view that receives nowhere near as great an emphasis in medieval poetry produced on the Continent. Late medieval English treatments of the story of Apollo and Daphne illustrate this point especially well, and are selected here in part because they may conveniently be weighed against the broadly European commentary traditions and Mediterranean literary approaches to the Daphne myth charted in Mary Barnard's 1987 monograph. In the classicizing love-visions popular in fifteenth- and early sixteenth-century England – a genre associated with Chaucer's influence and often connected to the Chaucerian apocrypha – Apollo's human suffering constitutes a frequent reference point for that of the lover-poet, in ways that often appear to compromise the validity of poetic authority itself. In Lydgate's *Complaint of the Black Knight*, for example, the title character's complaint against the cruelty of the God of Love draws upon the precedent of Apollo's unrewarded efforts as a lover – '[y]wounded' by Cupid's dart and faithful to a 'lady' who 'toke of him non hede' – as an analogue of his own situation (361–4).[132] Tellingly, the Black Knight emphasizes Apollo's debasement as a lover by featuring him as the only god in a list of *human* lovers, drawn from classical, Arthurian, and Chaucerian literature, whose erotic ventures caused them to meet bad ends.[133] Lydgate invokes the example of Apollo again in *Reson and Sensuallyte*, this time (in a speech by Venus) to prove the overwhelming power of love over those who would resist it. Apollo's fall into the world of mortal suffering – particularly servitude and disease – illustrates that Love precipitously reduces its subjects to 'servitute, sorwe, and woo, / Vnder hys yokke to be bounde,' and inflicts wounds '[m]ortal and perilouse many folde' (2462–5).[134] In Venus's account, Apollo is a diminished god utterly without resources, having 'loste al worldly plesaunce' (2485), bereft even of the questionable success of his Ovidian appropriation of Daphne's body in its new arboreal form.

Skelton's *Garland of Laurel* (begun c. 1495, revised in 1523), a meditation on poetic fame that bears comparison to Ovidian treatments of the
subject in *Amores* 1.15 and 3.9, restores to Apollo his role as the leader
and 'formest' (foremost) of poets (*Laurel* 287), marching first in a procession that includes 'poetis laureat of many dyverse nacyons' (324),
from Homer and Ovid to Petrarch and Boccaccio to the English triad of
Gower, Chaucer, and Lydgate.[135] Apollo's command of this lineage of
poets is radically defined, however, by his Ovidian failure as a lover,
which even more explicitly than in Ovid results in a critical appraisal of
a poetic authority that founds itself on such an etiology. Skelton presents Apollo at the head of the procession of poets proudly wearing the
laurel, deep in lamentation for the loss of Daphne, 'sith I have lost now
that I entended, / And may not atteyne it by no medyacyon' (318–19).
Like Ovid in exile, his songs are sorrowful – 'Meddelyd with murnynge
the moost parte of his muse' (295) – and replay verbally the frustration
of his desire in the face of Daphne's chastity ('Daphnes, my derlynge,
why do you me refuse?' [297]). What occurs next follows logically from
Ovid's presentation of events in *Metamorphoses* 1 yet manages to out-
Ovid Ovid. Skelton's Apollo chastises his own sister Diana, 'the goddes
inmortall' (303), for perversely influencing the virgin Daphne, who in
Ovid's account had emulated Diana's chaste lifestyle (*Met.* 1.476, 487).
Still more outrageously, Apollo curses 'the goddes' and 'fatall Fortune'
for being cruel to him (*Laurel* 309, 316), and bemoans the Ovidian paradox that 'I contryvyd first princyples medycynable / ... But now to
helpe myself I am not able' (310, 312). Speaking as a mere mortal subject
to Fortune and victimized by gods – including, ironically, his own sister
– Skelton's Apollo comically elaborates the Ovidian tropes of the self-
willed exile and the unhealed healer, while much more explicitly claiming the laurel as a (dubious) consolation prize for poetic posterity: 'Yet,
in remembraunce of Daphnes transformacyon, / All famous poetis en-
suynge after me / Shall were a garlande of the laurell tre' (320–2).[136]

Apollo's authority as god of medicine also invited appropriation and
interpretation in the Middle Ages. Isidore of Seville's *Etymologiae* 4.3
influentially transmitted the classical commonplace that Apollo was
'[m]edicinae ... artis auctor ac repertor' [author and discoverer of the
art of medicine], followed by Aesculapius and Hippocrates, who further expanded the techniques of medical practice.[137] As the father of
Aesculapius, Apollo sometimes appears in biographies of Hippocrates
and some versions of the Hippocratic Oath.[138] Apollo's authority as

healer is significant enough in the Middle Ages that medical treatises are on occasion attributed to him,[139] and vernacular English poetry assumes a familiarity with his status as the god who 'fonde first the craft of medecine / By touche of poues [i.e., pulse] and vryne Inspections.'[140] Perhaps because of his association, as god of poetry as well as healing, with *carmina*, Apollo becomes identified after Isidore with the sect of Methodist medicine (*Etymologiae* 4.4), which was linked with divinely revealed medical doctrine and incantation in contrast with rational (Hippocratic) medicine.[141]

Apollo's claims to authority as healer and poet converge in an unusual but revealing twelfth-century text written in England that has only very recently seen light in a modern edition: the herbal of Henry, archdeacon of Huntingdon and celebrated historian. As its editor A.G. Rigg observes, Henry's herbal is as much 'a vehicle for his poetic imagination and skills,' and particularly his awareness of classical precedent, as it is a scientific treatise;[142] accordingly, Henry seeks Apollo's aid in his endeavour as 'Vatum magne parens, herbarum ... repertor' [mighty father of bards and finder of herbs] (I Prologue, line 11). Throughout his herbal Henry looks to Apollo's inspiration and example to authorize his own transmission of medical knowledge, and more specifically, to contextualize his unique amalgamation of scientific detail and poetic ornament. In doing so, Henry rewrites Ovid's 'composite' Apollo – recognizable only in his piecemeal rejection of his own attributes – as a powerfully organic figure that *serves* rather than subverts the discourse of health. Apollo appears in Henry's herbal as the familiar 'deus et medicus et amans' [god, physician, and lover] who vainly attempts to save Hyacinthus from death (IV.1–2, line 19). Yet, unlike the fallen boy who in Ovid's treatment is little more than a sterile pretext for textual commemoration, Henry's Hyacinthus – as the medicinal hyacinth – paradoxically becomes in death a healer himself, surpassing the powers of his lover Apollo: 'periit quia vulnere, curat' [Because he perished by a wound, Hyacinth cures wounds (particularly battered limbs)] (IV.1–2, line 25).

Henry furthermore reshapes Ovidian precedent when, at several points in the text, he names himself as *vates* and claims inspiration by Apollo (I.21, line 17; IV Epilogue 2, lines 1–2; V Prologue, lines 14–21), placing himself in an Apolline lineage that verifies his authority as a receptacle and transmitter of the medical art. Just as Apollo sees and knows the secret causes of things, so does his son Aesculapius, and so, in turn, does Henry (III Prologue, lines 10–17); this is enough to guarantee the truth-value of the herbal (IV. Epilogue 2, lines 7–22). On this basis Henry, like Ovid before him, merits fame: 'Sic medicis Phebi similis gratissimus omni / Orbe legar toto nomenque perenne tenebo!' [Thus, like the doctors of Phoebus, I shall be read throughout the whole world, most pleasing to everyone, and I will have an eternal name] (V Interlude, lines 5–6). In an overt reconstruction of Apollo's ambivalent Ovidian legacy, Henry bases his own program of medico-poetic authority on the very balance of therapeutic identity that eluded Ovid's Apollo as 'deus et medicus et amans': 'Si non vis aliis, saltem tibi disce mederi: / Te quoque <si> spernis, cui bene fidus eris?' [If you do not wish to heal others, at any rate learn to heal yourself. If you reject yourself, to whom will you be trustworthy?] (VI Prologue, lines 3–4). In these ways, Henry of Huntingdon acknowledges Apollo's ambivalences and self-contradictions as a source of authority in the Ovidian tradition – a trend that becomes especially pronounced, as later chapters will demonstrate, in English poetry of the later Middle Ages – yet he displays a determination to recircuit these weaknesses into conceptual strengths that serve his own vision of authority as something at once practical, moral, and spiritual. Such an appropriation of Apollo prepares us for the concerns of the next chapter: the uneasy medieval cohabitation of Apolline and Christian systems of reference, and the intricate relevance of the pagan god of truth to a culture founded upon the imperative of a singular revealed Truth.

2 The Medieval Apollo: Classical Authority and Christian Hermeneutics

Co fu Bladud ki volt voler
Pur faire plus de sei parler;
Ço se vanta qu'il volereit
E a Londres sun vol prendreit.
Eles fist si s'apareilla
Voler vout e voler quida.
Mais il avint a male fin,
Kar desur le temple Apolin
Prist un tel quaz que tut quassa,
Issi folement trespassa.

[It was (Bladud) who wanted to fly, in order to be more talked about. He boasted he would fly, and would begin his flight in London. He made wings and put them on, wanting and intending to fly. But he came to a bad end, because on top of the temple of Apollo he had such a fall that he broke every bone in his body and thus, in his rashness, he died.]

Wace, *Roman de Brut*, lines 1645–54

As an inspirer, prophet, and healer, the classical Apollo was, first and foremost, an *interpres*. It is as such – part mediator, part go-between – that the god continued to be imagined in the Middle Ages, but with an added complication: the new hermeneutical burden of negotiating the radical distance between the pagan and the Christian worlds of which he was both a figure and a casualty. Consequently, the classical

Apollo's concerted metamorphosis in early Christian and medieval hermeneutics is far from straightforward. On one hand, Apollo enjoyed an 'exalted position' in mythographic handbooks and sermon exempla as a morally sublimated image of Wisdom, Learning, Truth, or even Christ.[1] On the other, Apollo's Ovidian association with debility and untrustworthiness percolated directly into vernacular poetic traditions, as observed in the previous chapter, and indirectly into a tenacious euhemeristic critique and an acute identification with the spiritual perils of idolatry. A striking but not unusual instance of the latter trend is Wace's account, above, of the legendary early British ruler Bladud, a magician and idol-worshipper whose ignominious crash atop Apollo's temple casts him at once as a latter-day Simon Magus misled by his own *ingenium* and as a second Icarus undone by the destructive heat of the sun, here the obsolete powers of an indifferent Apollo. Apollo's afterlife in medieval Christian tradition was not, however, confined to the two extremes of allegorical whitewashing and moral dismissal, for he was just as frequently imagined as a transitional figure whose complex mythical constitution and association with 'truth' limns a dynamic continuity between the teleologies of pagan learning and Christian virtue, concealment and revelation, destruction and vitalization. These tensions and this transitional impulse, I argue, epitomize problems of interpretation, exegesis, and representation by which medieval scholars and poets mediated antiquity and rendered a figure like Apollo intelligible, framing him as an aspect of their own hermeneutic self-image. My objective is to assess the most significant developments in Apollo's fraught relationship with authority as the intricately aesthetic interests of Ovid give way to equally pressing ethical and ontological concerns in the medieval Christian transmission and translation of classical material. It is not my intention here to offer a focused account of any one (not necessarily representative) aspect of the tradition, such as allegorical commentary, in isolation.[2] Instead, I map a number of salient forms in which Apollo's authority was confronted, undermined, and reinscribed in various literary and non-literary traditions in which Chaucer's vernacular appropriations of antiquity may broadly be situated: mythographic manuals and scholarly commentary on the pagan gods, iconography, popular sermons, ritual language, and biblical testimony, as well as literary formulations of paganism in romance, *chansons de geste*, and hagiography.

The Resurrection of Apollo

Alternate traditions of Apollo influential to varying extents in the
Middle Ages ran starkly against the grain of Ovid's approach to the
god. Hyginus's *Fabulae*, an eclectic mythological compendium from the
first or second century CE that structurally anticipated the handbooks
of myth popular in the later Middle Ages, supplied a series of learned
vignettes centred upon genealogy, metamorphosis, and aetiology indebted to Greek legend and Hellenistic procedures.[3] Hyginus's strikingly un-Ovidian manner, which is dry, factual, and often rationalistic,
shapes an Apollo with a radically different status as a powerful deity
who appears in an overwhelmingly flattering light. In the *Fabulae*,
which preserves a number of otherwise unattested variants of common
myths, episodes such as those of Apollo's birth and the punishments of
Coronis, Niobe, and Marsyas evince none of Ovid's ethical ambiguity
or outright scepticism; instead, Apollo safely enjoys the authority of the
Olympian elite throughout the collection and appears equally capable
of vengeance and mercy. In the fable of Marsyas, for example, a nameless Scythian, rather than Apollo, flays the defeated satyr (fab. 165);
similarly, the raven's failure to guard Coronis, rather than Apollo's rash
punishment of the bird for telling the truth, results in its banishment
(fab. 202). The North African grammarian Fulgentius's *Mitologiae* (late
fifth or early sixth century), an exceedingly influential Christian, allegorical mythography centred upon natural and physical interpretations, also privileges Apollo and dissociates him from his Ovidian
affiliation with failed erotic love. In the *Mitologiae*, Apollo's love for
Daphne functions simply as an introduction to the natural properties of
the laurel (1.14), and his protection of the raven is explained without
reference to his love for Coronis (1.13).[4] In Martianus Capella's fifth-
century *De nuptiis Philologiae et Mercurii*, Apollo's marriage to Mantice
(Prophecy/Divination) positively refigures his rape of the prophetess
Cassandra. In this text that allegorizes marital ceremony as a 'philo-
sophic concept of cosmic and microcosmic union,'[5] Mantice, overwhelmed by 'forte immensi amoris' [inordinate passion], *herself* seeks
Apollo, reprising the tradition of the god's forceful aggression toward
the unwilling Cassandra.[6]

This ethical renovation of Apollo in late antique and early medieval
moral allegory paved the way for the Christian allegorization of Apollo
and other figures that became popular later in the medieval period.
Mary E. Barnard and Stella P. Revard have expertly delineated the range

and longevity of the identification of Apollo and Christ from the early Christian iconographic adoption of ancient prototypes, to the exuberantly drawn typological networks of the *Ovide moralisé*, to the syncretism of classical learning and Christianity by Renaissance humanists.[7] This figurative alliance, as Barnard observes, is 'based chiefly on Apollo's ancient roles as sun-god, the god of healing, and the philosopher-god, whose identifying trait is wisdom. All three roles bear easily identifiable parallels with Christ in his Messianic mission.'[8] The Christ-Apollo identification was perhaps most ingeniously developed in the monumental *Ovide moralisé*, which centres upon the unfolding of salvation history within a mythologically generative framework in which 'the Incarnation of Christ ... represent[s] the ultimate metamorphosis.'[9] The idea that Apollo typologically prefigures Christ was not, however, confined to the *Ovide moralisé*'s flamboyant allegorizations; it also crept subtly into as innocent a text as the school commentary on the *Metamorphoses* composed by one Johannes Bolent, the *Constructio Ovidii magni* (1348), which eschews allegorical interpretation in favour of basic grammatical explication and literal summary. Bolent's relation of Apollo's plea to Daphne regarding why she should love him slips into quasi-Christian language: Ovid's straightforward 'Iuppiter est genitor' [Jupiter is my parent] (*Met.* 1.517) becomes 'ego sum filius dei. quia sum filius iouis' [I am the son of God. Because I am the son of Jove]; later, Bolent clarifies: Apollo is 'filius magni dei scilicet iouis.'[10] Still different in spirit is the approach by the Oxford Franciscan John Ridewall to the Christ-Apollo identification in his *Fulgentius metaforalis* (c.1330–4), a scholarly handbook that adapts Fulgentius's *Mitologiae* as a loose framework for a vast homiletic exposition of the chief ethical faculties of the soul.[11] Ridewall presents Apollo as synonymous with Veritas and thoroughly plumbs the god's various iconographic attributes for Christian significance; accordingly, Ridewall incorporates numerous references to points of doctrine culled from the Bible and the Church Fathers. Ridewall begins his verbal 'picture' by highlighting Apollo's status as the first and most distinguished son of Jove, making reference to a central passage in the second book of Martianus Capella's *De nuptiis* that led medieval commentators to stress Apollo's role as mediator of Jove's will, counsellor to mankind, nourisher and modulator of life. In this passage, Philology en route to her heavenly marriage hails Apollo as 'ignoti uis celsa patris uel prima propago, / fomes sensificus, mentis fons, lucis origo' [the exalted power of the Father Unknown, his first offspring, the spark of sensation, source of mind, beginning of light], and as 'uultusque paterne' [countenance of the Father] reflecting and beholding the agency that encompasses the universe (2.185, 193). Ridewall draws out the Christological undercurrents of this thickly Neoplatonist speech:

> Nota quod Philologia in ista sua oratione vocat Apollinem virtutem dei Iovis sicut nos Christiani dicimus de dei filio quod (sic) est virtus dei patris quia omnia per ipsum facta sunt. Qui (sic) iupiter ideo dicitur ignotus quia hominibus est incomprehensibilis.

> [Note that Philology in this speech calls Apollo the power (virtutem) of the god Jove just as we Christians say about the son of God, who is the power of God the Father, because through him all things are made. Therefore Jupiter is called 'unknown' because he is incomprehensible to men.]

For Ridewall, both Christ and Apollo mediate and reflect the will of their otherwise inscrutable fathers, at once embodying and facilitating access to the creative source of life. Pierre Bersuire [Petrus Berchorius]'s contemporary mythographic handbook, *De formis figurisque deorum*, which formed the detachable first chapter of the *Ovidius moralizatus* (itself the fifteenth book of the encyclopedic natural history the *Reductorium morale*), adds to the mix another connection between Apollo and Christ: both are associated with wisdom and divination ('ingenii & divinacionis') because they communicate the secrets of God ('occultis Dei') to humanity, revealing 'illis que ad salutem anime pertinent' [those things that pertain to the salvation of the soul].[12]

Two late medieval English sermons that attest rather unusually to the creative influence of the kind of classicizing exegesis performed by friars like Ridewall at Oxford and Cambridge demonstrate how this scholastic theory could be put into homiletic practice.[13] The early fifteenth-century Worcester Chapter Manuscript F.10 preserves an English sermon attributed to Hugo Legat, a monk of St Albans, which illustrates God's rewards and punishments according to merit by means of an exemplum of Apollo drawn from '[t]hus auteres þat treten *de picturis deorum*' (a reference to the work of scholars like Ridewall) (120–1).[14] Legat equates three iconographic details associated with Apollo's 'picture' – his bow and arrow, harp, and laurel – with the respective promises of divine punishment for the rebellious, mercy for the repentant, and heavenly bliss for those who love God. Apollo himself is '*deus sapientie*': 'This Apollo, þat is God of wit & of dome, is Crist, Goddes sone of heuene, for he is þe wisdom of þe fadir, springing owt of þe welle of glorius Godhede' (125–7). This wisdom informs God's very judgment, as expressed by Christ/Apollo: 'This is an hiȝe wit, a good discreciun of God, þis to reward eueri man aftir his deseruing' (144–5). A second sermon, from a Benedictine collection of the same period connected to Durham priory, commemorates the enclosure of a woman named Alice Huntingfield in a religious order through analogy with Ovid's account of Scylla's containment in her father's tower, during which time she becomes entranced by music from Apollo's lyre that reverberates in the stones (*Met.* 8.11–20); in the sermon's adjusted version, Apollo more dramatically flies through the air playing his lyre. As Siegfried Wenzel has shown, the English preacher adapted this fable to show that 'Alis' ('Silla' spelled backwards) can expect Christ, as 'Deus veritatis' – a phrase also used of Apollo – to 'ipsam confortabit cithera' [comfort her with his lyre] in the same manner. Christ will refresh his virgin bride with his sweet and truthful song just as Apollo moved the heart of Scylla with his lyre.[15]

Apollo as *Interpres*: Two Poetic Battles

Apollo's special proximity to Christ as a deity who embodies prophetic enlightenment and bridges the divine and human did more than distinguish him as a liaison between pagan and Christian forms of wisdom. It also marked him as an index of cultural rupture, a phenomenon situated by this chapter in theological and mythographic discourse and, in the next, traced in poetic representations of the civic sphere. The allure of illumination that surrounded Apollo demanded refutation or redirection if Christian truth was to reign supreme, and the already unstable character of Apollo's propensity for illumination in classical tradition, glaringly elided by the English homilist's account of Scylla's virginal enclosure,[16] made him a natural target. Apollo's authority was appropriated both by covert reinscription with competing forms of truth – the polemical, rather than merely allegorical, substitution of Christ for Apollo – and by overt ventriloquism of the god as humbled witness of his own irrelevancy. The culture wars that took Apollo as ideological victim also made him a popular antihero and poetic device, as later parts of this chapter will demonstrate. The present section explores a range of biblical and early Christian appropriations of Apollo as a figure of truth and harmony, and then considers Apollo's embattled role in two anonymous literary contestations between paganism and Christianity, from different milieux and with different aims, of the high and later Middle Ages: the *Eclogue of Theodulus* and the *Assembly of Gods*.

Early Christians writing for a Greek-speaking audience with an active knowledge of classical myth found a ready analogy for the agon of Christianity and paganism in the widely circulated episode of Apollo's defeat of Python, the antiquity of which stretches back, as we have seen, to the *Homeric Hymns*. The representation of the dragon who pursues the Woman clothed with the sun as she gives birth to a child (identified with Christ) in the twelfth chapter of the Book of Revelation, for example, appears to be directly indebted to the legend of Apollo's mastery of Python, who in some versions persecutes the pregnant Latona.[17] The Revelation-author's amalgamation of Near Eastern and Greco-Roman elements facilitates the strategic transfer of 'activities and images associated with Apollo ... to Christ while significant distinctions between them are retained' – not least the distinction between the 'verba prophetiae hujus' that testify to the word of God (Rev. 1:3) and the kind of false (pagan) prophecy exemplified by Apollo.[18] By reshaping the combat myth involving Apollo and Python as an allegory of Satan's defeat by forces aligned with Christ, the author polemically underscores the inadequacy of pagan values and their unambiguous replacement by Christian ones. In the same motion in which Apollo 'becomes' Christ, this very act of substitution paradoxically necessitates the pagan god's precipitous descent in the order of being, leading to a new identification not with the hero-figure but his nemesis, the conquered serpent.

Around the end of the second century, Clement of Alexandria similarly appropriated the Pythian Apollo as the template of a Christian apologetic in his monumental *Exhortation to the Heathen*. Clement begins by contrasting pagan art and festivity, represented by 'Helicon and Cithaeron,' with the celestial pleasures of 'Sion.'[19] Once the superiority of Christian enlightenment is established, Clement denounces the fables of the pagans and their practices of sacrifice and idolatry in his second through fourth chapters, after which he interrogates the testimonies of pagan philosophers and poets, and, finally, celebrates the benefits of worshipping Christ as the impetus of a final exhortation to conversion. A unifying motif in Clement's argument emerges in the first chapter's account of the lyre-player Eunomos performing at a musical contest in commemoration of the slaying of Python. One of the strings of Eunomos's lyre breaks, but a chirping grasshopper comes to

his aid, 'singing not to that dead dragon, but to God All-wise.' Clement
equates Eunomos's doomed song – whether 'a hymn in praise of the
serpent, or a dirge, I am not able to say' – with the cunning music of the
archpoets Amphion, Arion, and Orpheus, which spreads the poison of
idolatry and superstition against nature's own instinct, embodied in
the grasshopper, to revere God Almighty.[20] In turn, Clement identifies
the Python celebrated by Eunomos with the serpent of Genesis who
'enslaves and plagues men even till now,' entwining them in error –
thus rendering the Python/serpent amalgam, in Thomas Halton's
words, 'the poisonous symbol of classical civilization, writhing in its
death-throes at the omphalos of Delphi, the dead center of the pagan
world.'[21] Clement's later presentation of Christ, who 'cloth[ed] Himself
with flesh ... vanquished the serpent, and enslaved the tyrant death,'
activates an identification of Christ with Apollo as victor that recalls
Revelation's adaptation of the combat myth. Not only does Christ supplant Apollo's role as dragon-slayer, but he lays claim to the reins of his
solar chariot as '"the Sun of Righteousness" who drives His chariot
over all.'[22] More implicitly, Christ repossesses Apollo's lyre, which is
the prototype of Eunomos's instrument and an essential attribute of
the god himself.[23] The music played by Christ on Apollo's lyre is the
'New Song'; the frame of this refitted instrument is humanity itself,
tuned by the Holy Spirit in harmony with the cosmos. Unlike the 'lifeless instruments' plucked by Eunomos and the other bards, which like
the Sirens' songs intoxicate and kill, its strings cannot be broken or its
tune disrupted.[24]

Aggressive adaptation of Apolline myth was not the only way in
which early Christian polemic annexed Apollo's authority as a pagan
god: the Church Fathers had no qualms about usurping Apollo's voice
as prophet to authenticate their claims for Christianity. The Latin
apologist Lactantius influentially incorporated in his *Divine Institutes*
(303–11) several oracles of Apollo, 'quem praeter ceteros diuinum
maximeque fatidicum existimant' [whom they think divine above all
others, and especially prophetic], as part of a larger consolidation of
Jewish and pagan testimonies concerning the coming of Christ.[25]
Lactantius aimed to appeal to non-Christians' powers of logical assessment by means of a discourse, duly clarified, that they already re-
spected as trustworthy. By appropriating Apollo's oracles to evince
Christian revelation, Lactantius neatly 'present[s] a pagan god as chief
witness against paganism.'[26] The oracles that Lactantius quotes, although murky in origin, are most likely genuine; their effectiveness

within Lactantius's apology, as Stefan Freund remarks, would have hinged on their recognizability to a sceptical audience. In each case, Lactantius reveals Apolline wisdom as potentially misleading – since Apollo's intent was to deceive rather than morally instruct – but, upon close study, affirmative of Christian truth. Apollo's cherry-picked oracles, for Lactantius, affirm the omnipotence of a monotheistic God, acknowledge his own subjection to that God, observe Christ's human nature and his wisdom, and corroborate the immortality of the soul.[27] Considerable rhetorical finessing is necessary for Lactantius to make the oracular Apollo into a Christian witness, and even he has less than full confidence in the relevance of Apollo's wisdom to other forms of divine testimony.[28] Moreover, the third-century Neoplatonist Porphyry of Tyre's fragmentary tract *On Philosophy from Oracles*, an anti-Christian work rebutted by Augustine in *De civitate Dei* 19.23, had cited similar, even identical oracles concerning the godhead to *discount* Christian doctrine, finding in them evidence that the god of wisdom himself had exposed as invalid a religion based on the worship of a crucified man. It is partly for this reason that a market developed within the early Christian community for more pliable utterances of Apollo that pointed without ambiguity to a Christian victory in the agon between creeds – a market whose demand for truth was readily met through fabrication.

Beginning in the late fourth century, strategically forged oracles attributed to Apollo proclaiming the end of his own power and the advent of a new dispensation became popular ammunition, especially in the Eastern Church, against the tradition of anti-Christian oracles attested by Porphyry. To those familiar with a range of oracular utterances, Apollo could be seen as a 'convert' from his own earlier opinions to a theologically sound recognition of Christ's supremacy; '[a]fter the unconditional surrender of the gods who had for so long fought against the new religion,' observes Pier Franco Beatrice, 'no further justification was left for those pagans who obstinately continued to refuse to embrace Christianity.'[29] In one such oracle, recounted by Eusebius of Caesaria (c. 260–341), the Delphic Apollo refuses to respond to Emperor Augustus's query about a successor, complaining that 'A Hebrew boy, a god who rules among the blessed, bids me leave this house and go back to Hades.'[30] Similarly, a poem by Saint Gregory of Nazianzus (c. 326–90) adapts an actual Apolline oracle to mount an otherwise fictional pronouncement in which Apollo predicts his own destruction, and that of other cult deities, by a man who is his own father and who was born without the stain of childbirth.[31] In similar fashion, John of

Euboea, writing in the eighth century, reports a response by Apollo to a group of Achaean envoys seeking advice regarding a battle strategy that shows concern only for a different battle:

> After a time one will come to this earth and will become flesh without sin ... and he will incur the ill will of an unbelieving people and be hanged on high, condemned to death, which he will willingly endure; and he will rise from death to eternal life.

The envoys retort with annoyance that they had inquired about the kingdom of a woman, not a man, and that 'instead of one war you bring another on us, not being immortal gods and true masters.'[32] A less overtly self-incriminating Apolline oracle is related by Jacobus de Voragine in the *Legenda aurea* (c. 1260), an account of which appears in a late Middle English sermon in British Library MS Royal 18 B. xxiii. In this narrative, Apollo predicts that the Temple of Peace in Rome will remain intact until a virgin gives birth to a child; the Romans logically assume that this impossible prospect guarantees the temple's permanence, only to find the sacred building in ruins on the night of Christ's birth.[33]

Not only did many of these pseudo-oracles show – from the horse's mouth, as it were – Apollo's authority to be subject to the Christian order, they actively co-opted it as propaganda for particular Christian doctrinal assertions. For example, the fullest textual tradition of the so-called Tübingen *Theosophy*, a Byzantine epitome of a lost Greek collection of oracles and universal history composed c. 500 CE, features an oracle in which Apollo laments his imminent defeat by 'a bright heavenly man' whose omnipotence encompasses 'every divine utterance and presage.' Following this statement is a detailed exposition of the nature of the Christian godhead – still in Apollo's voice – that is noteworthy for its theologically precise expression of a monophysite heretical viewpoint regarding Christ's single divine nature.[34] The same forged oracle, in a tenth-century manuscript collection, was in turn reshaped to support the orthodox Christological position of Chalcedonianism, which stood opposed to the monophysite heresy.[35] In these ways, the silencing of Apollo spoke volumes: the god's voice, debased but also renovated as a field of articulation for newly competitive vocabularies of truth, still commanded the omphalos of cultural expression.

The bold polemicism of these oracular appropriations of Apollo's authority reflects the pronounced struggle, actual and rhetorical, between pagans and Christians – as within Christianity itself – in the first several centuries after Christ's death. As the conflict with paganism lost its historical immediacy, to become increasingly a matter of poetic and philosophical cultivation, the urgency of these early Christian reinscriptions of Apollo was supplanted by an interest in the creative capacity of Apollo as a surrogate or bridge-figure *nonpareil* in the negotiation between classical fable, which brazenly celebrates itself, and Christian poetry, which celebrates God as source of creation.

Salient traces of Apollo's contentious survival in discourses of illumination are found in the Carolingian *Eclogue of Theodulus*, a Latin poem by an unidentified author that assesses in pithily mnemonic terms the continuity and contrast between pagan and Christian wisdom. The broad affinity of the *Eclogue of Theodulus* – by the twelfth century a popular school text – with the apologetic traditions surveyed above is evident in its agonistic structure, framed within a bucolic milieu modelled on Virgil's *Eclogues*, as a poetic contest between the female Alithia (Truth), representing Judaeo-Christian revelation, and the male Pseustis (Deceit), an image of pagan wisdom.[36] The contest is judged by the ostensibly nonpartisan Phronesis (Wisdom or Prudence). The musical bearings of the competition – Alithia plucks King David's harp and Pseustis plays the rustic flute – evoke Clement's distinction between old and new song on the one hand, and Apollo's contests with Pan and Marsyas as presented in Ovid's *Metamorphoses* on the other.[37] Indeed, the whole contest between the two figures is built around such tiered comparisons: Pseustis tells stories drawn from classical mythology, and Alithia responds with matching narratives from the Old Testament. Alithia 'plays fair' by invoking the concealed wisdom of the Old Testament rather than the revealed mysteries of the New Testament, which are certain to overwhelm her opponent and thus ruin the game. A sense not only of equivalency but allegorical fulfilment underscores Alithia's narrative rebuttals of Pseustis's mythological fancies: the garden of Eden, for example, correlates with the Golden Age; Noah's flood matches the inundation survived by Deucalion and Pyrrha; and Delilah's betrayal of Samson parallels Deianira's deception of Hercules.

Strikingly, Apollo is one of only a very few pagan figures acknowledged by Alithia in her Hebrew epitomes: in a rare classicizing touch, she refers to the sun as Phoebus when it stands still at Joshua's command at Gibeon (169–72).[38] This story counters Pseustis's tale about Phoebe, as the moon, who prolonged the night for Jove when he begot Hercules. Later, when Pseustis realizes he is losing the competition because he is running out of stories, he revives Alithia's earlier reference to Phoebus's enduring power in complaining that the god's chariot will not descend, hindering nightfall and thus the end of the contest:

Quadrupedes Phoebi quae cogit causa morari?
Experientur item Phaëtontis saecula cladem.
Quid, vesper, cessas? saturarunt prata capellas,
Ruminat omne pecus, nescit procedere Phoebus.   (245–8)

[What is delaying the four-footed steeds of Phoebus? The world will suffer the same disaster as it did with Phaethon. Why delay, Evening? The meadows have filled the goats full. The whole herd is chewing the cud. Phoebus does not know how to make shift.]

In a neat bit of irony, the overlap of Pseustis's complaint with Alithia's earlier story shows him inadvertently adopting her superior language to describe, and thus confirm, his own inevitable defeat. At the same time, as we have seen, Alithia's account of the miracle at Gibeon itself had unusually absorbed the language and ideology of her competitor. One is tempted to approach this paradox as a kind of hermeneutic spiral in which the terms of Pseustis's defeat do not so much affirm Alithia's position as vindicate his own classicizing rhetoric while exposing Alithia's unacknowledged entrapment by it.[39] This reading, which would make a horizontal debate of a vertical one, is foiled, however, by Alithia's next move, which is to re-allegorize the sun as the light of truth and align it with God's wisdom as creator (249–52).

The last several quatrains of the *Eclogue* pivot upon the relative speed with which night ought to overtake day. Both speakers personify the day as a virgin, pressed into submission by the sky; Pseustis goads the ravishing sky, while Alithia prays for the virgin to triumph over darkness (293–316). When the sun finally does set (325–58; 342–4) – whether its course was miraculously prolonged or just seemed that way to the desperate Pseustis is unclear – Alithia moves on to higher truths: she promises now to elucidate the '[q]uatuor imprimis evangelicae rationis /... codicibus' [four books of The Good News], and specifically the Incarnation (330–1). This new scope of spiritual illumination supersedes the merely *natural* light of the setting sun and its affinity with the language of fable; the *virgo* whose cosmic tenacity had protracted the daylight now becomes the Virgin in whose body God took on human shape (329–32). By means of this series of conceptual transformations, the sun emerges as the image and guarantor of Alithia's narrative superiority and Pseustis's defeat. Insofar as the sun, as Phoebus, is initially evoked in the *Eclogue* with recourse to a pagan vocabulary, it bridges pagan and Judaeo-Christian worldviews – and this connection, with its potential for integration as much as friction, is on one level the subject of the poem. Ultimately, however, the sun's setting, which occasions Alithia's first mention of the Incarnation of Christ, marks not only the defeat of Pseustis, but the limitations of a hermeneutic that attempts to place pagan and Christian knowledge on an equal footing. As a named figure, Apollo enables Alithia and Pseustis temporarily to share a common discourse and move beyond simple binaries; by the end of the poem, he is rendered anonymous, his authority recircuited as an image of the spiritual radiance of Christ and the superior musical skill of Alithia. As winner of the contest, thanks to her inspiration by Christ-as-sun, Alithia stands firm in Apollo's own mythic role as musical victor.

Our second example of Apollo's cultural position as the iconic focus of medieval anxieties surrounding literary paganism is the *Assembly of Gods*, a learned Middle English poem from the late fifteenth century associated in different periods with the canons of Chaucer and Lydgate. Like the *Eclogue of Theodulus*, the *Assembly of Gods* explicitly combines pagan subject matter with pious Christian instruction through the framework of a battle between right and wrong, in this case employing a dreamer rather than a judge as the ethical consciousness at the centre of the action. The transition between pagan and Christian ways of knowing thus proceeds as a reflection of the moral and psychological regeneration of the Christian dreamer-narrator, who awakens instructed in how reason and sensuality can be united within the individual soul.

Apollo is the central pagan figure of the *Assembly*, and his prominence therein reflects the influence of Martianus Capella's *De nuptiis*, which, like the *Assembly*, features the sun-god as master of ceremonies at an allegorical banquet of divinities. The *Assembly*, however, concerns a divine dispute rather than a wedding, and instead of uniting the human intellect with divine (pagan) sources of knowledge by means of apotheosis, it establishes the superiority of Christian virtue to a pagan value system founded upon deceit and unchecked sensuality.[40] In this framed critique of the pagan world, Apollo functions both as host and mediator. First, he mediates a quarrel, introduced early in the poem, between Eolus on the one side and Diana and Neptune on the other, who complain that Eolus's chaotic influence has destroyed the peace of forest and sea, causing them to be reproached by their worshipers. Apollo convenes a banquet of the gods to settle the argument and personally enjoins his sister Diana to recognize Eolus's repentance; he further promises to favour Diana with his generative properties so as to counteract any future destruction wrought upon the land by Eolus.

A major turn in the plot occurs when Attropos, one of the Fates (here identified with Death) wins over the entire pagan pantheon to support his vendetta against Vertu, who alone eludes his grasp. Apollo is the first among the deities to boast, like a battle-hungry hero in a *chanson de geste*, that he will destroy Vertu imminently: 'yef he on erthe bee, / Wyth my brennyng chare I shall hym confound' (505–6). But when Vyce prepares to lead his army of colourful vagabonds against Vertu's off-guard forces, Apollo alone shows scruples by attempting to warn Vertu of the impending attack, reinforcing his role as mediator. Vyce, however, wants none of this, preferring the advantage of treacherous assault; Vertu is instead tacitly warned by Morpheus, through his messenger Ymaginacion, without the aid of Apollo. Apollo's position here is interestingly double-edged: as leader of the ranks of gods who wholeheartedly support the cause of Vyce, he nonetheless proves himself superior to the lot of them in attempting to play fair and warn Vertu. Apollo, in other words, subtly figures the potential transition from pagan Vyce to Christian Vertu which is the poem's larger subject, although the process is, in him, unfulfilled. Notably, this drama of conversion *is* played out within the diegesis of the poem's mythological narrative in the figure of Attropos, who, after Vyce's defeat by Vertu, abandons the failed pagan gods in decidedly Christian language – 'then I se well / That all ye goddes be but counterfete' (1331–2) – and vows, as Dethe, to serve the true God (whom, it is revealed, he has always unknowingly served [1394–8]).

The concurrent enlightenment and limitation of Apollo with regard to the supremacy of Christianity in the *Assembly* echo a number of Apolline postures with which this book is concerned – the unhealed healer, the prophet who predicts his own demise, the human god – and take shape in Apollo's exchange with Attropos upon his dismissal of the gods as comrades. Attropos's complaint is initially legalistic: the gods, led by Apollo, granted their 'patent of offyce' (494) that Vertu would be defeated with the provision that 'a goddes wrytyng may nat reversyd be' (492), and yet they have reneged upon their agreement by losing the battle. Apollo responds as *interpres*, explaining that the gods' jurisdiction – and hence the legal boundaries of the 'patent' – is the realm of Nature, but Vertu supersedes Nature and hence death. Clearly and coolly, Apollo explains to Attropos the limitations of the gods' power, the superiority of Vertu, and indeed the very reason that the battle was doomed to fail from the start despite his full-fledged support. Although this Apollo, like the defeated Apollo of the Christian oracles, articulates key restrictions on the gods' power, he betrays no awareness of what lies beyond that power or what is superior to Nature. For this reason, his response is legally valid but morally void. Attropos, dissatisfied, vows instead to serve the 'Lorde of Lyght' (1384, 1390), specifically impugning the supremacy of Apollo, whose 'beames bryght' at the banquet 'shone so fervently / That he therwith gladyd all the company' (382–3). Much like Phoebus the sun in the *Eclogue of Theodulus*, Apollo in the *Assembly of Gods* is displaced by the Christian God; at the same time, he is the only deity to see the pagan pantheon's status for what it is and to lead Attropos toward participation in the eternal. This paradox receives further attention in a moral gloss on the content of the dream provided at the end of the poem by Doctryne. The destructive path of Eolus, according to Doctryne, represents unbridled wealth; the complaints of Diana and Neptune, 'fooles reson' (1645); and Apollo, in a common mythographic identification, the wise man who corrects fools (1655–9). A mere three stanzas after Doctryne identifies Apollo with wisdom, however, she denounces the banquet over which he presides as a feast of idolatry: 'And as for all tho that represent / To be callyd "goddys" at that banket, / Resemble false ydollys' (1674–6). Scruples or not, Apollo is cut from the same cloth.

Apollo, Apollos, and Apollyon

Most any Greco-Roman 'deity theoretically could be appropriated in such ways to serve Christian interests, but Apollo was unique in sharing cultural space with two similarly named analogues in the New Testament, both of whom were absorbed into his conceptual apparatus in the early Christian and medieval periods. These two linguistic cousins, Apollos and Apollyon – Apollo's biblical alter egos, if you will – are brought together in relation to the classical deity in Bersuire's influential *De formis figurisque deorum* to support moralizations *in bono* and *in malo* of the god, who like other pagan figures in this preacher's handbook is rendered symbolically consistent with principles of Christian understanding and biblical wisdom.[41] Bersuire's multiple interpretations in the *De formis* of Apollo's iconography, the details of which are derived sequentially from Petrarch's *Africa* and Ridewall's *Fulgentius metaforalis*, culminate in two images forming a diptych around the concept of Apollo *exterminans*. One is positive – Apollo as the just man who exterminates all evil in himself – and the other negative – Apollo as the tyrant who exterminates innocent subjects by inflicting evil. The allegorization *in bono* draws parallels between the four wheels of Apollo's chariot and the four cardinal virtues, Apollo's affection for the laurel and the just man's devotion to the cross, and so on; finally, these analogies are sealed by a scriptural citation that bears a typically forced and provocative relation to the pagan image: 'Iudaeus autem quidam, Apollo nomine, Alexandrinus genere, vir eloquens, devenit Ephesum, potens in scripturis' [Now a certain Jew, named Apollo, born at Alexandria, an eloquent man, came to Ephesus, one mighty in the scriptures] (Acts 18:24). Bersuire applies this biblical reference to Apollo *exterminans* as the just man who annihilates the enemy's power through his preaching. The subsequent allegorization *in malo* of Apollo as tyrant likens that same chariot to worldly pomp, the laurel to frivolous pleasure, and more in this vein, and is collated in turn with its own biblical analogue: Apollyon of Rev. 9:11, angel of the abyss and king of the locusts.[42]

These two biblical loci aptly reflect Apollo's complex, often ambivalent relation to an interpretive culture circumscribed by Christian truth – an ambivalence, later chapters will demonstrate, that saturates even Chaucer's 'demoralized' treatments of him in texts such as *Troilus and Criseyde* and the *Manciple's Tale*.[43] The god's association with the preacher Apollo of the Book of Acts ('Apollos' in the Greek but 'Apollo' in the Vulgate) merits closer consideration. Most strongly emphasized in Acts, and underscored by Bersuire, is this Apollo's oratorical eloquence: as an Alexandrian Jew who converted to Christianity, the biblical Apollo is at once an image of Hellenistic learning, a namesake of the quintessential Greek god of the arts, and a paradigm (like Paul) of Jewish conversion. However, Apollo's preaching exposes his deficiency in certain essential articles of the faith; he knows only the baptism of John ['tantum baptisma Ioannis'] (Acts 18:25), not that of the Holy Spirit, and must be corrected by Paul's associates Priscilla and Aquila. The well-educated Apollo's doctrinal correction by a woman casts the limitations of his learned eloquence into strong relief, as the fifth-century Alexandrian commentator Ammonius notes.[44] In Acts 19, Paul visits Ephesus and remedies the deficiencies of Apollo's teaching by re-baptizing his disciples in the name of Jesus, thereby filling them with the Holy Spirit and causing them to speak in tongues. After his correction by Priscilla and Aquilla, Apollo goes on to preach at Corinth, where he makes many converts among the Jewish population and, as a passage in 1 Corinthians attests, comes to rival Paul in popularity:

> Cum enim quis dicat: Ego quidem sum Pauli. Alius autem: Ego Apollo, nonne homines estis? Quid igitur est Apollo? quid vero Paulus? ... Ego plantavi, Apollo rigavit: sed Deus incrementum dedit. (1 Cor. 3: 4, 6).

> [For while one saith: I indeed am of Paul; and another: I am of Apollo; are you not men? What then is Apollo and what is Paul? ... I have planted, Apollo watered; but God gave the increase.][45]

According to St Jerome, Apollo fled to Crete with the lawyer Zenas (mentioned together at Tit. 3.13) because of the tensions at Corinth; he was later to be called back by Paul.[46] These tensions could indicate, as a modern biblical authority has suggested, that 'some Corinthians may have been opting for what sounded like greater wisdom [represented by the eloquent Apollo], whereas Paul without eloquence had preached a foolishness really wiser than human wisdom, namely, Christ and him crucified ([1 Cor.] 1:18–2:5).'[47] Taking this implicit possibility to the extreme, the tract *De verbis scripturae: Factum est vespere et mane dies unus*, possibly written by the fourth-century Roman African scholar Marius Victorinus, cites the Apollo of Acts as an example of those who resist a simple, harmonious understanding of Scripture in favour of vain wisdom associated with 'syllogisticus sermo' and 'omnis superstitiosa adinventio.' Just as Priscilla and Aquila corrected Apollo, so 'Facile ... sapientes reprehenduntur. Scit enim Dominus cogitationes sapientium quoniam vanae sunt' [Wise men are refuted easily. For God knows that the thoughts of wise men are vain].[48]

Like many of Bersuire's associative references to Scripture, this one thus quickly loses its moral clarity as a homiletic or pedagogic point of reference for Apollo as the just man. Instead, the closer one looks at the context of Apollo as *vir eloquens* in Acts and related New Testament texts, together with their commentaries, the more one is reminded of alternate interpretations of Apollo rehearsed by Bersuire himself in nearby sections: namely, those that emphasize the god's moral association with 'verba placencia' [pleasing words] and destructive, worldly wisdom.[49] If these less than fully positive aspects of the Apollo of Acts only distantly unsettle the biblical text, the proximity of the sacrally malleable character of Apollo of Acts to the position of the pagan god Apollo on the cusp of a new dispensation asserts itself more dramatically in a late antique moralized world history from creation to the late fourth century known as *De aetatibus mundi et hominis*, composed by Fulgentius. Fulgentius's clipped overview of the miraculous events following Christ's resurrection draws heavily upon the Book of Acts and cryptically relates an episode in which 'Expetitur Paulus ad mortem dum Apollo futurorum praedicator perderet deitatem, et quia apostolos clamoribus sectabatur spiritus, ut recedat praecipitur' [Paul was threatened with death when Apollo(s), the proclaimer of things to come, lost his claim to divine powers; and because his spirit strongly pursued the apostles with outcries, he was cast down to make him cease].[50] It has been suggested that Fulgentius here conflates Acts 18:24–8, the account of Apollo's ministry in Ephesus, with Paul's punishment of the false prophet Bar-jesu in Acts 13:6–11 and the humiliation of false exorcisers in Acts 19:13–16.[51] This forced explanation is unnecessary, however, in light of the very real potential – already latent in Apollo's connection with Greek learning – for association between the preacher Apollo and the Apollo of the Delphic oracle. Like Fulgentius's Apollo, the Delphic Apollo is a 'futurorum praedicator' who, according to early Christian apologists, loses his claim to 'deitas' concurrent with the advent of Christ. In the *Divine Institutes*, a seminal text, as we have seen, for the appropriation of Apollo as witness of the truth of Christian monotheism, Lactantius employs similar language to describe the Delphic Apollo in his account of an oracle that ostensibly praises the Christian God and identifies the speaker as a demon rather than a deity – one who will be subdued by the coming of Christ. The fabricated oracles of Apollo in the Tübingen *Theosophy* further illustrate how polemical Christian accounts of the silencing of the oracles could resonate with Fulgentius's representation of the defeated Apollo of Acts. In the *Theosophy*, Apollo's oracle not only identifies the Christian God as the supreme king, but predicts that

> [t]his Spirit against my will will shortly drive me out of this temple, of which the prophesying threshold will be left deserted ... Apollo goes away, he goes away, because a bright heavenly man presses me with violence.[52]

Fulgentius's dispossessed 'Apollo futurorum praedicator' bears a striking affinity to this Apollo as demon cast out violently from his own temple. This multidimensional Apollo would seem to function for Fulgentius, therefore, not as a bridge between faiths, as in Acts 18, but as a casualty of the new religion.

The conceptual lineage of Bersuire's just man leads us, then, most unexpectedly in the direction of his reading *in malo* of Apollo *exterminans* as Apollyon of Revelation. In the passage to which Bersuire refers, the infernal locusts, let loose upon the earth, are said to have in their company 'regem angelum abyssi cui nomen hebraice Abaddon, graece autem Apollyon, latine habens nomen Exterminans' [A king, the angel of the bottomless pit (whose name in Hebrew is Abaddon and in Greek Apollyon, in Latin Exterminans)] (Rev. 9:11). Apollyon is memorably depicted in John Bunyan's *Pilgrim's Progress* as one of the builders of Vanity Fair and a monstrous, Geryon-like challenger of Christian, who heroically defeats him.[53] An identification of Apollyon with the Greco-Roman Apollo was, in fact, made well before Bersuire's *De formis*. One sixth-century Syriac manuscript of the New Testament contains the reading 'Apollo' for 'Apollyon,' a scribal slip consistent with the author's strategic representation, earlier in Revelation (6:2), of the rider of the white horse by means of solar and martial imagery traditionally associated with the pagan god Apollo.[54] Medieval mythographers had long explicated Apollo by means of etymological connection to the Greek root shared with Apollyon – i.e., to destroy, *exterminans* in Latin.[55] An equation of Apollyon with Apollo does not appear to have been common in medieval Scriptural exegesis, but it was not too recondite to surface in a formal curse of ritual excommunication added to the English missal known as the Red Book of Darley (Cambridge, Corpus Christi College MS 422, first half of the twelfth century), associated with the Austin canons of St Helen in Darley, Derbyshire.[56] Among the loathsome punishments verbally conferred upon the excommunicant is 'inmisionem per angelos malos usque deducatur in profundum inferni' [the letting loose of evil angels until he is drawn down into the depths of hell], where the subject is doomed to cohabit with a multitude of infernal villains featuring 'lucifer et satanas apollo astaroth ama, sama omnesque socii' [Lucifer and Satan, Apollo, Astaroth, Ama, Sama, and all their associates].[57] This curse formula strikingly enrols 'Apollo' within a legion of devils, all of whom have certifiable demonological pedigrees in biblical and apocryphal sources.[58] The casual nature of Apollo's inclusion in this demonic list attests to the popular association of Apollo with Apollyon,[59] and also sheds light on Apollo's virtually reflexive association with medieval conceptions of idolatry – in essence, demon-worship – and cultural difference more generally, contexts that will be explored later in this chapter in relation to depictions of the pagan pantheon in hagiography and romance.

One hermeneutic thread of Bersuire's allegorization of the Apollo and Daphne narrative in *Ovidius moralizatus* serves as a final illustration of the staying power of the association of Apollo with Apollyon exegetically activated in the *De formis*. Bersuire indicates that Daphne's flight from Apollo can be understood as an image of the human soul resisting the temptation of the devil, represented by Apollo; when she is transformed into a laurel, she becomes a 'persona religiosa, uirtuosa et perfecta' [religious person, virtuous and perfect].[60] Next, Bersuire cites Ecclesiasticus 21:2, 'Quasi a facie colubri fuge peccata' [Flee from sins as from the face of a serpent], in support of his reading of Daphne's escape from Apollo.[61] In so doing, he implicitly but unmistakably associates Apollo with the Python he earlier defeated, and thereby reshapes Ovid's myth to make Daphne the true victor over serpentine forces of evil and chaos, now allied with Apollo as persecutor. A second biblical analogy, this time between Daphne and the Woman clothed with the sun (Rev. 12:14), again identifies Daphne, *mutatis mutandis*, with imagery elsewhere attached to Apollo (e.g., in Bersuire's separate interpretation of him as *sol justiciae*).[62] Far from his solar glory here, however, Apollo is presented as an Ovidian analogue of the *serpens* or *draco* from whose face, in the biblical account, the Woman clothed with the sun flees (Rev. 12:14–17). Unable to shake his affiliation with Apollyon, Apollo emerges, here as in the *De formis*, as an apocalyptic demon and an image of Satan – this time even becoming the prey of his own heroic identity, radically appropriated and redefined as an emblem of Daphne's 'Christian' chastity.

'Whan Phebus dwelled heere in this erthe adoun' (*MancT* 105): The Euhemeristic Assault

Bersuire's mythographic superstructure attests to the ethical extremes that Apollo's cultic identity could be made to support in a theological context, but Apollo's instability as a figure of authority was also a matter of historical interest. Perpetually shifting in classical as well as medieval treatments between humiliation and heroism, exile and exaltation, Apollo readily lent himself to critiques of ancient worship based on a euhemeristic rationale: namely, that the pagan gods are no more than human beings deified in reputation. The Judaeo-Christian pedigree of the euhemeristic theory begins with Wisdom 14:15–20, which describes a grieving father who worships an *imago* of his dead son, establishing a cult of idolworship. The apparatus of euhemerism was broadly disseminated for mythographic purposes by Isidore of Seville's survey of the pagan gods in *Etymologiae* 8.11, which influentially recounts the Babylonian king Ninus's worship of a memorial image of his father.[63] The idea that the ancient gods were deified mortals originated with Euhemerus (third century BCE), whose intention was to define and justify, rather than discount, the constitution of the pagan pantheon. The euhemeristic theory lent itself more readily, however, to those who opposed on philosophical or theological grounds the validity of polytheism and its supporting fables; hence euhemerism's widespread co-option by early Christian apologists including Clement of Alexandria, Tertullian, and Lactantius, who condemned pagan idolatry as the false celebration of gods whose 'divinity' is, quite literally, manmade.

Apologists in the early Christian period relished pointing out the inconsistencies of the pagan gods and pagans' strategies of defending their gods, appropriating argumentative techniques earlier deployed in the framework of Academic scepticism in the third book of Cicero's *De natura deorum*. As we might expect, given his Ovidian associations with human imperfection and impotence outlined in the previous chapter, Apollo offered Christian apologists a particularly rich field for mockery. Among the most commonly encountered examples of the disreputability of the pagan gods in the writings of the Church Fathers – who took every opportunity to point out that the incriminating evidence was furnished by pagan authors themselves – is the episode of Apollo's servitude to Admetus, which neatly encapsulates the absurdity of an all-powerful god being subject ('turpissime' [most disgracefully], adds Lactantius) to the whims of a mere mortal.[64] To this example several apologists link the story of Apollo's and Neptune's humiliating servitude to Laomedon, mocking in turn the gods' constraint by a pecuniary arrangement and Laomedon's cavalier disrespect for their service.[65] Clement of Alexandria quips that, while some regard Apollo as a righteous counsellor and sage, the various women he raped would not likely agree, with the possible exception of Daphne, who 'alone escaped the prophet.'[66] According to Origen and John Chrysostom, even Apollo's oracles are distorted by his sexuality: when Apollo inspired the Pythian priestess, he did so by penetrating her private parts, resulting in an orgasmic ecstasy that is no conduit of truthful utterance. For this reason, claims Origen, Apollo chose as his mouthpiece a 'common woman' – not even a virgin – rather than a wise man, 'as though he could only find pleasure in the breast of a woman.'[67] Other apologists find amusement in the sheer illogicality and fatuousness of the cult of Apollo: for example, the irony that Apollo is smooth-cheeked while his son Aesculapius is bearded;[68] the multiple, conflicting genealogies of Apollo (which suggest that numerous deities confusedly pass under the same name);[69] and the glamourlessness of Apollo's cultic image as god of mice (the Sminthian) in the Troad and his obscure local appellations elsewhere as 'yawning Apollo' and 'guzzling Apollo.'[70]

These jeeringly polemical Christian invectives often sound like nothing so much as the stump speech of Ovid's Niobe. Ovid's far-reaching irreverence toward Apollo – unsubtly encapsulated, as we have seen, in Niobe's harangue against Latona and her family (see above, p. 30) – thickly endows the apologetic tradition with ready-made objections to the validity of Apollo's deity. Like Niobe, Arnobius mocks the inauspicious birth of Apollo and Diana on a floating island sought by a spurned mother in exile.[71] The powerlessness of the terrible twins to punish Arnobius for his 'blasphemy' is, in a sense, precisely his point. Lactantius, who was substantially acquainted with classical poetry and rhetoric, provides a mini-anthology of unflattering Ovidian episodes involving Apollo, embedded in a withering mythographic survey of the lives and deeds of various Olympians in *Divine Institutes* 1.9–11. In addition to observing Apollo's shameful servitude to Admetus and Laomedon, Lactantius highlights the disgraceful circumstances of Aesculapius's birth ('non sine flagitio Apollinis' [not without disgrace to Apollo]) – apparently an allusion to Apollo's murder of Coronis – as well as his responsibility for the death of Hyacinthus, implying that it was less an accident than a crime of passion: 'idem formosum puerum et dum amat, uiolauit; et dum ludit, occidit' [And he also, while in love with a beautiful boy, offered violence to him, and while engaged in play, slew him].[72] Lactantius's later epitome of his *Divine Institutes* gives a rather different, more fully Ovidian account of this last episode as an unintentional ('imprudens') murder followed by Apollo's regret, on account of which he 'gemitus suos inscripsit in flore' [inscribed his own lamentations on a flower].[73] This second account summons a pathetic image of Apollo mooning over a flower, after an *imprudens* action that proves not merely his unluckiness but his lack of foresight – the defining quality of a prophet. Unlike in the *Metamorphoses*, where Apollo's flower-writing was associated with prophecy and the eventual recuperation of artistic identity, Lactantius suppresses any hint of the restoration of Apollo's divine prerogative. But this too, with its suggestion of Apollo's fraudulence, is a legitimately 'Ovidian' reading: in effect, Lactantius could be said to defy the letter of Ovid's episode in favour of the spirit of his treatment of Apollo as a failed artist and unconvincing arbiter of illusion.

It comes as no surprise that Apollo's supposed wisdom and prophetic skills – the basis of his reputation as a conduit of truth – especially aroused the vituperation of Christian moralists. This aspect of Apollo either had to be turned against itself and made witness to its own demise, as in the self-defeating oracles discussed earlier, or it had to be exposed as intrinsically faulty, morally vicious, or abusive. The notion that Apollo spoke not as a god but a demon (cf. Augustine, *De civitate Dei* 8.23–4) offered one means of support for this second argument. Euhemeristic critique, broadly deployed to associate Apollo with human error and sin, provided another, proving most influential for medieval understandings of the god in his oracular aspect. Tertullian, for example, referring to Socrates' legendary gratitude to Apollo for (according to Plato) designating him the wisest of men, ironically contrasts Socrates' wisdom with that of 'Apollinem inconsideratum' [absent-minded Apollo], who '[s]apientiae testimonium reddidit ei viro qui negabat deos esse' [bore witness to the wisdom of the man who denied the existence of gods].[74] To Augustine, Apollo as god of prophecy is not only a fool but a drudge who wasted a good deal of hard work because he failed to predict that Laomedon would refuse to pay him for his labour.[75] In a clever twist, Clement of Alexandria, discussing Apollo's cruelly ambiguous oracle to Croesus, observes that the Apollo of the Delphic oracle was as miserly toward his suppliants as Laomedon was to him:

> Your Phoebus was a lover of gifts, but not a lover of men. He betrayed his friend Croesus, and forgetting the reward he had got (so careful was he of his fame), led him across the Halys to the stake ... He whom you worship is an ingrate; he accepts your reward, and after taking the gold plays false.[76]

Although some medieval mythographies, for example the commentary on the *Aeneid* attributed to Bernardus Silvestris and Boccaccio's *Genealogie deorum gentilium libri*,[77] preserved euhemeristic accounts of Apollo in neutrally antiquarian contexts, the patristic spirit of mockery of Apollo's human qualities remained popular late into the Middle Ages, reflecting a contemporary trend toward 'historical' rather than allegorical interpretation of pagan myth.[78] For example, John Capgrave's *Life of St. Katherine* (composed in the 1440s) features a spirited euhemeristic critique of paganism by the heroine, who reprimands Emperor Maxentius of Alexandria for reviving the worship of gods who once were men ('erdely as we bee / Were thei sumtyme' [4.8.634–5]).[79] Buttressing a tour de force of theological disputation is Katherine's wholesale debunking of the pagan pantheon as a rogues' gallery that has swindled the ignorant into mindless worship. Her condemnation of Apollo emphasizes the lying and ambiguous nature of his prophecies, which come off no better than the Latin of Chaucer's marble-mouthed Summoner (GP 637–46):

Youre godd Apollo, whan he was drunk of wyne
Than wold he jangyll in manere of prophecye,
Ful sotyll lesyngys wold he thoo dyvyne
To hem that knew not his trescerye.
Sumetyme soth sawed, sumetyme dyd he lye.   (4.23.1541–5)

A long digression on the euhemeristic origins of the pagan gods in Book Five of Gower's *Confessio amantis* (on avarice) presents an especially amusing portrait of Apollo as 'deus Sapiencie,' as he is identified in Gower's marginal gloss. Genius describes Apollo as a roving hunter who resorts to singing for his supper and gains followers by pretending to know the future, though his prophecies are 'sleyhtes alle' which 'hath the lewed folk deceived' (5.930–1). Thus, this deified beggar and charlatan 'cleped is the god of wit / To suche as be the foles yit' (5.935–6).

A particularly suggestive medieval variation on these durable euhemeristic critiques is the exemplary association of Apollo with his half-mortal son Phaethon within the *de casibus* tradition of moral counsel. A conceptual parallel between Apollo and Phaethon resulted from a common transposition of the episode of Apollo's servitude to Admetus from the aftermath of Aesculapius's death to that of Phaethon – a shift invited by the fact that both sons of Apollo are stricken by Jove's thunderbolts, resulting in Apollo's rebellious anger.[80] Once Apollo's servitude was linked with Phaethon's death, an analogy between their respective 'falls' suggested itself and invited development within the *de casibus* tradition, shaped by the same trends that, by the fifteenth century, occasioned pictorial depictions of the powerful cast down from Fortune's wheel in conformity with conventional iconography of Phaethon's fall from the solar chariot.[81]

In Walter Map's popular antimarital tract *Dissuasio Valerii* (c. 1180), later inserted into his *De nugis curialium*, the fall of Solomon from the height of wisdom to idolatry is brought to bear on a demonstration of the dangers of lust and female sexuality. To round out his point, Map introduces a surprising analogy with the downfall of Apollo, asserting that Solomon in his loss of wisdom was 'maiore … detrudi precipicio quam Phebus in casu Phetontis, qui de Apolline Iouis factus est pastor Admeti' [thrust down a sheerer precipice than was Phoebus after the fall of Phaethon, when from being the Apollo of Jove he became the shepherd of Admetus].[82] The classicizing friar Robert Holcot, commenting on Ecclesiasticus 3:29 – which discusses the effects of curiosity and pride as compared with wisdom – expands upon Map's conflation of Phaethon's and Apollo's *casus* from their respective precipices to prove the instability of honour. Holcot's approach to Apollo as a type of the fallen prince adopts an implicitly euhemeristic vocabulary introduced by the thesis, '[S]ic est de potentibus et robustis, immo qui ut dii colebantur, in miseria sunt depressi' [Thus it is that the powerful and strong – or rather, those who are worshiped as gods – are driven down into misery].[83] The specifically idolatrous nature of this worship emerges in the exemplum's moral application to 'modernis temporibus,' which holds that Apollo's enslavement is the fate of '[m]ulti principes et prelati que plus honorabantur ab hominibus quam Dei filius in altari' [many princes and prelates who are more honoured by men than the son of God at the altar] – an image evocative of medieval conceptions of political statuary as a tool of idolatry.[84] Apollo, like these earthly princes, was worshipped 'propter suam eminentiam' [on account of his excellence] 'ut deus' [as a god] – a comparative phrase that echoes the earlier censure of 'qui ut dii colebantur' (referring to those who only *think* themselves gods) and hints grammatically, as Judson Boyce Allen observes, that Apollo 'is not even clearly a god.'[85] Like his half-mortal son Phaethon, who foolishly overreaches in an attempt to prove his divinity, Apollo errs, in Holcot's estimation, by attempting to become more than he is.[86] In avenging Phaethon's death, Apollo transgresses upon the divine order represented by Jove and as a result is stripped not of his 'divinitate' – the formulation widely used in explications of Apollo's exile beginning with Servius – but of his 'dignitate divina.' The fact that it is merely Apollo's dignity, or office, that makes him 'divine' confirms that he, like his son, is no more than a puffed-up mortal with delusions of grandeur. Significantly, Holcot does not state that Apollo is condemned specifically to tend Admetus's flocks as a slave-labourer; instead, he makes the more homely suggestion that the destitute Apollo does so of his own accord, like Gower's street entertainer, to earn a living: 'et ad tantam devenit inopiam quod Admeti … regis pastor ovium est effectus' [and he became so impoverished that he became the shepherd of the flocks of King Admetus].

The arch humour of Holcot's moralization of Apollo, also characteristic of the other euhemeristic treatments surveyed, derives from the
ease with which the mythology of Apollo could be rewritten in wholly
'human' terms – a revision for which, as chapter 1 demonstrated, Ovid's
frequently scathing imputations of Apollo's lasciviousness, narcissism,
and incompetence provided a substantial, if morally incomplete, foundation. Another focus of the previous chapter – Ovid's contiguous association of Apollo with self-defeating artifice and illusion – corresponds
with a second polemical trend in medieval views of antiquity: the
understanding of Apollo as an idol which, in its materiality, is not only
undivine but *less* than human.

Apollo, Idolatry, and Empty Art

The ontological distinction between idols and men, as between men
and gods, was of utmost importance in medieval views of ancient worship (and contemporary image-making), and so demands clarification
before we turn to Apollo's honorary role as 'head idol' of the pagan
pantheon. Idols were, in medieval artistic theory, 'hollow men.' The
epistle of Jeremiah within the Prophecy of Baruch, which together with
the sapiential books of the Old Testament contributed seminally to
medieval understandings of idolatry, likens idols to 'in cucumerario
formido' [a scarecrow in a garden of cucumbers] that 'nihil custodit'
[keepeth nothing] (Bar. 6:69). Idols, moreover, are vulnerable to rust,
moths, and vermin (Bar. 6:11, 19). They are covered with dust and
smoke (6:12, 16, 20); defenceless from thieves (6:13–14, 17); unable to
stand without support (6:25–6); and lack all agency to give or receive
(6:33–7). Powerless to protect themselves even from the most banal of
adversities, idols cannot be expected to offer aid to those who worship
them (6:49, 52–5). Idols are lifeless objects fabricated by men, who were
themselves formed in God's likeness out of dust; because no creature
can be greater than its creator, idols by definition cannot be immortal
(Bar. 6:45–6; Sap. 14:14, 15:8–11, 16–17). Even beasts, which were cre-
ated by God, are higher in the scale of being than man-made idols (Bar.
6:67). Idols are a perversion of creation: they have mouths but cannot
speak, eyes but cannot see, ears but cannot hear, noses but cannot smell,
hands but cannot feel, feet but cannot walk (Psalm 113:[b]5–7).[87] Those
who trust in idols become like their creations (Psalm 113:[b]8), suc-
cumbing to a kind of self-petrification like the stony hearts of the idol-
worshiping Israelites in Ezechiel 36:25–6.[88] In a climactic segment of his
denunciation of the City of Man as epitomized by Rome in *De civitate*

Dei (3.17), Augustine exposes the failure of the pagan gods to provide lasting civic protection. The only powers possessed by idols, insists Augustine, are illusory: the effect of demonic manipulation licensed by human credulity.

Although such generalized condemnations of idolatry pertain as a matter of course to the pagan pantheon as a whole, portrayals of Apollo as idol facilitate an especially acute image of religious hypocrisy; seen in their full range, they reflect an extraordinary attention to Apollo's status in relation to prophecy and image-making that attests to particular tensions surrounding the contiguity of Apollo and Christ as mediators and disseminators of truth. A striking example of Apollo's association with idolatry is found in Lactantius's *De mortibus persecutorum* (first quarter of the fourth century), a tract that provides grist for Augustine's mill in its demonstration of the punishments providentially inflicted upon opponents of Christianity. Lactantius recounts that one particularly destructive persecutor, the emperor Maximian Galerius, was struck with a deadly cancer beyond medicine's power to heal. Turning to idols, Maximian sought aid from Apollo and Aesculapius, but despite Apollo's efforts at a cure – a familiar Ovidian turn of phrase – the disease only worsened, leading to the gruesome disintegration of his entire body from the internal organs outward, until the emperor dissolved into a festering sack of maggots.[89] Wace's account of the sickening thud of Bladud's body on Apollo's insentient temple, quoted at the beginning of this chapter, makes a similar point about Apollo's perverse way of providing remedy.

The rigid conventionality of medieval iconographic representations of Apollo as idol makes his incompetence, if anything, more chilling. London, British Library MS Harley 1766, an elaborately illustrated fifteenth-century manuscript of Lydgate's *Fall of Princes*, portrays the Apollo to whom Laius, Oedipus, Pyrrhus, and Cadmus pray as a horned, golden figure bearing a spear and shield, mounted on a pedestal.[90] Apollo's doll-like stature in these images renders him inherently ridiculous as an object of reverence by grown men twice his size. The effect of such worship takes brutally ironic shape in a miniature (fig. 1) depicting Pyrrhus, while sacrificing in Apollo's temple 'that god to magnefie' (*FP* 1.6822), being stabbed by Orestes as the idol of Apollo nonchalantly looks down at the crime (fol. 88r). Pyrrhus kneels below Apollo's feet, hands raised in prayer to a golden statue depicted with grossly elongated, donkey-like ears. The supplicant's defenceless position contrasts ironically with the shield and spear held

Fig. 1 Death of Pyrrhus in the temple of Apollo. John Lydgate, *Fall of Princes.* English, c. 1450–60. © The British Library Board. All Rights Reserved. London, Brit. Lib. MS Harley 1766, fol. 88r.

by the Apollo-idol, focusing the viewer's attention on Pyrrhus's pathetic, unbuffered vulnerability as he is impaled by the enormous sword of Orestes.

Apollo's untrustworthiness is underscored even more vividly in a densely illustrated early fifteenth-century French manuscript of Statius's *Thebaid* (London, British Library MS Burney 257), which in the first book develops an iconographic program that runs against the grain of the epic's panegyric celebration of Apollo's cultic powers at 1.696–720. This manuscript represents the pagan gods both as statuesque idols and as noble human figures in medieval dress, the latter technique being common in late medieval manuscripts of the prose *Ovide moralisé* and Christine de Pizan's *Epistre Othea*. The logic behind these shifts in portrayal can be difficult to untangle and owes in part to the protocols of multiple artists, but it is nonetheless probable that different degrees of moral distance from polytheistic subject matter on the part of a Christian readership stand behind such inconsistencies. These disparate representative strategies produce strange effects, as with a miniature in the third book of the *Thebaid* portraying Jupiter's instructions to Mars by means of an awkward image of two idols standing stiffly on pedestals yet engaged in animated conversation, while a crowned Venus, pleading with Mars not to destroy Thebes, kneels to the idols like a mortal woman (fol. 41v). Whatever distinction the artist may wish to draw between Venus and her fellow Olympians in this scene, it is clear that idols – as opposed to human figures – are typically enlisted to represent the pagan gods in morally suspect circumstances, such as the scene in which Laius's shade emerges from hellmouth while an idol (either Mercury or Jupiter) looks on (fol. 20v).

Three miniatures of Apollo found in close sequence in the first book form a case in point; of these, the first two depict an idol, while the third portrays a human king granting a boon. The first image (fig. 2) illustrates an oral account by Adrastus, while at table with Polynices, Tideus, and his daughters, of the legend behind Apollo's feast day, which begins with the story of Apollo's defeat of Python (fol. 15r; cf. *Thebaid* 1.557–71). In the miniature, the dinner guests 'look on,' as it were, at the content of the story, represented by an idol of Apollo atop a pedestal, just to the right of the table, aiming bow and arrows at a serpent almost under their feet.[91] Turning over the folio, the reader encounters a second image of Apollo (fig. 3), representing the next part of Adrastus's narration; this one, again framed by listening 'spectators,' seems baldly to reverse the first (fol. 16v). Here, the idol of Apollo

E quoza larans q3 ðiu tamen aura fuperftes

mmoutur uelis paftifubicie penates.

ic primum luftrare oculis cultus qz uettor.

Fig. 2 Apollo's defeat of Python, narrated by Adrastus to guests. Statius, *Thebaid*. French, early fifteenth century. © The British Library Board. All Rights Reserved. London, Brit. Lib. MS Burney 257, fol. 15r.

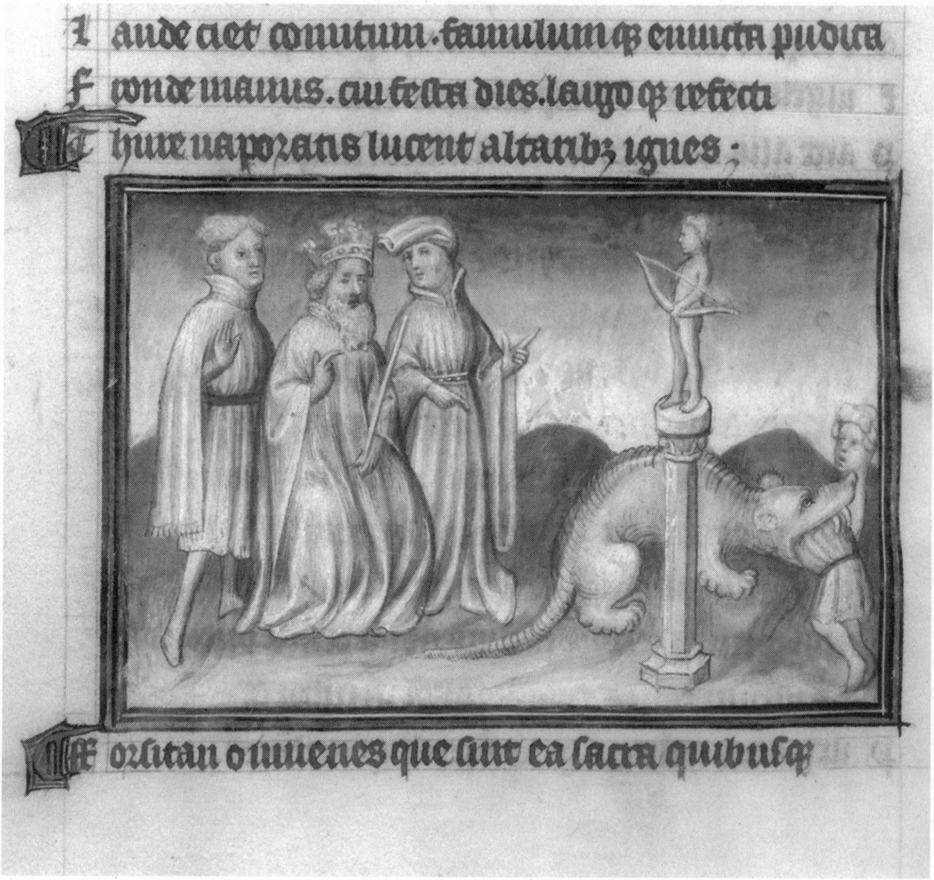

Fig. 3 Monster devouring Argive child under statue of Apollo. Statius, *Thebaid*. French, early fifteenth century. © The British Library Board. All Rights Reserved. London, Brit. Lib. MS Burney 257, fol. 16v.

stands on his pedestal holding his bow while, under *his* feet, an even larger serpent fastens its jaws around the upper torso of a child. Weapons in hand, Apollo coolly looks away, as if oblivious to what is taking place. Depicted here is the grisly low point of the events following Apollo's slaughter of Python in Statius's account: his own incitement of a Python-like monster upon the innocent children of Argos out of anger at King Crotopus's murder of his daughter, whom Apollo loved (see chapter 1, n. 121). The iconography of this scene, centring upon Apollo not merely as wrathful god but as torpid idol, appears conceptually related to an episode in the life of St Philip recounted in the fifteenth-century *Speculum sacerdotale*, in which the demonic character of an idol of Mars reveals itself in the form of a 'grete dragon' that 'stirte oute fro vnder the false mawmet' and devours a child, later restored to life by the saint.[92] By visually cueing a fairly conventional hagiographic association of the false power of idols with demons in serpentine form, the artist of the *Thebaid* manuscript image activates a polemically Christian view of antiquity that equates Apollo's failure to protect the child with the morally ruinous economy of idolatry itself.

In the first book of Statius's epic, after the god-sent monster is slain by a group of heroes led by the brave Coroebus, Apollo takes vengeance a second time by sending a pestilence upon Argos. Apollo's outrage finally abates when Coroebus appeals to Apollo's mercy – portrayed here in a third miniature (fol. 19r), in which Apollo appears as a bearded king (not an idol), and Coroebus kneels barefoot at his feet. This manuscript sequence, then, advances two very different perspectives on Apollo, each of which isolates an undeveloped implication in Statius's text: first, of Apollo as a hypocrite who (literally) turns his back on a destructive circumstance identical to that from which he had previously protected the people; and second, of Apollo as a dignified model for earthly kings who must balance justice with mercy. By the end of Book One of the *Thebaid*, the notion of Apollo's duplicity and irrational selfishness has been muted by a renewed celebration of the god's multifarious powers. In MS Burney 257, however, these tendencies remain iconographically unresolved, allied with discourses of idolatry that provide multiple coordinates for Apollo's inability – or unwillingness – to lift a golden finger for the children devoured under his watch.

This manuscript's extensive artistic deployment of idols to visually translate the worldview of the *Thebaid* into a cultural grammar intelligible to a Christian reader – who would find the Thebans' tragedy to unfold coextensively with their habitual reliance on false, material images – reflects a late medieval preoccupation, particularly in England, with the image-making habits of antiquity in relation to iconoclastic anxieties newly circulating within Christianity itself. Lollard denunciations of the church's traffic in images of saints, the Virgin Mary, and the crucifix, formalized in the *Twelve Conclusions of the Lollards* (1395), boldly applied biblical condemnations of idol-worship to mainstream Christianity, provoking a 'counterwave of treatises aimed at elucidating and justifying the position of images in Christianity' as well as a sizable body of hagiographic exonerations of Christian image-making (legitimized by the Incarnation) as distinct from literalistic pagan idolatry.[93] Recent critics tend to approach this complex phenomenon in visual and literary art through the broad lens of cultural analysis rather than considering how particular pagan gods figured into late medieval England's newly self-conscious apprehension of antique idolatry. Late medieval representations of idolatry, including MS Burney 257, stress the multiplicity of pagan idols – what Augustine called a 'deorum turba' [crowd of gods][94] – aiming at once to reinforce the moral disorder of an impossibly complicated genealogy rife with treachery, incest, and internal rivalry, and to underscore the ideological contrast between pagan polytheism and the triune unity of Christian worship.[95] The persecuted Christians of medieval saints' lives are commanded to worship various idols collectively (and sometimes anonymously) more often than they are forced to revere one god in particular; furthermore, their condemnations of idolatry gain rhetorical strength by means of lengthy, derisive catalogues of the gods like the one in Lydgate's double saints' life, *Saint Albon and Saint Amphibalus* (1439), that denigrates 'Satorn, Iubiter, Mars, and Appollo, / With fals goddessis Dian and Iuno' (2.399–400). Similarly, 'the fyn and guerdoun for travaille / Of Jove, Appollo, of Mars, of swich rascaille' is bitterly exposed at the end of Chaucer's *Troilus and Criseyde* as the comeuppance for anyone gullible enough to enlist in a doomed fraternity with a bunch of thugs (5.1852–3). Lydgate interpolates a much expanded version of Chaucer's critique of paganism at the emotional climax of the *Troy Book* (composed 1412–20), just after the brutal sacrifice of Polyxena in Apollo's temple that caps the fall of Troy. After denouncing the pagans' 'myscreaunce' and their devil-infested 'statues of stokkes & of stoon,' Lydgate imprecates the pagan idols with an almost bellicose vengeance, vowing not to let a single member of 'þe false route' escape his censure (4.6932, 6941, 6950).[96] What follows is an astonishing, forty-plus-line catalogue of the pagan gods and their attributes, succeeded by more general reflections on idolatry and its false rewards. The sheer comprehensiveness of this list, which includes not only the Olympians but various elves, fauns, and water-nymphs as well as mythological characters not worshipped as gods (Daphne, Ixion, Sisyphus, Tantalus),[97] betrays Lydgate's obvious delight in pagan mythology at least as much as his Christian instinct to condemn it. In Lydgate's moral dilation, Chaucer's bunch of thugs is reincarnated as a wholly dysfunctional, comically frivolous army of demons who laugh as Troy weeps.

Despite these impulses to generalize pagan idols into anonymity or multiply them into incoherence, poets and hagiographers did not hesitate to single out a particular god in their portrayals of idol-worship when they saw the potential for increased dramatic effect.[98] The consequences of this strategy could be relatively incidental, as with the use of the 'ymage of Juppiter' to provoke the Christians in Chaucer's *Second Nun's Tale* (364; cf. 413) – a choice of deity that has no special significance in context. A somewhat more calculated personalization of a pagan idol occurs in Osbern Bokenham's life of St Agnes in his *Legendys of Hooly Wummen* (composed 1443–7). The heathen prefect tempts Agnes, a virgin bride of Christ, by asserting that she can pursue a life of virginity within the bounds of paganism, by serving the goddess Vesta (4253–9). Because the idolatrous threat is particularized and correlates with Agnes's own personal outlook, the temptation is greater and her resistance to it more ideologically profound. In appealing to Agnes's connection with Vesta, the prefect cultivates an illusion of the pagan pantheon's *lack* of multiplicity – an illusion that Agnes rejects by indignantly lumping Vesta together with all the other 'doum ydols' (4264) – and thus promises the kind of intimate, individualized relationship with a deity that she claims to enjoy with Christ.[99]

It is significant, then, that when medieval writers *do* particularize the 'frauded fantasie' that is pagan idolatry,[100] Apollo appears frequently and in formative contexts as idol of choice. Insofar as idolatry was understood as the 'structure on which paganism itself is built,' [101] Apollo's prominence in medieval treatments of idol-worship indicates that his fallible authority could be regarded as an image of paganism itself – especially to the extent that antiquity constituted not only a benighted past but a framework of intellectual and cultural inheritance. Jacobus de Voragine's life of St Christine in his *Legenda aurea* offers a relatively straightforward example of the hagiographic appropriation of Apollo, describing Christine's forced procession naked through the city of Tyro to the temple of Apollo, where she causes the idol miraculously to shatter into dust.[102] Writing some two hundred years later, when images were under new scrutiny, Bokenham develops the dramatic implications of Voragine's scene: the prefect Zyon commands Christine to 'worship ... appoloos hye reuerence' (*LHW* 2761), at which point she prays to Christ for the idol to be pulverized, then challenges the pagans to make it whole in a speech that itself figuratively reconstitutes the shattered statue, as a wholly coherent sign of pagan degeneracy:

> Thou seyist þat appollo shuld a god be,
> Be whom meny soulis erryn greuously.
> And yete be mannys hand made was he.
> Swych a god is noht, as þinkyth me.
> Lo where he lyth; his eye is owte.
> But to reysyn hym up ye yow now dresse;
> And yf ye ne moun, wyth-owtyn doute,
> Knowyth þat swych godhede is fonnydnese.   (2792–5, 2799–2802)

Strikingly, in Bokenham's version of events, when Christine is eventually martyred, one of her Christian kinsmen constructs a memorial to Christine 'in appolloos temple,' depositing her relics there in hope 'to haue heuene to mede' (3103–6). As often happens in hagiographic texts, the idol's den is ideologically refashioned as the saint's shrine;[103] here, Apollo's temple also becomes a site of spiritual renovation for both Christine (whose resurrection is confirmed) and her devout kinsman. In contrast, the pile of dust that once was the idol of Apollo, physically demolished and disconcertingly unregenerated in his own temple, is left abandoned like a martyr without a cause.

The *Life of Saint Katherine* by John Capgrave, an East Anglian contemporary of Bokenham, grants an even more significant role to Apollo. In what is by far the most ambitious version of the legend in the Middle Ages, Capgrave portrays the emperor Maxentius duly worshipping the entire Olympian pantheon but paying special obeisance to Apollo, whose generative beneficence, it is implied, should be most difficult for the Christian Katherine to deny.[104] When Katherine first rebukes Maxentius, she finds him in the midst of a sacrifice to Apollo, 'oure god the sunne – / Whech every man for a god hath take' (4.752–3). In fact, Maxentius stakes his own authority, somewhat like Augustus, on the gods in general and Apollo in particular, and thus regards the threat posed by Katherine as both political and social. He accuses Katherine, who consistently professes faith in Christ, of blaspheming Apollo and warns her of the god's power to destroy her beauty (a motif that antici- pates the central action of Henryson's *Testament of Cresseid*):

> Apollo graunt that ye no venjauns have
> For youre blaspheme newly here i-sowe!
> He may you dampne and eke he may yow save[.]   (4.757–9)

Later, enraged by Katherine's conversion of the philosophers who were supposed to disprove her Christian convictions, Maxentius goads his pagan soldiers in the name of 'swete Apollo' to '[f]rye hem in her grece' (5.3.166–7) – an unsubtle intimation of the less-than-beneficent capaci- ties of Apollo as sun god. Failing to bait Katherine with the prospect of a statue in her likeness, Maxentius desperately attempts to reassert the urgency of worshiping Apollo (whom even his wife concludes is infer- ior to Christ [5.1441–4]) in his final temptation of Katherine:

> Than shal ye now with hey devocion
> Thurifye to that magesté
> Of grete Appollo. His exaltacion –
> As ye knowe wele, for it is no secré –
> Redressith this word [i.e., world] with hete whech that he
> Spredyth upon iche mayde. Obey thertoo!   (5.533–8)

Capgrave's Apollo serves not merely as a pretext for the legend's af- firmation of Christian faith, but also as an idol par excellence, an em- blem of paganism in its most attractive, threatening form – and thus a self-conscious image for the Christian reader of the misuse of images. Lydgate's contemporaneous *Saint Albon and Saint Amphibalus* similarly highlights Apollo's special culpability in the error of pagan worship while complicating this phenomenon with an obsessively classicizing rhetorical overlay that draws frequent attention to Phebus's astro- logical manoeuvrings. Lydgate individualizes Apollo in a complex and self-reflexive fashion that contrasts with the legend's various casual references to named and unnamed idols, while recalling the kind of rhetorical contestation examined earlier in the *Eclogue of Theodulus*. Apollo's role in the legend is concentrated around the series of events surrounding the climactic moment of St Albon's martyrdom, further embroidered by a denunciation of idolatry in the *verba translatoris*.

Ultimately, Albon figuratively earns his youthful epithet as 'Phebus souereyn / Thorugh all Itaile, and day sterr of Bryteyn' (1.636–7) through the mediation of a sun-like Christ.

When God dries up a great river at Albon's request so that the Britons can pass through, the pagans wrongly attribute the event to 'the glorious Phebus with his stremys cleer,' whom they praise as 'our god most myhti' (2.1677, 1680). After a collective prayer to the sun as 'our saviour' (2.1790), the narrator intervenes to condemn idolatry as an active rejection of Creator for creation. Instead of worshipping the 'sonne of liff,' which cannot be eclipsed or obscured, the pagans esteem 'werdly Phebus' (mentioned in the company of Jupiter, Saturn, Mars, and Venus), whose brightness lasts only until 'the nyght comyth on,' when 'his liht is from you ferr' (2.1817, 1824, 1825). The 'trouthe' and 'rihtwysnesse' of Christ as (true) sun prevail, however, just as Phebus shines 'most cleer' after 'stormy wedris' (2.1992–3, 1996). After Albon's martyrdom, a beam of light issuing from his tomb floods the sky, 'briht as the sonne bem,' miraculously illuminating the city all night long (2.2003). This miracle occasions a mass conversion of the pagans, who renounce the 'clowdy ygnoraunce' of idolatry and their 'fals errours, enclipsed with dirknesse, / Don to mauhmetis' (3.27, 65–6).

The miracle at Albon's tomb possesses such ideological scope precisely because it rewrites the naturalistic powers of Apollo as 'our god most myhti' on a superlative universal scale. The image of Apollo/sun as an object of widespread reverence – and thus a chief symbolic threat to the Christian order – is rhetorically annexed to delineate both Albon's and Christ's unparalleled power. Appropriately, when Amphibalus, Albon's spiritual mentor, is persecuted by the same hostile forces that targeted the protomartyr, he experiences a mystical vision of Albon united with Christ in glory, in which, by comparison with Christ's luminosity, 'Phebus was nat so briht / At mydsomer in his mydday speer' (3.1153–4). In these ways, Albon earns his reputation as 'Phebus soveryn' first by contributing to the rhetorical reduction of Phebus to a pile of rubble and an untenable force of nature, and finally by his own establishment as *imago* of Christ's truly restorative light.

Examples of Apollo's challenge to Christian sanctity in hagiographic tradition are easily multiplied, though not all share the intricacy of Capgrave's and Lydgate's treatments. For instance, St George is shown, like St Christine, to confront and humiliate an idol of Apollo, causing it to burst into flame, fall to the ground, or announce its own subjection (or fraud).[105] Apocryphal variants of this saint's legend include the revival from the dead and subsequent baptism of a virtuous pagan who had been a worshipper of Apollo, 'whose name he blushes to mention,' as well as the saint's ministry to a woman made destitute by her worship of Apollo and his healing of a sick child at Apollo's temple while the god himself falls into the abyss.[106] In the *Legenda aurea*, St Felix approaches worshippers of Apollo and challenges them to persuade their god to reveal what he is holding in his hand (a text of the Lord's Prayer); when Apollo fails to provide the answer, the pagans are converted.[107] Voragine also includes accounts of St Benedict overcoming demonic interference in order to convert a temple of Apollo into a chapel in honour of John the Baptist,[108] and the conversion of a Jew eavesdropping upon a convention of scheming demons in a Roman temple of Apollo.[109]

The most seminal literary identification of Apollo with idolatry, however, was found not in a saint's life but a 'history': Guido delle Colonne's *Historia destructionis Troiae* (1287), in the tenth book of which Achilles and Calchas meet by chance at Apollo's temple at Delphi, where they seek forecasts of the war's outcome for the Greek and Trojan forces, respectively. Guido transforms the bare edifice of earlier accounts of this scene into a lengthy authorial digression on the mythographic attributes of Apollo and his family, followed by an analysis of the origins of idolatry, a euhemeristic survey of the Olympians and other pagan gods, and a mini-demonology that traces the course of falsehood from Lucifer's fall to the demonic manipulation of idols (10.79–252). Much of Guido's material in this section is drawn from book 8, chapter 11 of Isidore of Seville's *Etymologiae*, which features a detailed catalogue of the major and minor pagan gods in the context of euhemerism and idolatry. Isidore's list, arranged to 'reflect the celestial hierarchy' as astrologically and genealogically ordained, begins with Saturn and treats Apollo roughly halfway through.[110] In contrast, Guido's handling of the archival material that he brings to bear on the Troy story revises Isidore's precedent to draw attention to the mythography of Apollo as springboard for a reflection on idolatry itself in all of its cosmic scope. In Guido's temple scene, the pagan pantheon becomes, in essence, a function of Apollo, whose historical position in Guido's narrative eclipses Saturn's pride of place at the head of the catalogue of Olympians. In the *Historia*, Apollo has theoretical, if not genealogical, authority.[111]

Guido's various Middle English redactors found this learned digression challenging; their efforts to engage even with the most basic aspects of its mythographic detail resulted in bunglings such as the identification of Diana as the sun and, just as absurdly, the daughter of

Apollo in the anonymous *'Gest Hystoriale' of the Destruction of Troy* (written after c. 1385),[112] as well as the iconographic portrayal of a female Apollo in one manuscript of Lydgate's *Troy Book* (Manchester, The John Rylands University Library MS Eng. 1).[113] In contrast to these amateurish textual and iconographic responses, Lydgate's influential version of the Troy legend rhetorically enhances Guido's account by adding substantial scholarly detail from Ovid and other sources, more than tripling the length of Guido's digression, in order to fashion a 'believable classical world' bounded by a decorous film of moral distance.[114] Typical of Lydgate's procedure in the *Troy Book* is the notably unmoralistic ornamental flourish with which he supplements Guido's mere mention of Apollo in his euhemeristic catalogue of the gods:

> And nexte Appollo, so cler, so schene & bri3t,
> þe daies eye & voider of þe ny3t,
> Cherischer of frut, of herbe, flour, & corne[.]   (2.5591–3)[115]

Lydgate reinforces his sense of the importance of Guido's dilation upon Apollo's Delphic temple, evidenced by such rhetorical lingerings, through an original addition of a companion passage later in the *Troy Book* that once again links a temple of Apollo (here the one in which Polyxena is sacrificed) with a prominent discussion of the 'false honour of ydolatrie' (4.6943).[116] At the end of the first passage, Lydgate accentuates the specific connection of Apollo's temple to his *auctor's* moral digression, underscoring its relevance to a contemplation of the 'grounde & gynnynge of ydolatrie' and 'remembraunce / of false goddis & of mawmetrie' (2.5927, 5932–3). Lydgate comes close to implying here that Apollo's temple – whose 'olde fundacioun' was earlier described (2.5421) – *is*, at least for the purpose of the present narrative, the 'grounde & gynnynge' of idolatry, a kind of architectural mnemonic in which to house 'in remembraunce' the dangers of image abuse.[117] Oddly enough, after such a thorough exposé of the deceptiveness of the demons who inhabit 'cursid ydoles' (2.5917), Lydgate returns to his main plot by directing our attention, in a line unparalleled in Guido, to the oracular capacity of 'gret Appollo, which may nat lye' (2.5940) – as if Apollo has crossed, in the space of a dozen lines, from the realm of cursed superstition to credible providence. If Apollo's multiple polarities in the *Eclogue of Theodulus, Assembly of Gods,* and even Lydgate's own *Saint Albon and Saint Amphibalus* were redeemed by their potential for positive transition, the *Troy Book's* awkward pivot here from moral philosophy to legendary history creates a diegetic rupture that leaves unresolved, and hence unserviceable, a series of pressing claims about Apollo's relation to truth.

Apollo as Saracen

As the fateful encounter of Trojan and Greek at Delphi in the Troy legends suggests, Apollo's synecdochic relationship with antiquity and idolatry endowed him with special powers of cross-cultural translation. In *chansons de geste* and chivalric romances involving the Islamic East, Apollo (usually spelled 'Apollin' in these texts; *MED* s.v. 'Ap[p]ollin, Apollo' [n.]) surfaces recurrently as the sole Greco-Roman deity amidst a pantheon of pseudo-Muslim idols. Indeed, Apollo served most often as the 'face' of the medieval West's ahistorical conflation of Islamic monotheism with classical polytheism.[118] Although chronicles and romances, unlike saints' lives and Guido's Trojan history, rarely show a depth of mythographic understanding in their treatment of a figure like Apollo – instead presenting the gods of the Saracens as largely interchangeable, without regard for their cultic particularities[119] – Apollo's multivalent associations with idolatry and demonic error made him an especially valuable device for writers who sought a cultural shorthand with which to 'sign' threatening religious difference. Within this milieu, Apollo's function takes shape within two distinct but equally unsavoury dramatic scenarios: mob rule and triune hoax.

In the first setting, Apollo features among an eclectic multitude of supposed Muslim gods including such figures as Mahomet, Tervagant, Ascarot, Alcaron, and Margog. Jupiter is the only other Greco-Roman god who appears in such lists with any regularity, but even this pagan patriarch does not rival the popularity of Apollo as a pseudo-Muslim deity.[120] The religious categories of non-Christians are notoriously fluid in these polemical contexts: Apollo and other Greco-Roman gods join the Norse Woden and the pseudo-Muslim Tervagant as gods of the Saxons in Layamon's *Brut*, and Apollo and Mahoun constitute the Saxon pantheon in Jean Bodel's Charlemagne romance, *La Chanson des Saisnes*, where the Saxons are repeatedly designated 'la gent Apolin.'[121] Similarly, the pagans of Roman Britain in *La Vie de Seint Auban* hold as their creed 'la loi Apolin' (line 65) but also worship Mahun, Tervagant, Satan, and a random sampling of Olympians. One manuscript family of the *Roman de Thèbes* identifies the gods of the Thebans as Mahon, Tervagant, Apolin, et al.[122] The title character of the *Sowdone of Babylone* makes an oath on Mahounde and Appolyne, while in the *Stanzaic Guy of Warwick* the Saracens variously appeal to Ternagaunt, Mahoun, and Apolin.[123] Similarly, Appolyn – which in context may refer to Apollo or Apollyon or both – is invoked by the Jewish torturers of Christ in the Towneley Crucifixion pageant; elsewhere they call upon Mahowne.[124]

Some writers gave this ever-shifting mob scene the illusion of order by developing a point-for-point pagan perversion of the Christian notion of deity: the worship (or, in luckless times, calumniation) of a mock 'trinity' featuring Mahomet, Tervagant, and Apollo. Variations on this formula did exist, but this particular configuration (or one closely related to it) including Apollo surfaced with impressive regularity in both French and English romance over the course of the Middle Ages. Both the *Chanson de Roland* and Jean Bodel's *Jeu de Saint Nicholas* feature this pagan trinity prominently, as does the fourteenth-century English romance *Bevis of Hampton* and, in the form of a trinity comprised of Termegaunt, Appolyn, and Margot (with Mahoun as asymmetrical fourth member) the contemporary Charlemagne romance *Firumbras*.[125]

In the *Chanson de Roland*, the triune force of Apollin, Mahumet, and Tervagan is invoked piecemeal and as a unit by the pagan King Marsile, and images of the three figures, in the form of a dragon standard and a statue, accompany the Emir Baligant of Babylon into battle.[126] Apollo is individualized here more than in other texts employing the pagan trinity motif, in ways that suggest he was intended as the Christ-figure of the trinity,[127] as the treatment of the gods by the pagan Queen Bramimonde reveals. Outraged at Charles's injury of her husband Marsile and certain that the Saracen cause is doomed, Bramimonde instigates the destruction of the idols who, she says, have 'mien seignur en bataille faillirent' [failed my lord in battle] and turned recreant ('Cist nostre deu sunt en recreantise') (2715, 2718). Her abuse of the gods begins with Apollo, whose statue she, along with an angry mob, chastises and physically abuses, ripping off its scepter and crown, tying its hands to a column, and kicking and smashing it to shards, before more briefly savaging the idols of Tervagan and Mahumet in turn (2580–91). Bramimonde's destruction of the Apollo-idol recalls the Scourging of Christ and foreshadows the torture of the traitor Ganelon, who later is bound to a pillar in similar fashion as he awaits his trial (3735–41). Just as Bramimonde, subsequently a Christian convert, sees through the false sanctity of Apollo, so does Charles's council recognize Ganelon's perfidy beneath his self-serving rhetoric. Once the pagan idols are shattered by Bramimonde – the Christians eagerly finish the job for her after she surrenders Sargossa to Charles (3661–5) – and Ganelon is denounced, like the gods, as a 'fel recreant' (3973), the Saracen queen is free to transfer her powers of devotion to the Christian order of which Apollo and his trinity had been a fallible, misleading image. By exercising her innate faculty of interpretation, Bramimonde successfully 'reads' in Apollo's failure to protect her city the familiar narrative of his exemplary corruptibility as a material object and hence a guarantor of material and spiritual well-being. By recognizing the 'mult grant folie' of worshiping such a god, she develops the 'veire conoisance' of a martyr (2714, 3987) – leading to her rebirth as Juliana, or St Juliana of Cumae (3986). The identification of Bramimonde with this saint who also overcame a pagan upbringing to become a Christian is, in fact, doubly appropriate: the *vita* of Juliana in the *Acta sanctorum* includes an account of the saint's resistance to the worship of Apollo and Diana.[128]

Writing in the Shadow of Apollo: From Exegesis to Aureation

The preceding pages have shown that Apollo, as half-man, false god, and artificial light, demanded careful interpretation by those who encountered him in medieval legend and visual art. This chapter concludes with a consideration of Apollo's concurrent status in the Middle Ages as a figure of interpretation itself: an image of exegetical elucidation and a purveyor of inspiration and eloquence. A widely circulated medieval mythographic commonplace maintains that Apollo is the god of divination and truth because, as the sun, he illuminates dark and obscure things: 'omnia obscura manifestat in lucem' [the sun turns into clear light everything obscure]; and 'occulta aperit eius splendor' [his brightness opens up what is concealed].[129] His rays, like arrows, cut through the cloud of doubt and pierce the Python, or false belief, with the light of *veritas*. A miniature in a fifteenth-century Flemish manuscript of the *Ovide moralisé en prose* (fig. 4) compactly expresses this analogy by visually juxtaposing Apollo's slaying of the Python with the sun scattering the surrounding clouds (Bibliothèque Nationale MS Fr.137, fol. 8). The very site of Apollo's birth epitomizes his illuminative powers: Delos, etymologized as *manifestum*, is so called because the island was once hidden beneath the waves but later became visible, or because Apollo's oracles, elsewhere *obscura*, are clear to the understanding (*manifesta*) at his Delian temple.[130] For medieval mythographers, Apollo's status as cosmic clarifier facilitates his identification with moral virtue, wisdom, or Christ. It also promises a clear and indubitable

Fig. 4 Combat of Phebus and Python. *Ovide moralisé en prose*. Flemish, mid-fifteenth century. Bibliothèque Nationale de France. Paris, Bibl. Nat. MS Fr.137, fol. 8r.

articulation of authority, as evidenced by as unlikely a witness as a scientific treatise on kinematics by the fourteenth-century French scholar Nicole Oresme, the *Tractatus de commensurabilitate vel incommensurabilitate motuum celi*. Like Henry of Huntingdon's herbal, treated in the previous chapter, which embellishes technical subject matter with a poetic fiction of Apollo's inspiration and stakes its own authority on Apollo's illumination of 'causas ... [p]rius absconsas' [causes that were previously hidden],[131] Oresme's *Tractatus* features Apollo as a disseminator of *auctoritas* suited to a treatise concerning the motions of heavenly bodies. Apollo appears prominently in the third part of the *Tractatus*, accompanied by the Muses and Sciences, as the chief figure in a dream-vision experienced by the confused narrator, who has reached the limits of his own logical capacities to resolve the question of the commensurability of celestial motions. Apollo commands Arithmetic and Geometry to debate the issue at hand, and Arithmetic begins by invoking Apollo in language redolent of the mythographers' association of the god with interpretive certainty:

> O veritatis actor eterne et defensor invicte te decet erroris efflare nebulas et obscuras ignorantie mentis tenebras effugare ut studiosis ingeniis veri splendor irradiet ipsius que sinceritas equitate tui iudicii patefiat divina auctoritate firmata[.][132]

> [Oh speaker of the eternal truth (lit., author of eternal truth) and defender of the unvanquished, it is proper for you to blow away the fogs of error and put to flight the dark shadows of the ignorant mind, so that the brilliance of truth should radiate with its very own zealous nature and its sincerity should be revealed by the equity of your judgment, supported by divine authority.]

In the *Tractatus*, a poetic device (dream-vision), harnessed to the authoritative yoke of Apollo as *veritatis actor*, serves the discourse of scientific fact – although, as we will see shortly, it does so incompletely. Elsewhere, the inverse occurs: poetic fiction or fabulation, potentially allied with the deceptive, artificial, or idolatrous dimensions of Apollo surveyed above, is rhetorically contained and sanitized by the truth-bearing, pedagogic hermeneutic of Apollo as solar exegete. The thirteenth-century scholar John of Garland, for example, begins his *Integumenta Ovidii*, a versified moralization of Ovid's *Metamorphoses*, by defining his duty as allegorist in terms that imagistically recall Apollo's role as penetrator of the obscure: where Ovid's work is dark and murky, John's commentary '[n]odos secreti denodat, clausa revelat / Rarificat nebulas' [unknots the knotty secrets ... reveals hidden facts ... scatters the mist (of obscurity)].[133] Apollo's wisdom offers a convenient self-image for the medieval exegete who, like Virgil's hero in the twelfth-century *Aeneid* commentary attributed to Bernardus Silvestris, must progress intellectually from poetic absorption, represented by the painted doors of the temple of the Cumaean Sibyl, to the fervour of philosophical learning that stirs inside the enclosure (*Commentary on the First Six Books of the* Aeneid, 6.14–34). In similar fashion, Book Two of Martianus Capella's *De nuptiis*, the most intensely mythical sequence of the text – relating, under Calliope's inspiration, Mercury's search for a bride and Philology's ascent to the assembly of the gods – coincides, in the author's account of his writing process, with the dark of night, while the approach of the morning sun (identified with Phoebus) marks his determination to leave behind fable (2.98, 2.219–20). Largely eschewing imaginative fiction, the last seven books offer a didactic exposition of the liberal arts, each of which is introduced by Apollo as master of wisdom. As a point of reference for exegetical theory, Apollo as light-bringer and moral expositor supplied medieval mythographers with an analogy for their own distillation of the light of learning from the shadows of fiction, their modulation of intellectual harmony from the din of fable.[134]

Yet uncertainties attend these very images of Apollo as elucidator of atmospheric and moral obscurity. Just as commonly as they present the solar Apollo as a beneficent life force and image of wisdom, medieval mythographies depict him as a destroyer whose excessive heat inflicts suffering and dries up the sap of plants. Remigius of Auxerre's commentary on *De nuptiis* (ninth century) compares Apollo's destructive rays with Jove's thunderbolts, and Macrobius's *Saturnalia* (early fifth century?) traces Apollo's cultic role as 'Lykos' to the fact that '[lupus] rapit et consumit omnia in modum solis' [the wolf, like the sun, carries off and devours everything.][135] In the mythographically detailed astrological tableau featured in Henryson's *Testament of Cresseid*, Apollo's benevolent role as '[t]ender nureis, and banischer of nicht' is juxtaposed with the destruction wrought by his chariot when driven by Phaethon and the brightness which burns rather than nourishes the naked eye.[136] Mythographers from Fulgentius to Boccaccio explicate this destructive figure associated with pestilence as Apollo *exterminans* or *perdens*, a desiccator of moisture, blackener of skin, and demolisher of untruth

– an appropriate centre point, Henryson may subtly hint, of a cosmos inclined toward 'seiknes incurabill.'[137]

Even Apollo's defeat of the Python is not as clear-cut an image of wisdom triumphing over error as it may first appear, as Bersuire's compression of the myth, considered earlier, to align Apollo with the serpent/devil suggested. One explanation offered in Macrobius's *Saturnalia* for Apollo's epithet 'Pythian,' for example, is that the sun's own motion at times appears serpentine; the myth of the Python's slaying thus arose to express the annual end of Apollo's course through the sky – that is, his 'put[ting] an end' to the serpent ['draconem confecisse'], which is himself.[138] Macrobius also refers Apollo's serpentine path to his epithet Loxias – in Latin *obliquus*, or winding,[139] a term applied to Apollo's obscure and circumlocutionary oracular speech in *De nuptiis* and routinely glossed by medieval commentators.[140] Others claim that Apollo at Delos appeared to his worshippers in the image of a serpent.[141] Similarly, Isidore remarks that Apollo's epithet 'Pythius,' and the Pythian games he institutes, commemorate not only the god's triumph over the serpent but his appropriation of its identity, since the name Python was among the 'spolia' (booty) taken by Apollo.[142]

Furthermore, mythographers indicate that Apollo cannot *only* be understood as a revealer of truth and penetrator of shadows because he himself is mutable, ambiguous, and requiring interpretation rather than unproblematically enacting it. Multiplicity and uncertainty define Apollo as a diffuser of signification: he is associated with divination because the rising and setting of the sun produce many significations; the raven consecrated to him has a voice bearing sixty-four interpretations; and his oracular counsel is ambiguous, 'multiplicitate sua huc et illuc trahunt mentem auditoris' [with its multiple meanings it leads the mind of the listener here and there].[143] Fulgentius fancifully derives one of Apollo's names, Sol, from 'solus' (unique or alone), but also from 'solite' (habitual, i.e., in his motion);[144] other mythographers note that Apollo is constant in age, always depicted as young and beardless, yet the sun's cycle of rising and setting reflects constant change, embodying the entire span of a life, from youth to old age.[145] According to Martianus Capella's commentators, Sol has twelve different appearances, a different colour for each hour of daylight.[146] Apollo is a single god but has an almost infinite pedigree of names and powers;[147] for Macrobius in the *Saturnalia*, all of the gods represent different cultic aspects of the sun, syncretistically embodying Apollo's multivalence.

Even a text as seemingly affirmative of Apollo's identification with the clarifying radiance of truth as Oresme's *Tractatus* ends by associating Apollo not with singular *veritas* but with unresolved *dubitatio*. After Arithmetic and Geometry debate celestial motion at length, Apollo orders silence; the dreamer, no more illuminated than he had been before the symposium, wonders 'cur sunt discordes iste veritatis parentes?' [in what sense are these disagreements the parents of truth?]. Apollo explains that the debaters' doubt is only a parody of human *scientia*, promising that he himself 'statim pronuntiabimus in figura iudicii veritatem' [straightaway ... shall announce the truth in the form of a judgment]. With this encouraging prospect the dream suddenly ends, and with it the *Tractatus*; the dreamer, bereft of enlightenment, laments that 'dubia conclusio restat' [the conclusion is left in doubt].[148] By employing the literary device of the *somnium* or 'middle vision,' as Steven F. Kruger has argued, Oresme does not intend to resolve a point of academic speculation but to 'explore the relation between divine and human ways of knowing ... focus[ing] attention again and again on the *problem* of attaining knowledge.'[149] What is even more significant, however, is that Oresme turns to *Apollo* within this dream-vision to make the point, to the dreamer's (and reader's) frustration, that although singular truth does exist, its dissemination is bound by doubt, discord, and caprice. Like the third book of Chaucer's *House of Fame*, another visionary text that founders upon the authority of Apollo (see *HF* 1091–109), 'tydynges' that promise enlightenment are jumbled with 'lesinges,' and the promised words of 'gret auctorite' fail startlingly to materialize (*HF* 2123–4, 2158).

Apollo's fertility within exegetical and pedagogic traditions as a figure for the hermeneutic process – both in its idealized form and its messier reality – also extended to imaginative literature, particularly the self-styled 'Chaucerian' (or Lydgatean) amalgam of classicizing and courtly discourse that flourished in the fifteenth century. In the prologue of the *Legend of Good Women*, as Lisa J. Kiser has shown, Chaucer develops an image of the God of Love's sun-like luminosity that allegorically configures the poetic process as the inspiring light of truth (here, Love) mediated by the 'poetic veil' of Alceste, the daisy vivified by the sun.[150] Lydgate and other fifteenth-century poets greatly expand and enrich this conjunction of the sun's rays, poetic expression, and truth/love, itself indebted to mythographic accounts of Apollo as solar exegete and vegetative agent, to develop the 'essentially decorative ... concept of eloquence' known as aureation.[151] In classicizing love-visions such as Lydgate's *Complaint of the Black Knight, Temple of Glas,* and *Floure of Curtesye,* the sun, as Phebus or Titan, recurrently appears as an inspiring agent in the poetic process. His light illumines, nourishes, and gilds, and his warmth generates the components of eloquence: *baum, licour,* and sweetness. In the theoretical vocabulary developed by Lydgate and adapted by other late medieval poets, especially the Scottish *makaris,* Apollo's illuminative power as the sun, allied with the gilding process of aureation, is analogous to the poet's own role as an embellisher and ennobler of language.[152] This is nowhere clearer than in William Dunbar's *Goldyn Targe,* which begins with a description of Phebus's morning rising suffusing the landscape with enameled colour, awakening the flowers, and drying the dew, and ends with a celebration of Chaucer's, Gower's, and Lydgate's 'fresch anamalit termes celicall,' which have the power to illuminate poetic matter and to 'fair ourgilt oure spech.'[153] Dunbar augments the aureate vocabulary present, for example, in Lydgate's *Temple of Glas,* which frames a vision of love with a meteorological conjunction of piercing sun and dark clouds, into a fully self-reflexive essay on poetic luminescence and inheritance that is a 'coherent metaphor for the poetic act by means of an analogy with the sun in the natural world.'[154] Instead of facing trepidation on a flight of steps or before a haughty lady, Dunbar's 'lytill quair' is enjoined in the last stanza to withdraw from the sight of its poetic betters and to 'be aferit of the licht' – that is, to humbly approach the engine of illumination, powered by Phebus and the three English poets, that gives rude matter the sheen of aesthetic value (lines 271, 279). Dunbar's profession of humility, around the turn of the sixteenth century, upon the poetic fertilization of 'Phebus tender bemes schene' (line 246) could be said to represent a high water mark within the English vernacular of Apollo's utility as a prism of authority and its relation to 'truth.' *Troilus and Criseyde,* a poem ostensibly written 'in derknesse' (*Tr* 1.18) – both of the soul and the bedroom – in many respects marks the beginning of such an enterprise, shimmeringly mapping the astrological and erotic manoeuvrings of Apollo against a tradition of national epic in which the god figures less as an inspirer or guide than a master civilizer, prophet, and poetic scapegoat.

3 Imperial Apollo: From Virgil's Rome to Chaucer's Troy

From Ovid's amatory works to the mythographic manuals considered in the previous chapter, Apollo's dissemination of *veritas*, crucial to the authenticity of vatic discourse and the dynamics of illumination, has recurrently emerged as fallible – even, in some instances, counterfeit. When Apollo's *veritas* did not, as in *Ars amatoria*, destabilize its own premises, it posed a threat to competing Christian structures of enlightenment that prompted tactics of neutralization ranging from overt denunciation to strategic cooption, paradoxically attesting to its continued allure. In Chaucer's *Troilus and Criseyde*, the mythology of *veritas* is redefined in erotic terms as the ideal of 'trouthe'; plagued by a similar instability, it is latently affiliated with feigning and fraudulence. Appropriately, problems of pagan 'trouthe' and truth-telling in the *Troilus* cohere around Apollo, potently informing the overlapping registers of the political, prophetic, and erotic out of which Chaucer shapes his historical romance. In sheer range, Apollo's influence in Chaucer's Troy overwhelms even that of a deity as close to every Trojan's heart as Venus. As god of the oracle, Apollo sets the plot into motion; as legendary builder of Troy's walls, he supplies its history; as the solar deity, his daily motions delineate its progress and propel it into the future. These levels of influence interpenetrate in richly paradoxical ways. The sun, frequently anthromorphized in the poem as Phebus, functions both as a measure of 'trouthe' upon which the lovers profess fidelity and an unwelcome intruder upon the darkness of the bedroom.[1] Similarly, Apollo's oracle, while nominally true in its predictions, is integrally linked with acts of treason and sexual untruth. Lurking behind the arc of the poem's action is the possibility that Calkas, in thrall to the ambiguities of Apollo's oracle, has *lied* – or at least failed to sort lies from truth – in his transmission of what Criseyde calls 'amphipologies' and Diomede, staking his own truthfulness on that of Calkas, 'ambages' (*Tr* 4.1406, 5.897).[2]

Apollo's poetic significance to Chaucer's *Troilus* does not end with this unsettling amalgamation of *veritas* with *dubitatio*. Among the many learned and complexly allusive topoi with which Chaucer enriches Boccaccio's *Filostrato* is Apollo's reflexive association with erotic misfortune, medical insufficiency, and counterproductive prophetic wisdom, all of which contribute to Chaucer's historical shaping of his pagans' worldview. In Chaucer's version of the story, all of the main characters (except for Diomede) are directly associated with an iconic aspect of Apollo: Criseyde in her radiant beauty, Troilus in his amatory experience, Pandarus in his role as healer, and Calkas in his profession as prophet.[3] Revamping Apollo's negligible role in the urbane world of Boccaccio's *Filostrato*, Chaucer highlights the god's intricate agency in his doomed ancient city on historical, cosmological, and visionary levels; in so doing, he reaches beyond Boccaccio to an earlier conception of Apollo as a *national* god, one that was seminally formulated in Virgil's *Aeneid* and critically revised in medieval Trojan legends from Benoît de Sainte-Maure's *Roman de Troie* (1150s) to Joseph of Exeter's *Ylias Daretis Phrygii* (1180s) to Guido delle Colonne's *Historia destructionis Troiae*. While Chaucer's treatment of Apollo in the *Troilus* is unarguably marked by the Ovidian and mythographic trends that have been the focus of the preceding chapters, his overriding concern is with the god's significance within a specifically Trojan context – and on this level, Virgil's treatment of Apollo as protector of the Trojans in their triumphant rebirth as Romans served as a master source and sounding board.

This chapter argues that, as a concerted study in the poetics of retrospection,[4] the *Troilus* conceives of the cultural and erotic significance of the Trojan Apollo within a contentious layering of authoritative and yet self-contradictory texts 'besy for to bere up Troye' (*HF* 1472). Chaucer, I will demonstrate, reads Virgil's epic through an Augustinian lens that not only critiques but appropriates the *Aeneid* as a 'building block' of Christian empire; it is with this trajectory in mind, ultimately, that Chaucer views the twinned falls of 'Troilus and Troie town' (*Tr* 5.768).[5] Reading the *Aeneid* in this light, Chaucer's attention turns particularly to discrepancies between Virgil's vision of a Trojan and a Roman Apollo that lead him to recognize that the imperial project that Virgil celebrates, as a model of civic and poetic construction, is fundamentally destabilized by the false securities associated with Apollo in the Trojan past. Chaucer's *Troilus*, then, offers an image of this unmoored Trojan history as it centres ambivalently upon Apollo and radiates outward to his 'children' in Troy, who live and love (and lie) under his influence. In a kind of reverse *translatio imperii*, Chaucer does not so much (as we might expect) respond in isolation to Virgil's Trojan material, contained in the first three books of the *Aeneid*, as read it back through the posterior text, forecast through the last six books, of an empire that has already come to be – one, enablingly for Chaucer's England, that has fallen in its turn. This second fall, in Augustinian terms, necessitates and elucidates a new model of Christian citizenship while at the same time delineating an impasse within pagan historical thought that inhibits successful renewal. In his poetic fantasy of Troy,[6] Chaucer excavates the archaeological remains of a fascinatingly benighted past but also, more significantly, a doomed cultural foundation of future civilizations – and the poets who 'bere' them up at their peril.

Of this cultural foundation Chaucer's Apollo is, strikingly, both artisan and antagonist:

> For certein, Phebus and Neptunus bothe,
> That makeden the walles of the town,
> Ben with the folk of Troie alwey so wrothe
> That they wol brynge it to confusioun,
> Right in despit of kyng Lameadoun;
> Bycause he nolde payen hem here hire,
> The town of Troie shal ben set on-fire.   (*Tr* 4.120–6)

Provocatively and unusually, Chaucer's Apollo, whose anger at Laomedon here stands unappeased, is the ritual *enemy* of Troy rather than its guardian. Moreover, Apollo's oracle – interpreted, misinterpreted, and manipulated – forms, we shall see, the mechanism of the epic's tragic progression, from Calkas's defection, to the lovers' first night of bliss, to Criseyde's eventual change of 'corage' (*Tr* 5.825). As the poem's insistent marker (as the sun) of passing time and 'dispitous' intruder upon the lovers' nocturnal bliss (*Tr* 3.1458), Apollo/Phebus carries ominous associations as the god who revealed to Calkas the fall of Troy, who supports the Greeks rather than the Trojans, and whose Delphic seat – which Chaucer discloses only through reportage and rumour – inspires, instead of clear vision, a problematic mix of conspiracy, shifts of loyalty, and brazen disbelief. These tensions infiltrate Apollo's status as city-builder, architect of the future, and, in the final account, exile from the heavenly city.

This chapter follows the motions of both retrospection and prophecy by first tracing Apollo's dimensions as a political and poetic agent in the *Troilus*, then moving backwards to explore the influence of a major medieval Trojan epic, Joseph of Exeter's twelfth-century *Ylias Daretis Phrygii*, upon Chaucer's conception of Apollo. Finally, it looks backwards still further – and at the same time into the 'future' – to Virgil's Apollo as he accompanies Aeneas, after the chronological moment occupied by Troilus's death, from Troy to Italy, and thence into Roman North Africa, where Augustine's polemical 'continuation' of Virgil's epic in his account of Rome's fall in *De civitate Dei* leaves both Aeneas and Apollo in a different place entirely. These various textual paths converge at a point outside of time, in the scene of spiritual homecoming that ends Troilus's wayfaring and serves as an injunction to would-be lovers, especially those who are storm-tossed like Troilus (*Tr* 5.638–44) and Aeneas, to '[r]epeyreth hom fro worldly vanyte' (*Tr* 5.1837) and become citizens of a city that is truly eternal.

The Bright Face of Troy: Apollo as Urban Planner

Apollo's untraditional enmity toward Troy in Chaucer's *Troilus*, instantiated in the passage from Book Four quoted above, is surprising on a number of levels. Apollo's first recorded appearance in literature, in Homer's *Iliad*, portrays him as the champion of the Trojans, especially Hector. A deliverer of plague upon the impious Greeks in the epic's first scenes, Apollo intervenes repeatedly to assist the Trojans in battle, demolishing the Greek rampart with the giddy enthusiasm of a child knocking down sandcastles at the seashore (*Iliad* 15.423–32).[7] Apollo's support of the Trojans in ancient literature is so well-rooted, in fact, that many scholars have theorized that this 'most Greek of all the gods' was actually Asiatic in origin. Dictys of Crete, representing the Greek perspective on the Trojan war, underscores Apollo's favouritism toward Troy in his account of the popular opposition to Agamemnon's rude dismissal of Chryses, a Trojan priest of Apollo: 'Having seen many evidences of Apollo's power and having learned of his popularity in the region nearby [i.e., Troy], we had made up our minds to serve this god devoutly.'[8] Virgil's *Aeneid* features Apollo, whom Aeneas addresses as the god who 'gravis Troiae semper miserate labores' [hast ever pitied the heavy woes of Troy], as the prophetic guide of the Trojans en route to their new homeland (*Aen.* 6.56). The epic's third book presents numerous oracles connected to Apollo, all of which are intended to direct Aeneas toward his Roman destiny:

Apollo's own oracle at Delos (3.90–8); the Trojan Penates's communication of Apollo's message to Aeneas on Crete (3.147–71); Anchises's memory of the prediction by Cassandra, who had been loved and granted her powers of prophecy by Apollo, of his family's Italian destination (3.182–8); the Harpie Celaeno's prophecy, transmitted from Jupiter via Apollo (3.245–57); and the prophecy of Helenus, priest of Apollo (3.369–462), within which is embedded an account of the future prophecy of the Cumaean Sibyl, Apollo's priestess (3.441–60). Fittingly, it is to Apollo, architect of the first Troy and patron of urban foundations, that Aeneas poignantly turns for counsel when journeying to found a second, more enduring city:

> da propriam, Thymbraee, domum, da moenia fessis
> et genus et mansuram urbem; serva altera Troiae
> Pergama, reliquias Danaum atque immitis Achilli.
> quem sequimur? quove ire iubes? ubi ponere sedes?   (*Aeneid* 3.85–8)

> [Grant us, thou god of Thymbra, an enduring home; grant our weary band walls, and a race, and a city that shall abide; preserve Troy's second fortress, the remnant left by the Greeks and pitiless Achilles! Whom should we follow? or whither dost thou bid us go? Where fix our home?]

In medieval Trojan legends and histories, a number of pivotal events pertaining to the Trojan cause transpire in temples of Apollo, most notably the defection of Calkas, the embalming and burial of Hector, Achilles's first sight of Polyxena, and Paris's treacherous ambush of Achilles.[9] These geographic locales were not matters of casual assignment: Guido, for example, draws attention to the irony that Achilles is erotically ensnared by Polyxena in the same temple of Apollo in which Hector's body is preserved – on the anniversary of his death, no less – and thus is conquered by love despite Hector's inability to defeat him on the battlefield.[10] In the same temple, in the twenty-seventh book of the *Historia*, Achilles meets his death, lured by the prospect of union with Polyxena. In most versions, Paris's murder of Achilles is not presented, as it was by Virgil and Ovid (who show Apollo guiding Paris's fatal arrow), as rightful retribution for Achilles's slaughter of the defenceless Hector.[11] Instead, the Dares-and-Dictys tradition regards Paris's deceitful slaying of Achilles in a holy place as a sacrilegious act in the presence of Apollo, which, according to Cassandra, leads Apollo and Minerva later to unpropitiously spurn the Trojans' sacrifices. In

Lydgate's *Troy Book*, the insult to Apollo even justifies the sacrifice of Polyxena.[12] Joseph of Exeter, less chary of mythological epic machinery than his contemporaries, portrays Apollo actively taking offence at Paris's impious action by preparing to shoot the offending Trojans as they ambush Achilles in his temple, until stopped by Jupiter. Apollo's temple is thus a significant site both politically and erotically in medieval Troy legends. The events associated with it indicate that the diminution of Apollo's special affection for Troy comes very late in the events of the war in most medieval accounts, and is meaningful precisely because the Trojans have so fully depended on his guidance up to that point.

Chaucer doubtless was aware of Apollo's traditionally positive associations with Troy, and he exploited these in a seemingly gratuitous detail introduced, surprisingly, a mere nine stanzas before the description of Apollo's prophecy to Calkas (in connection to which the god's ancient antagonism toward Troy is related). In the fateful battle in which Antenor is captured by the Greeks, Chaucer recounts that the efforts of a group of Trojan warriors – including Polydamas, Monesteo, Santippe, Sarpedoun, Polynestore, Polite, Rupheo, 'and other lasse folk as Phebuseo' – could not prevent the loss of such an important hero (*Tr* 4.50–4). Three of these names ultimately derive from the *Aeneid*, on which more later, and all but 'Phebuseo' are paralleled in the *Filostrato*. Chaucer's phrasing asserts the historical priority of Benoît's and Guido's accounts, however, over that of the *Filostrato*, in which the various Trojans are captured *along with* Antenor. In the pre-Boccaccian versions, Antenor is taken *despite* (Chaucer's 'maugre' [*Tr* 4.51]) the efforts of his fellow Trojans, only one of whom is named. Chaucer's unique inclusion of 'other lasse folk,' along with a Boccaccian catalogue of names rendered factually consistent with earlier accounts, advertises his own scholarly bona fides as a chronicler who not only has sought out and collated all available testimonies but, thanks to Lollius, brought to light new material, all the more convincingly 'historical' for its supposed insignificance. The supererogatory name 'Phebuseo,' then, requires explanation, and Stephen A. Barney's assertion that he is a character 'who appears to have been invented by Chaucer' and represents 'an Italianate name based on Apollo's name Phoebus,' seems most plausible, especially in the absence of alternative theories.[13] Chaucer's casual yet textually fraught inclusion of Phebuseo could be taken as a signpost of Apollo's traditionally positive affiliation with Troy as founding father – such that a civic-minded Trojan soldier could legitimately be named after him (one could compare the symbolic connotations of Troilus's own name). At the same time, the presence of Phebuseo calls attention to Apollo's significance within the mythic landscape of Book Four, where the god's status as a onetime Trojan advocate, now on the Greek side, substantiates Calkas's conflicted expression of his own national identity as a former citizen (Tr 4.71–2) of the city that, he assures the Greeks, 'in a stownde / Ben...ybrend and beten down to grownde' (4.76–7).

Calkas's revelatory (and oddly lyrical) words remind us that, as a tragic narrative, Chaucer's poem pivots only secondarily upon Criseyde's betrayal of Troilus; what shapes this circumstance historically, and situates it within the history of Trojan civilization, is the manifestation of and arbitration over Apollo's prophetic knowledge at key moments that intersect with the lovers' private experience. Chaucer encourages us in the *Troilus* to regard Apollo both as an urban planner and an architect, so to speak, of destiny, whose designs are repeatedly subjected to – if never in fact overcome by – human calculation. Unlike in pre-Boccaccian versions of the Troy story, which dwell on the content of various Apolline oracles directly and at length, Apollo's prophecies in the *Troilus* are the subject of recollection, commentary, and fabrication, but never unmediated experience. Calkas, in the poem's first stanzas, derives his status as 'a lord of gret auctorite' from his ceremoniously named master, 'Daun Phebus or Appollo Delphicus' (Tr 1.65, 70). Yet the precise content of Calkas's certain knowledge of Troy's doom 'by answere of his god' (Tr 1.69) is situated beyond the boundaries of the text and strategically withheld from our view. Calkas's reaction to Apollo's once-removed oracle, furthermore, lacks the pious cast given it by Benoît and Guido, who are more interested in the scene than Boccaccio. In those earlier versions, Apollo's Delphic oracle specifically commands Calkas to join the Greeks, making clear that defection is the encompassing will of the gods.[14] Benoît and Guido even allow Calkas to defend his sincerity when Briseida later accuses him of treason and Apollo's oracle of perversity. In contrast, Chaucer emphasizes Calkas's selfish cowardice as he 'stal anon' to the Greek camp 'softely' and 'ful pryvely,' like a thief in the night, without any specific injunction from Apollo to defect (Tr 1.81, 78, 80). In this version, the seer's elaborate plotting to save his own skin contrasts starkly with his lack of concern for his city and his daughter, whom he blithely abandons in her sleep (Tr 4.93).[15] As A.J. Minnis rightly notes, Chaucer's treatment of Calkas in Book One amounts to 'a thorough assassination of the character of this priest of Apollo' through the establishment of an unflattering connection 'between his supposed piety and his selfish behaviour.'[16] A pointed correlation, in fact, links Calkas's treachery with that of Aeneas as scathingly represented by Chaucer in the 'Legend of Dido': like Calkas, the 'traytour' Aeneas, upon receiving a dubious message from the gods (which, as in the scene involving Calkas, is not reported directly), 'shapeth...to stele awey by nyghte,' cruelly setting sail while Dido is 'slepynge' in bed (*LGW* 1328, 1289, 1326). In the 'Legend of Dido,' Mercury's counsel merely provides an excuse for Aeneas to do what he is already itching to do; in the same way, the truth-value of Apollo's oracle in the first book of the *Troilus* is obscured beneath the indirection of its representation and the deception it encourages in its custodian.

In the third book of *Troilus*, another oracle *manqué* fatefully punctuates the action. This one, in ironic contrast with Pandarus's Machiavellian 'purveiaunce' of the night's events (*Tr* 3.533), constitutes Troilus's alibi should anyone seek him while he is at Criseyde's house making love:

> If that he were missed, nyght or day,
> Ther-while he was aboute this servyse,
> That he was gon to don his sacrifise,

> And moste at swich a temple allone wake,
> Answered of Apollo for to be;
> And first to sen the holy laurer quake,
> Er that Apollo spak out of the tree,
> To telle hym next whan Grekes sholde flee –
> And forthy lette hym no man, God forbede,
> But prey Apollo helpen in this nede.   (*Tr* 3.537–46)

Multiple ironies inform this passage, which is original to Chaucer. There is a strong implication that if Troilus, like Calkas, had sought Apollo's oracular counsel he would have received some alarming news about the future of his city – perhaps the same eventuality signified by the monumental astrological conjunction that produces for the lovers such auspicious 'weder for to slepen inne' (*Tr* 3.657). Moreover, Apollo's own erotic history, which converges with Troilus's characterization in Chaucer's poem, supplies another level of poetic suggestion. The fact that Troilus chooses an alibi involving Apollo's oracle to 'cover up' love recalls Ovidian accounts of Apollo's neglect or ignorance of his own oracles when pursuing his erotic goals, particularly his abandonment of Delphi while in love with Hyacinthus (*Met.* 10.167–8) and the failure of his oracles during his attempted seduction of Daphne (*Met.* 1.491). Troilus's exploitation of Apollo's oracle to advance a secret but doomed love affair, furthermore, reinforces Apollo's own association with amatory deceit and misfortune.[17] It may well be significant that when Troilus in Book Four finally does seek ethical clarity concerning the gods' foreknowledge, he retreats to a nameless temple that is *not* associated with Apollo (*Tr* 4.947), thus reinforcing the inaccessibility and opacity of Apollo's prophetic counsel throughout the poem.

Apollo's oracle reemerges, again at a remove, in Calkas's entreaty for Criseyde's exchange at the beginning of the fourth book, where the god's counsel (*Tr* 4.114) is corroborated by other forms of prediction as well as historical evidence (Apollo's and Neptune's anger at Laomedon) that collectively serve as the rhetorical foundation of Calkas's request. Criseyde's reaction to her divinely sanctioned exchange is to convince Troilus, with some difficulty, that she will find a way to undermine her father's interpretation of the doubtful 'amphibologies' of the Delphic oracle (*Tr* 4.1406), adding yet another layer of machination to what is already a well-insulated technology. Criseyde's irreverence, interestingly enough, reflects a scepticism associated with the character of *Troilus* in Joseph of Exeter's *Ylias Daretis Phrygii*,[18] in which the young soldier ridicules an alarming prophecy, upon Helen's abduction, by the Trojan priest Helenus, as deceptive oracular speech – 'tenebris antri … loquacis' [darkness of the babbling cave].[19] According to Joseph, Troilus epitomizes the Trojans' foolhardiness and lack of prudence ('potens nec mensa futurum / Audet, cum presens metuat nichil' [Having no regard for the future, they dared everything, since in the present they feared nothing]) (*Ylias* 3.75–6) – a paradigm that aptly could be extended to the self-assessment of Chaucer's Criseyde after her plan to unravel her father's prophetic certainty fails.[20] Here Criseyde herself acknowledges that, despite the impulse of (hereditary) self-preservation, she failed to inherit that very inclination that made her father such a judicious prophet of Apollo:[21]

> Prudence, allas, oon of thyne eyen thre
> Me lakked alwey, er that I come here!
> On tyme ypassed wel remembred me,
> And present tyme ek koud ich wel ise,
> But future tyme, er I was in the snare,
> Koude I nat sen; that causeth now my care.   (*Tr* 5.744–9)

Criseyde's image of the three-eyed Prudence, which probably derives from canto 29 of Dante's *Purgatorio*, may also recall a widely circulated mythographic equation of the three prongs of Apollo's tripod with the dispensations of past, present, and future, linking Criseyde's failure of judgment even more closely to Calkas's role as soothsayer and engineer of the poem's action.[22]

The foresight that Criseyde lacks and her father commands, the impetuous Diomede insists upon: in the whole muddled complex of considerations that sways Criseyde toward accepting her Greek suitor's proposition, his conversational reminder of Apollo's prophecy of the fall of Troy makes the most significant impact upon the fearful Criseyde's resolve to return to Troilus. If Troy and all of its citizens are doomed, and Greeks are equal to Trojans in worthiness but superior in their odds of survival – so runs Diomede's logic – why shouldn't Crisyede choose to survive along with them? In response to this argument, Criseyde finally becomes her father's daughter: just as Calkas had, upon consultation of Apollo's oracle in Book One, changed allegiance from Troy to Greece and in the process left behind a loved one, so does Criseyde shift civic identities and abandon *her* beloved when Apollo's prophecy is strategically reinforced in Book Five. Our last image of Criseyde is brutally ironic: finally a prophet in her own right, Criseyde recedes from view only after bewailing her own textual 'future' with the accuracy of an accredited visionary (*Tr* 5.1058–66). By the time that Criseyde bleakly prophesies the loss of her 'name of trouthe in love,' the unwelcome, largely opaque 'truth' embodied by Apollo's oracle, which recurrently has been commodified, provides a point of reference not only for civic upheaval but damaged sexual property (*Tr* 5.1055).

The Children of Apollo

Despite Apollo's ostensible enmity toward Chaucer's Troy, one that is deepened by his prophetic identification with the broad and unsympathetic perspective that 'the tyme is faste by' for Troy's cataclysmic demise (*Tr* 4.117–18), the god's presence is so fully marked in this doomed city whose walls he erected that it sometimes seems embossed upon its very core. Apollo is not only a city-builder and harbinger of misfortune in the *Troilus*, he is also a shifting reflection of the various egos that comprise Chaucer's Troy before they become fossilized, in the city's final hours, in their respective literary reputations. The thematic significance of Calkas's professional affiliation with Apollo requires no further elaboration; the more subtle resonances of Apollo in the outlooks and behaviour of Criseyde, Troilus, and Pandarus, however, merit our attention before we consider the legacy of ambivalence surrounding Apollo as Trojan god in prior epic traditions – and, by connection, the cultural faultlines in the pagan worldview embodied in 'the forme of olde clerkis speche' (*Tr* 5.1854).[23]

Chaucer's Criseyde is a luminous beauty of almost cosmic powers of attraction; she spins through the poetic firmament as a bright star cloaked under the 'cloude blak' of a widow's garments (*Tr* 1.175), her very mood-swings leaving the perspectival surface of the poem awash in chiaroscuro (2.764–70).[24] In Troilus's expression of endearment, Criseyde is 'myn owen lady bright' (3.1485), and the narrator twice describes her blond hair as 'sonnyssh' (4.736, 816). The 'sonnyssh' quality of Criseyde's hair – the word's first recorded usage in English[25] – does not merely connote 'bright' or 'golden' but reflects a mythological context that anchors it in the poem's erotic vocabulary; namely, the 'gold-tressed Phebus' whose circuits mark the three years of the love affair (5.8). The iconic association between Criseyde and 'gold-tressed Phebus' derives from a mythographic commonplace, *Apollo auricomus*, marginally noted in relation to *Tr* 5.8 by the scribes of London, British Library MSS Harley 3943 and 2392 and centring upon imagery of cephalic radiance. In Macrobius's *Saturnalia*, Apollo is called 'Golden-Haired' and 'Unshorn' on account of the brightness of his rays (1.17.47), and Martianus Capella derives Apollo's epithet *auricomus* from the observation that 'Solis augustum caput radiis perfusum circumactumque flammantibus uelut auratam caesariem rutili uerticis imitatur' [the august head of the sun, streaming and surrounded with flaming rays, is like a gleaming head of golden hair] (1.12–13).[26] A contemporary iconographic correlative to Chaucer's Criseydan analogy, in fact, is found in Christine de Pizan's *Epistre Othea* in London, British Library MS Harley 4431, which depicts Apollo with golden flames radiating from his head instead of hair (fig. 5).[27]

The sunniness of Crisyede as *auricomus*, however, is set off by darkness and eclipse; like the sun, her countenance darkens and brightens (*Tr* 1.293) along with her 'slydynge … corage' (5.825), and in the fifth book her deserted house, no longer '[e]nlumyned with sonne of alle blisse' (5.548), becomes an image of day overtaken by night (5.544). In effect, Criseyde, initially an embodiment of Apollo's solar *veritas*, metamorphoses over the course of the poem into a figure of inconstancy

Fig. 5 Apollo *auricomus* slaying Coronis. Christine de Pizan, *L'Epitre Othea*.
French, c. 1410 – c. 1414. © The British Library Board. All Rights Reserved.
London, Brit. Lib. MS Harley 4431, fol. 117v.

mythically aligned with 'Phebus suster, Lucina the sheene' (4.1591). This metamorphosis is anticipated by the bifurcated *aube* of Book Three, in which Criseyde chides the withdrawing night with its familiar 'derke wede' (like the 'blake wede' that offsets Criseyde's sunniness [1.177]) and Troilus verbally accosts Titan, the rising sun (3.1431, 1464). During their last night together, Troilus pledges his faith on the regularity of the sun's rising – 'also soth as sonne uprist o-morwe' – while Criseyde insists, 'for the love of Cinthia the sheene,' that she is trustworthy, and measures the date of her return by the motions of the moon (4.1443, 4.1608; cf. 4.1591–6).

Criseyde thus ends far from where she began, reduced from an inscrutable illuminator of all that surrounds her to a figure, like the moon, capable only (she believes) of reflecting the will of others and passively reacting to forces beyond her control.[28] Troilus, by comparison, enjoys a more than ornamental connection with Apollo, who in certain Greek and Byzantine strands of myth was his father instead of Priam, or, in other versions, his lover.[29] It is remotely possible that Chaucer's innovative alibi for Troilus regarding his solitary worship at Apollo's temple in Book Three (where some of the same eastern sources place his death at the hands of Achilles) indirectly reflects one of these traditions of Apollo's mythic intimacy with Troilus, but it is certain that Chaucer modelled Troilus's early erotic experience upon that of Apollo in the first book of Ovid's *Metamorphoses*, reaching beyond the more recent precedent of Amant's encounter with Amors in the *Roman de la rose*. Apollo's mythic status as a young man (*ephebus*), which Isidore and later mythographers etymologically connect with his name Phoebus,[30] very likely led Chaucer to discern a link between Apollo's and Troilus's experiences as star-crossed young lovers, a link Troilus himself invokes during his first night with Criseyde when he seeks Apollo's aid (within a larger catalogue of divine *amours*) based on the god's love for Daphne (*Tr* 3.726–8). As John V. Fleming has convincingly demonstrated, Troilus's scornful nose-thumbing at Cupid as he saunters through the Palladium in Book One is answered by the same 'divine archery' with which Apollo himself was archetypally humbled in *Metamorphoses* 1 (like Ovid in the *Amores* and Petrarch in the *Canzoniere*), resulting in a similarly urgent desire for a woman who has not herself been struck by Cupid's amorous dart.[31] Like Ovid's Apollo, furthermore, Troilus ultimately loses his (more willing) Daphne through her father's intervention (cf. *Met*. 1.545).

Chaucer's suggestive alignment of the erotic histories of Troilus and Apollo elicits Ovidian irony at the expense of a latently problematic

Virgilian moment of heroic affirmation. In the *Aeneid*, Virgil also links his lover-hero and Apollo – both of whom he describes as 'pius'[32] – in a densely allusive simile that draws a parallel between Aeneas as he goes out hunting with Dido and Apollo as he departs from his winter home in Lycia to grace the altars of Delos and tread its hills, arrows rattling on his shoulders (*Aeneid* 4.143–9). Although this simile's referentiality potentially darkens Aeneas's character,[33] it also exonerates him as merely a *temporary* resident, like Apollo in Delos, of the idyllic world of celebration that is Dido's Carthage. Aeneas's departure for his homeland – authorized by Apollo's Lycian oracles themselves (*Aeneid* 4.345–6, 376–7) – is part of the divine plan as much as Apollo's return to Lycia is a function of the annual cycle. If Aeneas's absorption of the geographic dynamic of Apollo's cult sanctions his behaviour in Carthage (as does Mercury's command more directly) with divine approval embodied in mythic axiom, Troilus's repetition of the Ovidian Apollo's actions interpellates him into a self-defeating and narcissistic crisis of identity. Chaucer's Ovidian counter-vision of Virgilian heroism, as later sections of this chapter will show, ultimately engenders an Augustinian conception of Troy as a ruined city abandoned by fickle gods, and of Troilus as an *anti*-Aeneas, doomed to die fighting for a lost cause.

In Book One, after Troilus, like Apollo, is cut down to size by a vengeful God of Love, Pandarus, the poem's erotic diagnostician and prognosticator, enters Troilus's bedroom cloaked in the decidedly unencouraging garb of an Apolline love-doctor. In a passage not in Boccaccio, Pandarus recklessly mistranslates an excerpt from Oenone's letter to Paris in *Heroides* 5, presenting Apollo (who, as Oenone's rapist, is a peripheral character in the Ovidian original) as the letter's protagonist, and himself as an inheritor of his medical skills:

> 'Phebus, that first fond art of medicyne,'
> Quod she, 'and couthe in every wightes care
> Remedye and reed, by herbes he knew fyne,
> Yet to hymself his konnyng was ful bare,
> For love hadde hym so bounden in a snare,
> Al for the doughter of the kyng Amete,
> That al his craft ne koude his sorwes bete.'   (*Tr* 1.659–65)

'Right so fare I,' continues Pandarus: just as Apollo can heal others but not himself, so is Pandarus – although himself sick in love – certain that he can 'cure' Troilus by bringing his desire to fruition (*Tr* 1.666). As chapter 1 demonstrated, a complex network of associations integrates Oenone's posture as a trustee of Apollo's medical skills who cannot heal herself of love with a number of salient textual moments: Virgil's invention of a similar predicament in the internecine context of *Aeneid* 12, Propertius's maxim regarding the intractability of lovesickness, and the amorous Apollo's own failures as a (self-)healer in Ovid's *Metamorphoses* and exile poetry. Reflecting this syncretism, Pandarus strategically conflates Oenone's letter, which describes her own erotic suffering, with Apollo's account of his lovesickness at *Metamorphoses* 1.521–4. At the same time, by adapting Oenone's letter in these ways, Pandarus shapes an appropriately porous position of authority for himself as Ovidian medical guru and, furthermore, distracts Troilus from very real warnings concerning the relation between unchecked desire, erotic deception, and the fall of Troy in the original text of *Heroides* 5.[34] The net effect of these allusions is that Pandarus's subject-position as self-effacing practitioner of Apollo's medical art in Book One is cut from precisely the same textual cloth as Troilus's punishment by the God of Love's 'certior' arrow – both derive from the same speech, Apollo's to Daphne, in *Metamorphoses* 1, which gives no indication whatsoever that Apollo's healing herbs have any power over love, whether his own or someone else's.

When Pandarus dusts off his box of Ovidian cures in Book Four, attempting to heal the heartbroken Troilus with salves recommended by the *Remedia amoris*, Troilus deserves credit for recognizing Pandarus's Apolline vocabulary of remedy for the scam it has always been, cleverly turning the tables on Pandarus by reminding him of his self-professed inability to cure himself:

> But tel me now, syn that the thynketh so light
> To changen so in love ay to and fro,
> Whi hastow nat don bisily thi myght
> To chaungen hire that doth the al thi wo?   (*Tr* 4.484–7)

Troilus's well-justified question is essentially the same as that asked by Henry of Huntingdon, whose moral restitution of Apollo's medico-poetic authority was noted in chapter 1: 'Si non vis aliis, saltem tibi disce mederi: / Te quoque <si> spernis, cui bene fidus eris?' [If you do not wish to heal others, at any rate learn to heal yourself. If you reject yourself, to whom will you be trustworthy?] (VI Prologue, lines 3–4). From the Christian perspective of the end of the *Troilus*, the model of true *remedium*, which displaces Pandarus's failed Ovidian *ars*, is sup-plied by Christus Medicus, whose self-sacrifice on the Cross – the re-fusal to heal himself when tempted by his torturers – paradoxically *becomes* the cure, 'oure soules for to beye,' for humanity in its unre-deemed, diseased state (*Tr* 5.1843).[35] In contrast to Pandarus, Christ – the ultimate unrequited lover, who died 'right for love' – heals others precisely by *not* healing himself (*Tr* 5.1842). In effect, Pandarus's vexed association with Apolline medical authority, itself known to be rad-ically inadequate, catalyses the poem's closing celebration of Christ's salutary love – to which the end of this chapter returns – much as early Christians' polemical substitutions of Christ for Apollo, examined in chapter 2, rectified Apollo's failures as Christian success. Upon discov-ery of Criseyde's infidelity the deceptive and spiteful Pandarus, like the Delphic Apollo of the Church Fathers, is silenced and forced to confront his own irrelevance. Cursing his own niece, Pandarus's bitter admis-sion of rhetorical defeat, 'I kan namore seye' (*Tr* 5.1743) – his last words – compels the narrator's abrupt modulation of the poem, in the last hundred-and-fifty lines, from direct discourse to detached commentary and, finally, moral panorama, wherein the sublimity of Christian speech expunges the toxicity of both Pandarus's and Apollo's words.

'[I]ch was / Troian' (*Tr* 4.71–2): Apollo in Joseph of Exeter's *Ylias Daretis Phrygii*

Thus far this chapter has demonstrated that Chaucer's *Troilus* displays an acute interest in the mythology of Apollo to historically shape the circuit of social customs, technologies, and personal outlooks that ani-mate his pagan world. It has also emphasized the extent to which the prophetic dimension of the action, identified with Apollo, is integral to the poem's (and its characters') practices of fabrication and contests of authority. Finally, it has observed the problematic nature of Apollo's hostile relationship with Troy in Chaucer's poem, which adds unusual cultural pressure to the god's reported oracular pronouncements and meshes curiously with his shadowy presence within the psychic linea-ments of the city centre. This section and the next contextualize these and other aspects of the multivalent Apollo of the *Troilus* in anterior epic traditions involving Troy – particularly Joseph of Exeter's twelfth-century *Ylias Daretis Phrygii* and the early books of Virgil's *Aeneid* – in order to highlight the nature of Chaucer's conception of Apollo as a source of authority for nation-building and poetic construction.

Chaucer's complex deployment of Apollo in the *Troilus* appears somewhat less extraordinary when viewed alongside the god's numerous appearances in Joseph of Exeter's *Ylias*, an Anglo-Latin Trojan epic that Chaucer likely identified with 'Dares,' to whose much earlier chronicle he twice refers the reader (*Tr* 1.146, 5.1771) but gives no indication of knowing directly.[36] Joseph, an English scholar based at Reims, directly influenced Chaucer's portraits of the central characters in Book Five and his development of Troilus as a heroic figure,[37] but critics have been less interested in the intertextual relationship between Chaucer's *Troilus* and Joseph's *Ylias* than in the creative influence of Benoît de Sainte-Maure, Guido delle Colonne, and Boccaccio, who constitute a coherent medieval tradition of Trojan narrative to which the *Ylias* is to some extent an exception. Even before the full-fledged resurgence of interest in the Troy story in the later Middle Ages, Joseph had attempted a project suggestively close to Chaucer's: a Trojan epic, with special emphasis given to the role of Troilus, suffused with classical allusions and symmetry, and modelled more than respectably upon the Silver Age Latin and epic style of Statius and Lucan.[38] Joseph, admittedly, focuses on Troilus's martial exploits rather than his erotic experience, but there was nonetheless much in Joseph's epic to commend it to a poet of Chaucer's interests. The *Ylias* offered Chaucer something stylistically distinct from Dares's workmanlike pseudo-war diary, Benoît's ahistorical courtly romance, and even Guido's authoritative and morally unflinching chronicle: a studious emulation of the 'forme of olde clerkis speche' epitomized by 'Virgile, Ovide, Omer, Lucan, and Stace' supported by a complex recreation of the gods' participation (metaphorical, cosmological, imaginary, and naturalistic) in the pagan universe as seen by a Christian poet (*Tr* 5.1854, 1792).[39] The rich body of criticism in recent decades on Chaucer's colloquy with the poets of antiquity leaves no doubt that Chaucer engaged with many of these classical sources in their own right; however, it is equally important to acknowledge the significance of later 'classicisms' – even intermittently articulated or eccentric ones – in nuancing Chaucer's poetic view of the ancient past. This section, then, highlights one active locus of classicism, exemplified for our purposes by the figure of Apollo, within an available medieval 'history' of the Trojan war that Chaucer definitely knew, and to which he even may have looked for a conceptual model.

Given the general neglect of Joseph's *Ylias* by Chaucerians, it is necessary to establish briefly its stylistic relevance to the *Troilus* – one aspect of which we have already noted in relation to Chaucer's conception of Criseyde's scepticism (above, p. 132) – before considering Joseph's and Chaucer's shared concern with Apollo's status as a national god implicated in the politics of the Trojan War. The first and most striking of these proto-Chaucerian features is Joseph's conscious development of a dualistic structure for his epic and its reinforcement with the repeated phrase 'double sorrow' or 'double anguish' – phrases arguably closer in context to Chaucer's 'double sorwe of Troilus' (*Tr* 1.1) than the recognized precedents in Dante's *Purgatorio* and, more casually, Boccaccio's *Filostrato*.[40] The evidence presented here for the influence of the *Ylias* upon Chaucer's 'double sorwe' is by no means sufficient to resolve the matter, especially when other points of reference for this phrase have been defended so capably, but it does alert us to the structural and linguistic proximity of Joseph's epic to Chaucer's and, at the very least, their common indebtedness to an ancient repository of ideas that was nowhere else explored as subtly in medieval Trojan narrative. The first of Joseph's six books begins, like Book One of *Troilus*, with a programmatic statement of epic theme and an invocation – here to 'sacra fides,' which Joseph opposes to the fictions of the poets (*Ylias* 1.7). Despite his denial of poetic fiction, Joseph's first three verses in themselves reflect a debt to Juvenal, Lucan, and Statius that impressively connects his matter to epic, tragic, and satirical form as derived from classical tradition.[41] Tears in abundant measure constitute the first image of Joseph's opening lines, followed by an announcement of the epic's symmetrical design, centred upon double war and double destruction, namely the first and second sacks of Troy during the reigns of Laomedon and Priam.

Yliadum lacrimas concessaque Pergama fatis,
Prelia bina ducum, bis adactam cladibus urbem
In cineres querimur[.]   (*Ylias* 1.1–3)

[My complaint is the tears of the Trojan women and Troy given up to its fates, the two wars of the leaders, the city twice reduced to ashes by destruction.]

Later in the *Ylias*, at the time of Troy's second, definitive fall, this theme of double ruin resurfaces in language even closer to Chaucer's tear-filled prospectus of 'the double sorwe of Troilus' (little Troy) in his own, equally symmetrical first stanza. At the rhetorical climax of Troy's collapse in Book Six, Joseph dwells on the paradox that, amidst the chaotic onrush of swords and flames, to flee death in one form was only to run into it in another; for this reason, 'Utraque passis / Funera fas multis *geminos* conferre *dolores*' [It was granted to many to suffer *double anguish* and die both types of death] (*Ylias* 6.770–1; emphasis added). Less than one hundred lines later, after the death of Priam, Hecuba laments her fate to have lived to see both her children and her husband slaughtered, a form of sorrow that she describes as 'gemino ... planctu' [two-fold lamentation] (*Ylias* 6.833).[42] According to Joseph, Hecuba's double sorrow was, in fact, caused by the same figure who, in the first stanza of *Troilus*, inspires Chaucer's narration of the double sorrow of 'the kyng Priamus sone of Troye' (*Tr* 1.2): the fury Thesiphone. In Book Two of Joseph's epic, Thesiphone in concert with Allecto initiated the events that would ruin Troy (*Ylias* 2.2, 29).[43] Joseph's epic, then, provides the only known precedent for the phrase 'double sorrow' within the context of the fall of Troy (and that of the royal family) specifically, a context made all the more inviting by the epic's self-professed twofold structure and its concertedly classicizing design.

If Chaucer did take an interest in Joseph's poetic elaboration of a twice-doomed Trojan world, he surely would have been struck by Joseph's deeply learned command of classical myth, appearing most notably in his transformation of Dares's skeletal account of the Judgment of Paris into a wickedly humorous four-hundred-line Ovidian catfight. Venus, as a 'symbol of all those things which men fervently desire, but which once attained destroy them,' is accordingly the central divine power in Joseph's representation of the fall of Troy,[44] but Apollo surfaces almost as powerfully in the imaginative texture of Joseph's epic – indisputably more prominently than in any other medieval version of the Troy story besides Chaucer's, even taking into account Guido's seminal treatment of Apollo's Delphic oracle as wellspring of idolatry. Like Chaucer, Joseph draws on Apolline myth at important moments in his epic, for example, when he compares the burning of the city of Troy to the conflagration caused by Phaethon's chariot (*Ylias* 6.837–8) – both, in Joseph's treatment, examples of the consequences of unchecked ambition. Even Apollo's inspiration, states Joseph, could not provide words enough to describe the utter disaster of Troy's destruction (*Ylias* 6.765). And in a rhetorical manoeuvre reminiscent of that of his contemporary Alan of Lille, Joseph at the end of his poem forecasts his authorship of a greater epic on a sacred subject (the Crusades) tuned to a superior lyre ('plectro maiore').[45] This second epic, which does not survive, will concern 'nostre signa Sibille' [the banners of our Sybil] – a formulation that most likely alludes to Augustine's account of the Erythraean Sibyl's prophecies of Christ in *De civitate Dei* 18.23[46] – and it will be inspired not by Cirrha (i.e., the Delphic oracle) but by a 'celsior ... Apollo' [a loftier Apollo] (*Ylias* 6.964, 966–7; my translations). In essence, Apollo as an image of poetic inspiration in its full spectrum from pagan *fabula* to Christian celebration (which demands the replacement of the pagan Apollo with a 'celsior' guide) frames the most intensive sequence of Joseph's account of the fall of Troy.

Joseph associates Apollo not only with his own writing but, uniquely, with various aspects of the Trojan scene. When Paris falls asleep on Mount Ida and experiences his fateful vision, for example, he rests in the shade of a laurel tree 'dignissima Phebo' [most worthy of Apollo]; no fewer than thirteen lines are devoted to the laurel's preeminence over all other trees and its particular association with Apollo's eternal youth (*Ylias* 2.214–27; qtd at 2.214). Joseph's incorporation of Apolline myth here is far from ornamental: it neatly brings together, on the one hand, the much-repeated mythographic commonplace that laurel placed on the head of sleepers inspires true dreams,[47] and on the other, the archetypal scene of Apollo's rape of Daphne that supplies the etiology of the laurel and prefigures Paris's disastrous abduction of Helen.[48] Indeed, Apollo's amatory experience, which, as we have seen, also allusively informs the early sections of the *Troilus*, is cited as an example of the cruel effects of Venus in Minerva's speech within Paris's dream (*Ylias* 2.425–6).

Apollo's participation in the world of Joseph's epic is problematized by the question of his loyalties, which, as in Chaucer's *Troilus*, are unusually conflicted. Apollo's political allegiances in the *Ylias* inform both 'historical' and cosmological levels of action. An international god of sorts, connected to both Trojans and Greeks and trusted entirely by neither party, Apollo at the crucial consultation of his oracle at Delphi by Achilles and Calkas is proclaimed (echoing a patristic imputation) to be 'venalis' – bribed by gifts to tell his inquirers what they want to hear (*Ylias* 4.247). Apollo's prophecies also come under attack in the Trojan parliament in Book Three, when Helenus and Panthus both transmit oracular wisdom endowed by Apollo concerning Troy's certain doom if Helen is abducted. As noted earlier, Troilus denigrates Helenus's prophecy as fraudulent, claiming that the Trojans know a different Apollo ('alius ... Apollo') who, the approving crowd adds, is a 'certior augur' [more reliable augur] in league with Venus (*Ylias* 3.69, 3.87).

Marshalling legendary history with all the gusto of a return volley, Helenus's fellow Trojans refute his Apolline prophecy with counterevidence of Apollo's support for Paris's mission, creatively found in his historical enmity against the house of Atreus, from whose cannibalistic crimes he (as the sun) shrank. Contestation over the ideological underpinnings of Apollo's prophecies continues in Antenor's response to Panthus's still more convincing revelation. Invoking the factual truths of history, which justify Troy's revenge on the Greeks, over 'bachantis fabula fani' [the fables of the mad shrine], Antenor suggests that Apollo's cultic association with Lerna, near Argos, has made him partial to the Greeks (*Ylias* 3.117). Apollo, claims Antenor, has been spreading lies ('ficta') through his oracles to divert the Trojans from battle so as to protect his own Greeks (*Ylias* 3.140–3). The dramatic irony inherent in this false statement is only increased by the fact that Antenor will later help the Greeks and earn a reputation as a liar himself. Apollo's prophetic wisdom, as regarded by different ideological contingencies in the *Ylias*, is in these ways significantly elastic, foreshadowing the intersections of Apollo's oracle with the destinal unfolding and private manipulation of events in Chaucer's *Troilus*.

If the truth that Apollo embodies, in the view of Joseph's Trojans, is historically contingent and politically biased, the god's stance on the war is more difficult to interpret. Joseph indirectly acknowledges Apollo's traditional sponsorship of Troy in his citation of the god's affiliation with Troy's allies from elsewhere in Asia: 'quicquid / Prima dies, orbis oriens, cunabula Phebi / Gentis' [people of the dawn, the east, the resting-place of Phoebus] (*Ylias* 4.18–20). Apollo also is said by Joseph to rule Troy's harbour (*Ylias* 1.543, 3.423). Nevertheless, the *Ylias* strongly emphasizes Apollo's unmitigated anger at Troy for Laomedon's shortchanging of him and Neptune – a theme that significantly resurfaces in Chaucer's *Troilus*. In the first war against Troy, Hercules vows to attack the inhospitable Trojans in the name of Apollo and Neptune, who like the Argonauts were wronged by Laomedon (*Ylias* 1.293–5). In most accounts, Hercules's sack of Laomedon's Troy assuages Apollo's anger and leads to his reestablishment of close ties with the city,[49] but in Joseph's epic, on the first day of the second war against Troy, Apollo (as Sol) rises more quickly than usual, outpacing his own morning star, eager to witness the (second) downfall of 'periura ... Pergama' [perjured Troy] (*Ylias* 5.95–6). The Greeks attribute Apollo's welcome alacrity to his continuing grudge against the city of Laomedon:

Vocat ecce deus, Sol letus hanelis
Instat equis, Neptunus aquas ac pervia mollit
Cerula. Credo equidem, vires augentibus ipsis
Laomedonteo poscunt ex hoste triumphum.   (*Ylias* 5.108–11)

[See, Apollo calls us on! He joyfully speeds his panting horses, while
Neptune makes gentle the dark-blue waters we are sailing on. I do indeed
believe that they too have joined our ranks, and are calling for a triumph
over the descendants of Laomedon(.)]

Just as when, in Chaucer's *Troilus*, the historical fact that 'Phebus and
Neptunus bothe / ... Ben with the folk of Troie alwey so wrothe / That
they wol brynge it to confusioun' cements Calkas's obsequious explication of Apollo's pro-Greek prophecy (*Tr* 4.120, 122–3), so does this cluster of passages in Joseph's epic create the implication that the wisdom
of Apollo's oracle is socially constructed, its partiality reflected in the
god's very cosmological framing of the war's progress.

Apollo's celestial motions in the *Ylias* are, in fact, fully integrated
with his mythic history. In this epic that follows medieval precedent in
eschewing the Homeric notion of gods fighting in the ranks of mortals,
Apollo mainly 'participates' in the action in the form of the personified
sun rising, setting, and lingering over the battlefield out of pity, rage, or
both. Similarly, Chaucer adds to the *Filostrato* numerous temporal
markers centred upon the movements of Phebus the sun, highlighted
in direct narration and internal discourse a remarkable eight times
throughout the poem.[50] Phebus's cyclic motions are concentrated in the
third and the fifth books of the *Troilus*, where they impinge upon the
nocturnal bliss of the bedroom and, later, punctuate Criseyde's slide
into infidelity and Troilus's temporally bound vigilance at Troy's walls
– an image of history inexorably overtaking romance in the last days of
the war, before the radical shift in perspective that sees Troilus ascend
through the planetary spheres. A pronounced conceptual similarity
underlies Joseph's and Chaucer's epic orchestration of Apollo's astrological circuits in relation to their poems' action – particularly their
'negative' portrayals of Apollo as Trojan god – highlighting their common interest in Apollo's connection to the natural order as a framework
for human affairs.

A review of the events of Joseph's *Ylias* from the perspective of
the heavens presents several striking points of correspondence with

Chaucer's *Troilus*, which traces a 'parallel movement of the heavenly bodies and the emotional action of the poem.'[51] First, when Paris prepares to carry off the coquettish Helen under darkness of night, he impatiently imagines that '[z]elotipum Titana' [the jealous sun (Titan)] – a phrase that evokes the *aube* genre – is delaying his descent in envy of the Trojan's good fortune (*Ylias* 3.268). Night then descends via an elaborate periphrasis evoking the effects of the 'radiis languentibus' [dying rays] of Phebus (*Ylias* 3.269–73). At the beginning of the war, a variation on this motif occurs when the eager Greeks blame the sun for delaying its rising rather than its setting; they chastise 'Titone' (Tithonus) for holding back the dawn, herald of Phebus, with his feeble embrace (*Ylias* 5.38–40). In response to their complaint, the firmament speeds up its motion, making audible the music of the spheres and hastening the journey of Phebus (*Ylias* 5.41–4). The result is the miraculously accelerated rising of Phebus, already noted, which the Greeks attribute to the god's eagerness to see Troy punished (*Ylias* 5.94–111). The motions of Joseph's Apollo (as Phebus or Titan) in relation to the moon and constellations mark a long list of events: the entry of the Greek fleet into the Trojan harbour, two truces, the night of Andromache's prophetic dream, and the beginning of the tenth year of the war. Notably, in the thick of the war, Apollo's sentiments are less clear than at the beginning: at one point, Phebus grieves so deeply for the losses on both sides that he plunges his chariot abruptly into the sea, ending the day's fighting with unexpected night (*Ylias* 5.421–4). Phebus's circuit endows the most intense sequence of the war, which sees the death of Hector and the flourishing of Troilus, with cosmic gravity:

> Torserat astrivagum pacta in vestigia Phebum
> Annua mobilitas bis senos mensa labores,
> Et iam mixte acies.
>
> (*Ylias* 6.115–17)

[The swift onward movement of the year, its twelve toils completed, had spun heaven-wandering Phoebus through the arc appointed for the truce, and now the armies clashed once again.]

When Troy finally falls, Phebus hides behind the clouds in grief, overcome by an ambivalent mixture of enmity and sympathy: 'et eversis, que struxit, menibus hostem / Ingemuisse putes' [although he was Troy's enemy, it was as if he was mourning for the walls which he had built and which had now been overthrown] (*Ylias* 6.855–6).[52]

Chaucer likewise goes to great lengths to weave the motions of Phebus into the trajectory of his epic's central matter: a tragic love affair itself woven minutely into the fabric of the Trojan war. In doing so, he employs poetic techniques remarkably similar to those of Joseph, including the conspicuous incorporation of *aube* imagery within an epic lexicon of astrological chronometry. In the *Troilus*, the motions of the sun and constellations frame everything from Pandarus's wooing, to the lovers' first night in bed, to the prospect of Criseyde's return to Troy.[53] When, in Book Five, the events of the war and the demands of history converge with the lovers' formerly private affair, the epic motions of Phebus mark both the diminishment of Troilus's hopes for Criseyde's return and, more implicitly, the ever-receding calendar of Troy's existence. The effect in this last book is particularly reminiscent of Joseph's interpolation of Phebus's motions into the unfolding progress of the war, as the following cross-section of passages illustrates:

> The gold-tressed Phebus heighe on-lofte
> Thries hadde alle with his bemes cleene
> The snowes molte, and Zepherus as ofte
> Ibrought ayeyn the tendre leves grene,
> Syn that the sone of Ecuba the queene
> Bigan to love hire first for whom his sorwe
> Was al, that she departe sholde a-morwe.   (*Tr* 5.8–14)

> ....

> On hevene yet the sterres weren seene,
> Although ful pale ywoxen was the moone,
> And whiten gan the orisonte shene
> Al estward, as it wont is for to doone;
> And Phebus with his rosy carte soone
> Gan after that to dresse hym up to fare
> Whan Troilus hath sent after Pandare.   (*Tr* 5.274–80)

> ....

> The laurer-crowned Phebus with his heete
> Gan, in his cours ay upward as he wente,
> To warmen of the est se the wawes weete,

> And Nysus doughter song with fressh entente,
> Whan Troilus his Pandare after sente[.]   (*Tr* 5.1107–11)

Like both Joseph's Paris and his Greeks, who impatiently wait upon Phebus's cycles, personifying the sun as envious, slow-footed, or blood-thirsty to rationalize their own perspectives on the passage of time, so does Troilus mythologize the sun's prolongation of the days as he waits for Criseyde to return:

> The dayes moore and lenger every nyght
> Than they ben wont to be, hym thoughte tho,
> And that the sonne went his cours unright
> By lenger weye than it was wont to do;
> And seyde, 'Ywis, me dredeth evere mo
> The sonnes sone, Pheton, be on lyve,
> And that his fader carte amys he dryve.'   (*Tr* 5.659–65)

The collusion of the solar Apollo in the down-spiral of the love affair in Book Five – presented in these passages alternately as vicarious and oblivious – stems conceptually from the lovers' *aubes* in Book Three. There, the complex, cyclic interplay of day and night, sun and moon, is first drawn into the rhythms and paradoxes of the love affair. Embedded within a larger tragedy that necessitates the lovers' separation, the *aubes* of the third book do not so much celebrate the transcendence of love over social forces that demean or oppress it (like Boccaccio's less fully developed *aubes*), as represent the fragility of sensual enjoyment in the face of historical reality and the future, devastating fact of infidelity.[54] Just as Joseph's Greeks and Trojans denounce the sun's purported jealousy and Tithonus's senility, so does Troilus, distraught over parting from Criseyde at dawn, mock the daylight as an 'envyous' spy – and 'Titan,' conflated with Tithonus, as an old fool who can't make his lover linger (*Tr* 3.1454, 1464–70). Troilus prays for God to 'quenche' the sun's light and declares in a tone verging on belligerence that 'us nedeth no day have' (*Tr* 3.1456, 1463), suggesting the ethically unsettling irony that, at least in Troy, the lovers' '"insight" into love requires darkness.'[55] A second *aube* later in Book Three represents the lovers outdoing each other to besmirch the sunrise, calling the day 'traitour, envyous, and worse, / And bitterly the dayes light thei corse' (*Tr* 3.1700–1). Rounding out this subjectivized view of Phebus's immutable cycles is Troilus's comically egocentric theory that the sun has tricked his horses into taking a shortcut out of resentment at the lovers' nocturnal joy:

> 'Allas, now am I war
> That Piros and tho swifte steedes thre,
> Which that drawen forth the sonnes char,
> Han gon som bi-path in dispit of me;
> That maketh it so soone day to be;
> And for the sonne hym hasteth thus to rise,
> Ne shal I nevere don hire sacrifise.'   (*Tr* 3.1702–8)

As in Joseph's epic, creative solar mythography is casually replotted upon unfolding events to suit particular rhetorical perspectives. Chaucer's reinscription of Apollo's astrological bearing on the action – which in the *Ylias* suggested the god's ambivalent loyalties to both warring nations – reveals much about the motivations of the characters through whose imperfect eyes the sun is perceived. Criseyde revises Troilus's first demand for the sun's envious light to be blotted out, for example, in her list of *impossibilia* – physically incredible events that will occur before Troilus loses his place in her heart. 'First shal Phebus fallen fro his speere,' insists Criseyde, and eagles mate with doves, and mountains come tumbling down, before *that* happens (*Tr* 3.1495–8). Whereas Troilus imagines the sun's demise as a condition of their uninterrupted bliss, Criseyde heralds the sun's stability – the regular daily motions that follow from its intactness – as an image of her constancy. In effect, Chaucer stages a contest of solar clichés with particular generic affiliations which, taken individually, are equally valid but in this context cannot help but reflect poorly upon Criseyde, whose sentiment defies the logic that celebrates their union as it has just been expressed. Criseyde bases her vow of fidelity, that is, on an image that *opposes* their continued love: the force of reality and the progress of time, embodied in the sun whose rising separates the lovers.[56]

Interestingly, Troilus makes a similarly revisionist move later in the third book, but for very different reasons. Celebrating love's power during a garden stroll with Pandarus, Troilus sings a *canticus* adapted from *Consolation of Philosophy* 2.m.8 that invokes the fact that 'Phebus mote his rosy day forth brynge, / And that the mone hath lordshipe over the nyghtes' to illustrate love's harmonization of discord (*Tr* 3.1755–6). This, of course, blatantly contradicts Troilus's own wish a short while earlier that the sun never again rise. Tempting as it is to attribute this slip to the mechanics of Chaucer's interpolation of this song from a peripheral source, the passage is better understood as Troilus's reordering of his earlier solipsistic gripe about the inconveniences of secret love into a larger, cosmic vision of love's power, in which the sun's and moon's motions themselves partake in – rather than occlude – the all-encompassing benevolence of love. Thus reconfigured, the Phebus of Troilus's song is not the inflexible force of reality imagined by Criseyde but the god who, in one of Joseph's Ovidian allusions, stands in awe of fires greater than his own (*Ylias* 2.425–6; cf. *Met.* 4.194–5).

This idyllic vision of cosmic harmony cannot be sustained, however; in Book Five it is all but cancelled by Troilus's cynical reprise of his second *aube* (concerning the detour of Phebus's horses) in his complaint that the chariot of the sun this time is making its circuits too *slowly*, driven awry by a revenant Phaethon (*Tr* 5.659–65).[57] In other respects, too, the astrological texture of Book Five ironically reverses that of Book Three: the sunlight that Troilus had once wished to 'quenche' (3.1456) becomes the light that is 'queynt' in Criseyde's deserted palace (5.543), for example, and the night, once the time of bliss too soon to end, becomes haunted by nightmares (5.246–59). Indeed, Chaucer develops the implication that the lovers' anger at Phebus's intrusion into the bedroom was always informed by anxieties about separation – for the misery of parting for the day implies unvoiced concern over the choices one or the other might make when alone – suspicions, appropriate to a tragedy, which had already been raised by the argument over the fictive Horaste in the third book. Ironically, in their *aubes*, Troilus and Criseyde are united against the fiction of an 'envyous' sun in a poem in which the real envy will be provoked and experienced by the lovers themselves. In a cruel twist of fate, the physical and emotional distance feared by the lovers in their respective delineations of their erotic geographies in Book Three culminates, in Book Five, in their permanent severance – a book that sees the same Phebus spin indifferently over Criseyde, warm in bed in 'hire fadres faire brighte tente' as she takes 'fully purpos for to dwelle' (*Tr* 5.1022, 1029), as well as over Troilus as he stands checking his math on walls that (impossibly) will soon come tumbling down (5.1107–13). Like his counterpart in Joseph's *Ylias*, Apollo – whose very astrological authority has become a source of rhetorical contestation and erotic propaganda – might well grieve for the losses on both sides.

'[A]nd after out of joie' (*Tr* 1.4): Troy's *falsa gaudia*

The ambivalent loyalties and generic multiplicity of Joseph's Apollo provide a point of reference for Chaucer's extraordinary integration of the god in his poem's historical and cosmological action. The idea of Apollo's radical incompletion as a Trojan god, however, stems less from medieval redactions of the Troy story than from Virgil's *Aeneid*, which has been somewhat overshadowed in its relation to the *Troilus* by other members of the elite procession of 'Virgile, Ovide, Omer, Lucan, and Stace' (*Tr* 5.1792).[58] Virgil's nightmare vision of '[h]ow Ilyon assayled was / And wonne' (as Chaucer paraphrases *Aeneid* 2 in *HF* 158–9) offers an appropriately tragic model for Chaucer's own book of Troy, which, despite its focus on a private affair, begins and ends with the public events of the war: a political defection and a heroic funeral.[59] In the *Aeneid* Chaucer would have found, of course, the germ of the Troilus legend (*Aen.* 1.474–8); he also would have encountered a problematic, even implosive point of origin for a great empire whose legacy underwrote the national myth of Chaucer's England – a myth controversially implicated, during the period of the *Troilus*'s composition, in the semi-official recognition of London as Troynovaunt.[60]

Apollo's positive association with Aeneas as the god who guides him to his Roman destiny and ensures the survival of his progeny was tempered in the Middle Ages by the reputation of Virgil's hero as a traitor (to Troy and to Dido)[61] – a reputation that Chaucer deliberately invokes in Book Two of the *Troilus* by implicating Aeneas in a circle of friendship with Antenor, maligned for his future treason in Book Four, and 'false Poliphete,' involved in a nebulous legal wrangle with Criseyde (*Tr* 2.1474–5, 1467). The Apollo of the *Troilus* is the god who in the *Aeneid* failed Virgil's Troy and, as we shall see, even sped along its fall, but offered new and greater security to Aeneas as founder of a new nation. Chaucer's *Troilus*, which revisits the *Aeneid* from the perspective of medieval adaptations of the Troy story inspired by the antithetical tradition of Dares,[62] imagines a Trojan god – and, in Troilus, a Trojan hero – circumscribed by tragedy and unredeemed by cultural translation.

An assumption behind my interpretation of Chaucer's Virgilianism as it pertains to the legacy of Apollo is that the English poet conceived of the *Troilus* not only as retrospective of but as a prequel to Virgil's *Aeneid*. On one level, the *Aeneid* is an ancient text that supplies a poetic precedent for the *Troilus*, as in the fateful rainstorm in Book Three that allusively evokes the similar circumstances of Dido's and Aeneas's union in *Aeneid* 4. But if the *Troilus* is 'subgit' to the *Aeneid* (*Tr* 5.1790), it also aims aggressively to gloss it: although written long after Virgil's epic, Chaucer's poem 'happened' before his and is, thus, in a way, more authentic (in the same sense that the belated Dares and Dictys were regarded as closer to the truth than Homer). Thus it is significant that the *Troilus* explores some of the same thematic concerns as the *Aeneid* – heroism, self-preservation, prophecy – but situates them in an earlier set of circumstances and directs them toward a different conclusion. Viewed in relation to the *Aeneid*, especially in its medieval incarnations as an allegory of spiritual education,[63] the historical world of the *Troilus* is notably 'untransmuted': like Criseyde, it knows its present and past but not its future. Chaucer offers absolutely no indication that Troy one day will be gloriously reborn as a new nation that in turn will become an imperial staging area for future civilizations, including the one that makes Chaucer's own poem possible.[64] In suppressing this fact, Chaucer resists both the arc of Virgil's narrative and the medieval tendency to view the Troy story within a larger historical cycle.[65] To the extent that Aeneas figures in Chaucer's narrative, he appears as a friend, and probably co-conspirator, of traitors – yet the political treason of the Aeneas faction, given so much less weight than Criseyde's sexual betrayal, remains unarticulated and inchoate, overshadowed by a more profound treason of cosmic scope: the fraud of Troy's pagan gods, the 'rascaille' who, at the end of the poem, are denounced for double-crossing those who trust them (*Tr* 5.1853). Whereas the marked failure of Troy's gods in the *Aeneid* to protect the city, and the inscrutable desire of some of them to harm it, ultimately advances a grand purpose for which Troy's fall was necessary – the restoration of a greater homeland in Italy – Chaucer envisions Troy as a *polis* unredeemed by gods who are themselves unredeemable. The *translatio imperii* in Chaucer's poem is not from Troy to Rome, but from the city of man to the city of God, and the point of contact between these cities is one of rupture and renunciation rather than continuity.

Chaucer's Trojans worship their gods and fight for their city within a pre-Roman Virgilian world which, unbeknownst to them, operates according to an Augustinian ethic: the same pagan gods that betrayed Troy will also, *mutatis mutandis*, fail Rome in its hour of need, enforcing a tragic rather than teleological model of secular history.[66] The concentration of Chaucer's creative interest in the first four books of the *Aeneid*, which span the period from Troy's fall to Dido's death, enables him to shape an Apollo, as we shall see, blighted by the failure of his own urban foundation and associated with dead-ended warfare rather than the cultivation of *pietas*. Chaucer's Troilus chooses the path that Virgil's Aeneas rejects: to remain in Troy until the bitter end and die fighting, albeit not 'in loyal service to his country but as a battlefield suicide only in the nominal service of a city he has in the end grown to hate.'[67] Unlike Virgil's Aeneas, who successfully escapes the undertow of his Trojan heritage as a potential second Paris,[68] Troilus, as little Troy, succumbs to an outmoded and infertile Trojanness associated with an Ovidian conception of Apolline cultural construction. Criseyde, on the other hand – as a traitor and a survivor – follows something broadly resembling Aeneas's trajectory of self-preservation, guided by her father's wisdom, Apollo's oracle, and the embryonic prospect of a new life.

Virgil's Troy book, as Gian Biagio Conte has observed, presents one of many sites of ideological inconsistency in the *Aeneid* that contribute to the epic's status as a network of contradictions to be examined rather than a consistently pro- or anti-imperialist iteration to be affirmed.[69] Aeneas's recollection of Troy's last days resoundingly illustrates that the gods as 'guarantors of justice [are] at the same time responsible for injustice':[70] as Venus herself explains to Aeneas when she momentarily lifts the cloud from his mortal vision, neither Helen nor Paris are at the root of this destruction, but 'divum inclementia, divum, / has evertit opes sternitque a culmine Troiam' [the gods, the relentless gods, overturn this wealth and make Troy topple from her pinnacle] (*Aen.* 2.602–3). Problematic indeed is the implication that Troy's own gods have been vanquished ('victosque deos,' *Aen.* 2.320) by rival forces oblivious even to the moral deserts of a figure like Ripheus, most just of the Trojans,[71] who was slain on Troy's last night but later merits for his sheer righteousness a spot in, of all places, Dante's Paradise (*Par.* 20.68). To seek a theodicy in Virgil's Troy book is to gaze into the abyss: if Virgil's epic ended at Book Two, his gods would seem more like the band of ungrateful and infectious demons described by Augustine than the numinous powers who in the fullness of time reward Aeneas's *pietas* with a new homeland.

One way that Virgil keeps the balance between the fall of Troy and the rise of Rome in check is to dissociate Apollo from the scene of Trojan devastation and implicate him instead in the progress of Aeneas's journey westward, into the future, which Apollo constructively generates through various oracles, his appearance on Aeneas's shield as an agent of Augustus's success in the Battle of Actium (*Aen.* 8.704–6), and his preservative counsel to Ascanius on the battlefield (9.638–60).[72] Virgil faced a significant challenge in negotiating the relation between the two main civic spheres of his epic: he was determined to give Apollo, Augustus's patron god, a substantial and positive role in this legendary history of the Julian family's ancestors – hence his substantial introduction of examples of Apollo's involvement into the existing tradition of Aeneas and his travels[73] – but he also wished to emphasize Rome's origins in the fallen city of Troy, a fact that necessitates the defeat of Apollo as divine sponsor of Troy. Accordingly, Virgil handles Apollo delicately. Whereas the *Iliad* is replete with episodes involving Apollo's assistance in battle, Apollo is conspicuously absent in the Trojan battle scenes of Virgil's second book. When Aeneas is granted a momentary vision of the various gods gleefully destroying Troy within a kind of parallel universe, he sees no gods defending Troy; Apollo is not mentioned at all. Significantly, Aeneas sees Neptune, traditionally hostile to Troy, shaking down the walls and crashing the foundations that he himself built (*Aen.* 2.610–12); elsewhere, reference to the construction of Troy is thrice made in the name of Neptune alone (2.625, 5.810–11, 9.144–5). Virgil studiously avoids reminding the reader of the widely known tradition in which Apollo shared the work of building Troy's walls equally with Neptune. Indeed, Aeneas's prayer at Delos to Apollo (quoted earlier), whom he invokes as 'Thymbraee' (i.e., Trojan), for a lasting city with enduring walls preserved by the god himself (3.85) would have been both deeply ironic and in bad taste were we encouraged to recall Apollo's former partnership with Neptune while the walls of Old Troy crumbled.

Virgil circumvents the embarrassment of Apollo's defeat at Troy, then, by presenting the god effectively as 'missing in action,' invisibly preparing to speed Aeneas along the next stage of his journey. Here as elsewhere in the *Aeneid*, however, 'other voices' (to echo the title of R.O.A.M. Lyne's classic study of the epic) can be heard which make Apollo's absence in Virgil's Troy more akin to a problematic presence. Apollo's first appearance in the *Aeneid*, appropriately for an epic motivated by Apollo's oracular guidance, occurs within a prophecy (2.114–15), but this particular prophecy, embedded within the lie of Sinon, is as suspect and fraudulent as the worst fabrications imagined in Joseph of Exeter's *Ylias*. This prophecy of Apollo, in fact, is delivered by none other than Calchas, a Greek seer in the *Aeneid*, and it is as fictitious as the manipulative ruse that contains it. According to Sinon, after the Greeks thought the war lost, foul weather prevented their departure.

An oracle of Apollo proclaimed that a human sacrifice was needed to calm the seas; Calchas, goaded by the spiteful Ulysses – who pressured the soothsayer to fulfil a personal grudge – interpreted the oracle to refer to Sinon. Sinon avoided his barbaric execution and, in return for refugee status in Troy, reveals to the Trojans (again invoking the guidance of Calchas) that the wooden horse is meant by the Greeks to expiate their crime of defiling the Palladium; if the Trojans bring it inside their walls, the glory will be theirs and not the Greeks'. Our introduction to Apollo is thus as the ethically vacuous centre-point of a kaleidoscopic series of fictions: the truth-telling god's false (invented and/or manipulated) oracle which aids the ruse of the lying Ulysses and in turn lends authority to the calculated lie of the 'periuri' [perjured] Sinon – an epithet elsewhere applied to Laomedon in his breach of contract with Apollo and Neptune (*Aen.* 2.195). The irony is augmented by the fact, revealed much later in Diomede's account of the Greeks' punishments since leaving Troy (11.255–77), that the Greeks indeed *should have* feared Pallas's outrage at their sacrilege. In using the name of Apollo and his oracles in the service of a cold-blooded lie, then, Sinon commits the very impiety which is the subject of his fiction. In this matrix of deception that repays perjury with perjury, it is difficult not to feel that the truth-value of Apolline prophecy, and the relationship of Apollo to Troy, is tainted from the start.

Apollo's prophetic wisdom remains deeply compromised in Aeneas's account of the destruction of Troy. Although Apollo himself does not take part in the final battle, his Trojan priest Panthus does. On the night that the wooden horse is admitted to the city, the dead Hector appears to Aeneas in a dream, informing him of the penetration of Troy and directing him to flee and seek a new home for Troy's gods, because the city is doomed. Aeneas, overcome by *furor*, prepares instead to fight. At this moment, he encounters Panthus carrying the images of the vanquished gods and frantically clutching his grandchild. The significance of Aeneas's encounter with Panthus is ambiguous: on one hand, it seems aimed to reinforce the content of Hector's message (since Panthus holds the Penates that are to be entrusted to Aeneas) and remind Aeneas of his own familial responsibilities. On the other, however, Panthus's words to Aeneas are despairing and shortsighted: 'venit summa dies et ineluctabile tempus / Dardaniae. fuimus Troes, fuit Ilium et ingens / gloria Teucrorum' [It is come – the last day and inevitable hour for Troy. We Trojans are not, Ilium is not, and the great glory of the Teucrians (alternatively: We were Trojans, there was an Ilium, etc.)] (*Aen.* 2.324–6)

– memorable phrasing that may be reflected in Calkas's 'ich was /
Troian' in the *Troilus*. Panthus's speech has the effect of futilely directing
Aeneas into the battlefield rather than toward the future proclaimed by
Hector. Impelled by Panthus's words ('talibus ... dictis') and, curiously,
'numine divum' [divine will], Aeneas rushes into battle not, at this
point, out of a sense of civic duty – Troy is already lost, even nameless,
in Panthus's view[74] – but driven by an urge to die in a way that maxi-
mizes the bloodbath for the enemy. In a voice of despair, Aeneas calls
his comrades to arms:

> excessere omnes adytis arisque relictis
> di, quibus imperium hoc steterat; succurritis urbi
> incensae: moriamur et in media arma ruamus.   (2.351–3)

> [All the gods on whom this empire was stayed have gone forth, leaving
> shrine and altar; the city ye aid is in flames. Let us die, and rush into the
> midst of arms.]

Later events, of course, cause Aeneas to renew his trust in the gods,
prompting him to regroup with his family and the Penates and flee the
burning city. Panthus's fate, however, follows without reprieve from
this self-destructive response to Troy's calamity: one hundred lines
after his address to Aeneas, Panthus is fatally wounded in battle, un-
protected, Virgil notes, by Apollo's fillet (2.429–30).[75]

As a priest of Apollo, Panthus's lack of foresight, which leads him
and, initially, Aeneas, to fight a lost war, contrasts ironically with
Hector's prophetic vision of Troy's rebirth through Aeneas.[76] Panthus's
mastery of Apollo's powers, furthermore, is inadequate to save him
from slaughter, just as Apollo's medical art is inadequate to heal Aeneas
on the Italian battlefield in Book Twelve (see pp. 62–3 above). In these
respects, seen especially in relation to the Greeks' deceptive appropriation of Apollo's authority to trick the Trojans into tearing down the
walls that the god himself built (a fact that Virgil cannot entirely sup-
press), Apollo's unexplained lack of support for the Trojans appears
almost antagonistic – at the very least, it suggests an impotence only
later to be reconstituted, in Aeneas's post-Trojan adventures, as a
strength. Apollo is, of course, chief among the gods on whose foundation, in Aeneas's address to his fellow citizens at 2.351–3, the 'imperium' of Troy had stood firm ('steterat') – the foundation on which, in
fact, it had *imagined* itself as a (proto-Roman) 'imperium.'[77]

The sequence consisting of the unprophetic speech of Panthus and Aeneas's fatalistic *cri de coeur* resonated deeply with Augustine as well as Chaucer, whose creative reworking of it in the *Troilus* will be the final concern of this chapter. In *De civitate Dei* 1.3, Augustine cites Virgil's description of Panthus to illustrate the perils of worshipping 'victos deos' – if gods can be conquered, reasons Augustine, they should not be looked for cultural sustenance. The first three books of Augustine's treatise focus on Rome as an example of an earthly empire whose lust for dominion made it vulnerable to dissolution. Augustine exhaustively refutes the idea that the Roman empire's embrace of Christianity, rather than other factors, led to its demise. Aeneas's lament that the gods have deserted the 'imperium' is taken by Augustine to represent the flawed pagan viewpoint that empires fall because of some default in their worship of the gods necessitated (for example) by fidelity to a single Christian God. Aeneas's speech, cited repeatedly, becomes a kind of refrain in this section of *De civitate Dei*. Augustine exposes Aeneas's legalistic logic as faulty, proving that pagan gods do not in fact reward good or punish bad faith but only flatter the fortunate and deceive the proud, fleeing one empire and supporting another because they are jet-setters, not jurists.[78] Indeed, empires fall *because* their moral fibre is weakened by dependence on false gods; in both Troy's and Rome's cases, 'cum uel sola esse potuerit causa pereundi custodes habere uoluisse perituros' [the only possible cause of destruction was the choice of such perishable defenders].[79] Apollo and Neptune, whose anger at Laomedon many blame for the fall of Troy, are themselves imposters who cannot even agree on which side to support once war breaks out; they certainly should not be trusted to sustain an empire.[80]

For Augustine, then, the gods' desertion of Troy cannot be attributed to infractions like the one committed by the stingy Laomedon against his divine employees: that would be to give the gods, quite literally, too much credit. Like Augustine, Chaucer evokes the pagan viewpoint, expressed by Calkas – whose wisdom is more suspect than ever upon returning to the *Troilus* from the *Aeneid* – that the spite of Apollo and Neptune has doomed Troy.[81] At the end of the poem, however, Chaucer revises this enduring pagan conception of the gods' revenge by advancing an enlightened Augustinian perspective that inverts the pagan concern over Laomedon's failure to 'payen [Phebus and Neptunus] here hire' (*Tr* 4.125) into a Christian reflection on the contemptible 'guerdoun for travaille' paid by 'rascaille' like Jove, Apollo, and Mars to the poor wretches who labour for *them* (5.1852–3). By this Augustinian logic, ironically, Laomedon was *right* to stiff Apollo and Neptune for their work, for as pagan gods they deserve no reverence.

In view of the broad literary contexts traced up to this point – Joseph of Exeter's politically ambivalent and propagandized Apollo, Virgil's absent Trojan protector, Augustine's vanquished betrayer of empires – Chaucer's delineation of Apollo at once as a submerged aspect of his Trojans' self-image *and* a force of unmitigated antagonism toward Troy emerges as clearer in design. By way of conclusion, then, this chapter traces some implications of the intertextuality of Chaucer's Apollo by returning in an exploratory spirit to the idea of *Troilus* as a belated prequel of the *Aeneid* – not, however, the *Aeneid* that ends with the notorious plunge of Aeneas's sword into Turnus's breast, but instead one capped by a fantasy 'thirteenth book' consisting of Augustine's account of the fall of Rome (which, as we have seen, correlates polemically with Troy's fall).[82] This composite epic, like Joseph's *Ylias*, is a tale of a twice-fallen, doubly sorrowed city, and its resolution is a roadmap for a city uncircumscribed by sorrow.

It is the last night of Troy's existence, before the Greeks' treachery is discovered: a time of giddy celebration, sweet slumber, and false security. The mutilated Deiphebus – a most gracious dinner party host in the *Troilus* – speaking later to Aeneas in the underworld reminds him 'ut supremam falsa inter gaudia noctem / egerimus' [how we spent that last night amid deluding joys] (*Aen.* 6.513–14). These are the joys of Chaucer's Troy before it is destroyed; they shimmer in the conviviality of Trojan society, the 'plesance and the joie' of high towers and grand halls, and the 'hevene blisse' of the bedroom (*Tr* 5.730–1, 3.1322). 'But al to litel, weylaway the whyle, / Lasteth swich joie,' and Troilus's safe haven is laid waste by bad news triggered by a downturn in the Trojans' military fortunes: 'The folk of Troie hemselven so mysledden [i.e., blundered *or* deceived themselves][83] / That with the worse at nyght homward they fledden' (*Tr* 4.1–2, 48–9). A group of Trojans – Polydamas, Monesteo, Santippe, Sarpedoun, Polynestore, Polite, Rupheo, 'and other lasse folk as Phebuseo' (*Tr* 4.54) – could not prevent the capture of Antenor, a circumstance that now makes advantageous Criseyde's exchange. Two of these warriors, Polite(s) and Rupheo (Ripheus), also appear in Troy's last battle in *Aeneid* 2; a third, Monesteo [Mnestheus], is mentioned at *Aen.* 4.288 and several other points. In Virgil's epic, Polites is slaughtered by Pyrrhus before the eyes of his father Priam as he crouches at a holy altar (*Aen.* 2.526–32), and Ripheus is among those soldiers who listen to Aeneas's 'deserted shrines' speech and follow him into futile battle, to be killed along with Panthus (2.339, 426–7). Phebuseo – who, as we have seen, Chaucer seems to have invented – is associated by end-rhyme with Rupheo, and this ghostly avatar of Apollo acts in league with a group of Trojan soldiers whose best efforts fail (in the *Troilus* as in the *Aeneid*). If Chaucer does intend us to think, if only in passing, of Apollo when he surprises us with the inclusion of Phebuseo, he may also invite us to trace a connection between the day's Trojan loss 'maugre' Phebuseo's exertion and the similar failure of 'what alle hire goddes may availle' in the 'Appollo' stanza of the epilogue (*Tr* 5.1850). Both passages strike an Ovidian vein of rhetoric that presents Apollo as perpetually too late, too far away, not powerful enough *despite* our expectation that he should be (a similar rhetoric is adopted by Phebus's crow in the *Manciple's Tale*, lines 249–52). Just as Rupheo and Phebuseo 'fail' Troy, so does Apollo.

It is, however, to the actions of Troilus that our look back – or, rather, forward – via Rupheo and Phebuseo to Troy's last night in *Aeneid* 2 ultimately directs us. Gazing at the shards of the only life he has known and seeing that the gods have deserted Troy, Aeneas advances the despairing counsel of false heroism: 'moriamur et in media arma ruamus' [Let us die, and rush into the midst of arms] (*Aen.* 2.353). This course of action, it is clear in the *Aeneid*, is wrong in every conceivable way: it denies the prophetic vision offered by Hector, neglects his familial responsibilities, and merely feeds the Greeks' annihilating flames with more Trojan flesh in the knowledge that nothing else can be accomplished. Yet this is precisely what Troilus determines to do once *he* receives ocular proof that 'al is lost that he hath ben aboute' (*Tr* 5.1645).[84] 'From hennesforth,' proclaims Troilus, 'as ferforth as I may, / Myn owen deth in armes wol I seche' (*Tr* 5.1717–18). Unlike Boccaccio's Troilo, who vows to seek out Diomede and fight to the death, Troilus approaches the battlefield as a suicide. Unlike Aeneas, Troilus will have no epiphany in this lifetime. He will not remember his family, recognize the design of the gods, or seek a way out; nothing will rise out of Troy's ashes. Whereas Mercury appears as a messenger-god to Aeneas in Dido's Carthage – another potential dead-end for Aeneas – to incite him toward his future mission, the same god approaches Troilus, who has already *reached* a dead-end, in his capacity as psychopomp. Mercury does not guide Troilus toward a new destiny that can salvage and ennoble his history, but calcifies him in a destiny that is both historically closed and obscured from our view: 'And forth he wente, shortly for to telle, / Ther as Mercurye sorted hym to dwelle' (*Tr* 5.1826–7). Troy's household gods are not preserved or redeemed but, in the *Troilus*'s third-to-last stanza, verbally pulverized – as if, when seeking out a new empire to deceive, they took a wrong turn into the domain of hagiography:

> Lo here, of payens corsed olde rites!
> Lo here, what alle hire goddes may availle . . .
> Lo here, the fyn and guerdoun for travaille
> Of Jove, Appollo, of Mars, of swich rascaille!   (*Tr* 5.1849–50, 1852–3)

Troy is denuded of its historical specificity and made an icon of any city – Rome, Carthage, London – that falls because of trust in 'false worldes brotelnesse' (*Tr* 5.1832), exemplified in this case by the brittle 'walles of [this] town' (4.121): walls that Apollo built, Troilus stood vigil at, and, in *Aeneid* 2, the Trojans themselves blindly tore down. The final geographic space of the *Troilus* is not any earthly realm predisposed to repeat Troy's mistakes but instead the 'holughnesse of the eighthe spere' (*Tr* 5.1809), where the temporality of Troilus's pagan world mystically converges with the narrator's Christian vision of Christ's love and humility, virtues that in the preface of *De civitate Dei* are said to 'soar above all the summits of this world, which sway in their temporal instability, overtopping them all with an eminence not arrogated by human pride, but granted by divine grace.'[85]

This abrupt Augustinian shift in scene at the end of the *Troilus* from Troy to the Heavenly City, and more cryptically from Mercury's opaque guidance to Christ's lucid reward, makes a harsh reality painfully clear: wherever Troilus's experience may have directed the narrator's heart – the narrator who has more than a little in common with the Augustine who once wept for Dido – Troilus himself got nowhere near this far. In Chaucer's fantasy Virgilian composite-epic, Aeneas's ability to imagine and create a new empire is tragically unfulfilled in Troilus, whose actions instead prefigure the bootless warfare associated with the shadowy Trojan Apollo lurking, as we have seen, behind the second book of the *Aeneid*. This Virgilian renovation *is*, however, in a sense undertaken by Criseyde, who elsewhere in the poem is intermittently and provocatively identified with male classical figures.[86] Criseyde, in the final account, shares with Aeneas a powerful instinct of survival as well as, for all her bluster, paternal obedience (*Tr* 5.193–4). Once she recognizes, in the Greek camp, the gravity of the threat to Troy, she, like Aeneas, becomes heedful of Apollo's oracle, even taking on a new lover, as does Aeneas in Latium, to stabilize her political circumstances. Yet Criseyde is hardly a heroic figure.[87] In fact, whereas the Virgilian vision of Aeneas seems to have been the strongest (counter-)influence on Chaucer's conception of Troilus as a warrior, the medieval view of Aeneas derived from Dares is more relevant to Criseyde – as it was, fittingly, to her father (see above, p. 131). Like the medieval Aeneas, Criseyde is a traitor as much as a survivor; her success in escaping the fate of other Trojan women, certain ruin or slavery, is framed as deceit – understandable, perhaps, under the circumstances, but nonetheless ignoble. Hers is a fame (like Dido's, in a neat intertextual twist) to be feared (*Tr* 5.1054–62; cf. *HF* 345–60), and her progeny will not seek the stars but curse their mother: 'And wommen moost wol haten me of alle./...Thei wol seyn, in as muche as in me is, / I have hem don deshonour, weylaway!' (*Tr* 5.1063, 1065–6) Chaucer does not, however, allow us to see Criseyde's wanderings any more than Troilus's eternal dwelling place. That enterprise would, of course, be left to Robert Henryson in the next century, who found licence to intervene in the poetic destinies of both Criseyde and Troilus by famously turning the questions of 'trouthe' raised by Chaucer's poem, considered at the beginning of this chapter, around on the poet himself.[88]

After sending his book on its own celestial journey and entrusting it to his intellectual peers for correction, Chaucer's last move in the *Troilus* is to dedicate his work to 'that sothfast Crist' both as an ideal reader and as a kind of fortifier of the heavenly city (*Tr* 5.1860). In so doing, Chaucer achieves closure for his poem both literally and figuratively, providing a resolutely Christian perspective on the inadequacy of the Trojan Apollo and the vulnerability of the city he built. Christ, as one who is '[u]ncircumscript, and al maist circumscrive' (*Tr* 5.1865), is evocatively associated in Chaucer's Dantean final stanza with the act of writing: to circumscribe, at its etymological core, is to 'write around.'[89] Part of the paradox contemplated in the poem's last stanza, therefore, is that Christ is unwritable, unable to be contained in writing ('uncircumscript'); and yet, as the Word, he lexically encompasses everything, encircling it like a palisade ('al maist circumscrive'). Indeed, Chaucer suggests in this most civically conscious of poems, Christ's words – and words founded in Christ – are a *wall* that circumscribes and civilizes the city of the text, forming a bulwark against 'visible and invisible foon,' rascally gods and lusty Greeks alike (*Tr* 5.1866). In effect, Christ is a builder of walls that bind and fortify the words of human poets, and his defence of these walls is the conceptual heart of the narrator's last prayer. Unlike the doomed walls that Apollo, pagan god of poetry, constructed for Troy, these walls can never be sabotaged; they are as intact as the undefiled body of Mary, 'mayde and moder thyn benigne' (*Tr* 3.1869).

For all the finality of this sequence, the end of *Troilus and Criseyde* is far from Chaucer's final word on the matter of Apollo; indeed, the hard-won conviction enjoyed here finds itself on less secure ground elsewhere in Chaucer's works. The remainder of this book delineates a contrasting trend toward irresolution, recidivism, and narrative crisis in Chaucer's later confrontations with Apollo in the *Canterbury Tales*, a trend first witnessed in the early *House of Fame*. Although the exigencies surrounding Apollo in the *Tales* are at important junctures poetically productive, they also haunt poetic identity and expression to a degree that Chaucer never again redresses as securely as at the end of the *Troilus*. Our concerns now shift from the classically charged world of Troy to the quotidian poetic realm of the *Canterbury Tales*. The following chapter explores Apollo's role in poetic self-construction and his agency in literary transmission at what is generally regarded as the centre-point of the story collection. In Fragment V of the *Tales*, two young male lover-poets – the Squire and the Franklin's Aurelius – call on Apollo for aid in fashioning themselves as makers of fiction, and Chaucer himself is drawn into the orbit of the god's contestable authority for future generations.

4 Fragmentary Apollo: The *Squire's Tale*, the *Franklin's Tale*, and Chaucerian Self-Fashioning

Everyone knows that the Miller, with his lecherous bagpipes and taste for smut, leads Chaucer's pilgrims out of Southwerk (*GP* 565–6). In fact, the Miller's physical position challenges the Knight's social and narrative position as leader well before Robyn usurps the Monk's place by 'quiting' the Crusade hero's tale. Chaucer's placement of this embodiment of entrepreneurial cunning and 'subjugated knowledge,' rather than a figurehead of monologic authority like the Knight,[1] at the head of the group evokes, for many readers, the poet's intimation of his concern with 'the unfixing of authoritarian judgement,' and hence the presiding spirit of 'game,' in the *Canterbury Tales* as a whole.[2] Indeed, the rival ordering schemes of the procession – narrative (Knight first) vs. physical (Miller first) – neatly introduces a tension, developed throughout the *Tales*, between competing forms of institutional discourse: in Bakhtinian language, between the '"eternal," "immovable," "absolute," "unchangeable"' truths of the chivalric ethos and the 'gay and free laughing aspect of the world, with its unfinished and open character, with the joy of change and renewal' that might be identified with the artisanal Miller.[3]

In privileging the Miller of the *General Prologue* in this way, and valuing the world of play and misrule which sets a pattern of requital and subversion within the game-world of the storytelling contest, Chaucer seems, in the beginning of his last great work, to invoke a very different kind of authority from the classical models of creation – 'olde thinges [that] ben in mynde' – to which he turned at the start of *Troilus and Criseyde* and the *Legend of Good Women* (*LGW* F 18). Despite the *Knight's Tale*'s appeals to traditional forms of authority and the *Parson's Tale* reinstatement of them at the end of the pilgrimage, recent critics have regarded the *Canterbury Tales* more as a heteroglossic text reflecting the carnivalesque spirit of the Miller than one engaged with classical models of poetic inspiration. By this reading, Chaucer in the *Tales* rejects what Bakhtin would describe as the 'authoritative word … located in a distanced zone, organically connected with a past that is felt to be hierarchically higher,' which 'is given (it sounds) in lofty spheres, not those of familiar contact. Its language is a special (as it were, hieratic) language.'[4] In this setting, Apollo, familiar haunt and arbiter of Chaucer's earlier poetry, would seem to be an unwelcome presence on the Canterbury pilgrimage.

It is all the more noteworthy, then, that William Blake, in his celebrated 1809 painting and subsequent engraving, *The Canterbury Pilgrims* (fig. 6), gives Apollo pride of place. First of all, Blake rejects the visual dimensions of Chaucer's narrative in favour of his rhetorical arrangement by portraying the Knight and Squire at the head of the pilgrimage and the Miller, nondescriptly, toward the rear.[5] More precisely, Blake positions the Squire who, we are told in the *General Prologue*, 'carf biforn his fader at the table' (*GP* 100), *first* in the procession, his rearing steed just outpacing his father's more sedate mount. Blake designs this arrangement out of the unconventional conviction that the Squire's character as a practising poet is superior to that of the Knight, containing 'the germ of perhaps greater perfection still, as he blends literature and the arts with his warlike studies.' Blake goes on, strikingly, to dub the Squire 'the Apollo' of the pilgrimage.[6] Blake's artistic portrayal of the blond, handsome Squire has indeed been regarded as 'Apollonian';[7] the red plumes of the beardless Squire's cap, in fact, recall medieval depictions of the sun's rays surrounding the blond head and smooth face of Apollo *auricomus*. Like the solar Apollo and his horse-drawn chariot, Blake's Squire, a figure of artistic illumination, rides closest to the rising sun.[8]

Blake's association of Chaucer's Squire with Apollo, while complicated by his own idiosyncratic mythology, registers the god's crucial importance to the textual debate concerning the function and perils of eloquence staged by the closely linked tales of the Squire and the Franklin. In this fragment, Apollo – heralded just as the *Squire's Tale* breaks off and invoked in a central prayer by the squire-figure Aurelius in the *Franklin's Tale* immediately subsequent – forms a mythological bridge between the Squire's and Franklin's conceptions of artistic identity. Fragment V, that is, replots Chaucer's poetic encounter with the poets of antiquity, epitomized by the *Troilus*, upon the social contest

Fig. 6 William Blake, *Chaucers Canterbury Pilgrims*. Engraving, 1810. McGill University Library. Lawrence Land William Blake Collection, Rare Books and Special Collections.

itself. Here, two 'modern' narrators differently appeal to the figure of Apollo to define their poetics in relation to textual authority. Their struggles in doing so suggestively underscore Chaucer's own confrontation with the unstable character of authoritative structures governed by Apollo which, as earlier chapters have shown, constitute the ill-fitting mantle of authorship. After exploring the link between Apollo and poetic inspiration in Fragment V, this chapter establishes its relevance to fifteenth- and early sixteenth-century mythologizations of Chaucer either as a font of Apolline inspiration or as an Apollo figure in his own right. This chapter turns, therefore, from the precedent of antiquity to the dynamics of literary reception, from the ancient formation of Apollo as a contested icon of authority – which we have already discerned, in the Chaucerian sphere, in the retrospective intertextuality of the *Troilus* – to a *forward* transmission of artistic identity and poetic praxis within the English vernacular, one that conceptually circulates around Chaucer's Apollo. In the tales considered here, Apollo's very fragmentariness invites reinscription; similarly, his failures of authority license assertions of authorship.

Because previous scholars have been more concerned with the literary relationship between the Knight and the Squire as an imaginative model of the 'infantilized' poetics of Chaucer's fifteenth-century followers,[9] the extent to which the literary debate regarding eloquence in the Franklin's and Squire's tales is reinscribed in later 'Chaucerian' poetry has been underestimated. Indeed, the terms of this debate were crucial to the conception of poetry in the Chaucerian style and to the new trends in authorial self-fashioning in the fifteenth century it helped shape. Attention to the rhetorical role of Apollo in Chaucer's poetics, then, also illuminates *Chaucerian* poetics, revealing an often surprising balance between Chaucer's critical awareness of his role as poet and his followers' mythologizing, reinvention, and usurpation of that pursuit.

Apollo in Fragments: Two Cruxes

The *Squire's Tale* breaks off in mid-course with the lines 'Appollo whirleth up his chaar so hye / Til that the god Mercurius hous, the slye –' (SqT 671–2).[10] The lovesick squire Aurelius in the *Franklin's Tale* invokes the sun as 'Appollo, god and governour / Of every plaunte, herbe, tree, and flour' (FranT 1031–2), and enjoins him and his sister Lucina together to submerge the hated rocks under a flood of water. These two moments stand alone in Chaucer's poetry as the only references to the solar body as

'Appollo' – as opposed to 'Phebus,' or simply 'the sonne' – and thus invite analysis as a pair.[11] Although it seems at first as if Aurelius invokes Apollo simply as the sun, his closing promise to make a pilgrimage to the temple of the Delphic 'Phebus' (*FranT* 1077–8), coupled with the provocative 'Ye may me helpen, save my lady, best' (1042) (because Apollo is sympathetic toward foolish young lovers, being one himself?), suggests that more is at stake here than simple meteorology.

Like Aurelius's prayer to Apollo, the final lines of the incomplete *Squire's Tale* raise several questions. Why does Chaucer atypically compel us to recall the non-astrological character of Mercury ('the slye') in the midst of an astrological periphrasis,[12] and does such mythological anthropomorphization imbue his unusual reference to 'Appollo' as well? Does the exuberant conjunction of Apollo, god of poetry, with his brother, god of rhetoric, pertain figuratively, as some critics have suggested, to the poem's abrupt termination? The critical impasse regarding the state of completion of the *Squire's Tale* (which centres, for obvious reasons, on the significance of this final couplet) is stubbornly shaped by antithetical understandings of the tale's quality: those who find the tale unsatisfying, strained, or dull believe it satirizes the Squire's narrative capacities and the superficialities of his *General Prologue* portrait, which, they argue, cause the exasperated Franklin to interrupt. Those who find the tale serious, unironic, and even innovative, endorse the opinions of the tale's early scribes and readers that it is genuinely unfinished, and that the Franklin link – which praises rather than denigrates, and does not suggest interruption – was designed to follow upon the *complete* tale (either lost or never executed). This chapter does not attempt to resolve this debate, or to review in any depth its critical history,[13] but isolates an assumption that has informed most defences of the 'interruption theory': that the *Squire's Tale* is a failed spectacle of poetic ambition or pretension, and that the ascendant Apollo of the final couplet dramatizes the certainty of its collapse. My reading of Fragment V and its influence proceeds from the unconventional view that the *Franklin's Tale*, which shares with the *Squire's Tale* a self-conscious concern with rhetoric and poetic ambition, ignores the Squire's actual *caution* toward 'high style' and the fantastical, instead indulging in a cult of poetic feigning in the service of cultured eloquence ostensibly based on the Squire's example. The crucial point in what I shall argue is indeed the Franklin's interruption is not the literary merit of the Squire and his tale, but the Franklin's reading, absorption, and rewriting of the Squire and his tale. Specifically,

the Franklin interprets the last two lines of the *Squire's Tale* as an image
of poetic ambition that he associates with the Squire despite the court-
ier's own qualification of such an image, and identifies this with his
squire Aurelius, whose prayer to Apollo reinforces the god's association with literary privilege. This, we shall see, is an ideal of courtly
learning and rhetoric to which the Franklin and the poets who write in
his wake aspire.

'Appollo whirleth up his chaar so hye': The *Squire's Tale* and Poetic Ambition

The Squire, as the only poet (besides Chaucer) on the Canterbury pilgrimage, 'koude songes make and wel endite' [*GP* 95–6]). His tale's narrative progress, however, is impeded and ultimately halted by a
self-reflective, even self-defeating fascination with the process of its
own creation.[14] The same thickly 'poetic' quality that led Milton to
group Chaucer with the *vates* Musaeus and Orpheus in *Il Penseroso* on
the basis of the *Squire's Tale* has seemed to twentieth-century critics ineffective, pretentious, or parodic.[15] The Franklin shares with the Squire
an intense concern, especially in his prologue, with poetic self-definition, colours of rhetoric, and astrological ornamentation associated
with high style. These concerns unify Fragment V, along with a preoccupation with magic and illusion, the genre of romance, and setting
in the pagan world (first contemporary, then ancient).[16] It is a commonplace, especially among those who assume that the Franklin interrupts
the Squire because of his tale's quality, to speak of the Squire's lofty
poetic ambitions and his tale as evidence of their failure, or, to put it
more courteously, as the 'poem of a young man, enchanted by excess,
and lacking in mature judgment.'[17] In point of fact, the ironic readings
that have dominated criticism of the *Squire's Tale* in the last fifty years
have, in exposing the narrative 'mess' of the tale, rendered it entirely
too tidy.

It is a testament to the peculiar power of the *Squire's Tale* that such
readings are prone to the very rhetorical excess that they critique. An
eclectic, if broadly representative, overview of critical opinion on the
Squire's ambition serves as an illustration. In an influential early essay
that set the stage for later dramatic readings, Marie Neville argued that
the Squire attempts to 'outdo' his father's rhetorical manoeuvrings by
augmenting certain aspects of the Theban tale, but finds himself 'out of
his depth.'[18] To Robert S. Haller, the Squire embellishes his tale with

rhetorical devices merely to show that he can use them (unlike the Knight, who uses such devices 'decorously'), and in doing so produces an incoherent story.[19] In Joyce E. Peterson's view, the Squire's shallow, or 'trivial,' poetic style – again, opposed to the 'proper perspective on courtliness' of the *Knight's Tale* – reveals the real subject of the tale to be its teller's moral corruption.[20] Jean E. Jost claims that the Squire, lacking his father's rhetorical 'honesty,' views the power of language idealistically but is 'oblivious to the fact of his narrative's failure.'[21] Robert P. Miller brings such readings of the Squire's unsuccessful 'high style' to bear upon the final couplet of the tale, in which 'the Squire is left dangling, like Apollo, in the middle of a "hye" figure'; elsewhere, the same author proposes that the couplet's conjunction of Apollo and Mercury alludes to the congruence of Wisdom and Eloquence in Martianus Capella's *De nuptiis*, and that the collapse of the tale on this note confirms that the Squire lacks both of these qualities.[22] This conjunction of Apolline 'poetic inspiration' and Mercurial 'eloquence' also impresses A.C. Spearing, who views it as emblematic of the *Squire's Tale*'s strained high style, thankfully exploded by the Franklin's interruption, 'as if Apollo has been shot down by a ground-to-air missile.'[23] Spearing might more aptly have chosen an archaic image, such as a lightning bolt, for it is with the myth of Jove's shooting down of the out-of-control Phaethon – the 'sonnes sone' (*HF* 941) who tried to drive his father's chariot – that these insistences on the Squire's poetic ambition culminate, in Dolores Warwick Frese's astrological reading of the *Canterbury Tales*.[24] Here, a critical assumption that has gone largely unquestioned, but has been much inflated, since Neville first advanced it – that the Squire, like Phaethon, an 'ambitious, but ungovernable' son,[25] immoderately attempts to surpass his father and brings upon himself utter disaster – has been ingeniously mythologized. Unfortunately, critical ingenuity has come to supplant careful reading of the tale itself and engagement with its own quietly sustained mythology.

The now-orthodox view of the Squire as arrogant, rhetorically over-inflated, fulsome, and inept is based upon three phenomena: first, a forced discernment of irony in certain key passages in the tale; second, an inherited obtuseness toward the Squire's real interests and intentions in telling his tale; and third, a characteristically modern distaste for rhetoric and 'high style.' In order to place the final couplet accurately within larger concerns regarding antiquity, authority, and the construction of the poetic self in Fragment V (and Chaucerian poetry), these issues must first be addressed.

As all critics have noticed, the Squire, like his father, frequently disclaims his own poetic ability by means of the modesty topos, the inexpressibility topos, and *occupatio*. Unlike his father, he often intends these passages to be taken straightforwardly, actually *not* describing Canacee's beauty because he feels unable to, rather than 'saying something while not saying it.' Critics have seen this either as a clever parody of rhetorical conventions on Chaucer's part or as a dramatic revelation of the Squire's supposed incompetence and preoccupation with the surface level of narrative. However, a fresh reading of these rhetorical passages fails so drastically to support the argument for ironic exposure of the Squire that a very different interpretation of the tale seems better justified: namely, that the Squire, far from following in Phaethon's footsteps, distances himself throughout the tale from images of poetic ambition or proficiency.

Two passages frequently taken as evidence of the Squire's pretension serve as illustration: the introduction of the knight-emissary's speech (*SqT* 89–109), which seems to encode a recognition of the rhetorical success of his father, the Knight, and the *occupatio* concerning the 'forme of daunces' at Cambyuskan's court (283–8). In these passages, the Squire suggests that his Eastern romance surpasses in spectacle the best of the Arthurian world: the knight's courteous speech and bearing exceed Gawain's, and no one but Lancelot, who 'is deed,' could describe the 'subtil lookyng and dissymulynges' of the dancers (287, 285). The ambivalence of the Squire's perspective is easy enough to grasp: while ennobling his material through association with an Arthurian lineage, he simultaneously dismisses Arthurian romance as something that is 'olde' (95) 'deed,' and inaccessible. 'Therfore,' says the Squire, 'I passe of al this lustiheed' (288). The gist of these two passages is: 'Since I lack the skills (and, in the second case, the interests) of these Arthurian paragons, I will have to abridge my description.' However, critics intent upon reading the tale ironically as an exposé of its teller insist that there is an 'implicit comparison between [the Squire] and Lancelot' which 'gives to the Squire's assumed modesty more than a tinge of fatuously admiring self-regard.'[26] Further,

The Squire, by alluding to these figures [i.e., the Arthurian heroes], is indicating that he acts and speaks in their image. Although he claims to be unable to come up to their perfections and will not attempt to describe those matters which are peculiarly their province, the rhetorical effect of the allusions is to make the reader identify the Squire with these knights

... The Squire wishes to be thought of as equaling Gawain in 'olde curtei-sye' and Lancelot in 'lustiheed.'[27]

If the Squire truly had felt himself not up to the task of telling his tale, such critics continue, 'he would not have plunged forward [like Phaethon!] with such headlong daring, such unrestrained recklessness ... If he actually believes the scene to be indescribable, he holds a mental reservation for himself.'[28] Despite the psychological licence taken by many critics in their readings of these Arthurian allusions, the fact remains that the Squire shows no hint of disingenuity: true to his word, he does *not* go on to describe the dance.

It need hardly be said that if all comparison were synonymous with equation, and all *occupatio* replaced by silence, our understanding of what little of Chaucer's works that would remain would surely be impoverished. Shortly before the Lancelot passage is another that has produced similarly strained readings: here, the Squire refrains from describing the revelry of the dance because anyone making the attempt 'moste han knowen love and his servyse / And been a feestlych man as fressh as May' (280–1). These lines, of course, closely echo both the language and the sense of the Squire's *General Prologue* portrait. Many have taken this correspondence as proof that the Squire's modesty regarding his poetic ability is disingenuous, since he disclaims an ability that we have already been informed he possesses. This is a neat and attractive theory – indeed, *too* neat and attractive – and a troublingly bold pronouncement upon a tale whose textual status is extremely uncertain and which, by all indication, lacks revision.[29] If a deliberate allusion to the *General Prologue* description of the Squire is intended in these lines, the least critically violent inference is that the Squire's denial of poetic and amatory skills that elsewhere we have been assured he possesses is a modest rather than a disingenuous gesture.[30] This interpretation accords perfectly with the interchange between the Host and the modest Squire in the Introduction to the tale, all but impossible to read ironically, in which the Squire shrinks from the supposition that he can 'sey somwhat of love,' promising simply to 'seye as I kan / With hertly wyl' (2, 4–5). The *General Prologue*, after all, presents the Squire not only as a lover and a poet but a respectful son who knows his 'lowely, and servysable' place (GP 99). Rather than mobilizing irony because, in disavowing rhetorical skill, the Squire often uses it (e.g., the *traductio* of lines 105–6), these moments make most sense as appreciative tributes to those who *are* rhetorically expert. In this light, the Squire's admiring presentation of the knightly messenger, most naturally read as an image of respect for his father the Knight as storyteller rather than an unmotivated attempt to outmatch him, suggests a self-presentation as 'lowely,' not 'hye' like Apollo's flight in the final couplet – indeed, one that is antithetical to Phaethon's failed attempt to drive his father's luminous chariot.

The problem of genre circumscribes the 'Phaethonic' readings the *Squire's Tale* has invited. Gardiner Stillwell, the progenitor of twentieth-century ironic interpretations of the *Squire's Tale*, decries the spirit of scientific realism that disrupts and undercuts the 'wide-eyed *naïveté* and quaint curiosity required by [the Squire's] theme,' and prevents it from 'achieving a uniformly romantic tone.'[31] Indeed, interpretations of the *Squire's Tale* run into problems – and, frequently, seek solace in irony – precisely where the *Squire's Tale* parts ways with the 'tapestry world' and 'wonderland' of magic and fantasy typical of romance,[32] and engages with historical and scientific realities.[33] In fact, the very circumlocutions and digressions that stall the tale's development – including, crucially, the astrological periphrases – cohere around a concern with rational and scientific inquiry. The Squire's main interest in Part One is the description of the gifts and their technological powers, not the details of courtly feasting or characterization of the members of Cambyuskan's family. Part Two begins on a note of exhilaration with the vocabulary of medical science and dream theory, widely regarded as an instance of fatuous poetic self-indulgence on the Squire's part but consistent with his enthusiasm for rational detail throughout the tale. Rhetorical style is also implicated in the scientific spirit of the tale, which contains the most astrological detail of any in the Canterbury collection.[34] Powered by a narrator more interested in tracing the motions of the sun than the thoughts and motivations of his characters, the tale incorporates four separate astrological periphrases (47–51, 263–5, 385–7, 671–2) and interlaces the motions of the sun, constellations, and stars with those of his characters (especially 263–7 and 384–7) in a way that positively encourages arguments for astrological allegory.[35]

These 'rational digressions,' then, are primarily outlets for the Squire's intellectual interests rather than failed attempts to flaunt his poetic ability, lifting him out of the idealized, conventionally romantic world of his *General Prologue* portrait into a scientific milieu in which Chaucer, whose autobiographic connections with the Squire run deep, was himself associated as translator of the *Treatise on the Astrolabe*.[36] The tale is an anti-romance in the sense that it embodies the Squire's challenge, rather than adoption, of romance naivety; as with the 'dreem of which ther nys no charge' (359) of the revellers, the Squire declines to narrate the details of ungrounded fantasy. It is, as one critic has claimed, an 'experimental tale of science fiction.'[37]

The celestial 'hye' of the final couplet, then, invites evaluation in light of the Squire's attitude toward rhetorical prowess in a way that is responsible to the tale's discursive constitution rather than the mythologies of critical hegemony. The Squire's development of imagery of elevation before the end of the tale offers a context for the propulsive force of Apollo in the final couplet; at the same time, it draws on a venerable tradition of caution toward physical or imaginary flight – of which Apollo's fiery chariot is one model – as a metaphor of artistic ambition and visionary perspective.[38] The Squire is indeed concerned with poetic ambition, but his tale's vocabulary of elevation shows him to be both conscious and wary of the dangers of rhetorical prowess, linked imagistically with height well before the end of the *Squire's Tale*. The prospect of describing Canacee's beauty, for example, is 'so *heigh* a thyng' that it should only be undertaken by a 'rethor excellent,' but the Squire retreats from such associations: 'I am noon swich, I moot speke as I kan' (36–41).[39] A *rime riche* similarly evokes effective rhetoric's *highness*, adding a physical image of its forbidding elevation: 'Al be that I kan nat sowne his stile, / Ne kan nat clymben over so *heigh* a style' (105–6).[40]

Rhetorical expertise, to the Squire, is not only a difficult and highly selective enterprise, but a potentially dangerous one, vulnerable to abuse and deceit. Its perils are dramatized in the falcon's description of the tercelet, a perverted reprise of the messenger in Part One, whom she meets 'ful *hye* under the sky' (503) and by whose verbal presentation she is deceived.[41] To the falcon, the heights of the sky represent the realm of desire, vulnerability, and deceit into which she was thrust after the sheltered period of her flightless youth 'in a roche of marbul gray' (500): 'I nyste nat what was adversitee / Til I koude flee ful *hye* under the sky' (502–3). It is 'over hire heed ful *hye*' (411) that Canacee finds the falcon lamenting, and her pitiful fall to the earth restores her to a realm of compassion, guileless communication (evoked in the transparency of language facilitated by Canacee's ring),[42] and natal shelter (the 'mewe' prepared by Canacee).

At the same time, the *Squire's Tale* contemplates the control and rechannelling of the thrilling dangers associated with the falcon's high flight in its description of the mechanical steed of brass given to Cambyuskan, which carries its riders 'hye in the air' (122). The steed protects its rider from both terrestrial and celestial peril – the former in the projection of Algarsif's winning of Theodora with the steed's help (663–6) and the latter in the messenger's description of the steed's capacity to carry the rider who has mastered the art of its operation '[w]her-so yow lyst, in droghte or elles shoures, / … Withouten wem of yow, thurgh foul or fair; / … Withouten harm, til ye be ther yow leste' (118, 121, 125). Indeed, the flying steed, which is compared with an 'egle' (123), promises a technological triumph over the 'adversitee' that for the falcon characterized flight 'hye under the sky.' It makes possible the natural but frequently compromised coordination of 'youre body' with 'youre herte' (119–20) – the disjunction of which undermines the tercelet's 'hewe of trouthe' (508) – to exert mastery over nature and human limitation.

If the optimistic art represented by the brass steed suggests a thematic continuity between the two intact parts of the tale, it also reflects upon the purely rhetorical commencement of the third. The golden steed, admired as 'so *heigh* … and so brood and long' (191) and granted astrological significance in its shining 'as sonne brighte' (170) and its travels 'in the space of o day natureel' (116), provides a counterimage of the 'hye' Apolline sun of the final couplet.[43] The skill required by the brass steed as flying chariot in effect insulates it from Phaethonic abuse, securing even its very mobility from those who 'kan nat the craft' (185), just as the *stile* of eloquence bars the unskilled from entry into the world of inspired poetry. As a Pegasus for the Squire's modern world, the 'magic' steed, in association with the ascendant Apollo, resituates poetic inspiration not in superstitious 'fantasies' or 'olde poetries' recklessly executed (205–6), but in a new, rationally informed art based in 'craft.' If the 'hye' path of Apollo freezes in suspension an important preoccupation of the Squire, it hardly leaves him as an ambitious rhetor eager to soar the heights. The solar 'Phebus,' subsumed by the poetic 'Appollo' in the last couplet, may well evoke Phaethonic artistic ambition such as that associated with Icarus in the *House of Fame*, who flew 'so *highe* that the hete / Hys wynges malt' (*HF* 921). It is an ambition, however, with which the Squire, like Geffrey in his ascent to the House of Fame, does *not* identify himself.

'[S]wiche colours as growen in the mede' (*FranT* 724): The Franklin, the Squire, and Poetic Authority

Does the Franklin, then, 'shoot down' the Squire? The manuscript evidence suggests that scribes, unlike most modern scholars, did not think so: five MSS contain scribal comments to the effect that Chaucer 'made no more' of the *Squire's Tale*; the Ellesmere MS leaves the rest of the page blank after line 672, as if hoping that more text would be found; and other MSS provide superficial closure by suppressing lines 671–2 (thus disguising the tale's incompletion) or, less commonly, adding a spurious promise in the Squire's voice that the tale will be resumed on the return journey.[44] No MS calls attention to the Franklin's words to the Squire as an interruption, as does occur with the endings of the *Monk's Tale* and *Sir Thopas*.[45] Nor do any of the early printed editions imply interruption in their presentation of the text, and from Caxton's second printing (1484) onward editorial comment indicates the tale's unfinished state.[46] Scribal opinion is an imperfect reflection of Chaucer's intentions, however, and internal evidence drawn from the pattern of Chaucer's other interrupted tales supports the theory that the Franklin does indeed intervene at line 672. Like *Sir Thopas*, the *Squire's Tale* breaks off early in its third section and ends in mid-sentence at a similar grammatical point ('Til on a day' [*Th* 918]; 'Til that the god Mercurius hous, the slye' [*SqT* 672]).[47] Whereas Chaucer's genuinely unfinished narratives (*House of Fame*, *Anelida*, and *Cook's Tale*) end with scant suggestion of what is immediately to follow, the *Squire's Tale*, which projects at length and in detail the remaining threads of its ambitious plot just before its termination,[48] is most like the interrupted *Sir Thopas*, which shortly before the Host's intervention promises 'anon' a 'spelle; / Of bataille and of chivalry, / And of ladyes love-drury' (896, 893–5), much as the Squire heralds 'aventures and ... batailles' (659) and a resolution of the love story begun in Part Two, along with two additional wooings.

That the Franklin discreetly interrupts to prevent the Squire from telling any more of a bad tale – in which case the *Squire's Tale* must be read as parody of the genre of romance or ironic exposure of the Squire as narrator – is not an inevitable conclusion. Instead of taking the complimentary tone of the Franklin's words to the Squire as evidence that Chaucer intended the Franklin's praise as a comment on a finished tale (either lost or never completed) rather than an interruption, as some critics have,[49] it is advantageous to move beyond an all-or-nothing approach to the Franklin's response to the Squire to consider why the Franklin might *both* admire and cut short the Squire's narrative. Length – as distinct from literary quality – is the issue most immediately at hand at the point of the tale's termination (which follows closely upon the Squire's projection of a very lengthy remainder), just as in the Knight's initial objection to the *Monk's Tale*: '"Hoo!" quod the Knyght, "good sire, namoore of this! / That ye han seyd is right ynough, ywis,

/ And muchel moore"' (*NPProl* 2767–9).[50] The *Franklin's Tale*, true to its genre, is tightly constructed, imagistically concentrated, and relatively short; as such, it indicates the Franklin's literary tastes and suggests why he may have lost patience with the Squire's sprawling romance, even had he admired it – or, at least, felt the duty to admire it as an enthusiast for all things *gentil*.[51] Not only are the Franklin's tact, praise, and conversational geniality appropriate to a suave intervention in the over-long discourse of a social superior, but they are consistent with the spirit of complimentary emulation with which the Franklin 'quits' the *Squire's Tale* in his own romance. In a sea of insult and one-upping, the Franklin stands alone in the *Canterbury Tales* in positively extending, rather than subverting or mocking, his predecessor's tale;[52] we should not object, then, that his interruption of that tale is no more like the other interruptions.

By acknowledging the ambivalence of the Franklin's response to the *Squire's Tale*, which his commendatory interruption dramatizes and his intervention in the midst of Apollo's cosmological progress encodes, we can begin to evaluate the Franklin's appropriation of the Squire's textual authority, an appropriation that later provides a model for the equally commendatory (and implicitly competitive) 'intervention' into Chaucer's oeuvre by fifteenth- and sixteenth-century poets. The Franklin establishes a parallel between Aurelius and the Squire that both subjects them to and equates them with Apollo as squire figures, lovers, and poets; at the same time, as we shall see, the Franklin maps his own poetic ambitions upon the Apolline cosmography to which his tale creatively responds.

As Martin Stevens has astutely observed, Chaucer's interruptions reveal more about the tales in question than poor quality: they playfully imply that 'what [the interruptors] found unbearable is, in the mind of the poet Chaucer, really intended to be given critical attention, and at some more remote level intellectual approval by the reader, who is the ultimate judge.'[53] Chaucer's interruptions, in fact, reflect more profoundly upon the interruptor than the interrupted, as the Knight's nervous interruption of the Monk's unbroken record of aristocratic tragedies attests. The Franklin's intervention in the *Squire's Tale* is no exception. In every other instance in the *Canterbury Tales* in which two tales, like the Squire's and the Franklin's, are dramatically situated in relation to each other – particularly when volunteered, usually in a spirit of 'quiting,' rather than commissioned by the Host (i.e., *MilT/RvT, FrT/SumT, ClT/MerT*) – Chaucer draws attention to the second tale's limited or perverse rescripting of the first. The Franklin, consistent with this pattern, wilfully misinterprets the *Squire's Tale*: in praising the Squire for his 'eloquence' and 'gentil' speech, the Franklin isolates the image of Apolline poetic ascendancy left hanging in the Squire's last couplet, plotting the first coordinate on a map of misreading that extends into twentieth-century criticism. The Franklin's intrusion at this moment magnifies what for him is the most salient aspect of the Squire's narration: *eloquence* as an aristocratic ideal.[54] Because the Franklin aspires to this ideal, he indulges it in his own poetic self-presentation and his creation of the squire Aurelius.

Like the Squire, the Franklin ostensibly distances himself from all claims to rhetorical prowess. Unlike the Squire, he is insincere. The Franklin's opening profession of poetic inexperience is conspicuously based on a passage from Persius's *Satires* (*FranProl* 721–2), and his contrast between rhetorical and natural colours ('Colours ne knowe I none, withouten drede, / But swich colours as growen in the mede' [723–4]) employs a *traductio* considerably more brazen than the Squire's *stile/style* rime riche. Furthermore, the Franklin's *traductio* works against itself by inviting association with rhetorical manuals' fondness for analogy between these two kinds of colours, as in Geoffrey of Vinsauf's injunction to 'let the mind's finger pluck its blooms in the field of rhetoric,' an association current as late as Henry Peacham's rhetorical treatise, the *Garden of Eloquence* (1577, revised 1593).[55] Further reinforcing the artificiality of the Franklin's profession of modesty is the noteworthy fact that in the *Franklin's Tale*, Apollo, god of poetry, is also god of the very flowers that 'growen in the mede,' as Aurelius's prayer to 'Appollo, god and governour / Of every plaunte, herbe, tree, and flour' (1031–2) reveals. The Franklin's self-styling as a 'natural man' in contrast, he implies, with experienced poets like the Squire, can therefore hardly be taken at face value, but instead must be regarded as part of a strategic appropriation of textual authority.[56]

The flowers of poetic style also place the Franklin as (disingenuous) poet in relation to the squire Aurelius, the tale's resident love poet, who 'fressher was and jolyer of array, / As to my doom, than is the month of May' (*FranT* 927–8), in turn reflecting the *General Prologue* portrait of the Squire, 'Embrouded ... as it were a meede / Al ful of fresshe floures ... / He was as fressh as is the month of May' (*GP* 89–90, 92).[57] Such an image in fact evokes one vein of medieval iconography of Apollo, represented by an illustration of Sol in a fifteenth-century manuscript of John de Foxton's *Liber cosmographiae* (fig. 7), which portrays the god

Fig. 7 Sol in a flowered tunic. John de Foxton, *Liber cosmographiae*. English, 1408. Cambridge, Trinity College MS R.15.21, fol. 35v. Courtesy of the Master and Fellows of Trinity College Cambridge.

as a young man wearing a short, flower-embroidered, wide-sleeved garment much like that of the Squire in *GP* 89–93. The recollection by Aurelius's brother of the ability of 'subtile tregetoures' to make 'floures sprynge as in a mede' introduces the all-important power of illusion to the events of the tale (*FranT* 1141, 1147). The world of romance and the rhetoric of illusion thus shape the Franklin's narrative outlook in ways that associate poetic composition with both Apollo and artifice.

Whereas the *Squire's Tale* rationalizes the 'magic' gifts within the sphere of the intelligible, adopting an essentially technological attitude toward poetic art, the *Franklin's Tale* conflates poetic creation with illusion and appearance. In so doing, the *Franklin's Tale* associates the squire Aurelius as well as the clerk of Orleans with 'the power and peril of illusion-making within poetic fiction,'[58] a concern that radiates outward from the prayer to Apollo near the midpoint of the tale, itself a reprise, I will argue, of the ending of the *Squire's Tale*. If the *Franklin's Tale* lacks the distracting narrative self-consciousness of the *Squire's Tale*, with which it shares a thick rhetorical ornamentation and astrological embellishment, it embeds concerns with artistic creation more subtly: in the capacity of the clerk 'to maken illusioun' (1264); in the textual associations of the remembered 'book,' whose physicality is emphasized, that leads Aurelius and his brother to seek the clerk's aid; and in the romance-like series of illusions summoned by the clerk 'in his studie, ther as his bookes be' (1207).[59] As, in V.A. Kolve's words, a 'figure of power, authority and mystery, a man *capable* [of] creating convincing illusion,'[60] the clerk of Orleans is a kind of Apollo figure, a centre of creative authority. The marvellous illusions with which the clerk entertains Aurelius and his brother in his book-filled study in fact resonate evocatively with an image of Apollo Medicus in an illustrated fifteenth-century English medical manuscript, London, British Library Sloane MS 6 (fig. 8), the first in a series of miniatures depicting the descent of the medical art from Apollo through Aesculapius, Asclepius, Hippocrates, and Galen.[61] This image portrays Apollo, in a study, prominently holding a cryptically inscribed book of medical art as he uses 'chermez & ynchantementez' (so the caption) to heal three men who, with eyes closed, appear to be levitating in a trance opposite Apollo. The powers of curative control over body and mind dramatized in this image, centred upon an authoritative book, evoke the therapeutic vision summoned in the clerk of Orleans's study. Likewise, the morally suspect association of medical charms with a pagan god recalls the Franklin's condemnation of the clerk's 'supersticious cursednesse' (*FranT* 1272).[62]

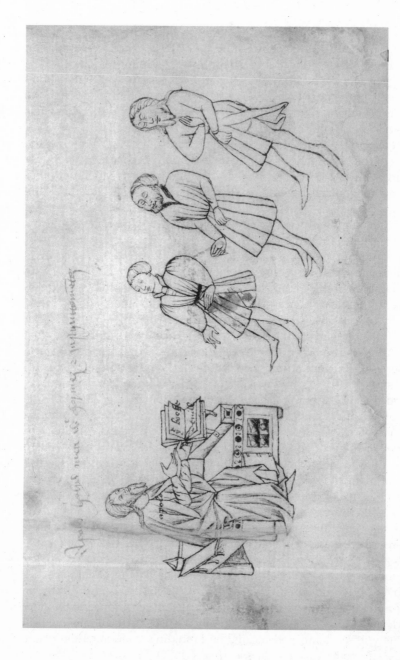

Fig. 8 Apollo Medicus healing three men in a trance. John of Arderne, medical treatise. English, second quarter of fifteenth century. © The British Library Board. All Rights Reserved. London, Brit. Lib. MS Sloane 6, fol. 175r.

The enchanted patients in the medical image also recall the 'traunce' (1081) into which Aurelius falls earlier in the tale after praying to Apollo. Aurelius, who suffers from a medically acute form of lovesickness ('He seeth he may nat fro his deeth asterte; / Hym semed that he felte his herte colde'), approaches Apollo, after all, for medical aid as much as meteorological assistance (1022–3; cf. 1111–15). No wonder, then, that Aurelius presents himself as supplicant to 'Appollo, god and governour / Of every plaunte, herbe, tree, and flour' (1031–2) – details otherwise irrelevant to his request for aid, but consistent with descriptions of Apollo Medicus. Henry of Huntingdon, for example, invokes Apollo as 'Vatum magne parens, herbarum ... repertor' [mighty father of bards and finder of herbs], and Chaucer himself refers in the *Troilus* to Apollo's '[r]emedye and reed, by herbes he knew fyne' (*Tr* 1.661).[63] In this tale in which the pagan gods are little more than unresponsive involucra of a (latently Christian) divine order, the clerk of Orleans usurps Apollo's role by becoming the true healer of Aurelius, the artist and poet-figure whose imaginary creations – in contrast to Aurelius's wasted 'songes, compleintes, roundels, virelayes' (948) – carry the authority truly to effect change, both over the visible world and Aurelius's ailing psyche.

The Failure of Invocation and the Poetics of Illusion

Such authority is an object of intense desire to the Franklin, who is a kind of surrogate of the clerk of Orleans: a householder who ensures that his guests 'lakked no vitaille' (*FranT* 1186; cf. *GP* 339–54) and a fellow creator of fictions.[64] Although the Franklin disapproves of the pagan clerk's indulgence of magic, his supposed ignorance of 'termes of astrologye' (1266), like his claim to be unschooled in rhetoric, is belied by his obvious technical familiarity with the art in lines 1273–91.[65] The *Franklin's Tale* itself has been seen as a 'cleverly concocted illusion' through which the Franklin rhetorically asserts himself within the privileged male discursive order to which he aspires.[66] This imaginative bond connecting rhetoric, art, and illusion, poet and magus, exposes the tale's reflection on itself as poetry, along with its assimilation and revision of the Squire's Apollo. In his very profession (itself allusive) never to have slept on Mount Parnassus, the Franklin introduces a classicizing vocabulary of inspiration to the tale's discourse, much as Chaucer's refusal of the laurel in the *House of Fame* styles him a conscious contributor to the poetic history of laureation. The poet Aurelius's prayer to Apollo, which is a kind of invocation, advances, we shall see shortly, this concern with poetic inspiration, and the tale's most noted astrological *chronographia*, which occurs just before Aurelius's prayer in the voice of the Franklin, reinforces it. As a gently ironic preface to Aurelius's prayer to the solar Apollo,[67] the Franklin relates the sun's setting in language that commonsensibly undercuts a swell of rhetorical ornament:

> Til that the brighte sonne loste his hewe;
> For th'orisonte hath reft the sonne his light –
> This is as much to seye as it was nyght –   (1016–18)[68]

That we have here in the Franklin's voice a self-aborted astrological periphrasis involving the motion of the sun, named 'Appollo' a few lines later, further supports the theory that the Franklin interrupts the Squire's similar periphrasis.[69] It also confirms the relevance of the last couplet of the *Squire's Tale* both to Aurelius's following prayer to Apollo and, more broadly, the Franklin's shaping of his 'poetic' voice in relation to the Squire's.

The Franklin's comic self-deflation, as has long been noted, is modelled on a (prose) line from the general prologue of Fulgentius's *Mitologiae* that tartly caps an ornate fourteen-line poetic periphrasis on the setting of the sun: 'et, ut in uerba paucissima conferam, nox erat' [And, as I can state in very few words, it was night].[70] The larger context of Fulgentius's line also bears importantly upon the Franklin's self-conception as poet.[71] This section of Fulgentius's Prologue dramatizes the exegete's rhetorical struggle for interpretive control of his own material; rather than defying the seductions of Calliope through rational allegoresis of pagan myth, Fulgentius succumbs, despite himself, to the pleasures of lying poetic ornament like an 'insanus uates' [frenzied bard]. Like the Franklin, Fulgentius fails to sustain a position of moral superiority over pagan story and rhetoric.[72] Before the astrological periphrasis in Fulgentius's Prologue is broken off with the abrupt words that the Franklin echoes, Fulgentius imagines a nighttime scene involving the motions of the sun, Phoebus, and *soror* Luna, details that will, in turn, resurface in Aurelius's address to the divine siblings in his prayer. The allure of pagan *fabula* reaches a climax at the end of Fulgentius's periphrasis in language of particular point to the *Franklin's Tale*, which describes the illusions [*simulacra*] that deceive the mind with 'falsidicis ... signis' [lying images]. This precedent for the *Franklin's Tale*'s central preoccupation with illusion, then, simultaneously links the dangers of appearance with the action of rhetoric, the ambition of the *vates*, and the solar activity of Apollo, further highlighting the contiguity between poet and magus.

The invocation of Apollo with which this Fulgentian section of the *Franklin's Tale* culminates is no less than the Franklin's answer to the *Squire's Tale*. The squire Aurelius is the Franklin's imaginative revivification of the Squire, whose fiction he usurped, and his prayer, as a sustained cosmological monologue, crucially glosses the Franklin's reading of the *Squire's Tale* in two respects. First, it reveals that the Franklin's squire, as an immature and somewhat frivolous lover, is closer in spirit to the idealized 'lovyere and … lusty bacheler' of the *General Prologue* (80) than to the more complexly intellectual Squire who tells the tale of Cambyuskan, as the several echoes of the Squire's *General Prologue* portrait in the *Franklin's Tale* confirm. Second, despite this difference in characterization, Aurelius's invocation of Apollo bears an important *rhetorical* connection to the Squire's discourse.[73] Like the *Squire's Tale* itself, Aurelius's invocation of Apollo fails notably: Apollo does not grant the prayer (or respond in any way), and the obscure astrological grounding of the clerk's later fulfilment of Aurelius's wish, which occurs in winter, when Apollo is at his weakest, seems unconnected to the summertime scenario Aurelius imagines in his prayer.[74] Like the Squire's unfinished final couplet describing the motion of Apollo, the squire Aurelius's prayer to Apollo stands unfulfilled. Chaucer goes to some lengths to highlight the anticlimactic nature of Aurelius's prayer, defying the precedent of analogous scenes: Arcita's prayer to Apollo in Boccaccio's *Teseida*, in which a sympathetic Apollo actively extends pity toward a fellow lover, and the magician Tebano's successful supplication to Nature, in Boccaccio's *Filocolo*, for aid in his occult creation of a winter garden.[75] On the one hand, the failure of Aurelius's prayer reinforces the impotence of Apollo: can Aurelius really expect Apollo, a healer who cannot heal himself, to disturb the universe for his sake? On the other, Aurelius's unfulfilled prayer necessitates the introduction of the clerk of Orleans, whose powers of illusion, associated with the Franklin's own artistic capacity, take on the cosmic scope erroneously attributed to 'Appollo, god and governour' in Aurelius's prayer.

The failure of Aurelius's presumptuous prayer to Apollo registers the Franklin's view of the *Squire's Tale*, interrupted at a corresponding point, as a failure in its own right.[76] The Franklin does not regard the *Squire's Tale* as such because he finds it pompous, incompetent, or insubstantial, however, but because it is, to him, a noble (indeed necessary) failure, and a springboard for his own self-assertion as a man of eloquence. Overlooking the cautious, experimental character of the Squire's attitude toward the poetic vocation, the Franklin marginalizes his squire Aurelius as a victim of transgressive ambition, and affirms for himself the role of the poet as master of illusions. He writes himself into the program of authority identified with the Squire by writing the Squire out: literally, by intervening in his tale, and figuratively, by causing the clerk of Orleans, with whom the Franklin identifies himself, to carry out a project–at once the magical illusion and the poem itself – which Aurelius, the Squire's alter ego, could not master.

In these ways, as Chaucer's most self-consciously poetic and most thoroughly classicizing fragment, Fragment V squarely confronts the problems of textual authority epitomized by Apollo. At the end of the *Squire's Tale*, Apollo is at once a centrifugal and centripetal force, poised both at the breathless edge of one tale and at the gravitational centre of the fragment. His function near the midpoint of the *Franklin's Tale*, by comparison, is to expose fractures in pagan habits of belief and the possibility of successful inspiration. If the Squire's failure is the Franklin's success – and the Franklin sees to that by appropriating the fragmented end of the *Squire's Tale* – it is a kind of success, a form of authority, that sustains itself by means of an illusion that conceals a precarious, contested centre. In this sense, the Franklin, as a model of the belated poet for later generations, is a true 'son of Apollo.'[77]

The strongest justification for observing such far-reaching implications in the fragmented ending of the *Squire's Tale* is the unmistakable tendency of Chaucer's poetry beyond Fragment V to associate Apollo with narrative discontinuity and, indeed, disaster. Next to the broken-off motion of Apollo at the end of the *Squire's Tale* and the unfulfilled prayer to Apollo in the *Franklin's Tale* we must place the *Manciple's Tale*, Chaucer's reworking of a forgettable Ovidian narrative into a stunning *coup de grâce* in which Phebus renounces his own art and peremptorily silences the poetic voice of the *Canterbury Tales*, leaving the only remaining possibilities of discourse to the Parson, a matter reserved for the next chapter. A similar breakdown occurs in the third book of the *House of Fame*, which begins with a neo-Dantean invocation of Apollo – 'This lytel laste bok thou gye!' (*HF* 1093) – and ends, like the *Squire's Tale*, in a state of incompletion. Despite Geffrey's prayer to the 'God of science and of lyght' (*HF* 1091), Apollo does not guide his third book to its proper end. If the invocations that open the three books of the poem (to Morpheus, Venus and the Muses, and Apollo) mark a journey of enlightenment, Apollo provides a manifestly unstable summit of wisdom.[78] And if, as Sheila Delany has observed, each of the first two books of the *House of Fame* proceeds from an invocation of a pagan god to a prayerful summons of Christian authority,[79] the third book – in the state in which it survives[80] – defies this balance: bookended by a tentative prayer to a temperamental Apollo and a faceless 'man of gret auctorite' (2158), it is a dark fantasy of a capricious Apollo who strands his subject Geffrey in a second desert, the surreal haze of unmediated and unverifiable knowledge.[81] Geffrey's prayer to Apollo fails, like that of Aurelius, and in both cases the *auctoritas* that eludes the human artist is revealed as a 'feble fundament / To bilden on a place hye' (*HF* 1132–3): an illusion perpetuated, like the rock of ice on which names melt and congeal, through constant reinscription.[82]

Dreaming of Parnassus: Apollo, the Squire, and Chaucerian Reception

Recent criticism has viewed the fragmented ending of the *Squire's Tale* as only the most obvious manifestation of its implicit urge toward self-fragmentation and metafictional reflection.[83] However seductive the incomplete state of the *Squire's Tale*, it invited surprisingly little scribal interpolation and scant continuation, critics widely assume, until an advanced era of print culture, when Spenser 'completed' the tale in his *Faerie Queene*.[84] In one respect, as Martin Stevens has argued, the putative interruption of the *Squire's Tale* by the Franklin supplies its own 'completion' of the narrative: a 'self-reflexive moment of closure, in which the nature of closure is itself being tested.'[85] In another respect, suggests Stephen Partridge, the 'Wordes of the Frankeleyn to the Squier' provide a retrospective gloss on the *Squire's Tale* that becomes a surrogate for the missing conclusion and thus forestalls scribal continuation.[86] These important observations, however, have largely preempted consideration of fifteenth- and early-sixteenth century forms of literary engagement with the *Squire's Tale*,[87] especially the tale's rhetorical self-awareness and its astrological texture, which, as we have seen, converge around the figure of Apollo as locus of poetic authority. Spenser's attraction to the *Squire's Tale* as a fulcrum of anxieties about 'the durability of written monuments, the limitations of an English poetic heritage, and the viability of poetic vocation'[88] pressingly requires contextualization in the prolific and intertextually sophisticated forms of engagement with the *Squire's Tale* soon after Chaucer's death.[89] Most striking in the literary appropriation of the *Squire's Tale* during this period – apart from the conspicuous tendency freely and select- ively to adapt, rather than literally complete, the unfinished tale – is the persistent fusion of rhetorical stances and mythological textures from the Squire's and the Franklin's tales. Fifteenth- and early-sixteenth cen- tury 'Chaucerian' writers commonly recognized the general continu- ities between the two tales of Fragment V; they also engaged, in certain cases, with the Franklin's interpretation of the *Squire's Tale* as an art of eloquence and his appropriation of the Squire's concerns with pagan creativity and wonder. That is to say, early readers of the *Squire's Tale* read it through the eyes of the Franklin, finding their own cultural con- cerns as poets mirrored in his emulatory and self-deprecatory stance toward the Squire, as well as his creative attraction to the ascendant, aureate Apollo as an image of poetic authority and eloquent style.[90] By tracing these paths of reception we will ultimately apprehend how Chaucer becomes, for Spenser, a locus of authority and inspiration – indeed, how Chaucer is transformed, via his self-defeating *Squire's Tale*, into the vatic Apollo with whom poet-Geffrey, in the *House of Fame*, never dared equate himself.

The first reader of Chaucer to observe a connection between the Squire's and Franklin's self-presentations as narrators was Lydgate, who in *Saint Albon and Saint Amphibalus* – noted for its attention to Apollo in chapter 2 – wove allusions to both tales into a characteristic- ally dazzling tapestry of self-debasement:

> – I nat acqueyntid with musis of Maro,
> Nor with metris of Lucan nor Virgile,
> Nor sugrid ditees of Tullius Chithero, [cf. *FranT* 721–2]
> Nor of Omerus to folwe the fressh stile,
> Crokid to clymb ouer so high a stile, [cf. *SqT* 105–6]
> Or for to folwe the steppis aureat
> Of Franceis Petrak, the poete laureat? [cf. *ClT* 31]
> …
> Dreedyng my labour shuld be in veyn
> That neuyr drank of Pegaseus welle[.][91]

Lydgate manifestly constructs his narrative voice out of a fusion of the humility topoi employed by the Squire and imitated by the Franklin.[92] Just as there is considerable artificiality in the Franklin's highly rhetorical self-portraiture as a 'natural man,' as we have seen, there is substantial disingenuity in Lydgate's lament for Chaucer in the *Troy Book*, which similarly absorbs the Franklin's pose of belatedness and self-distance from aristocratic eloquence (here placing Chaucer in the position of the Squire, with a touch of the Clerk's Petrarch):

> And Chaucer now, allas! is nat alyue
> Me to reforme, or to be my rede,
> For lak of whom slouȝer is my spede –
> þe noble Rethor þat alle dide excelle;
> For in makyng he drank of þe welle
> Vndir Pernaso, þat þe Musis kepe,
> On which hil I myȝt[e] neuer slepe –   (*Troy Book* 3.550–6)

The desert-like world in which Lydgate claims to live, set against Chaucer's 'golden age' of aureate eloquence,[93] is, like that of the Franklin (who 'sleep nevere on the Mount of Pernaso'), a world of negation and voyeuristic longing. The fountain in the Chaucerian garden in the *Complaint of the Black Knight* is '[n]e lyche the pitte of the Pegace / Vnder Parnaso, wher poetys slept' (92–3);[94] elsewhere, Lydgate 'may assay for to countrefete / [Chaucer's] gay[e] style, but it wyl not be; / The welle is drie, with the lycoure swete, / Bothe of Clye and of Caliope' (*Floure of Curtesye* 239–42).[95] In Lydgate's poetic mythology, as observed in chapter 2, eloquence is presented in 'essentially decorative' terms through an imagery of aureation, illumination, and embellishment related to Apollo the sun as inspiring agent, and the idea of the poet as illuminator.[96]

Osbern Bokenham also adopts the Franklin's pose as unskilled in rhetoric in his 'Legend of St. Anne,' where he distinguishes himself from the increasingly mythical Chaucer, here grouped with Gower and Lydgate:

> For tullyus wolde me neuer non teche,
> Ner in parnase wher apollo doth dwelle
> I neuer slepte, ne neuer dede seche
> In ethna flowrs ...
>   nor of þe sugird welle
> In elicona, my rudnesse to leche,
> I neuer dede taste ...   (1453–9)

Bokenham turns to the Franklin's disingenuous pose as part of his programmatic flirtation with classical eloquence, exposed throughout his legendary as seductive yet morally inadequate compared with plain Christian speech.[97] Representing Chaucer as the Squire figure whose poetic skill inevitably overshadows that of the belated poet, Bokenham's critique of eloquence registers, in an explicitly Christian key, some of the same concerns with the perils of 'high speech' embedded in the *Squire's Tale* itself.

The lexicon of rhetorical self-deprecation introduced by the Franklin and substantiated by Lydgate and Bokenham persisted even into the sixteenth century, when Skelton parodied it in gendered terms in *Phyllyp Sparowe*, which features a mock-heroic lament for a dead sparrow in the voice of Jane Scrope, who claims to be unequal to the task of literary mourning because

> ....I am a mayde,
> Tymerous, halfe afrayde,
> That never yet asayde
> Of Elyconys well,
> Where the muses dwell[.]   (607–11)

As if to cue her source, Jane turns humorously, after this disclaimer, to her acquaintance with the *Canterbury Tales* as proof of her limited literacy, followed by a lengthy catalogue of other vernacular texts. Finally, Skelton, speaking *in propria persona* as 'laurigerum / Britanum ... vatem' [laureate poet of Britain] (834–5),[98] asserts his authorial control over Jane's elegy, in all of its Squire-like rhetorical paralysis, with an over-the-top ebullition of aureate diction (847–51) followed by not one but two invocations of Apollo (863–70, 970–6). No schoolgirl's blushing admission not to have done her homework, Jane's apology, but a strategic preface of an authorial pose on Skelton's part wholly consistent with the series of disingenuous, self-promoting uses of the 'sleepless on Parnassus' commonplace instigated within English tradition by Chaucer's Franklin.

The eloquence for which the Franklin praises the Squire in the transition between their tales and in his prologue is, of course, the very quality for which Chaucer, 'flour of eloquence,'[99] was most often commended in the century and a half after his death.[100] From this current of praise the Italian humanist Stefano de Surigone, in a Latin epitaph inscribed on Chaucer's tomb at Westminster and featured at the end of Caxton's 1478 edition of Chaucer's *Boece*, heralds Chaucer, *mutatis mutandis*, as 'Galfridus Chaucer vates.' More precisely, de Surigone daringly represents *Chaucer naming himself* a *vates* from beyond the grave: 'Galfridus

Chaucer vates: et fama poesis / Materne . hac sacra sum tumulatus humo' ['I, Geoffrey Chaucer the bard, glory of my native poesy, am buried in this sacred ground'].[101] While the eulogy speaks less to any real acquaintance with Chaucer's works than to a mutually advantageous commercial relationship between Caxton and a professional author,[102] it is noteworthy for absorbing Chaucer into a thoroughly classicized vocabulary through such devices as invocation of the Muses, apostrophes to the Fates, and the trope of poetic immortality. For Seth Lerer, this eulogy and Caxton's editorial project more generally mark a transition in Chaucerian reception from the 'self-imagined childhood of Lydgatean abnegation to the laureate adulthood of humanist scholarship,' and from 'evocation to invocation' of Chaucer as a literary authority, newly associated with a distant, antique past rather than a broadly permeable, vernacular present.[103] It is oversimplistic, however, to dismiss de Surigone's poem as mere ideological exploitation of 'the poet of scalded *toutes*,'[104] an interpretation that perpetuates a carnivalesque reading of Chaucer and ignores Fragment V's insistent concern with classical vocabularies of inspiration, eloquence, and authorial self-fashioning. That a late fifteenth-century Italian humanist praises Chaucer in invocatory terms that Chaucer himself had introduced into English, through his own transformative engagement with an earlier generation of Italian humanists, is enough to give us pause.[105] That de Surigone associates Chaucer's 'last words' within the heart of the eulogy with Latin rather than the vernacular that he so ennobled reappropriates Chaucer's achievement within the new scholarly values of a laureate culture, but just as significantly endorses the classicizing world of poetic refinement out of which Chaucer carved his own vernacular space and articulated his poetic self-conception. 'Chaucer''s out-of-character self-designation as *vates* and reflexive association with *fama* in de Surigone's eulogy is, of course, a matter of humanist projection of current poetic values onto the earlier poet, but it is a stance occasioned, crucially, by Chaucer's own critical experimentation with classically based conceptions of poetic vocation and ambition in his poetry.[106] As we shall see later in this chapter, this conception of Chaucer as *vates* leads, in the case of Spenser's *Faerie Queene*, to an identification of Chaucer with Apollo himself, derived both from Chaucer's own poetic supplication of Apollo in the *House of Fame* and, more obliquely, that of the squire-figures of Fragment V.

David Lawton's observations on the cult of 'dullness' as a self-conscious socio-political strategy in the century after Chaucer's death help account for fifteenth- and early sixteenth-century interest in the textual dynamics of Fragment V. Lawton's paradigm, unlike Spearing's and Lerer's models of infantilized fifteenth-century readership, regards the tenacious disclaimers of rhetorical ability in so much fifteenth-century poetry as 'a politic response to princely or royal command' that prefigures the rhetoric of Renaissance prince-pleasing.[107] In this light, it is wholly appropriate that the Franklin's self-effacing deferral to the aristocratic sensibility of his superior, the Squire, influenced the early modern poet's stance vis-à-vis his royal patron. In both cases, the denial of poetic ability and status serves both to integrate the poet into a privileged social fabric, and transparently (if paradoxically) to assert a claim to professional eloquence – one that Chaucer, like his Squire, in reality never made. The Squire's caution toward high style and rhetoric thus mirrors the double stance toward poetic ambition for which Chaucer, who develops a cult of authority and poetic fame in English poetry even while disowning his own inclusion in it, is notorious. In this way, the paradoxes of the *Squire's Tale* crystallize the ambivalences of Chaucer's own poetic position, subtly articulated by Chaucer in this tale told by one surrogate poet and, as would become typical of the post-Chaucerian era, imaginatively 'continued' by another.

Sitting in Apollo's Chair: Lydgate to Skelton

As we have seen, the final couplet of the *Squire's Tale*, far from being a random point of dissolution, calls attention to the problematic construction of authority in connection to Apollo, a phenomenon advanced by the Franklin's interruption of the *Squire's Tale* and his creative appropriation of the Squire-Apollo link in his own tale. Just as the Franklin's reception of the *Squire's Tale* as an art of eloquence shapes the legacy of fifteenth-century poetic modesty, creative adaptation of the *Squire's Tale* in the years after Chaucer's death follows the Franklin's lead in appropriating the Squire's final couplet as shorthand for self-authorization as well as cue of the dangers of poetic ambition. In dramatizing a liminal moment of poetic authority through the image of Apollo's motion, this problematic couplet invites completion – beginning with the *Franklin's Tale* and continuing, in various forms, up to Spenser's time – precisely by evoking the formation and transfer of authority. Support for this claim is supplied by three fifteenth- and early sixteenth-century responses to the Squire's fragmentary Apollo: Lydgate's *Temple of Glas* (c. 1400–20?), the apocryphal *Floure and the Leafe* (c. 1460–80), and Skelton's *Garland of Laurel*. All suggest that the Squire's final lines, despite their grammatical incompletion and partial obscurity, were deemed significant enough to take on a textual life of their own as an epitome of elevated poetry.

Our first example is drawn from Lydgate's visual 'anthologization' of Chaucer on the walls of the central edifice in his *Temple of Glas*, on which is imaginatively depicted a vast range of amatory subjects delineating 'the possibilities of the Chaucerian encounter with the classics.'[108] Lydgate ends his list with a seemingly incongruous reference to the *Squire's Tale*, as if in homage to – and competition with – the tale's own lack of an ending.[109] In reinscribing the 'open' ending of the *Squire's Tale* as a device of closure for a central Chaucerian episode in his own poem, Lydgate animates the suspended Apolline circuit of the end of the *Squire's Tale* in a manner just as enterprising as that of the Franklin, and, like him, engages in strategic dialogue with the Squire's commentary on poetic authority. Lydgate's erotic ecphrasis of 'ful many a faire image / Of sondri louers' (*TG* 45–6),[110] which begins with the Ovidian Dido and culminates in an eight-line summary of the *Knight's Tale*, ends by turning to the loves of the gods – Apollo, Jove, Mars, and Mercury – and finally to the human adventures of the *Squire's Tale*. Lydgate's rehearsal of details from the *Squire's Tale* curiously elides all reference to love (rather than invoking, for example, the erotic subject matter of the falcon's speech, or the marital object of Algarsif's prospective adventures), dwelling instead on the technical efficacy of the marvellous gifts:

> And vppermore depeint men myȝt[e] se,
> Hov with hir ring, goodli Canace
> Of euere foule þe ledne and þe song
> Coud vndirstond, as she welk hem among;
> And hou hir broþir so oft holpen was
> In his myschefe bi þe stede of bras.   (*TG* 137–42)

Although it may seem as though Lydgate's catalogue of lovers has become purely associative here, the erasure of the link between such details from the *Squire's Tale* and the point of their inclusion in the list highlights the sheer authoritative value of the tale in the *Temple of Glas*'s reshaping of Chaucer's oeuvre and Lydgate's self-conception as heir to Chaucer's literary authority. Lydgate visually positions the matter of the *Squire's Tale*, moreover, above ('vppermore depeint' [137]) an account of the marriage of Mercury, 'god of eloquence' (132), and Philology, identified with 'sapience' (131), and the bride's ascent '[h]igh into heuen' (134) with the help of the Muses.[111] Lydgate's image here of a high-flying figure of wisdom in association with eloquence strikingly captures the unsustainable imagery of the *Squire's Tale*'s last couplet involving Apollo and Mercury. Simultaneously, Lydgate grants the tale an 'vppermore' status representative of a Chaucerian aesthetic capable of integrating the rhetoric of humility with the authority of poetic elevation.[112] In this way, Lydgate follows the Franklin's lead in providing closure for a tale wary of the rhetorical cost of its own completion, even while appropriating the concerns with eloquence that it had cast in the most cautious of moulds to affirm his own poetic project.

The apocryphal *Floure and the Leafe* (c. 1460–80) invests the *Squire's Tale* with closure not by reshaping it as an ending but reenvisioning it as a beginning. The *Floure* commences, in effect, where the *Squire's Tale* left off: 'When that Phebus his chaire of gold so hie / Had whirled up the sterry sky aloft …'[113] These familiar lines introduce a fourteen-line springtime periphrasis modelled upon the first sentence of Chaucer's *General Prologue*, signalled by the opening 'When that.' The full opening passage is studiously Chaucerian in its references to Taurus, the regenerative effect of 'shoures sweet' after a dead season, and the animation of the reawakened individual. In effect, the anonymous poet co-opts the Squire's curtailed lines as the first move in adopting a characteristically Chaucerian persona and rewriting one of Chaucer's most rhetorically elevated passages. This reprise of the frame of the *Canterbury Tales* is further enriched through deliberate assimilation with a genre (dream-vision) and verse form (rhyme royal) associated with Chaucer's high-style poetry. Like Blake, the *Floure*-poet associates the Squire, if not as visionary then as poet and literary astrologer, with the motivating spirit of the *Canterbury Tales*, positioning the Squire poetically at the 'head' of the pilgrimage by rewriting the opening lines of the *General Prologue* in language drawn from his tale. Rather than circulating disjointedly as a mark of poetic failure, or the failure of poetic ambition, the Squire's final couplet generates successful 'Chaucerian' poetry.

If Lydgate and the *Floure*-poet variously appropriate the fragmentary Apollo of the *Squire's Tale* in fabricating poetic authority and placing themselves within a consciously Chaucerian lineage, Skelton most fully exploits the concerns with poetic ambition and authorization represented by the *Squire's Tale*'s final couplet. Like Lydgate, Skelton turns to the Squire's Apollo in a dream-vision, the *Garland of Laurel*, whose conceptual focus, as noted in chapter 1, is a definition of the poetic vocation. In this poetic manifesto, in which Apollo's association with the laurel is extensively dramatized, Fame refuses to admit Skelton into her house (which contains Chaucer, among others) until Occupacioun, Fame's registrar, reads the titles of all of the works Skelton has written, for better or worse, from a 'boke of remembrauns' (1149). The fact that many of the titles in Skelton's list are otherwise unattested leads John Scattergood to suggest that Skelton, deploying a Chaucerian topos of self-cataloguing, may also engage in Chaucerian self-parody by listing his actual works along with (perhaps invented) 'lost works,' thus identifying himself with an almost impossibly enormous corpus.[114] Very near the end of this long and bizarre list, Occupacioun cites a title of an otherwise unknown work by Skelton, which takes its name from the Squire's penultimate line:[115]

> Item Apollo that whirllid up his chare,
> That made sum to snurre and snuf in the wynde;
> It made them to skip, to stampe, and to stare,
> Whiche, if they be happy, have cause to beware
> In ryming and raylyng with hym for to mell,
> For drede and he lerne them there A B C to spell.   (1471–6)

Upon hearing this title, Skelton, who had been silent throughout Occupacioun's recital, suddenly panics:

> With that I stode up, halfe sodenly afrayd,
> Suppleyng to Fame, I besought her grace,
> And that it wolde please her, full tenderly I prayd,
> Owt of her bokis Apollo to rase.   (1477–80)

But Fame refuses, reminding Skelton that words, once uttered, 'must nedes after rin all the worlde aboute' (1483). A dejected Skelton concedes, 'I did what I cowde to scrape out the scrollis, / Apollo to rase out of her ragman rollis' (1489–90), after which several more titles are rehearsed and the dreaming narrator awakes.

Whereas Lydgate rewrote the non-ending of the *Squire's Tale* to bestow (self-promoting) closure upon Chaucer's canon, and the *Floure*-poet manipulated it to achieve rhetorical authority over a Chaucerian love-vision, Skelton creates from it an intentional crisis in his own poem, exposing the problematic lability of his own canon and his (rarely confronted) insecurities with his role as laureate. Once again, the Squire's fragmentary Apollo is associated with a moment of poetic liminality. Indeed, what occurs on mention of 'Apollo that whirllid up his chare' is, in effect, a *self*-interruption: wishing that he had not completed or circulated a poem whose title derives from the truncated ending of a poem that Chaucer did not complete, Skelton belatedly disrupts notice of that poem within yet another poem (the *Laurel*) over which he exerts authorial control. However, as a dream-vision, the *Laurel* controls Skelton – fictionally speaking, he has no power over the content of the dream – as much as he controls it, hence Occupacioun's refusal of his request. Skelton's adoption of the Squire's final couplet as a beginning for his (lost) poem thus reaffirms its original status as an unsuccessful 'ending,' a fragment to be broken off, refused, or reclaimed. Resisting further mention of the 'Apollo' after Occupacioun forbids its erasure, Skelton dismisses it as a matter that 'erkith me lenger to wryte' (1491). Reflected in this awkward statement is both Skelton's defeat respecting his primary act of composition and his imperfect power to abridge and revise that act of composition by *writing no more of its existence* in the present poem. Although Occupacioun's list continues for another two stanzas, Skelton's self-interruption – like the interruption of the Squire by the Franklin – results in an important shift in narrative voice and perspective. After this contest of wills, Occupacioun no longer recites the details of Skelton's dossier in her own voice; instead, Skelton shifts to third-person narration and *tells* us what she reads, for the first time exerting rhetorical ownership over the texts named (i.e., 'my devisis,' 'my translacyon,' etc. [1494, 1498]). This shift expresses the imminent success of Skelton's claim to the laurel – which all of the preceding has, of course, been marshalled to prove – and leads inexorably to the atemporal citation of the very poem in which the dream is contained ('when of the laurell she made rehersall' [1503]), a collective cry of triumph, and the dissolution of the dream (1504–11). As a narrative or autobiographical crisis, then, the notice of Skelton's 'Apollo' evinces a rupture in his own canon even as it is constituted and celebrated, displacing the voice of Occupacioun in a way that empowers the poet's own. 'Apollo that whirllid up his chare' is both a threat to Skelton's claim of authority and the pivot upon which its recovery in the *Laurel* turns. The absence of the 'Apollo' poem itself ultimately matters little; its title is enough to summon a range of associations with literary tradition and self-criticism that crystallize around Skelton's complex play with the construction of authority in the *Laurel*.

More needs to be said, however, about *why* Skelton wishes to 'rase' the 'Apollo' out of his own book of Fame, and what should be made of the audience reaction he describes in lines 1472–6. The problem is conspicuous in part because the trenchantly satirical Skelton elsewhere is more wont to gloat over hostile audience response or mock the inferior intellect of those who misunderstand his poetry, than to appear contrite or, worse, 'afrayd' (1477).[116] Despite the obscurity of Skelton's account of the 'Apollo,' the poet's evocation of the snorts and snuffles with which the lost poem was met suggest it was an unpopular work because perceived as haughty or pretentious, an impression captured by the grandiloquent air of the title, swelling with the force of poetic ambition. It is deliciously ironic that a poem critiqued for its arrogance is singled out for its infamy within a larger poem that, with its extended fantasy of laureation and self-enrolment in the classical canon, is in many ways the epitome of arrogance: as Skelton's nineteenth-century editor Alexander Dyce wryly observed, 'the history of literature affords no second example of a poet having deliberately written sixteen hundred lines in honour of himself.'[117] Indeed, Skelton's embarrassed memory of the 'Apollo' is more tactical than autobiographical: it draws critical attention to, and trains an ironic eye toward, the very image of poetic ascendance that the *Laurel* projects and defends.[118]

As in the *Squire's Tale* itself, the lofty image of Skelton's high-whirling 'Apollo' must be viewed in its lexical and figurative context. Skelton recurrently associates the rhetoric of height with pride and pretension, as when his enemy Garnesche's heart is said to be 'to hawte, iwys, yt wyll nat be alowde' and he is warned, 'Loke nat to hy' (*Agenst Garnesche* 2. 26, 42b). False prelates are 'so haute' and, like so many precarious Apollos, 'loke so hye / As though they wolde flye / Aboute the sterry skye' (*Collyn Clout* 71–4). Notably, Skelton equates this language of elevation with faults of poetic composition in his heroine Jane's critique of Lydgate's aureate style in *Phyllyp Sparowe*:

> Also Johnn Lydgate
> Wryteth after an *hyer* rate;
> It is dyffuse to fynde
> The sentence of his mynde …
> Yet some men fynde a faute,
> And say he wryteth to *haute*.   (804–7, 811–12; emphases added)

Provocatively, Skelton implicitly equates such 'haute' style with the poetic attitude that nearly unseats the poet from Apollo's rising chariot in the *Garland of Laurel*.

This constellation of imagery – 'haute' aspirations, aureate language, the critique of poetic pretension – identifies the laureate Skelton with the ascendant Apollo in the context of 'Apollo that whirllid up his chare,' and suggests the arrogance of such a poetic stance. In this light, Skelton's disaffected competitors, mentioned in the 'Apollo' passage, find themselves in the position of Marsyas: like the presumptuous satyr, they 'have cause to beware / In ryming and raylyng with [Skelton] for to mell, / For drede and he lerne them there A B C to spell.' Support for this reading is offered by Skelton's *Agenst Garnesche*, a *flytyng* composed nearly a decade before the completion of the *Laurel*, which reads like a comic impersonation of how Apollo might have taunted Marsyas in the moments before flaying him. Painting Garnesche as a 'gawdy, gresy' beast of slovenly carriage (3.120), the poem mocks its target's feeble attempts at poetry –

> For reson can I non fynde
> Nor good ryme in yower mater.
> I wondyr that ye smatyr,
> So for a knave to clatyr;
> Ye wolde be callyd a maker ...
> Ye lernyd of sum py-bakar.   (3.104–8, 111)

– emphasizing the folly of challenging a laureate like himself:

> Yower termys ar to grose,
> To far from the porpose,
> To contaminate
> And to violate
> The dygnyte lauryate.   (3.96–100)

In short, 'It ys for no bawdy knave / The dignite lawreat for to have' (5.114–15). Condescendingly parading his credentials before Garnesche – his degree from 'Oxforth, the universyte' (5.81) and the personal favour of Calliope, among other distinctions – Skelton interestingly employs the same vocabulary and rhyme pattern as in the 'Apollo' stanza of the *Laurel*. It would be better for Garnesche to drive a dung cart '[t]han with my poems for to *melle*' (5.94; emphasis added), for Skelton 'lernyd to *spelle*' the most important man in England, the young Henry VIII, and 'yave hym drynke of the sugryd welle / Of Eliconys waters crystallyne' (5.95, 98–9; emphasis added). Skelton issues an unsubtle threat to Garnesche, who lacks such 'lernyng primordiall' (5.105): 'Thow ar frantyke and lakkyst wyt, / To *rayle* with me that the can hyt'; one who stands high may 'in a throw /... fale downe and ebbe full lowe' (5.118–19, 122–3; emphasis added). Returning to the *Laurel*, one can better appreciate the problematic nature of the 'Apollo' in a poem that advances the ideology of laureate superiority in a sublimated dream-sphere that otherwise excludes the world of plodding Marsyases. In registering broader concerns about the perils of poetic ambition, the last couplet of the *Squire's Tale* offers Skelton an economic yet subtle way of exploring such issues within and across his most poetically self-aware fictions.

The Latin glosses to the *Laurel*, of which at least some, if not all, are likely authorial,[119] deepen the significance of the lost 'Apollo' by placing it in allusive dialogue with the biblical and Virgilian Apollos. The gloss to line 1473, 'Factum est cum apollo esset Corinthi' [Acts 19:1], activates an association between the 'Apollo' of Skelton's title and the well-intentioned but theologically faulty Jewish Apollo of Acts, examined in chapter 2 in association with misleading eloquence. Another gloss, to line 1476, adduces the Sibyl's frenzy at *Aeneid* 6.101, in which the invisible Apollo, riding her like a horse, violently fills her with inspiration, summoning an appropriate enough association between Skelton's titular 'Apollo' and the god's jurisdiction over prophetic inspiration.[120] The Virgilian gloss strikingly evokes the violent, even violative, nature of Apollo's inspiration of the Sibyl, who tries to resist the god who 'fatigat / os rabidum, fera corda domans, fingitque premendo' [tires her raving mouth, tames her wild heart, and moulds her by constraint] (*Aen.* 6.79–80). Apollo's mastery of the wilful Marsyas stirs just beneath the surface here, especially as boldly reimagined by Dante in the invocation to Apollo in *Paradiso* 1, which conflates Apollo's violent flaying of Marsyas with an almost erotic image of poetic inspiration reminiscent of that experienced by Virgil's Sibyl: 'Entra nel petto mio, e spira tue / sì come quando Marsïa traesti / de la vagina de la membra sue' [Enter into my breast and breathe there as when you drew Marsyas from the sheath of his limbs] (*Par.* 1.19–21).[121] Chaucer's *House of Fame* – a poem very much in Skelton's mind when composing the *Laurel* – adapts Dante's invocation in a way that nervously highlights Apollo's imperiousness ('Nat that I wilne, for maistrye, / Here art poetical be shewed' [*HF* 1094–5]) and encodes the poet's fear of reliving Marsyas's fate.[122] Skelton's vaguely ominous-sounding threat in the 'Apollo' stanza to teach his challengers their A B C's places the numinous poet himself in the position of Chaucer's fearsome Apollo, torturing rather than teaching his challengers. Skelton's Chaucer, unlike Chaucer's 'Geffrey,' *is* one of the privileged denizens of Fame's house, a peer rather than a peon of Apollo. Despite Skelton's coy, Chaucerian stance in needing to be shoved (by Chaucer!) into Fame's court (444–8), and notwithstanding his embarrassment over the reception of 'Apollo that whirllid up his chare,' Skelton does not hesitate to eulogize himself, in Latin, as a second Homer who has surpassed his predecessors in dignifying English verse (1524).

Skelton's failed attempt to erase the 'Apollo' from Occupacioun's book creatively weaves the Apollo of the *Squire's Tale* into Chaucer's vision of the contingencies and perils of poetic composition, centred around Apollo, in the *House of Fame*. Furthermore, Fame's refusal of Skelton's request in lines 1481–3, quoted above, loosely echoes the eagle's lesson on the multiplication of sound and Eolus's distribution of good and bad fame around the world in the *House of Fame*. It also echoes another Chaucerian poem featuring Apollo, the perils of speech, and the adventures of a poet-figure (in this case avian): the *Manciple's Tale*. The ironically verbose lesson bequeathed by the Manciple's mother – 'Thyng that is seyd is seyd, and forth it gooth, / Though hym repente, or be hym nevere so looth' (*MancT* 355–6) – captures precisely the point of Skelton's Fame that words spoken in her court 'must nedes after rin all the worlde aboute' (*Laurel* 1483). Viewed in relation to the *Manciple's Tale*, the *Laurel* shows Skelton playing out the experience both of Chaucer's crow, whose ill-considered words cannot be revoked, and Phebus, the master poet who breaks his musical instruments and regrets teaching his crow the art of language. As in Chaucer's *Retraction*, a likely influence on Occupacioun's list, the obvious futility of Skelton's attempt in the *Laurel* to 'recall' a work already in circulation is made increasingly ironic by the fact that the 'Apollo' *has* been lost from the book of Fame, retaining ontological status only by Skelton's ostentatious attempt at its erasure in the *Laurel*.[123] Skelton's appropriation of 'Apollo that whirllid up his chare' from the end of the *Squire's Tale* thus functions both to place the poet in Apollo's ascendant but never-stable seat and to rewrite the *Squire's Tale* around the dangers of speech, poetic ambition, and fragmentation that similarly frame Chaucer's Apollo in the *Manciple's Tale* and the *House of Fame*. Turning to Chaucer's Apollo enables Skelton to write himself (literally) into the tradition of English eloquence and to contemplate critically the precarious position of the human poet, in his role as *vates*, within that tradition.[124]

Mastering Apollo: Spenser's *Squire's Tale* and Chaucerian Infusion

Viewed in conjunction with these fifteenth- and early sixteenth-century appropriations of the *Squire's Tale*, Spenser's attraction to the unfinished tale as a stage for an almost occult induction of 'vatic continuity' [125] between himself and Chaucer, through which he claims 'infusion sweete / Of thine owne spirit, which doth in me surviue' (*FQ* 4.2.34), seems less anomalous. [126] Spenser, first of all, follows the rhetorical lead of his Chaucerian forebears in dramatizing his own 'interruption' of the *Squire's Tale*, which sets the stage for his reinscription of the tale into his own allegorical landscape. Spenser's Squire of Dames, a minor figure in the *Faerie Queene*, encounters Chaucer's Cambell and Canacee on horseback – in a time warp reminiscent of Lydgate's encounter with Chaucer's pilgrims in the prologue of the *Siege of Thebes* – recognizes them, and prepares to recount their story. At this point Spenser intervenes in his own voice, summons the inspiring spirit of Chaucer, and proceeds to narrate his own conclusion of the *Squire's Tale* at length. As William J. Kennedy observes, 'Spenser's displacement of his Squire amounts to a displacement of his Chaucerian prototype in *The Canterbury Tales*' at the same time as it implicitly equates the Squire with Chaucer, over whom Spenser exerts his own poetic authority. [127] Craig A. Berry characterizes the intertextual dynamics of Spenser's continuation of the *Squire's Tale* as a kind of post-Chaucerian 'quiting,' the construction of a tale that 'responds to and dilates on the meaning of its predecessor' [128] – much as I have argued that the Franklin does to the Squire's tale and his Apollo in particular. [129]

Why, however, does the *Squire's Tale* figure so centrally in Spenser's 'very direct appeal to Chaucer's reputation as a serious poet,' [130] and how does this tale facilitate Spenser's bold claim of Chaucerian 'infusion'? A. Kent Hieatt has plausibly suggested that Spenser epicizes the sprawling *Squire's Tale* by associating it with the *Knight's Tale*. [131] Berry, on the other hand, claims that the *Squire's Tale*'s 'self-consciousness about literary inheritance and audience reception' makes it a natural site of commerce between Spenser and the Chaucerian heritage of poetic authority. [132] Chaucer was important to Spenser as an English model not only of elite romance tradition, however, but also of the lexicon of inspiration and anxieties regarding the poet's role – and role models – as prophet. Like Skelton, Spenser 'completed' Chaucer by conflating the Apollos of two fragmentary texts, the *Squire's Tale* and the *House of Fame*. After his 'interruption' of the Squire of Dames, Spenser summons an image of Chaucer as a laureate worthy of registration '[o]n Fames eternall beadroll,' who speaks from Helicon's depths ('well of English vndefyled') (*FQ* 4.2.32), but who, paradoxically, is vulnerable to the radical instability of texts and the ignorant ravages of 'Eld' (4.2.33). The ending of the *Squire's Tale* – which Spenser believes, or pretends to believe, once existed and was by his day lost – exemplifies poetic contingency itself, and thus places Spenser, in this crucial moment of self-definition, squarely in the midst of a Chaucerian refusal to separate a poetics of inspiration from association with failure, loss, or impermanence, by which it is always threatened and on which it is predicated.

No wonder, then, that Spenser next invokes Chaucer in language moulded by one of Chaucer's most overdetermined and covertly prevaricating invocations:

> Then pardon, O most sacred happie spirit,
>   That I thy labours lost may thus reuiue,
>   And steale from thee the meede of thy due merit,
>   That none durst euer whilest thou wast aliue,
>   And being dead in vaine yet many striue:
>   Ne dare I like, but through infusion sweete
>   Of thine owne spirit, which doth in me surviue,
>   I follow here the footing of thy feete,
> That with thy meaning so I may the rather meete.   (*FQ* 4.2.34)

What is most striking about this invocation is not Spenser's Pythagorian fantasy of Chaucer having been transformed into himself, but his creative rewriting of Chaucer's invocation of Apollo in the *House of Fame* in such a way that Chaucer, startlingly, becomes the Apollo-figure, the inspiring presence toward whom Spenser is careful not to appear a usurper.[133] Like Chaucer's invocation of Apollo in the *House of Fame*, Spenser's is a guarded, emphatically apologetic summons, with its opening plea for pardon and its rejection of such Marsyan symptoms of poetic competitiveness as daring, stealing, and striving (cf. Chaucer's 'Nat that I wilne, for maistrye, / Here art poetical be shewed' [*HF* 1094–5] and Skelton's disdain for those who 'melle' with his 'Apollo'). Spenser's invocation, like Chaucer's, qualifies its request for inspiration with a more homely emphasis on guidance in prosody ('I follow here the footing of thy feete'; cf. *HF* 1096–8, 1102–3) and meaning over detail ('That with thy meaning so I may the rather meete'; cf. *HF* 1099–1100).[134] What is more, Spenser cannily reveals his appreciation of

Chaucer's own dramatization, in his invocation to Apollo, of his relationship to *his* immediate poetic predecessor – Dante, who, in a sense, is the Apollo figure by whom Chaucer is inspired, and to whom Chaucer does not want to appear presumptuous. In the same way, Dante, before Chaucer, fashioned his own plea to Apollo for inspiration at the beginning of the *Paradiso* as a summons, or perhaps exorcism, of Ovid's presence in his epic of spiritual transformation.[135] Even while Spenser takes the radical step of identifying Chaucer with the icon of inspiration that Chaucer himself once feared, he confirms his supposed rebirth in Chaucer's spirit by channelling, as it were, his cautionary stance toward authority before embarking upon his extended reinvention of the Squire's tale post-Apollo. Spenser's placement *here* of a reworking of Chaucer's invocation to Apollo from the *House of Fame*, then, displaces and rewrites the famous image of the ascendant Apollo that up to this point stood as a textual reminder of the *Squire's Tale*'s incompletion. In one motion, Spenser secures for himself permission to enter Fame's house and to sit in Apollo's whirling chair: if not a new Chaucer, then a licensed Phaethon.

No such poetic optimism emerges from Chaucer's own final, momentous encounter with Apollo in the *Manciple's Tale*, the subject of the next chapter. As noted earlier, the *Manciple's Tale* in close conjunction with the *House of Fame* mediated Skelton's appropriation of the last lines of the *Squire's Tale* in his *Garland of Laurel*. Activating this complex of texts that feature Apollo in a position of rhetorical authority allowed Skelton – and, in a different manner, Spenser after him – to reflect upon problems of poetic ambition and fragmentation while facilitating self-inscription within a continuous, perfectible poetic lineage. The poetic energies that link these texts for early modern poets also circulate within Chaucer's own corpus. The *Manciple's Tale* brings us abruptly from the superlative heights of the Squire's celestial Apollo to a set of all-too-familiar lows surrounding the god 'in this erthe adoun' (*MancT* 105). At the same time, it ushers us into a house of *in*famy, saturated with 'tidynges, wheither ... false or trewe' (*MancT* 360) and governed by Apollo, inevitably recalling the houses of Fame and Rumour poetically opened to the narrator of the *House of Fame* by the same impetuous god.[136] In the *Manciple's Tale*, the last receptacle of pagan myth in the *Canterbury Tales*, Geffrey's earlier progress toward 'auctorite,' broken off frenetically in the *House of Fame*, is rendered wholly unwritable, while his guide, the 'God of science and of lyght,' rejects illumination and shutters his own house from any glimmer of truth (*HF* 1091).

5 Domestic Apollo: Crises of Truth in the *Manciple's Tale*

Tell the emperor that my hall has fallen to the ground. Phoibos
no longer has his house nor his mantic bay nor his prophetic
spring; the water has dried up.

> Oracle of Apollo delivered to an envoy of Julian the
> Apostate upon his attempt to revive the defunct
> Delphic oracle in 361–2 CE, as reported by Philostorgius

Among the concerns of the previous chapter was the problem of beginnings – iconographic, rhetorical, memorial – and their connection to Apollo as *origo* of poetic production. The final chapter of this book focuses, fittingly, upon endings. Like the preceding chapter, this one dwells upon a moment of textual crisis in the articulation of Apollo's authority, but instead of generative poetic effects and a burgeoning lexicon of authorship, this crisis results in permanent fragmentation and a rejection of poetic transmission itself. The poetic journey of the *Canterbury Tales* does not end at Becket's shrine or, strictly speaking, in the long shadows cast by the Parson's prose sermon, but at the doorstep of a fallen, obsolescent Delphi: the house of Apollo when he 'dwelled heere in this erthe adoun' (*MancT* 105). For all its spareness of description, Phebus's house,[1] imaginatively situated for the pilgrims in the suburbs of Canterbury, reeks of the quotidian, the banally domestic; certainly it is a far cry from the bellowing cave at which Aurelius wistfully imagines himself a barefoot supplicant. Despite the resonances, for many critics, of Phebus's house with the medieval courts in which Chaucer himself negotiated the fraught demands of servitude, poetic production, and princely counsel, the setting of the *Manciple's Tale's* action more directly evokes a rather tawdry 'house next door,' an image readily affirmed by comparison with the god's sonorous, bejewelled *sale* in Machaut's *Voir dit* and the vaguely defined locales that float in and out of the narrative in most other analogues.[2] In the *Manciple's Tale*, Phebus's house is a starkly delineated space where crow and wife, their desires and instincts pent up, are kept by a jealous master. We have a dim but tangible sense of it as a physical place: a nondescript dwelling with a door through which Phebus comes home from a long day's work and, later, flings out the family pet in rage. In a sense, the *Manciple's Tale* returns us, in our end, to our beginning: like the Knight, with his 'olde stories' of the pagan past (*KnT* 859), the Manciple begins by invoking the record of 'olde bookes' as they illuminate the mythic history of Apollo, the very avatar of paganism (*MancT* 106). Indeed, the Manciple moves beyond the Knight's account of the aftermath of the Theban civil war to a still more ancient ur-history, when Amphion raised the walls of Thebes with his song, an event recalled by the Manciple at the beginning of his tale (*MancT* 116–17) as if in direct counterpoint to the *Knight's Tale*, in which Theseus 'rente adoun' these very walls (*KnT* 990). It follows, then, that in the *Manciple's Tale*, the chivalry of Phebus, rather than Theseus, supplies the ceremonious occasion that inaugurates the narrative.[3] In one sense, the *Canterbury Tales* is a Christian journey from Southwerk to Canterbury; in another, it is a literary journey from a generative, forward-looking paganism to a self-consuming and sterile one that can be salvaged only by the Parson's caustic medicines, which reject fable altogether.

The sheer tawdriness of Phebus's house and the events that occur within it might tempt us to read the *Manciple's Tale*, following James Dean, as a 'de-mythologized' travesty of a god, idealized elsewhere, 'who but slenderly knows himself, who acts by extremes in failing to curb his spirit, and who keeps neither his wife nor his tongue under control.'[4] Yet this is precisely the Apollo we have come to recognize so acutely in Ovidian tradition, mythographic convention, and Chaucerian poesis – indeed, this *is* Apollo's 'mythology.' For this reason, the *Manciple's Tale* may be the most genuinely Apolline and hyper-Ovidian of all the texts examined thus far; as such, it demands to be treated not only as a sociopolitical parable, as it has been capably and often, but as what may well be Chaucer's 'final use of ancient lore' – as a tale, that is, more than simply parodic or superficial in its engagement with classical precedent, reflecting an intrigue with the poetics of antiquity that encompasses much of Chaucer's pre-*Canterbury Tales* poetry and significantly punctuates the *Tales* themselves.[5] Indeed, we need not choose between a social and a mythic reading of the *Manciple's Tale*: it can profitably be understood as a mature reflection on the confluence of the ideology of literary paganism on the point of breakdown and the labile social repertoire of the here and now. Just as, in the *Manciple's Prologue*, the numbing effect of Bacchus's palliatives jestingly collapses fourteenth-century professional conflict into ancient ceremony, so does the Manciple, after his altercation with the Cook, instinctively construct an analogical relationship between contemporary and pagan experiences of the dangers of jangling through his choice of tale.

This chapter resituates the *Manciple's Tale*, as it were, on a road of pilgrimage inclusive of pagan *and* Christian trajectories, arguing that Apollo's house should be viewed at once as the corrupt locus of adultery, murder, and self-deception for which it is well-recognized, and as what amounts to a Delphic destination.[6] Specifically, Phebus's house becomes a site of revelatory performance by the crow, one that I will argue evokes association with oracular discourse both in its capacity for ambiguity and in precipitating an impasse of interpretation that leads to ethical crisis. Crucial to this reading is the second metamorphosis that Chaucer extraordinarily superimposes upon the transformation of Phebus's crow from white to black: the silencing of the crow's intelligible speech and, with it, the voice and materials of poetic expression. While the tale's metatextual concern with language has often been noticed, those critics who have focused on the vocal metamorphosis specifically have mostly viewed it within a framework of gender politics or of penitential and contemplative practice.[7] The following pages propose instead that the silencing of the crow and the connected issue of the disputed truth-value of the crow's report (which Phebus first believes, then disbelieves)[8] relate importantly to Apollo's status as god of prophecy and mythic presider over the issue and suppression of voice. Literary accounts of oracular activity known to Chaucer offered a suggestive precedent for the convergence of garrulousness, truth-telling, interpretation, and silence which he uniquely orchestrates in the *Manciple's Tale*. Furthermore, the literary genealogy of prophetic discourse overlaps pointedly with two of the tale's main thematic registers: testimonial birdsong – in classical terms, augury – and political counsel. Tracing the circulation of these diverse topics around the matter of oracles and the figure of Apollo as thwarted prophet, this chapter begins by considering the enduring association between oracles and *vox*, a motif present in the very sequence of Ovid's *Metamorphoses* from which the *Manciple's Tale* ultimately derives. Next, it examines the apparent ambiguity that surrounds Phebus's crow's act of truth-telling in light of pagan custom and epistemology, and then highlights a quasi-oracular crux (recognized after the fact) that turns Phebus's confrontation with the informing crow into a crisis of interpretation as well as a debacle of courtly counsel. The chapter concludes by reflecting on the intertextuality of the *Manciple's Tale*, and of prophetic discourse more generally, offering some observations regarding the structural position of the story of Apollo and Coronis in the *Canterbury Tales* and the *Metamorphoses*, in which the presence or absence of Aesculapius ultimately defines the success and salvific power of the poetic artefact.

Voicing the Oracle

From the Cook's silent, gaping mouth to the dental fortress out of which no 'tidynges' are to escape, the Manciple's prologue and tale are fixated upon the mouth as site of vocal expression, error, gossip, truth, and lies. The fragment's oral encasement finds thematic focus in the crow's possession and subsequent loss of his sweet song and fluent speech, matched in turn by Phebus's monumental shattering of his 'mynstralcie, / Both harpe, and lute, and gyterne, and sautrie' (*MancT* 267–8). No precedent exists for this emphasis on the crow's voice and its metamorphic deprivation or, for that matter, the cessation of Phebus's artistic designs; instead, the tale's sources and analogues focus solely on the bird's change of colour and the dangers of misplaced speech. A point of reference for the centrality of voice in the tale is readily apparent, however, when we consider the mythological apparatus of its central figure, Phebus, rather than seeing him merely as a human shadow of the glorious Apollo we (think we) know from other contexts. Historically, oracles were closely associated, like Phebus's crow, with the power of speech. Martianus Capella, for example, describes Apollo's Delphic cave as 'loquacia,' surrounded by an arboreal grove whose stirring replicates the music of the spheres.[9] Martianus's medieval commentators point out an etymological relationship between *fanum* (oracular temple) and *fone* (Gr. *phone*: sound, voice) or *for*, *fari* (to speak), and the past participle of the latter (*fatum*) in turn forms the root of *fatum*, i.e., fate or prediction.[10] The Cumaean Sibyl, in the *Aeneid*, prophesies from a hundred-mouthed cave from which as many voices issue, and in the *Metamorphoses*, she retains only her voice after her aged body has withered away.[11] Appropriately then, the decline of the oracles was figured as the silencing of the oracles, a topos that forms a conceptual counterpart to the early Christian ventriloquism of Apollo's 'last words' as a strategy of Christian self-authorization, explored in chapter 2 (pp. 83–5). The silence of the oracles was described influentially by Plutarch, Lucan, and Martianus Capella as well as by Christian writers, like the one responsible for this chapter's epigraph, who viewed the oracle's transformation from vocal to mute polemically, as confirmation of the new dispensation of Christ as the Word incarnate. 'The oracles are dumb,' proclaims Milton in a much-quoted passage in 'On the Morning of Christ's Nativity,' 'No voice or hideous hum / Runs through the arched roof in words deceiving.'[12] In fact, Chaucer need have looked no further than the second book of Ovid's *Metamorphoses* – the same book that relates the legend that evolved into the *Manciple's Tale* – to have found an example of truthful oracular utterance, associated with Apollo, emptied of its vocal power.

In *Metamorphoses* 2, after Apollo's raven (in Chaucer's version, a crow)[13] is metamorphosed from white to black the god delivers his son Aesculapius from the dead Coronis's womb, and then entrusts him to the centaur Chiron for rearing. This section of Ovid's narrative centres upon the prophetic outcry and subsequent metamorphosis of Chiron's irreverent daughter, the mantic Ocyroe, who is transformed from a half- to a full horse and deprived of her speaking voice. In this scene, Ocyroe's lengthy and vociferous prophecy concerning the fates of Aesculapius and Chiron angers Jupiter, who resists such a full unfolding of his designs. The specifically vocal dimension of Ocyroe's prophetic powers is identified with her garrulousness, underscored by her rambling oral description of the progressive experience of her physical transformation even as it is happening. Ocyroe's prophecy merges seamlessly into an account of her own metamorphosis, which continues until her human language also changes, first into the sounds of a person trying to imitate a horse, and finally into bona fide, unintelligible whinnies:

> ... 'praeuertunt,' inquit 'me Fata, uertorque
> plura loqui, uocisque meae praecluditur usus.
> non fuerant artes tanti, quae numinis iram
> contraxere mihi; mallem nescisse futura.'   (*Met.* 2.657–60)

[The Fates forestall me and I am forbidden
to say more and my use of speech is blocked.
The skills by which I have provoked god's anger
were not worth so much; I would rather not have known the future.]

As with Chaucer's crow, Ocyroe's silencing results from her imprudent truth-telling and, furthermore, specifically entails a reduction to
bestial noise. Similarly, in the *Manciple's Tale*, the crow's sweet song
is transformed into a harsh caw unsuited to linguistic communication (see *MancT* 300–1, 305–6). If Chaucer's crow is transformed in
appearance (colour) as well as voice, so is the metamorphosis of
Ocyroe dual in effect, changing both 'uox et facies' [voice and like-
ness] (*Met.* 2.675).

The end of the Ocyroe episode, considered in light of Ovid's debasement of Apollo's authority in chapter 1, returns Apollo to the story:
Chiron, distraught, calls out for the absent Apollo's help as his daughter
is metamorphosed, but Apollo is preoccupied elsewhere with his own
erotic affairs. Chiron's request for aid was regarded by later commentators as appropriately directed: the *Narrationes fabularum Ovidianarum*, an
epitome of the *Metamorphoses* of uncertain date attributed to Lactantius
Placidus, refers Ocyroe's gift of prophecy to Apollo's sponsorship, and
Arnulf of Orléans associates her with Cassandra, who was loved by
Apollo.[14] Ocyroe's Apolline associations are corroborated by the related
story of the Thracian prophet Phineus, also given the gift of prophecy by
Apollo but punished by Jove for revealing the future too clearly.[15]
Indeed, the reduction of Ocyroe's too-clear voice to brutish incoherence
may represent the enforcement of the ambiguity appropriate to prophecy, a register that both Ocyroe and Phineus lack. In the *Aeneid*, prophetic ambiguity carries traces of bestiality in a comparison, noted in
chapter 4, of the inspired Cumaean Sibyl to a raging *horse* (*Aen.* 6.100–1)
– an analogy validated, as it were, by the forthright Ocyroe's equine
metamorphosis.

At the same time, the silencing of Ocyroe on account of her indiscreet
speech evokes the classical topos of loss of voice as punishment for
challenging the gods, usually artistically.[16] A salient example of this motif is the myth of Thamyris, hubristic competitor with the Muses, first
related in the *Iliad* (2.691–3) and repeated in Statius's *Thebaid*, where
Chaucer could have encountered it:

> hic fretus doctas anteire canendo
> Aonidas mutos Thamyris damnatus in annos
> ore simul citharaque – quis obvia numina temnat?   (*Thebaid* 4.182–4)

[here Thamyris made bold to surpass in song the skilled daughters of
Aonia, but doomed to a life of silence fell on the instant mute with voice
and harp alike – who may despise deities met face to face?]

Statius goes on to relate Thamyris's transgression to that of Marsyas against Apollo; in fact, the legend of Marsyas – who loses his skin rather than his voice as a result of challenging Apollo to a musical contest – may inform the very words of Ovid's Ocyroe (*Met.* 2.259–60), which anticipate the memorable lament of Ovid's Marsyas: '"a! piget, a! non est" clamabat "tibia tanti"' ('Ah! I am sorry, ah! the flute,' he cried, 'it is not worth so much') (*Met.* 6.386).[17] Arnulf of Orléans invokes this motif of punishment-by-silencing with particular reference to Apollo in his gloss on Phoceus, grandson of Cephisus, whose metamorphosis receives brief notice at *Met.* 7.388–9. According to Arnulf, Phoceus's voice was silenced and he was transformed into a seal – the most silent of all fish – as punishment for foolishly disputing with Apollo.[18]

The second book of Ovid's *Metamorphoses*, then, engages directly with a creative vocabulary widely circulated in ancient literature that associates vocal expression and transgression, and the silencing of *vox*, with the discourse of prophecy as well as the perils of interfering with the divine order. The Ocyroe episode incorporates Apollo within this complex of motifs, and is, moreover, of direct relevance to the *Manciple's Tale* in its concluding relationship to the events of the Coronis story. An overly narrow view of the perimeter of Chaucer's Ovidian source has obscured for most critics the proximity of the Ocyroe episode to the element of vocal punishment that Chaucer adds to all prior versions of the Coronis legend. Such textual conservatism is dangerous: as I have shown elsewhere, the trend in medieval commentaries on *Metamorphoses* 2 is not to detach Ovid's narrative of Apollo, Coronis, and the raven from the episodes that surround and structure it, as occurs in vernacular poetic renditions of the story,[19] but to interpret it fully in the context of these peripheral narratives, which include the warning issued to Apollo's raven by Minerva's crow, the story of the crow's metamorphosis and banishment embedded in her warning, the delivery of Aesculapius after Coronis's murder, and the events involving Chiron and Ocyroe.[20] If anything, Chaucer's conspicuous elimination of both Coronis's pregnancy and the birth of Aesculapius from the story would presumably have sent the learned readers in his audience scurrying to their 'olde bookes' and the crutch of their commentaries, where they not only would have found the missing pieces but recurrently been encouraged to draw logical and moral connections among the various episodes that constitute the Coronis sequence. With considerable energy and frequent ingenuity, commentators conflated, telescoped, and repackaged these related

episodes in order to untangle them, encouraged by the dense inter-
weaving of this material already present in Ovid's text.[21]

The story of Ocyroe, as A.M. Keith has shown in detail, is closely
linked to the preceding episodes of the sequence, for example in the
prophetic status that she shares with the crow who warns the raven not
to divulge Coronis's misdeed and urges the credibility of its 'praesagia
linguae' [tongue's forewarning] (Met. 2.550). In fact, the theme of 'indiscreet loquacity' – the use and abuse of the voice, and the propriety and
utility of speech – unites this whole sequence of episodes as well as
later sections of Metamorphoses 2.[22] Just over fifty lines after the metamorphosis of the raven from white to black comes the tale of Mercury's
theft of the lovelorn Apollo's cattle, in which the herdsman Battus (i.e.,
'Chatterbox') reveals Mercury's secret and is transformed into a stone.
Later in Book Two, the maiden Aglauros, who first appears in an inset
narrative in the crow's warning, is also changed to a stone on account
of her envious compulsion to betray Mercury's secret desire for her sister Herse, as well as her verbal resistance of the god's will (Met. 2.812–
32). Like Apollo's raven, Aglauros is literally blackened by her verbal
transgression – 'nec lapis albus erat, sua mens infecerat illum' [But the
stone was not white, her mind had infected it] (Met. 2.832) – and like
Chaucer's crow, she is silenced through metamorphosis, her vocal passages horrifically petrified as creeping stone grips, then becomes, her
throat.[23] Seen in relation to such contexts, Chaucer's coal-black, laryn-
gitic crow invites understanding as a densely Ovidian creature formed
by the amalgamation of the core narrative of the raven with the vocal
punishment of Apollo's prophetess Ocyroe and the various irreverent
(but truth-telling) abusers of vox with whom she is associated in the
surrounding episodes of Metamorphoses 2.

White Lies, Black Ravens

The classical topos of vocal punishment, which as we have seen is tied
closely to the phenomenon of oracular truth-telling, would seem naturally relevant to the most pressing moral difficulty of the story of Apollo's
raven, in all of its versions: the fact that the raven is punished – and
usually disparaged by the narrator – for telling the truth about Coronis's
infidelity. This point is of particular importance in the Manciple's Tale, in
which Chaucer, far from shrugging off the problem as a vestigial inconsistency, takes pains to thematize the crow's truth-telling by introducing the loss-of-voice motif, causing the plot to turn upon Phebus's

vacillation over the truth of the crow's report, and showing Phebus to draw the conclusion – more explicitly and shockingly than in any other version – that the crow lied about his wife's adultery. It is easier, first of all, to regard the raven as justly punished when we see him as a meddler or a malicious tattle-tale rather than a faithful servant giving good counsel. Ovid, for example, tarnishes his character by making him stubborn (he refuses to listen to the crow's warning and dismisses her rudely) and his motives pecuniary (he expects a reward). Gower, in comparison, presents the raven as Coronis's pet bird, not Apollo's, implying that he owes a debt of loyalty to his mistress rather than to Apollo. And while Chaucer portrays a much more sympathetic crow than Ovid or Gower, evoking the social vulnerabilities of the medieval court poet, his expansion of the crow's characterization, particularly his direct speech, highlights the crow's affect, which has seemed to many readers mocking, malicious, even spiritually bankrupt.[24]

A closer look at the legendary and poetic traditions through which Apollo's raven reached Chaucer indicates that Phebus's mistrust of the crow in the *Manciple's Tale* has more than a purely irrational cause. A rival version of the story of Apollo's raven within Ovid's own oeuvre supports an alternate tradition of a lying bird – rather than a deliverer of an unwelcome truth – in relation to which the *Manciple's Tale* can be read as a kind of palimpsest, haunted by an unrealized narrative contingency. In *Fasti* 2.243–66, Apollo, preparing for a sacrifice to Jove, sends his raven to fetch water, but the raven, tempted by hunger, delays until the figs on a tree near the spring ripen; finally, he returns bearing 'ficta verba' [a lying tale] concerning an invented attack by a water-serpent to excuse his tardiness (*Fasti* 2.258). Apollo, unconvinced by this lie, curses the raven to suffer thirst while the figs ripen from that day forward, and later stellifies him.

Not surprisingly, Ovid's two divergent accounts of Apollo's punishment of the raven by means of metamorphosis in the *Fasti* and the *Metamorphoses* were sometimes juxtaposed and conflated by later mythographers.[25] Furthermore, the notion of the raven as lying traitor, and its impingement upon the separate tale involving the raven's change of colour, was inevitably shaped for the Middle Ages by Judaeo-Christian legendary tradition, which also featured a tale of an untrustworthy corvid in the account of Noah's ark in Genesis 8:6–7.[26] According to Genesis, after the deluge had calmed, Noah sent the raven as a messenger to determine whether the waters had receded from the land; when the raven failed to return, Noah sent the dove twice on the same errand,

and the second time she returned with the olive branch, signalling the end of the flood. Although some positive interpretations of the absence of Noah's raven did exist, the more common view deplored its treachery and selfishness, attributing its dereliction of duty to distraction by carrion.[27] In a Jewish legend related by Louis Ginzberg, the raven balks at Noah's command, claiming that Noah secretly wants to dispose of the raven, an unclean animal, and also to defile the raven's wife (!) while he is on his journey; when the raven finally accepts the mission, he fails to return to Noah with news because he is distracted by a floating corpse, which he sets about to devour.[28] The notion that the raven failed to return because of his gluttony became a standard feature of the legend, and strikingly mirrors the story in Ovid's *Fasti* involving the raven's distraction from his task (which similarly involves water) by his appetite. Particularly in Christian thought, the raven of Genesis represented the foul sensuality of humanity that the Flood had been designed to wash clean. Hugh of Fouilloy's moralized Aviary (c. 1132–52), for example, equates Noah's raven with despairing sinners, who feed on 'carnalibus desideriis' and 'curis exterioribus' instead of tending to their own souls.[29] The Church Fathers interpreted the raven as representative of the Jews who alienated themselves from the church, which is the ark, or as an image of backsliding Christians who fail to reform themselves spiritually despite their baptism, represented by the ark's immersion in the flood.[30] In the longer version of Guillaume de Deguileville's *Pèlerinage de vie humaine* (c. 1355), a work known to Chaucer and translated by Lydgate, the raven is associated with procrastination and spiritual sloth and presented as a proxy of the figure Apostasy.[31] The York mystery cycle, reflecting these views, portrays the raven as a 'fayland frende' cursed by Noah to suffer for his 'werkis wrange.'[32] Appropriately, in the Wakefield Noah pageant, Noah's rebellious wife chooses the raven as the most trustworthy bird for the errand, while the more prudent Noah favours the dove.[33]

Intriguingly, Eastern legends apparently unknown to the medieval West recorded a version of the Flood story in which Noah punishes the treacherous raven by changing its colour from white to black, reflecting an international folktale motif that also informs the Greco-Roman legend of Apollo and the raven transmitted in the *Metamorphoses*.[34] Without knowledge of this tradition, the twelfth-century English scholar and theologian Alexander Neckam felicitously linked all three raven-scenes under consideration (from Genesis, *Fasti*, and *Metamorphoses*) to create a similar implication. In his *De natura rerum*, a prose compendium of moralized scientific lore, Neckam juxtaposes the treachery of Noah's raven with an account of the raven's thirst in Ovid's *Fasti*.[35] Neckam's later poetic redaction of this treatise, *De laudibus divinae sapientiae*, explicitly points out that the raven betrayed both Noah and Apollo ('Tam Noe quam Phoebum decepit Apollinis ales'), and goes a step further to make the obvious connection between the garrulous raven's oral punishment of thirst in *Fasti* and 'ficta linguae mendacia' [the false lies of his tongue]. Finally, turning to the *Metamorphoses*, Neckam adds that the same raven's 'vitium linguae' [sin of the tongue] resulted in the wrongful murder of Apollo's lover Coronis, and, ultimately, in the raven's change of colour.[36] This cross-fertilization of traditions regarding the raven is damning: the nominal truthfulness of the raven's report in the *Metamorphoses* is almost completely elided under the pressure of these impinging contexts. Whether or not the fault is his, Apollo's raven carries mythic and literary associations that quite literally darken his reputation as a messenger in a given narrative before he even has a chance to open his beak.

The influence of the Ovidio-biblical figure of the treacherous raven, coupled with the irony that the raven in the *Metamorphoses* is condemned for telling the truth, encouraged implications in some postclassical versions that the raven may actually have lied to Apollo about the actions of Coronis.[37] The plausibility of the raven's mendacity is essential to understanding the central scenario of the crow's revelation and Phebus's unexpected reaction in the *Manciple's Tale*, in which the appearance (if not reality) of multiple interpretive possibilities, as we shall see, cuts to the heart of Phebus's role as god of prophecy. A brief survey of some of the complications that underlie the raven's disclosure of Coronis's adultery in versions of the narrative contemporary with Chaucer's enables us to see the logic of Phebus's self-deception more clearly. Evrart de Conty's *Livre des eschez amoureux moralisés* (c. 1390–1405), a commentary on the *Eschez amoureux* that contains ample mythographic material, relates the story of Coronis without offering the reader a moral foothold in independent verification of Coronis's adultery, such as a third-person narrative account or the dying Coronis's acknowledgment of her guilt (both of which occur in Ovid). Instead, we are told only that Apollo 'le soupeçonnoit et mescreoit d'avoir adultere commis' [suspected and evilly (or incorrectly) believed that she had committed adultery].[38] The raven's message again emerges as suspect in Machaut's *Voir dit* on account of the motives of Toute-Belle, who relates the story of Coronis to Amant in an effort to persuade him that she has not been faithless, and so should not be the victim of overhasty judgment. Although the fact of Coronis's infidelity in tradition – which, unlike in Evrart de Conty's commentary, is confirmed by Toute-Belle's own narratorial admission that Coronis slept with another man (7816–24) – clearly undercuts the narrator's attempt to exonerate herself by means of the story, the space for ambiguity found in the events of the story is significant. Upon cursing the raven, Apollo raises the possibility that the jangling bird lied: 'Et puet estre quelle estoit monde / De ce fait et que menti mas' [And it could be she's innocent / In this matter and that you've lied to me] (8119–20). In fact, Coronis's dying speech departs from the Ovidian source on which it is otherwise closely modelled by enigmatically, even cruelly, leaving open the possibility that Apollo has punished her for a crime she did not commit:

En morant dist lasse dolente
Bien voy que la mors mest presente
Et se nay pas mort desservi
Sen gre ne vous ai bien servi[.]   (8070–3)

[Dying, she said: 'Alas, miserable one!
I see well I'll die soon,
And yet I've not deserved death
If I have served you well in good faith.']³⁹

A provocative inversion of this apocryphal tangent involving a loved one falsely accused is found in a fabliau rendition of the Coronis narrative in the French and Middle English versions of the *Seven Sages of Rome*. Here the cast of characters features a magpie rather than a raven and a nameless 'burgeis' and his wife rather than Apollo and Coronis, and the plot unfolds differently from the classical version of the legend. The wife, who is guilty of adultery, frames the magpie by concocting an elaborate scheme meant to ensure that her husband will not believe the bird's revelation of her tryst. The husband falls for the trick and, believing his wife falsely maligned, kills his beloved bird in anger. ⁴⁰ The husband, however, later discovers his wife's ruse, recognizes her sexual and verbal treachery, and casts her out of the house while lamenting his rash murder of his pet magpie, whose good counsel he disbelieved. Indeed, the unfailingly truthful nature of the magpie's speech had been emphasized early in the narrative – 'Et il l'en créoit moult bien, qu'ele ne savoit mentir'; 'And þe burgeis louede his pie, / For he wiste he couþe nowt lie' – accentuating the shortsighted irony of the husband's later conclusion that the bird *did* lie.[41] Despite the fact that the wife is guilty in this version, the bird, who assumes the role of the murdered wife in the classical strand of the legend, is innocent. Yet another precedent is supplied here, then, for the ambiguous interplay of female treachery, the possibility of error, and a lying informer.[42]

In the *Manciple's Tale*, Phebus's bitter repentance and self-loathing after murdering his wife are not prompted, as in most other versions, by any pathetic dying words or the revelation of her pregnancy – both narrative elements are conspicuously lacking in Chaucer's version – but by Phebus's sudden, unexplained conclusion that the crow's words were false, and his wife true:

> 'Traitour,' quod he, 'with tonge of scorpioun,
> Thou hast me broght to my confusioun ...
> O deere wyf! O gemme of lustiheed!
> That were to me so sad and eek so trewe,
> Now listow deed, with face pale of hewe,
> Ful giltelees, that dorste I swere, ywys ...
> O trouble wit, O ire recchelees,
> That unavysed smyteth gilteles!'   (*MancT* 271–2, 274–7, 279–80)

This peripeteia on Phebus's part, centring on the validity of the crow's act of verbal reportage, seems related to Chaucer's subsequent addition of a specifically *vocal* metamorphosis – one that resonates, as we have noted, with the classical topos of the misuse of *vox*. Lacking any dying words from his wife to corroborate the crow's story, Phebus suddenly regards the truth of the bird's report as open to question. '[F]oolish naïveté' and 'warped recollection' indeed define Phebus's egotistical volte-face,[43] but at the same time, Phebus's doubt cannot so readily be isolated from the traditions of the deceptive informer, the treacherous raven who tries to delude his master with *ficta verba*, and the potentially innocent accused. On the one hand, we readers, having witnessed the adultery in third-person narration, are assured of the truthfulness of the crow's revelation, but on the other, we can appreciate why Phebus, god of poetry in its last gasps, subscribes to a kind of textual paranoia: over-reading the crow's message to compensate for having under-read his own narrative experience, Phebus's tortured response is shaped by the pressures of those widespread traditions that associate the raven with lies and deceit.[44] If we give these traditions their due as spectral presences in the *Manciple's Tale*, we can better understand Chaucer's aims and procedure in re-imagining the exchange between Phebus and crow to raise complex issues of perspective, truth-telling, and interpretation at the heart of this last, heartless tale.

'Trouthe thee shal delivere'

Why would Chaucer wish to open the authenticity of the crow's revelation to doubt, if only in Phebus's mind, by activating literary contexts that are ultimately incompatible with the events of the *Manciple's Tale*? To answer this question, we must look closer at the crow's speech to Phebus as it unfolds after his initial, jarringly interspecial 'Cokkow!'[45] In choosing not simply to summarize the crow's revelation, but to grant it nine full lines of direct discourse, all the more conspicuous for their rhetorical nuance, Chaucer compels us to consider the issue of language as a mediating force in a way that is unparalleled in all other versions of the tale, which studiously avoid representing the raven's words to Apollo. Part nostalgia, part bitterly ironic flattery, the crow's speech reads like a hymn of praise from which the bottom devastatingly drops out:

> 'By God,' quod he, 'I synge nat amys.
> Phebus,' quod he, 'for al thy worthynesse,
> For al thy beautee and thy gentilesse,
> For al thy song and al thy mynstralcye,
> For al thy waityng, blered is thyn ye
> With oon of litel reputacioun,
> Noght worth to thee, as in comparisoun,
> The montance of a gnat, so moote I thryve!
> For on thy bed thy wyf I saugh hym swyve.'   (*MancT* 248–56)

Phebus at first believes the crow; then, after having committed murder, changes his mind and declares his wife 'giltelees.' There is no doubt, as critics have observed, that the tyrannical Phebus's sense that his ego is at stake compels him to 'ventriloquize' his silent and silenced wife as a paragon of chastity in order to 'protect the myth of his wife's innocence,' and by extension his own reputation as 'fulfild of gentillesse, / Of honour, and of parfit worthynesse' (*MancT* 123–4).[46] The garrulous crow's association with prophetic discourse, however, encourages a somewhat different reading of the scene, one in which Phebus, who we recall is introduced as 'Delphice' at the beginning of Ovid's version of the story (*Met.* 2.543), first acts out, then deconstructs, his own mythic province as god of oracular interpretation. Embedded in the crow's revelation, I argue, is an 'oracle' of sorts, delivered not through but *to* the oracular divinity himself. Phebus's multiple reactions to the crow's words prove what victims of Apollo's oracles have always eventually discovered: that oracles are *'about* equivocation,' and that 'the ultimate question about an oracle ... is not whether it tells the truth but what we will allow to count as the truth.'[47]

We need not look far past the horizon of Fragment IX for a deliberate link between oracular prophecy and transgressive utterance. The *Parson's Tale* details several forms of transgressive speech, a branch of wrath, which are potentially relevant to the crow's discourse in the *Manciple's Tale.*[48] Especially striking is the Parson's inclusion of divination as a sin of the mouth (specifically, a form of swearing), a categorization without precedent in Peraldus's *Summa vitiorum* or the 'Quoniam' redaction, Chaucer's two primary sources in this part of the tale.[49] '[H]em that bileeven on divynailes,' according to the Parson, make predictions *'as by flight or by noyse of briddes*, or of beestes, by sort, by nigromancie, by dremes,' and other signs (*ParsT* 604; emphasis added). This passage makes clear that Chaucer not only was aware of the pagan practice of augury, divination through the voice or flight pattern of birds – also referenced in *Tr* 5.380–2 – but was attuned to its close connection with the medium of speech.[50] Indeed, the *Manciple's Tale's* scenario of a bird advising a human being about a pressing circumstance by means of a vocal utterance that necessitates interpretation is on one level strongly suggestive of augury. This level of significance is by no means far-fetched: in fact, it is supported by no less an authority than Boccaccio's *Genealogie deorum gentilium*, which contains a euhemeristic treatment of the Coronis myth in which Apollo reacting to the report of the raven is explicated as a mortal who detects his wife's adultery through augury ('augurandi peritia fornicationem novisse Coronidis').[51]

These are not the only ties that bind Phebus's crow to a literary context of augury. Ovid's account of the prophetess Ocyroe, as we have seen, supplies one model for the vocal punishment of a garrulous truth-teller within a narrative sequence of demonstrable relevance to the *Manciple's Tale.* Ovid's crow, a prophet whose forewarning of disaster is ignored by the raven, supplies another precedent – especially if, as I have suggested elsewhere, the exemplary self-promotion of Ovid's crow influenced Chaucer's unique designation of his tale's avian protagonist as a 'crowe' rather than a raven.[52] Both crows and ravens were associated with prophecy in the ancient world (see, e.g., Horace, *Odes* 3.27.11, 16), and both were used in Roman augury.[53] In medieval bestiary and encyclopedic lore, the crow was, if anything, more closely linked to prophecy than the raven, as Phebus's pronouncement that the crow henceforth will 'crie agayn tempest and rayn' indicates (*MancT* 301).[54] An influential account of the crow in Isidore of Seville's *Etymologiae*, repeated by Rabanus Maurus, the *Bestiary*, and Bartholomaeus Anglicus, emphasizes the crow's association not only with meteorological prediction but the foretelling of a range of human affairs: 'quam aiunt augures hominum curas significationibus agere, insidiarum vias monstrare, futura praedicere' [Augurs say that this bird by its signs is attentive to the concerns of humans, and shows the paths where ambush lies, and predicts the future].[55] Guillaume de Deguileville's *Pèlerinage de vie humaine* presents the crow, which '[m]akyth noyse and cryeth ofte,' as a dark agent of Necromancy's company.[56] Finally, an etiology provided in Ovid's *Fasti* for the sacrifice of birds to the gods provides an interesting inversion of the story of Apollo's punishment of the crow. In Ovid's account, avian sacrifice was instituted to check the powers of birds who, through a fault of the tongue ['linguae crimen'], revealed too clearly the thoughts of the gods to augurs (1.445). Viewed within the context of augural practice, the *Manciple's Tale* enacts a revealing counter-instance of this legend: instead of suffering punishment for divulging the hidden designs of the gods to men, Chaucer's crow is cursed for revealing the secrets of men to a god.

Much irony here lies in the fact that Phebus, rather than acting as master of the auspices, is himself subject to their signifying power; his reversion to divine prerogative in punishing the crow, then, is distinctly unconvincing. Phebus's status in the *Manciple's Tale* as an earthly prince as well as Olympian god further deepens his participation in the discourse of prophecy. In ancient and medieval culture, prophecy was closely connected both with poetic expression and political counsel. The earliest oracles allegedly were delivered in verse, an inherently ambiguous form that, according to Plutarch, functioned as a protective measure for prophets who had to deliver unwelcome truths obliquely, shifting uncertainty about future events into the realm of interpretive uncertainty.[57] Oracular ambiguity, however, also invited abuse, as Nicole Oresme illustrates in contemporary medieval terms in his *Livre de divinacions* (c. 1361–5), a work to which Chaucer turned for scholarly detail in his treatment of pagan divination in the

Troilus.[58] Building on Cicero's *De divinatione* and a panoply of classical and Christian authorities, Oresme discusses prophecy in relation to princely counsel, stressing the danger that divination poses to 'personnes d'estat comme sont princes et seigneurs auxquels appartient le gouvernement publique' [those of high estate, such as princes and lords to whom appertains the government of the commonwealth].[59] The treatise's twelfth chapter, which supplies Chaucer with his definition of 'ambages' at *Tr* 5.897–8, inveighs against the propensity of court diviners to mislead princes with their flattering prophecies, which are premised on the Senecan notion that 'the truth is hateful' to rulers.[60] Furthermore, Oresme states, court diviners

> make secret enquiries into the state of persons and things hidden and then, what they know only by hearsay, or what they have guessed by human wit ['par conjecture humainne'], they pretend to divine by their science … And, when they have predicted and are doubtful as to whether their prediction will be verified, they bring it to pass by any means in their power, by treason, fraud, or by nigromancy, malefice, or otherwise. And there are some among them who, when they have prophesied misfortune to their own lord, would rather the misfortune happened to him than that they themselves should be rebuked and found wanting[.][61]

Some court prognosticators, by Oresme's reckoning, tell their princes what they want to hear rather than advancing truth,[62] while others pass off gossip as prophecy, using their influence treacherously to malign their enemies and advance their own interests.

Present as well as future events were very much under the purview of court prophecy and ancient oracles; indeed, many of the surviving Delphic oracles concern current events. Prophets, according to Theodore L. Steinberg, are properly speaking 'forthtellers rather than foretellers,' for whom the future is part of a continuous present.[63] Oresme implies as much in his critique of prognosticators' expertise in exploiting petty grudges and simmering scandals to 'reveal' supposed threats to the well-being of the auditor:

> When they [diviners] feel that a man is inclined to think ill of another, they instil into him unfounded suspicion of the other and say in their divinations, for instance, that he has planned such and such, or has plotted treason against him, so that hatred or vengeance or other great misfortune is the result.[64]

Returning to the *Manciple's Tale* from this Oresmian vantage point, we find the princely Phebus receiving counsel from a figure elsewhere linked to prophetic expression. Oresme's scenario of a diviner accusing an innocent person of treason on account of a perceived distrust could very well describe the central sequence of the *Manciple's Tale*, with the exception of the innocence of the accused – an exception that Phebus, of course, finally chooses to ignore. We are made aware from the beginning of the tale, in true fabliau style, that Phebus is 'inclined to think ill' of his wife: 'Jalous he was, and wolde have kept hire fayn. / For hym were looth byjaped for to be' (*MancT* 144–5). The crow's disclosure, it is important to note, plays on suspicions that Phebus already had of his wife; when an act of 'hatred or vengeance or other great misfortune' indeed results from the crow's report, it is as if Phebus is living out the ill effects denoted in Oresme's *précis* of false prophecy. The point is not that the crow's revelation is false – it is not – but that an arsenal of scholarly and literary rationalizations exists for Phebus to exploit when he convinces himself that no wife of *his* could have been unfaithful. These contexts, which seem to be part of the mental apparatus of the god of poetry, tarnish the crow by associating him with legendary avian deceit and self-interest, and by aligning him with devious uses of prophecy in a courtly setting. If the crow's 'oracle' is not already ambiguous, Phebus will do his best to make it so.[65] No great stretch of the imagination is necessary to refurbish Phebus's house as the House of Rumour, in which truth and lies cavort at will.

The case for a 'prophetic' reading of the climax of the *Manciple's Tale* is more than circumstantial; textual support from elsewhere in Chaucer's works gives it notable authority and substantiates the tale's participation in a Chaucerian poetics of antiquity. A familiar Chaucerian scene in which a famed prophet counsels a prince – Cassandra's interpretation of Troilus's dream of the boar in Book Five of *Troilus and Criseyde* – mirrors the crow's exchange with Phebus in a way that strongly suggests that Chaucer regarded the two scenes as a conceptual pair. Cassandra was, of course, the locus classicus of the seer whose true prophecies were denied, and her cursed prophetic powers, we recall, were granted by her lover Apollo. Both Phebus's crow and Cassandra reveal an act of adultery to idealistic male lovers, and both prove their interpretations of circumstance 'by sadde tokenes and by wordes bolde' (*MancT* 258): the crow with a luridly detailed eyewitness account and Cassandra with an exhaustive cultural history that elucidates the erotic symbolism of Troilus's dream. Troilus dreams of a boar

'[t]hat slepte ayeyn the bryghte sonnes hete' (*Tr* 5.1239), an image repeated in the Manciple's account of the Python slain by Phebus 'as he
lay / Slepynge agayn the sonne upon a day' (*MancT* 109–10). Both
prophet-figures expose a current and ongoing, rather than future, betrayal. Furthermore, the crow's and Cassandra's speeches, for all their
truthful authority, share a distinctly patronizing tone and a rhetorical
delight in the act of narrating bad news that does their message no
good.[66] Cassandra begins her interpretation of Troilus's dream by in-
wardly admiring the depths of her own knowledge in a gesture that can
only be described as condescending ('She gan first smyle, and seyde,
"O brother deere ..."' [*Tr* 5.1457]) and ends it, more than a little pleased
with her meticulous exposition, by cavalierly dismissing emotion altogether: 'Wep if thow wolt, or lef, for out of doute, / This Diomede is
inne, and thow art oute' (5.1518–19). In a similar way, Phebus's crow
turns information that he knows full well will be cause for Phebus's
devastation into an opportunity for delivery of his magnum opus, a
bloated panegyric of Apolline virtues built up only to be cut down as
indiscriminately meaningless and brutally ineffectual. These prophets'
revelations of truth are similarly blunt, half-gleefully unfeeling, and
both are divulged pithily in the last line of their lengthy narratives:
'This Diomede is inne, and thow art oute'; 'For on thy bed thy wyf I
saugh hym swyve' (*Tr* 5.1519; *MancT* 256). The former line, with its
transparent sexual innuendo, is nearly as coarse as the latter, and stabs
at the ear similarly with its abundance of monosyllables.

   Like Phebus, Troilus rejects the truth with which he is confronted
against his better knowledge, after having initially believed it. Upon
waking, Troilus himself had interpreted his dream as indicative that
'My lady bryght, Criseyde, hath me bytrayed' (*Tr* 5.1247); however,
Troilus resolutely denies this same interpretation when Cassandra advances it. Again like Phebus, Troilus projects the fact of his lady's sexual
falseness onto the truthful prophet herself,[67] claiming that the interpretation is false and Criseyde true; then he orders the prophet to depart:

   '*Thow seyst nat soth*,' quod he, 'thow sorceresse,
   With al thy *false* goost of prophecye!
   Thow wenest ben a gret devyneresse!
   Now sestow nat this *fool of fantasie*
   Peyneth hire on ladys for to *lye*?
   Awey!' quod he. 'Ther Joves yeve the sorwe!
   Thow shalt be fals, peraunter, yet tomorwe!'   (*Tr* 5.1520–6; emphases added)

Strikingly similar is Phebus's condemnation of the crow, whom he similarly regards as false in order to avoid believing the same of his wife:

And to the crowe, 'O *false* theef!' seyde he,
'I wol thee quite anon thy *false tale.*
Thou songe whilom lyk a nyghtyngale;
Now shaltow, *false* theef, thy song forgon'[.]

> (*MancT* 292–5; emphases added)

When, in line 1526, Troilus caps his outburst with a prediction that Cassandra's falseness will continue tomorrow, he brilliantly mocks the integrity of Cassandra's prophetic discourse, which he insinuates is the hobby of a crackpot rather than a gift of the gods.

Perhaps the most enticing of all these links between these passages from *Troilus* and the *Manciple's Tale,* however, is Troilus's particular offence at Cassandra's inclination 'on ladys for to lye' (*Tr* 5.1524). What Cassandra said cannot be true, reasons Troilus against his better judgment, because no one can be right in saying such crude things about the ins and outs of *ladies* – and Cassandra, king's daughter though she may be, is no lady.[68] This, of course, is precisely the line of thought that so disturbs the Manciple, who insists that '[t]her nys no difference, trewely' between a woman of high degree and a 'povre wenche,' if they are both lecherous, other than the arbitrary linguistic custom that calls one a 'lady, as in love' and the other a 'lemman' (*MancT* 212, 215, 218, 220). Both, in the Manciple's acrid view, are whores, their bodies equally defiled. Troilus's objection to Cassandra's bad-mouthing of ladies suggests that he recognizes that her news regarding Criseyde similarly threatens the distinction between *lady* and *lemman,* on which culture itself rests. Cassandra talks about Criseyde the way that the Manciple, and even more pointedly the crow, talk about 'ladies': as a wench to be 'swyved.' On virtually every level – the manner and structure of their revelations, the harshness and forthright nature of their delivery, and the reaction they provoke in their once-believing auditors – Cassandra and the crow emerge as prophetic alter egos.

Eating Crow: Oracle and Aftermath

On the face of it, the crow's sing-song iambic-pentameter bombshell, 'For on thy bed thy wyf I saugh hym swyve' (*MancT* 256), like Cassandra's last and greatest line, could not be more straightforward, and it has consistently been regarded as such in the tale's criticism. The syntax of the crow's line, however, is strikingly artful. The crow's with-holding of the main verb 'swyve' until the last word not only maxi-mizes the punch-in-the-gut,[69] but tantalizes and taunts – as his whole speech has done – by withholding meaning until the last possible mo-ment. Setting, protagonists, and perspective are all established in this last line before the action that structures and defines them. In this sense, the line could be said to induce (temporary) interpretive vertigo. Although the point may seem academic, it is not immediately clear from the syntax *who* is doing the swyving; the main verbal phrase 'I saugh' could take either 'thy wyf' or 'hym' as direct object, either of which in turn could govern 'swyve.'[70] Despite the comparable syntax, no such ambiguity inheres in the line that shortly follows, 'And in his ire his wyf thanne hath he slayn' (*MancT* 265), though the echo suggests the close, even causative relationship between the last line of the crow's revelation and Phebus's rash action.[71] Two MSS (BL Lansdowne MS 851 and McCormick MS, University of Chicago Library 564) corroborate a reading of male agency in the details of the crow's report at lines 311–12: 'Ne telleth nevere no man in youre lyf / How that another man hath *swyved* his wife' (the Riverside editors, following majority textual opin-ion, print 'dight' here). Nonetheless, it is apparent that the syntax of the crow's line presents the power dynamics, and hence the context and significance, of the scenario ambiguously. Granted that it does not ul-timately matter who was the sexual aggressor, the introduction of ambiguity and multiple possibilities into the events upon which Phebus's murderous reaction is based is significant. That is to say, the crow's language demands 'wit' and 'discrecion' on the part of the aud-itor—qualities that Phebus later laments he did not exercise when lis-tening to the crow (*MancT* 282) – and gives force to Phebus's chilling regret, not that he killed his wife, but that he did so without under-standing all the facts: 'Smyt nat to soone,' he enjoins, 'er that ye witen why' (*MancT* 285).

Divinatory wordplay, the technical name for which is kledonomancy, as enacted in classical literature played ingeniously on puns and double meanings, 'revealing an extent of meaning greater than what any hu-man listener could have suspected or foreseen.'[72] The mechanism of kledonomancy is frequently activated by overhearing a chance word or phrase and mining it for submerged meaning predictive of the subject's own future. In an example cited in Cicero's *De divinatione*, Marcus Crassus, preparing to embark on a doomed expedition against the

Parthians, hears a fruit seller call out to him to buy some *cauneas* (figs), but fails to recognize the punning omen *Cave ne eas* [Beware how you go] embedded in the word.[73] In the *Manciple's Tale*, the crow's 'Cokkow!' functions similarly, signalling the thickening of language into something other than the literal. Phebus comes home and overhears the crow singing this unprecedented song, which on one level is nothing more nor less than non-referential bird music, a 'natural irrational [song]' without human significance.[74] Alarm sets in, however, when Phebus, drawing on human resources of rational association and cultural knowledge, detects the potential for a double meaning in the crow's 'cokkow,' one that demands association with the word 'cuckold' and finds confirmation in the literary genre of *caccia* or *chasse*, 'a standard fourteenth-century musical type in which the cuckoo-cuckold pun is commonplace,' which the crow's song closely matches.[75] In response to Phebus's request for clarification, the crow delivers the 'oracle' proper, culminating in the grammatically multivalent, if not genuinely equivocal, 'For on thy bed thy wyf I saugh hym swyve.' If the crow's revelation does not seem as ambiguous as we would expect of a genuine oracle, it must be remembered that, conventionally, oracles are ambiguous only upon second glance, as is the case with Mars's seemingly straightforward promise of 'Victory!' to Arcite in the *Knight's Tale*.[76] The inquirer's instinctive initial reaction to an oracle, or apprehension of a chance remark, is usually at odds with the *lectio difficilior*, which turns out to be the correct interpretation. Furthermore, a 'straightforward response' from an oracle 'is not necessarily unambiguous,' and 'a reputation for knowing the truth ... is not the same as a reputation for telling the truth.'[77] Phebus's self-contradictory reaction to the crow's revelation, first believing then disbelieving its implication that his wife was unfaithful, completes the tale's delineation of the traumatic unfolding of oracular narrative, 'in which obscurity becomes a name for a clarity you can't bear.'[78]

Before turning to Phebus's reaction itself, let us consider the possibility that the 'ambiguity' attached to the final line of the crow's speech – who was on top – pertains less to misinformation than perspective. Given the overlap between the climax of the *Manciple's Tale* and the interchange between Cassandra and Troilus, it is perhaps not coincidental that a similar erotic ambiguity appears in the dream that Troilus presents to Cassandra for interpretation. It has been argued that the interspecial embrace of the boar and Criseyde in this dream, unlike in Boccaccio's version, presents an intentionally ambiguous 'locus of sexual energy and initiative,' reflected in the confused textual transmission of a crucial pronoun: 'And by this bor, faste in his [many MSS read *hire*] armes folde' (*Tr* 5.1240), which foregrounds 'genuine interpretive alternatives.'[79] The syntactical ambiguity in *MancT* 256 is similar in form, and could further be compared with that exemplified by the notorious oracle of Pyrrhus, also discussed by Cicero: 'Aio, te Aechida, Romanos vincere posse.'[80] The ambiguity of this oracle derives from a cruel semantic trick: 'te' can either be the subject ('you can defeat the Romans') or the object ('the Romans can defeat you'). The accusative case ('te') necessitated by the indirect discourse ('Aio' = I say) in Pyrrhus's oracle occludes grammatical clarity just as the insistence upon perspective in the crow's words ('I saugh') obscures meaning by presenting the subject of the action (whoever that is) as object of the crow's gaze. In both cases, it is the ego, the subjective perspective ('I say,' 'I saugh') that simultaneously authorizes the statement – by claiming omniscience and privileged access to truth – and deranges it, initiating a dangerous game in which the auditor must recover and recreate meaning in order to recognize the truth. But while the burden of correct understanding is placed upon the interpreter, the promise of absolute truth as object of the game is compromised by the speaker's own subjectivity: it is always possible that the 'I' has gotten in the way of the 'it,' not just in the process of communication, but in the act of perception itself. This is precisely the implication with which May, in the *Merchant's Tale*, taunts Januarie out of believing that he witnessed her adultery:

> Ful many a man weneth to seen a thyng,
> And it is al another than it semeth.
> He that mysconceyveth, he mysdemeth.   (*MerT* 2408–10)

If even ocular proof is insufficient to convince this doting cuckold that his wife copulated with another man – like Phebus, Januarie first believes then disbelieves the reality of the adultery – how much more tenuous is the potentially ambiguous verbal report of a potentially biased and, after all, historically untrustworthy eyewitness related in the *Manciple's Tale*.

All this is pure rationalization, of course, but in my view Phebus is guilty of it, driven by a desperate instinct to preserve a self-image of which no perceptive reader is convinced in the first place. When Phebus suddenly decides, albeit belatedly, that his wife was innocent and the crow's words either a straight-out lie (the Oresmian interpretation) or misleading in their ambiguity (the Delphic interpretation), he acts as if he has just epiphanically discovered, after the fact, the real solution to an oracular riddle, like Oedipus making the sickening discovery of his real parentage. In a sense, Phebus is overdetermined by his own mythic history: having been so intent on epistemologically challenging or, in the Christian view, deceiving inquirers at his own oracle, Phebus here believes himself deceived, instinctively viewing the crow's advice as a kind of oracular trick – when, in reality, the only deception that has occurred is Phebus's self-deception.[81] Phebus's regret at having assumed the truth-value of an act of verbal reportage is to an extent appropriate in the context of a tale that explicitly interrogates the correspondence between words and the things they signify, between 'lemmans' and ladies, cuckoos and cuckolds, Coronises and Criseydes. Phebus's initial belief in the crow's report represents a fulfilment of his worst fears about his wife, while his later revision of his interpretation enacts an indulgence of his wishes, grounded in a nominal ambiguity within the crow's words that sheds doubt on the actual circumstances of the witnessed event as well as on the trustworthiness of the crow's perspective. But if Phebus doubts the proximity of the crow's linguistic representation to factual reality, he replaces that faulty linguistic representation with one of his own by mythologizing his dead wife as a paragon of truth – much as Troilus, in reaction to Cassandra's counsel at *Tr* 5.1527–33, transforms Criseyde into Alceste (with whom the narrator, notably, *contrasts* her at *Tr* 5.1778).

In silencing the crow and shattering his musical instruments, finally, Phebus not only negates the possibilities of poetry but, in effect, silences his own oracle, setting the stage for a contrast between the contingent nature of pagan truth and its Christian antithesis in the *Parson's Tale*. In the last breaths of the *Manciple's Tale*, I would suggest, before Phebus's house is smothered by the prolix, quotidian lesson deriving from the narrator's mother, Chaucer stages a figurative idol-smashing to match the one rhetorically accomplished at the expense of 'payens corsed olde rites' at the end of the *Troilus*, discussed in chapter 3 (*Tr* 5.1849). Remarkably, even while at this moment Chaucer prepares ineluctably for the Christian ending of the pilgrimage, he does not force a Christian army upon the unfortified plain of the *Manciple's Tale*. No crusading Parson is required to smash the idols and shut down the oracles: Phebus, crushing and blasting his own icons, then wishing for death (*MancT* 291), does it himself.

Coda

Prophecy, writes Alessandro Barchiesi, 'create[s] an interface not only between different time periods inside and outside the narrative, but also between different texts.'[82] In the *Manciple's Tale*, prophecy offers Chaucer an opportunity to explore in an almost nihilistic spirit the wrinkles within and recombinative possibilities of literary tradition regarding Apollo. The oracular subtext of the tale licenses, in a way, Chaucer's radical innovations regarding the well-known story of Apollo and Coronis, showing it to equivocate and rewrite itself in the very act of narration, to always risk becoming a story other than the one it is. The tale's concern with prophetic discourse also acts as a spur to an intratextual reflection on Chaucer's own poetics, reminding us that if it is the storyteller's responsibility to make the 'word ... accorde with the dede' (*MancT* 208) – an epistemological absolute that itself emerges as paradoxically double in its two appearances in the *Canterbury Tales*, first to open up and then to close down the possibilities of poetry – it is our own act of interpretation as readers (to an extent, an oracular act) that *constitutes*, and must ultimately bear responsibility for, meaning. We are faced in Chaucer's poetry with a range of interpretive possibilities of which Apollo's mythographic role as a diffuser of signification – a god whose oracular raven, according to Fulgentius, has a voice bearing sixty-four different meanings – is a nightmare scenario. 'Blameth nat me,' writes Chaucer with deadpan oracularity, 'if that ye chese amys' (*MilProl* 3181).

When Phebus breaks his instruments and silences his crow at the end of the *Manciple's Tale*, Chaucer explodes and perhaps exorcises his poetics of their saturation by the superannuated matter of Apollo: the Apollo who failed to provide lasting inspiration in the *House of Fame*, whose vacillating authority underwrote the epic history of Troy, who functioned as a frangible mirror of poetic production in Fragment V of the *Canterbury Tales*, and who, at the end of his literary journey, required an informer to gain awareness of the goings-on in his own house. In this final, bleak vision of Apollo, the crises and anticlimaxes that elsewhere empowered Chaucer's reflection on his poetics, their envelopment by the literary past, and his own identity as author come to a head in a way that inhibits textual transmission: both the crow's ability to relay events it witnesses and the growth of stories out of stories within the poetics of pilgrimage are brought to a halt. Chaucer's final encounter with the god of poetry in the *Canterbury Tales*, it could be said, appropriates the legacy of Apollo to contemplate the death of the author, and thus prepares not only for the *Parson's Tale* but the *Retraction*.

The *Manciple's Tale* accomplishes all this so powerfully in large measure because of its placement in the closing sequence of the *Canterbury Tales*, where it provides the last and bleakest instance of a diseased world in need of the Parson's spiritual remedies, more powerful even than Becket's health-bringing relics.[83] Like the *Canterbury Tales*, Ovid's *Metamorphoses* is framed by a concern with the healing arts situated within an Apolline trajectory. As noted in chapter 1, Apollo's demoralizing failures as a medical practitioner, emphasized throughout the *Metamorphoses*, are epitomized early in the epic by his inability to revive Coronis. The medical successes of Ovid's Aesculapius, then, reverse and correct his father Apollo's shortcomings, even leading, in the case of the risen Hippolytus, to a cure for death. Boccaccio's *Genealogie*, sensitive to this pattern of reversal, observes that while Apollo 'cum remediis suis illam [Coronis] nequiret ab Inferis revocare' [was not able with his remedies to call her (Coronis) back from the Underworld], Aesculapius succeeded in the equivalent enterprise: 'mortuum hominem ab Inferis revocaret in vitam' [he called back a dead man to life from the Underworld].[84] Our first view of Apollo in the *Metamorphoses* dramatizes his painful wounding by Cupid, from which he cannot heal himself; at the end of the epic, in a scene that confirms Ocyroe's prophecy of the future glory of Apollo's son, Aesculapius exercises his healing arts successfully to cure Rome of plague. Following this medical triumph, a series of Roman apotheoses culminates in that of Ovid himself as artist. By placing as unlikely an Ovidian narrative as that of Apollo and Coronis at the *end* of the *Canterbury Tales*, Chaucer encourages us to read his story collection structurally against Ovid's. Eliminating the birth of Aesculapius in the *Manciple's Tale*, Chaucer strips the myth, quite literally, of its fertility and potential for self-correction. In positioning this narrative thus aborted of possibility at the end of the *Canterbury Tales*, the very place where, in its Ovidian correlative, the *triumph* of Aesculapius is found, Chaucer stages a metamorphosis of omission that sets his poetry in an Ovidian lineage even while superseding it. For all his exposure of the limitations of *ars*, Ovid ends by granting it a voice, healed of earthly corruption, that will last forever, immune to the wrath of Jove and the oblivion of change. Chaucer, in contrast, silences poetry, providing as a final image an Apollo who is broken and without issue, leaving future readers to wonder if it is only the sound of their own voices within his temple walls.

Notes

Introduction

1 The 'classical tradition,' as treated in this book, is simultaneously fixed
   and permeable; in Helen Cooper's characterization, it is 'a corpus of
   literature that carried authoritative status, but whose authority [Chaucer]
   increasingly challenged' while obliquely interpolating himself within its
   discursive structure to claim for his own poetry a comparable authority
   ('The Classical Background,' 255, 264). It should not be forgotten that the
   term 'classical,' like 'medieval,' was unavailable to Chaucer, who called
   the works of classical authors, with no great premium on historical
   exactitude, 'olde bokes,' or, still more broadly, 'poesye.' Textual authority,
   cultural prestige, and the exoticism of the ancient, therefore, define the
   medieval conception of classical poetry more than the rigid temporal
   criteria employed in later periods. For all their referential imperfections,
   the terms 'classical' and 'classical tradition' are an integral apparatus of
   the critical discourse to which this book contributes, with the addition of a
   third concept: 'classicizing.' By this I mean the intentional colouring of a
   medieval (or later) work with mythological allusions, devices such as
   invocations to pagan deities, and/or setting in the ancient past, with the
   aim of transmitting, reinventing, or conversing with the *idea* of ancient
   literature, often by means of modernizing and assimilating it into newly
   readable forms. 'Classical' is used in this book with reference to a fixed
   body of Greco-Roman cultural forms from a period broadly spanning the
   eighth century BCE to the fifth century CE. 'Classicizing' is used in
   contexts that highlight the permeability and dynamic appropriation of
   classical forms.

2 As Cannon has observed of the formation of Chaucer's iconic status in the fifteenth century, 'Chaucer had made himself conduit to a hieratic litera-ture by joining his own writing to a privileged line of earlier poets, and his successors were more than willing to endorse his claim because, in their endorsement, they, too, partook of the fruits of his achievement' (*Making of Chaucer's English*, 185).

3 Chaucer, 'The Complaint of Chaucer to his Purse,' line 22. All Chaucer citations are from the *Riverside Chaucer* and will hereafter be documented in the main text by line number.

4 Keats, *The Letters of John Keats*, 384–5.

5 Citations of Keats's poetry, by line number, are from *The Complete Poems*, ed. Barnard.

6 Letter to Richard Woodhouse, 27 October 1818, in Keats, *The Letters of John Keats*, 227. On Apollo's dramatization of Keats's theory of negative capability, see Bode, 'Hyperion, *The Fall of Hyperion*, and Keats's Poetics.'

7 Bernstein, 'Subjectivity as Critique,' 50. For a broader view of the import-ance of Apollo to Keats's understanding of the poetic imagination and the artist's identity, see Evert, *Aesthetic and Myth*, 23–87; on Apollo's role in *Hyperion* specifically, see White, *John Keats*, 119–38.

8 Bernstein, 'Subjectivity as Critique,' 48.

9 See, for example, Miller, 'The Origin and Original Nature of Apollo'; Gagé, *Apollon Romain*; Kerényi, *Apollo*; and Gershenson, *Apollo the Wolf-God*.

10 Solomon, *Apollo*, xii.

11 A condensation of the argument of Detienne's book in an earlier form is available in English translation as 'Apollo's Slaughterhouse.' Detienne reads Apollo as a dynamic, composite figure, rather than attempting to separate older, cthonic elements of his cult from its 'essential nature'; for a similar approach to a single Apolline myth, see Sourvinou-Inwood, *'Reading' Greek Culture*, 217–43.

12 Poetic treatments of the Muses in the Middle Ages have received histori-cist attention by Curtius, *European Literature*, 228–46; Ziolkowski, 'Classical Influences'; and Verbaal, 'Invocatio Musae.'

13 An excellent overview of this shift in critical interest is Blumenfeld-Kosinski, *Reading Myth*, 1–14. This trend within the circuit of the study of medieval vernacular poetry coincides with a burgeoning interest in recent years in the theory and practice of reception within the discipline of classical studies, the bibliography of which is already considerable. Important chapters in the ongoing critical narrative of classical reception in the last fifteen years include Martindale, *Redeeming the Text*; Hinds, *Allusion and Intertext*; and Martindale and Thomas, eds, *Classics and the Uses of Reception*.

14 Blumenfeld-Kosinski, *Reading Myth*, 9.

15 The post-medieval Apollo has, of course, been more fully studied, e.g.,
    in Revard, 'Christ and Apollo.'

16 For the argument, with which I tend to agree, that Chaucer was familiar
    with the *Canzoniere* more broadly, see Fleming, *Classical Imitation*, 119–21,
    and Stillinger, *Song of Troilus*, 172–8.

17 Cottino-Jones, 'Myth of Apollo and Daphne,' 176; see also Hainsworth,
    'Myth of Daphne,' and Sturm-Maddox, *Petrarch's Laurels*.

18 Huot examines the role of Apollo in the works of Machaut and Froissart
    in 'Daisy and the Laurel,' 244–6, and *From Song to Book*, 307–14. For an
    overview of fourteenth-century French poets' development of new models
    of vernacular authority, see Brownlee et al., 'Vernacular Literary
    Consciousness,' 465–8.

19 The antagonism of these figures is rooted, for the Middle Ages, in Cupid's
    angry defeat of the obstreperous Apollo in Book One of Ovid's *Met.*
    (1.452–73), and in Apollo's revelation (as the sun) of the affair of Venus
    and Mars to Vulcan – an interference for which Apollo is duly punished
    by Venus (*Met.* 4.169–92).

20 Froissart, *La Prison Amoreuse*, ed. and trans. de Looze, 'Letter' 9.136–46,
    12.67–88.

21 Huot, 'Daisy and the Laurel,' 244; on the *Roman de la rose* interpolation, see
    Huot, *The* Romance of the Rose *and its Medieval Readers*, 134–6.
    Iconographic evidence of this conflation of Apollo and Cupid survives in a
    miniature in an important early fifteenth-century manuscript of Christine
    de Pizan's *Epistre Othea* (BN fr. 606, fol. 25v) discussed by Desmond and
    Sheingorn, *Myth, Montage, and Visuality*, 112–18. Depicted here is Apollo's
    accidental slaying of his male lover Hyacinthus (confused with
    Ganymede), not with an ill-aimed discus but with a 'long iron bar that
    pierces him in the eye,' recalling images of the God of Love in the *Roman
    de la rose* shooting Amant in the eye with his arrow (112).

22 Wimsatt, *Chaucer and his French Contemporaries*, 85; see also Brownlee,
    Poetic Identity, 13–23, and Blumenfeld-Kosinski, *Reading Myth*, 168–9. For
    an alternative account of Froissart's conflation of Love and Apollo, not as
    a self-authorizing move but an ironic exposure of lovers who redefine
    'truth' in erotic terms, see Heinrichs, *Myths of Love*, 198–206.

23 Huot, 'Daisy and the Laurel,' 246.

24 Minnis, '*De vulgari auctoritate*,' 49–51; cf. Minnis, *Medieval Theory of
    Authorship*, 190–210. For a recent argument that 'the speech of a clerkly "I"
    that defines itself in writing' featured in the *dit* genre positively influenced
    Chaucer, see Spearing, 'Textual Performance,' 33.

25 Minnis, *'De vulgari auctoritate,'* 61–3; cf. Minnis, *Medieval Theory of Authorship*, 177–90. On the influence of the *dits amoureux* upon Gower's *Confessio amantis*, see Burrow, 'Portrayal of Amans.' On Gower's engagement with humanist attitudes toward rhetoric, see further Copeland, 'Lydgate,' 239–42.
26 Tinkle, *Medieval Venuses and Cupids*, 201–3.
27 Ibid., 135.
28 Ibid., 203–4.
29 Ibid., 122.
30 As Machan notes, literary authority in Middle English textual culture was 'unstable' and 'contested,' neither 'an issue beyond critical examination nor . . . one to be taken for granted' (*Textual Criticism*, 112).
31 Brownlee et al., 'Vernacular Literary Consciousness,' 428.
32 Kiser, *Truth and Textuality*, 1–2, 5; cf. Taylor, *Chaucer Reads 'The Divine Comedy,'* 41–9.
33 Lynch, *Chaucer's Philosophical Visions.*
34 Patterson, *Chaucer and the Subject of History*, 83.
35 Galloway, 'Authority,' 29, 34.
36 Ross, for example, likens the Franklin's proclamation (which is more than a little tongue-in-cheek) to Geffrey's own rejection of the lofty House of Fame for its less elite neighbour, the House of Rumour (*Making of the English Literary Canon*, 42). Significantly for the present study, Ross dismisses Geffrey's invocation of Apollo in *HF* as an incongruent part of this picture.
37 See also Hanna et al., 'Latin Commentary Tradition,' 363–421.
38 The classic defence of the affinity between Chaucer's 'poetics of uncertainty' and the self-reflexiveness of postmodern writing is Jordan, *Chaucer's Poetics*, qtd at 10.
39 See also Percival's extension of Copeland's reading in *Chaucer's Legendary Good Women*, 130–48.
40 Copeland, *Rhetoric*, 195.
41 See Fumo, 'God of Love.' The argument that Chaucer adopts a stance of 'father-figure' toward his works in his palinodes, precisely because of his concern with God the Father's judgment, revises Spearing's influential claim (*Medieval to Renaissance*, 88–110) that Chaucer thoroughly resists a stance of paternal authority in his poetry. On Chaucer's development of an affirmative position of literary authority, see also Utz, 'Writing Alternative Worlds,' 121–32.
42 Minnis, *Medieval Theory of Authorship*, 210.
43 Minnis writes thus of Chaucer's *Retraction*: 'the "shield and defence" of the compiler has slipped, and for once we see Chaucer as a writer who

holds himself morally responsible for his writings' (*Medieval Theory of Authorship*, 208).

44 Watson, 'Politics of Middle English Writing,' 347.

45 Carlson, *Chaucer's Jobs*, 66.

46 Ibid., 1.

47 Because it unites under a single rubric the rich grammar of fable with which Chaucer engages and the ways in which his classicizing posture in turn gives shape to a cult of English authorship, I use the term 'mythologize' rather than the more intentionalist 'invent' in discussing Chaucer's contribution to the discourse of English authorship. On the power, and capacity for historical distortion, of a Chaucerian 'myth of origin' in the development of English poetic tradition, see Cannon, *Making of Chaucer's English*, 179–220.

48 Quotation from Minnis, '*De vulgari auctoritate*,' 63. Cf. Machan, *Textual Criticism*, 132.

49 See Green's seminal discussion of the courtly education that a fourteenth-century man of letters like Chaucer would have received in the royal household (*Poets and Princepleasers*, 71–100). Like scholastic literary theory, however, the polite, francocentric milieu of the court is only one of several shaping influences upon Chaucer's wide-ranging engagement with classical poetry and ideas of authority. It is partly for this reason that Carlson's argument, that Chaucer's professional (i.e., courtly and bureaucratic) life implies an aggressively public value-system for his poetry ('writing as alienable labor, producing literary commodities to be traded for reward'), underestimates Chaucer's independent-mindedness as an author (Carlson, *Chaucer's Jobs*, 44).

50 Cf. Copeland's observation that Chaucer's 'play on authoritative postures' in *LGW* 'is a sign of the control that Chaucer, as a vernacular writer and translator, exerts over the academic tradition, a control that allows the free play of a self-reflexive comedy' (*Rhetoric*, 186).

51 The term *vates* was influentially defined by Isidore of Seville, in *Etymologiae* 7.12.15, 8.7.3, as a priest-prophet-poet amalgam inspired by divine *furor*; on this concept of *furor poeticus* and its relation to insular traditions of the visionary bard, see Ziolkowski, 'Classical Influences,' 30–1. For a cross-cultural overview of manticism, see Leavitt, 'Poetics.'

52 Fyler, *Chaucer and Ovid*, 22; cf. Fyler, '*Omnia vincit amor*,' 202.

53 Spearing, *Medieval to Renaissance*, 28–9. Cf. Spearing's observation that Chaucer 'is fascinated by this new conception of the vernacular poet as prophet, yet he cannot quite adopt the role as wholeheartedly as Dante does' (24).

54 Ebin, *Illuminator*, 1–18, 133–62. Notably, Ebin does not engage with Chaucer's classicizing poetics.
55 Ibid., 139.
56 Milton, *Paradise Lost* 9.44–7, cited here and subsequently from Hughes's edition.
57 Although not exclusively devoted to these issues, Dean, 'Ending of the *Canterbury Tales*,' 26–7, deserves mention as containing a brief but highly useful review of Apollo's mythic identity in Chaucer's works and elsewhere.
58 Striar, '"Manciple's Tale,"' 198.
59 Kensak, 'Apollo *exterminans*,' 153, 156; see also Kensak, 'Silences of Pilgrimage.'
60 My approach thus unfolds the implications of Wakelin's observation, in his recent study of fifteenth-century English humanism, that classical allusion in the century after Chaucer's death frequently adopts Chaucerian rhetoric as a way of mediating antiquity, rather than engaging in a direct, humanist fashion with classical poetry. It is thus 'hard to disentangle whether Chaucerian poetry made readers amenable to the humanist fashion for antiquity, or the humanist fashion altered the reading and writing of courtly verse' (*Humanism*, 66).

1 Apollo as Human God

1 Of Leucothoe and her rival Clytie (*Met.* 4.195–270), Isse (*Met.* 6.124), Dryope (*Met.* 9.331–2), Deione (*Met.* 9.443–4), Chione (*Met.* 11.303–17, a gang rape with Mercury), the Cumaean Sibyl (*Met.* 14.130–42), and Paris's first wife Oenone (*Her.* 5.145–52).
2 Of Apollo himself into a raven (*Met.* 5.329), a hawk, and a lion (*Met.* 6.123–4); of Cephisus's grandson into a seal (*Met.* 7.388–9); and of Daedalion into a hawk (*Met.* 11.339–45).
3 For the former position, see Leach, 'Ekphrasis,' 128, and cf. Frécaut's claim that 'Apollon est incontestablement, dans les *Métamorphoses*, le dieu le plus sensible, le plus apte à éprouver des sentiments humains' ('La Métamorphose de Niobé,' 142 n. 50), affirmed in Le Bonniec, 'Apollon.' For the latter view, see Anderson, ed., *Ovid's* Metamorphoses: *Books 1–5*, note to 2.626–7.
4 See especially Haight, 'An "Inspired Message,"' 360–5, and Gosling, 'Political Apollo' and 'Augustan Apollo.' Gosling well articulates Apollo's function as a bestower of authority in the realms of literary theory and politics (see in particular 'Political Apollo,' 512). Cf. Putnam's contention

that Ovid's Apollo functions as an 'emblem of Roman martial strength, exerting its might against ineffectual opponents so as to gain its ends by force' ('Daphne's Roots,' 80).

5 Armstrong, 'Retiring Apollo,' 528, 535, 543. For a similar argument with respect to Apollo's role in *Ars amatoria*, see Sharrock, *Seduction and Repetition*, 226–9. On Apollo's marginality in *Remedia amoris*, see Hardie, '*Lethaeus Amor*,' 178–9.

6 Janan, 'The Book of Good Love?' 134. Cf. the cautions expressed by Miller, 'Ovid and Augustan Apollo,' 165–6, regarding critical enthusiasm for Augustan interpretations of Ovid's Apollo.

7 In my attention to the importance of the reader's imaginative reception of Apollo in Ovid's works I am especially influenced by the approaches of Sharrock, *Seduction and Repetition*, and Wheeler, *A Discourse of Wonders*, as well as the expert analyses of Ovid's narratological procedures in Keith, *A Play of Fictions*; Barchiesi, 'Narrative Technique and Narratology'; and Rosati, 'Narrative Techniques and Narrative Structures.'

8 For a recent Nietzschean critique of *MancT*, see Astell, 'Nietzsche, Chaucer, and the Sacrifice of Art.'

9 Nietzsche, *Birth of Tragedy*, 115.

10 Otto, *The Homeric Gods*, 61, 78.

11 Sallis, *Crossings*, 29.

12 Shelley, 'Hymn of Apollo,' lines 31–6, in *Complete Poetical Works*, ed. Hutchinson, 682–3 (hereafter cited parenthetically by line number).

13 Zanker, *Power of Images*, 3, 50. On the anti-Augustanism of Ovid's generally unflattering treatment of Apollo, see Haight, 'An "Inspired Message,"' 360–5 (which suggests that Ovid's treatment of Apollo resulted in his banishment); Barnard, *Myth of Apollo and Daphne*, 19, 31, 42; Gosling, 'Augustan Apollo,' 4, and 'Political Apollo,' 504; and Ahl, 'Apollo,' 118–26.

14 Cosgrove, *Apollo's Eye*, xi.

15 Ibid., 5, 27; on the Apollo space missions, see 254–67. It is not far from Cosgrove's account of Apolline geospatial imperialism to science fiction's memorable rendition of Apollo in Episode 33 of *Star Trek* ('Who Mourns for Adonais?' [1967]) as the last surviving Greco-Roman deity, now facing extinction on his own planet (the ancient gods were early space travellers!). As Winkler insightfully demonstrates, this extraterrestrial Apollo is associated with the rhetoric of mid-century totalitarianism, 'in which an all-powerful individual, accorded quasi-divine status, receives unquestioning obedience from his subjects so that a new and perfect race of supermen may achieve their earthly paradise in a new order under his leadership' ('Neo-Mythologism,' 403).

16 Foucault's remarks were made in a 1976 interview ('Truth and Power,' 133) that reflects upon several major currents of his career; a later, definitive examination of power in relation to systems of communication is Foucault's 'The Subject and Power' (1982). See also Gosling's discussion of propagandist appropriations of Apollo among rival political factions in republican and imperial Rome, where 'laying claim to Apollo's special favour sanctioned one's bid for power' ('Augustan Apollo,' 1).

17 Bierl, 'Apollo in Greek Tragedy.' See further the discussion of Apollo's perversion of sacrificial ritual in Greek tragedy by Gibert, 'Apollo's Sacrifice.'

18 Detienne, 'Apollo's Slaughterhouse,' 53. Other, more commonly noted, 'un-Apolline' features of Apollo's cult include the deranged frenzy of the Pythia, the myth of Gaia's possession of the Delphic oracle before Apollo (on which cf. Sourvinou-Inwood, 'Reading' Greek Culture, 228), and Apollo's and Dionysus's sharing of Delphi as a cultic centre. On the complex system of exchange between Apolline and Dionysian cults, see Detienne, 'Forgetting Delphi.'

19 Detienne, Apollon le couteau à la main, 234, 240; translations mine.

20 See Spentzou, 'Introduction,' 14–15; cf. Sharrock, 'An A-musing Tale.'

21 Tentatively dated thus by Athanassakis, ed., Homeric Hymns, 79, rejecting the sixth century BCE date given by a later chronicler, Hippostratos.

22 On Ovid's appropriation of the Homeric Hymn to Apollo in Met. 6, see Barchiesi, 'Venus' Masterplot,' 124.

23 On this point, see Miller, From Delos to Delphi, 37–47.

24 Text and translations of Met. are from Hill's multivolume edition unless otherwise indicated. Ovid refers here to a version of the myth (found, e.g., in Callimachus's Hymn 4 [to Delos] in which Delos was a drifting island before Apollo's birth; the divine siblings later moored Delos in the sea in gratitude for its hospitality.

25 Niobe does not appear in the Homeric Hymn to Apollo, but she does feature in two Callimachean hymns concerning Apollo. In Hymn 2 (to Apollo) the weeping rock that once was Niobe delays her tears in awe of the song of praise sung to Apollo by his worshipers. Hymn 4 (to Delos) includes a prophecy by Apollo while still in his mother's womb that condemns the city of Thebes as home of the impious Niobe and her children, thus establishing Apollo's powers of foresight at the expense of one whose future scepticism toward his divinity can only be taken as foolish. For discussion of Ovid's use of these Callimachean hymns elsewhere in Met., see Wills, 'Callimachean Models'; on the Ovidian Niobe's own manipulation of hymnic precedent to glorify herself, see Feldherr, 'Reconciling Niobe,' 133–4.

26 Anderson, *Ovid's* Metamorphoses: *Books 6–10*, 194.

27 *Met.* 6.333, missing in Hill's edition, is supplied from Tarrant. Ovid's source for this little-known story was most likely Nicander's lost *Heteroioumena* (late third century BCE?), which can tentatively be reconstructed from a post-Ovidian version of the story by Antoninus Liberalis. For analysis of Ovid's adjustments to this inherited story, see Van Tress, *Poetic Memory*, 150–3; cf. Clauss, 'Episode of the Lycian Farmers,' 310–11.

28 'To Apollon,' lines 123–5, in Athanassakis, ed., *The Homeric Hymns*. Line numbers from this edition are hereafter indicated in the main text.

29 On Apollo's '*double* birth' (first as an infant and then as a god) in the *Homeric Hymn*, and the broader currency in archaic poetry of ambrosia as divine nourishment, see Miller, *From Delos to Delphi*, 47–50. Apollo's regeneration in Keats's *Hyperion* is treated in the Introduction, p. 5.

30 For these views, see Leach, 'Ekphrasis,' 127, and Le Bonniec, 'Apollon,' 154–6.

31 Ovid's unusual emphasis on Apollo's overreaction in this version of the story stands out especially in relation to his treatment of the same episode in the *Fasti*, which clearly specifies that Marsyas 'superbus erat' and 'provocat' Apollo (*Fasti* 6.706–7). All citations and translations of the *Fasti* are from the edition of Frazer and Goold.

32 As Jacobsen has argued ('Apollo and Tereus'), Ovid also establishes a suggestive parallel between Apollo's pursuit of Daphne and Tereus's lust for Philomela.

33 Miller, *From Delos to Delphi*, 42 (cf. 106–8).

34 *De deorum imaginibus libellus*, sec. 4; cf. Seznec, *Survival of the Pagan Gods*, 175–9.

35 Some variants on this exist ('quadrigam,' 'scribemeum,' 'clipeum'), since the scribes struggled with the word 'gryphen.'

36 VM II 28; VM III 8.16 (cf. 6.34); Boccaccio, *Genealogie*, 4.3. All citations of VM I and VM II (Vatican Mythographers I and II) refer to the text and numbering of Kulscár's edition; those of VM III (Vatican Mythographer III) follow Bode's edition.

37 These possibilities arise in an episode in the preceding book, 9.394–438. As Fulkerson observes, Ovid may have been aware of other versions of the story in which Hyacinthus was rendered immortal ('Apollo,' 400).

38 Detienne, *Apollon le couteau à la main*, 196.

39 On the ritual commemoration of this event known as the Septerion, see Fontenrose, *Python*, 15, 453–6.

40 Plutarch, 'Obsolescence of Oracles,' in *Moralia* 418; cf. 421.

41 Citations of Servius and the glosses by the later redactor known as Servius *Danielis* are from Servius Grammaticus, *Servii Grammatici qui feruntur in*

Vergilii carmina commentarii, ed. Thilo and Hagen, translations mine. On the medieval substitution of Admetus's daughter for Admetus as object of Apollo's affections, see Tournoy, 'Apollo and Admetus,' and Fumo, '"Little *Troilus*,"' 289–90, esp. n. 28.

42 The notion of Apollo's transfiguration by passion as a metamorphic phenomenon is implicit in Ovid's text; see Anderson, 'Multiple Change,' 6–8.

43 *Allegoriae* 2.12; cf. 6.21–4. Citations of Arnulf are from Ghisalberti's edition; translations mine.

44 Arnulf of Orléans, following Lactantius Placidus, states in regard to this episode that 'Neptunus et Apollo [mutati] in homines' (*Allegoriae* 11.7).

45 Apollodorus, *Library*, 2.103.

46 See Barnard, *Myth of Apollo and Daphne*, 3, and Calvino, 'Ovid and Universal Contiguity.'

47 For the early history and evolution of Apollo's combat with the Python, see Fontenrose, *Python*, 13–22.

48 For discussion of these features, see Williams, 'Augustus and Daphne,' 251; Knox, 'In Pursuit of Daphne,' 200; and Wills, 'Callimachean Models,' 154.

49 The (failed) narrative competition between the voices of Apollo and Ovid for which I argue in this paragraph bears comparison with Nagle's observation of the paradox that Apollo's unconvincing rhetorical advances toward Daphne serve Ovid's successful narrative seduction of the reader by calling attention to the act of storytelling as a performance shared by poet and characters. See Nagle, 'Erotic Pursuit,' 38.

50 As Feldherr argues, Daphne's metamorphosis evinces a 'process of occlusion and possession' by Apollo rather than a crystallization of her own identity. Feldherr points to Ovid's subversive identification of the evergreen laurel with divine power and civic triumph rather than, as one would have expected, Daphne's preserved virginity, as well as the analogy drawn between the laurel's leaves and Apollo's flowing hair rather than Daphne's ('Metamorphosis,' 172–3; qtd at 172). Cf. Solodow, *The World of Ovid's* Metamorphoses, 180.

51 Hardie, *Ovid's Poetics of Illusion*, 48.

52 Cf. Miller, 'Ovid and Augustan Apollo,' 177.

53 On the close, if largely implicit, connection between laurel and text/poetic fame in Ovid's scene, see the excellent analysis in Hardie, *Ovid's Poetics of Illusion*, 49–50.

54 On Apollo's inflexibility in comparison to Mercury in *Met.* 1–2, see Fredericks, 'Divine Wit,' qtd at 248.

55 Although the strict identification of Apollo with Phoebus/Sol/Titan in Ovid's Phaethon episode has been a matter of debate among classicists (see Fontenrose, 'Apollo,' and McKay, 'Solar Motifs'), no distinction was made among these figures in the Middle Ages, which favoured a 'composite' understanding of Apollo. In *Met.*, the problems surrounding Apollo's naming only intensify the episode's concern with the revelation of identity.

56 Fredericks, 'Divine Wit,' 247.

57 Phaethon's upheaval of Apollo's neatly ekphrastic cosmos thus supports Leach's contention that 'the power and permanence of artistic creation' as depicted in various other parts of *Met.* 'is answered only by a glimpse of the limited perspectives of the poem itself with all its emphasis upon dissatisfaction, uncertainty and mutability' ('Ekphrasis,' 133).

58 The Thessalian setting of the Daphne narrative is evident in the fact that Daphne's father is the river Peneus, a Thessalian river. This setting is made explicit at *Met.* 1.568, where Thessaly is referred to, as in the Coronis episode, as Haemonia. Ovid's version of the Daphne narrative is unique in setting the story in Thessaly and making Peneus the father of Daphne (see Knox, 'In Pursuit of Daphne,' 194). The implications of this change of setting will be treated later in this chapter, but it is worth noting here that one effect of Ovid's emphasis upon the Thessalian setting is an alignment of the Daphne episode with that of Coronis, which traditionally takes place in Thessaly.

59 Ovid's second reference to Apollo as 'Delphice' at *Met.* 2.677, at the end of the sequence involving Chiron and his daughter Ocyroe that follows the death of Coronis, is similarly ironic: the point it introduces is that Apollo's Delphic powers are not available or potent enough to give aid.

60 Cf. Le Bonniec, 'Apollon,' 164. Apollo's prophetic abilities are similarly critiqued in the Daphne episode, which capitalizes upon the irony that Apollo, who at the end of the episode prophesies Augustan Rome's uses of the laurel, did not also foresee that he would fail to attain Daphne's love (cf. *Met.* 1.491). On this point, see Hardie, 'Ovid into Laura,' 259, and *Ovid's Poetics of Illusion*, 46–7, and cf. Augustine's cynical comment on the story of Apollo's servitude to Laomedon, discussed above.

61 *Amores* 1.7 makes a particularly suggestive comparison, as Le Bonniec notes in 'Apollon,' 165–6.

62 All citations and translations of the *Amores* are from *Heroides and Amores*, trans. Showerman.

63 On Ovid's use of imagery of the hunt in the Apollo and Daphne episode, see Davis, *Death of Procris*, 25–42. In a complementary reading of the link between Python and Coronis in *MancT*, Herman concludes that by

juxtaposing these scenes Chaucer reveals that '[i]nstead of ordering the chaos [represented by Python], Phebus adds to it' ('Treason,' 325).

64 As Barnard observes in her analysis of Apollo's erotic induction in *Met.* 1, the form of love experienced is the 'violent and irrational' emotion known as *furor*, which entails 'the lover's total self-pitying submission to his malady' ('Ovid's Apollo and Daphne,' 356).

65 Anderson, *Ovid's* Metamorphoses: *Books 1–5*, notes to 2.623–5, 626–7.

66 One might regard Apollo as a hyperbolically advanced 'student' of Ovid in the *Remedia amoris*, proving the maxim that '[s]uccessore novo vincitur omnis amor' [all love is vanquished by a succeeding love] (*Rem. Am.* 462) with such parodic force that Coronis has been wiped out of Apollo's mind before the extended account of her death and Aesculapius's birth has even ended. Cf. Fulkerson's observation of 'the short space between Cyparissus and his replacement Hyacinthus' as lovers of Apollo in *Met.* 10 ('Apollo,' 400).

67 Indeed, as Nicoll points out, the Alexandrian tradition of Apollo's servitude to Admetus may well have served as a conceptual basis for Ovid's humiliating presentation of Apollo in the Daphne narrative ('Cupid,' 177 n. 24).

68 On Apollo's association with the Roman elegiac topos of love's slavery, see Copley, '*Servitium amoris*.' All citations and translations of *Ars Amatoria* are from Mozley's edition.

69 As argued, for example, by Armstrong, 'Retiring Apollo,' qtd at 532.

70 See Myerowitz, *Ovid's Games of Love*, 73–9, on Ovid's conception of *ars* and its relation to *cultus* and *ingenium*.

71 Sharrock, *Seduction and Repetition*, 212.

72 Nicoll, 'Cupid'; see also Knox, *Ovid's* Metamorphoses, 14–15.

73 Newman, *Augustus and the New Poetry*, 182–6, regards such flippant Ovidian treatment of the priestly role of the bard as the death-knell of the *vates*-concept for Augustan poetry, sacrificed to Ovid's 'essentially light, fluent, polished and superficial' vision of the poet's role as eroticist (193). My argument, in contrast, is that Ovid *expands* the concept of *vates* by summoning it in erotic contexts, and that his reasons for doing so are not merely parodic but indicative of a sustained exploration of *ars*, inspiration, and poetic authority.

74 See also Ovid's invocation of his status as 'Musarum purus Phoebique sacerdos' [unstained priest of Phoebus and the Muses] to amplify his attractiveness as a suitor at *Amores* 3.8.23, and his inclusion of his praise of his girlfriend among the fables of *vates* at 3.13.41.

75 Armstrong suggests that Apollo here is parodically likened to the cup-bearer Ganymede serving Jove ('Retiring Apollo,' 537).

76 On Ovid's simultaneously vatic and empirical presentation of his own authority in this passage, see Ahern, 'Ovid as *Vates*.' For a literary genealogy of Ovid's truth-claim, which one might extend to Chaucer's Wife of Bath, see Miller, 'Callimachus,' 29–32, and 'Disclaiming Divine Inspiration,' 157–9.

77 Ovid's strategies of deception and their perpetration upon the reader are profitably analysed in Allen, *Art of Love*, 15–37.

78 Sharrock, *Seduction and Repetition*, 245–56, qtd at 245. Armstrong, 'Retiring Apollo,' 541–2, further substantiates Sharrock's reading of the redundancy and occasional inappropriateness of Apollo's advice, concluding that 'Apollo has demonstrated that he has little, if anything, new to offer either to the poet or to the novice lover, and the *praeceptor*'s order to obey his instruction becomes tinged with sarcasm' (542).

79 Casali, 'Apollo,' 25.

80 Text and translation from King's edition. Le Bonniec, 'Apollon,' 173, notes the connection of this passage with Apollo's counsel in the *Ars*. On Cicero's conception of self-knowledge, see Courcelle, *Connais-toi toi-même*, 1:27–38.

81 Observed by Anderson, *Ovid's Metamorphoses, Books 1–5*, note to 3.346–8, who cogently describes Narcissus's plight but does not connect the scene to *Ars amatoria* 2.

82 Hardie, *Ovid's Poetics of Illusion*, 30.

83 Hardie aptly comments that Apollo in this scene 'cannot escape from self-knowledge into a relationship with another, in an ironical and blinkered obedience to the Delphic maxim "know thyself" that will be closely paralleled by the disastrous self-knowledge of the Ovidian Narcissus' (*Ovid's Poetics of Illusion*, 48). Hardie does not, however, trace this motif of narcissistic self-knowledge to its conceptual core in Apollo's epiphany in *Ars amatoria* 2. On Apollo's egotism in his seduction of Daphne, see also Gross, 'Rhetorical Wit,' 307.

84 Janan, 'The Book of Good Love?' 114–16.

85 Cf. ibid., 119. Hardie also notes that the Hyacinthus episode shows Apollo to defy the second Delphic admonition, 'nothing to excess' (*Ovid's Poetics of Illusion*, 64).

86 The blurring between Apollo as *auctor* and as object of writing here is conceptually linked with his wish at *Met.* 10.202–3 to exchange fates with Hyacinthus.

87 Janan, 'The Book of Good Love?' 120.

88 As implied by Miller, 'Lamentations of Apollo,' 420–1. For the contention that Ovid's attitude toward *ars* in general is optimistic in this sense, see Lateiner, 'Mythic and Non-Mythic Artists,' 21–3, and Myerowitz, *Ovid's Games of Love*.

89   The argument regarding Apollo and gender put forth in this and the
       following paragraphs supports Sharrock's observation of links between
       Apollo's advice in *Ars* 2 and imagery of effeminacy and feminine vanity
       developed elsewhere in the poem (*Seduction and Repetition*, 249–52).

90   Although Ovid uses the name 'Phoebe' for 'Diana' rarely, its appearance at
       Met. 6.215–16 in the Niobe episode stresses the unity of purpose and
       twinned identity of brother and sister. Apollo's hair (along with that of
       Bacchus) also serves as a model for female coiffure at *Amores* 1.14.31, and
       is compared with that of Narcissus at *Met.* 3.421. On Apollo's androgyn-
       ous beauty, see Gibson, ed., *Ars Amatoria Book 3*, 152–3 (note to 3.141–2),
       and McKeown, *Ovid: Amores*, 2:378 (note to 1.14.31–2).

91   This paragraph's argument bears comparison with Hardie's observation
       of the Diana-like Daphne's status as an object of incestuous intrigue for
       Apollo in *Met.* ('Approximative Similes,' 90–1, 109). On the medieval
       association of Daphne and Diana and the incestuous possibilities that
       result in one Chaucerian narrative, see Fumo, 'Aurelius' Prayer,' 630.

92   Propertius, *Elegies* 2.1.57–8; text and translation from Goold's edition.
       Medicina amoris is well defined with reference to Ovid by Knox, *Ovid's*
       Metamorphoses, 15–17; Sharrock, *Seduction and Repetition*, 53–61; and
       Casali, 'Enone.'

93   Ovid's narrative of Cupid's wounding of Apollo was greatly influential in
       medieval romance, particularly the *Roman de la rose* and its descendants (in
       which the lover is pierced through the eye), wherein the 'medical' dimen-
       sions of Ovid's scene are commonly amplified by medieval optical science.

94   In *Heroides* 5, Oenone claims to have been loved by Apollo, who instructed
       her in the art of healing. A true student of her master, however, Oenone is
       unable to heal herself of love: 'deficior prudens artis ab arte mea' [skilled
       in an art, I am left helpless by the very art I know] (*Her.* 5.150). Both
       passages are indebted to Tibullus 2.3, in which Apollo's devotion as
       servitium amoris to Admetus derives from an inability to cure his own
       desire: 'nec potuit curas sanare salubribus herbis: / quidquid erat medicae
       vicerat artis amor' [nor could he cure his trouble by health-giving herbs. /
       Love had triumphed o'er all resources of the healer's art] (2.3.13–14). All
       citations and translations of the *Heroides* are from Showerman's edition,
       and of Tibullus from the edition of Cornish et al.

95   Sharrock defines this paradox with reference to Propertius's 'solus amor
       morbi non amat artificem': 'The cure for love is sex … but homoeopathy
       for sex (more sex) creates more desire (more sex, more of the disease)'
       (*Seduction and Repetition*, 59).

96 Cf. Miller, 'Lamentations of Apollo,' 413–21, which emphasizes the pathetic dimension of Apollo's erotic failures, and Fulkerson, 'Apollo,' 388–402, which stresses Apollo's deferral of responsibility in such cases.

97 On this motif see Jackson, 'The Wounded Healer,' qtd at 2. Jung coined the phrase in his 1951 'Fundamental Questions of Psychotherapy'; see Jackson 21–3.

98 Text and translations of *Tristia* and *Ex Ponto* are from the edition of Wheeler and Goold.

99 See Nagle, *Poetics of Exile*, 55–70; Williams, *Banished Voices*, 69–70, 122–8.

100 This passage in *Ex Ponto* appears to be modelled on Propertius 2.1.57–70, which states that lovesickness is immune to the healing arts of Machaon (also mentioned in the *Ex Ponto* 1.3 passage), Chiron, and Aesculapius. Cf. Nagle, *Poetics of Exile*, 62–3.

101 See the detailed discussions in Arn, 'Three Ovidian Women,' 6–8; Fleming, *Classical Imitation*, 122–3; McInerney, '"Is this a mannes herte?"' 228; Fumo, '"Little *Troilus*"'; and Hagedorn, *Abandoned Women*, 131–7.

102 Baswell, *Virgil in Medieval England*, 16.

103 Hinds, *Allusion and Intertext*, 106. Relevant also is Richard F. Thomas's account of the dynamic by which 'a problematic aspect of a Virgilian passage is activated in the later text [i.e., in Ovid] … amounting to affirmation of the problematic aspect.' This is not simply subversion on the part of a later author, Thomas argues, but a kind of collaboration through exposure of a 'subversive potential already in Virgil' (*Virgil and the Augustan Reception*, 78).

104 On this point, cf. Miller, 'Virgil,' 111.

105 Text and translations of the *Aeneid* are from Fairclough's edition.

106 *Met.* 14, which eliminates the Iapyx episode, may rework this imagery indirectly in the scene (without counterpart in the *Aeneid*) in which Venus deifies her son by sprinkling his body with 'ambrosia cum dulci nectare mixta' [ambrosia mixed with sweet nectar] (*Met.* 14.606). On dittany, see Pliny, *Natural History* 26.87.142–45, and Cicero, *De Natura Deorum* 2.50.

107 Fairclough translates, 'a mightier one – a god – works here,' but it is equally plausible, given that two gods are involved in the scene, that 'maior' directly modifies 'deus,' and that the comparison is of Venus to Apollo.

108 Harrison, 'Vergil and the Homeric Tradition,' 221–3.

109 Miller, 'Virgil,' 108–12. The gulf between Apollo's private aim of seduction and Iapyx's civic-minded intentions for his medicine increases the irony.

110 Ibid., 112.

111 Cf. Gillis, *Eros and Death*, 89–92.
112 Morgan, 'Dido the Wounded Deer,' 67–8. This understanding of the Dido/deer simile was current in the Middle Ages: Isidore of Seville (*Etymologiae* 17.9.29) and Bartholomaeus Anglicus (*De rerum proprietatibus* 17.49) cite this very passage from *Aeneid* 4 as evidence of *dictamnus*'s healing powers.
113 Citations refer, by line number, to de Grave's edition of *Eneas*; translations from Yunck, *Eneas*.
114 Some of the relevant lines here (*Her.* 5.140–5, 151–2) are considered spurious by modern editors, beginning with Merkel in 1888. Medieval readers, however, would not have doubted these lines' canonicity. See Stinton, *Euripides*, 42 n. 1, and Jacobson, *Ovid's* Heroides, 185–7 for a defence of their textual propriety.
115 For an overview of pre-Ovidian treatments, with bibliography, see Stinton, *Euripides*, 40–50; Jacobson, *Ovid's* Heroides, 176–7; and Knox, ed., *Ovid's Heroides*, 140–1.
116 As Spentzou notes, 'the very moment that Oenone expresses doubts about the adequacy of her medical skills to cure her wretched love, a future inadequacy of these skills is already deposited in the text for the learned reader: Oenone's herbs will indeed be notoriously unavailable when needed to cure Paris' fatal wound' (*Readers and Writers*, 193–4). Cf. Casali, 'Enone,' 91–3.
117 The fact that these lines concern Apollo's love for Admetus reinforces the influence of Tibullus 2.3 (or, if not genuine, the recognition of Tibullus's influence by a scribe or later reader) upon this section of the poem. Chaucer's Pandarus registers the proximity between Oenone's and Apollo's unhealed love in his convenient distortion of *Heroides* 5 to centre upon Apollo's predicament: see *Tr* 1.659–65 and, for detailed discussion, Fumo, '"Little *Troilus*"' and chapter 3 below, pp. 137–8.
118 See the excellent discussions of narrative technique and character in Jacobson, *Ovid's* Heroides, 176–94; Stinton, *Euripides*, 40–50; and Bradley, 'Ovid *Heroides* 5,' 158–62.
119 On these variants of the Daphne story, see Knox, 'In Pursuit of Daphne,' 188–9; Williams, 'Augustus and Daphne,' 251–3; and Barnard, *Myth of Apollo and Daphne*, 15–16.
120 Barnard, 'Ovid's Apollo and Daphne,' 358.
121 Statius achieves a similar effect in his account of the aftermath of Apollo's slaying of Python in the first book of the *Thebaid*. In order to expiate his blood-guilt, Apollo becomes a servant to king Crotopus of Argos and falls in love with his daughter (a scenario that suggests

cross-pollination with the separate tradition of Apollo's service to
Admetus after murdering the Cyclops). Apollo's ensuing impregnation
of Crotopus's daughter leads to a series of destructive events including
her murder (by her father) after the unfortunate death of the child
produced by her union with Apollo, the ravaging of Argos by a second
Python-type monster sent by an enraged Apollo, and a pestilence
inflicted upon the country by Apollo's arrows. Statius thus carries
forward the Ovidian association of Apollo's supposed purification with
new cycles of contamination activated by erotic passion, cued by familiar
rhetoric surrounding Apollo's careless failure to protect his lover: 'sero
memor thalami maestae solacia morti, / Phoebe' [too late remembering
thy union, O Phoebus, thou dost devise a solace for her miserable fate]
(*Thebaid* 1.596–7). All citations and translations of the *Thebaid* are from
Mozley's edition.

122 As Fulkerson observes, by enjoining the lover to replace old love with
    new Ovid ironically discloses that 'the way to "cure" yourself of love is
    to recognize that there is no cure at all and so to throw yourself into the
    lifestyle' ('*Omnia vincit amor*,' 222). Rosati, 'Art of *Remedia Amoris*,'
    similarly argues that the intentional futility of *dediscere* (unlearning)
    results in a therapeutic program that is both corrective and supplement-
    ary, 'assum[ing] the integration of the previous teaching' (155). Ovid
    himself points out the continuity between the *Ars* and the *Remedia* at
    Rem. Am. 12, as well as in the *Ars*'s occasional anticipations of the
    Remedia's medical vocabulary in the context of *obtaining* love (*Ars Am.*
    1.357 and 2.735–8; cf. *Rem. Am.* 131–4). Citations and translations of the
    Remedia are from *The Art of Love*, trans. Mozley, rev. Goold.
123 That is, in Amor's aspect of 'Lethaeus,' i.e., Lethean, 'forgetting'; see
    Hardie, '*Lethaeus Amor*,' 178–9.
124 As claimed by Durling, 'Ovid as *Praeceptor Amoris*,' 164–5.
125 Cf. Rosati's argument that the *Remedia*'s stance on love is ultimately
    elegiac, reinforcing the topos of '*amor non est medicabilis* familiar from
    Heroides 5' ('Art of *Remedia Amoris*,' 164–5).
126 Text and translations are from Tester's edition of the *Consolation of
    Philosophy* (hereafter abbreviated *CP*)..
127 See Javitch, 'Rescuing Ovid,' and Ginsberg, '*Ovidius ethicus*.'
128 On Ovid's transformative review of his earlier works in the *Tristia*, see
    Hinds, 'Booking the Return Trip.'
129 Cf. O'Daly, *The Poetry of Boethius*, 107; Crabbe, 'Literary Design,' 245–7;
    and Claasen, *Displaced Persons*, 246–51. Hexter provocatively reads Ovid's
    exile as a 'thrust' into 'posterity,' in which Ovid's sense of geographical

distance from Rome prefigures the cultural distance from which Ovid's medieval readers encountered him – rendering Ovid, as it were, the first 'medieval' poet ('Ovid in the Middle Ages,' 416–24; qtd at 416).

130   Also cf. Ovid, *Tristia* 5.1.5, noted by Gruber, *Kommentar zu Boethius*, 51 (*ad* 1 m.1.2).

131   Fish, 'Physician, Heal Thyself,' 872.

132   All references to the *Complaint* cited by line number are from *Minor Poems*, ed. MacCracken.

133   Lydgate's reference to Phebus's servitude to Daphne 'When that he went her in erthe lowe' (359) echoes Chaucer's introduction of Phebus in *MancT*, when he 'dwelled heere in this erthe adoun' (*MancT* 105). It seems likely that Chaucer's wholesale humanization of Phebus in *MancT* as 'the mooste lusty bachiler / In al this world' (107–8) influenced Lydgate's inclusion of Phebus among mortal lovers.

134   Cited by line number from Sieper's edition.

135   Citations of Skelton's poetry, by line number, are from Scattergood's edition of *The Complete English Poems* unless otherwise noted.

136   Cf. *The Book of the Laurel*, ed. Brownlow, 74, and Spearing, *Medieval to Renaissance*, 242.

137   All citations of Isidore from Lindsay's edition; translations from Barney et al.

138   See MacKinney, 'Medical Ethics,' 19 n. 29.

139   Voigts, 'The Significance of the Name Apuleius,' 217 n. 16.

140   Robbins, *Secular Lyrics*, no. 79, 1–2.

141   I am grateful to Faith Wallis for this information in a personal communication; she indicates further that one family of twelfth-century commentaries on the *Aphorisms* of Hippocrates claims that the word 'methodos' means 'incantation.'

142   'Henry of Huntingdon's Herbal,' ed. Rigg, 221. Rigg details the herbal's contents at 225–46 and presents a partial critical edition at 247–88, from which citations in the main text hereafter refer (by book, section, and line number). Translations are Rigg's.

2 The Medieval Apollo

1   Barnard, *Myth of Apollo and Daphne*, 53.

2   A sense of the formal range of Ovidian commentary in England, which includes moralizing interpretations as well as 'largely unadorned literal summaries,' can be gathered from McKinley, 'Manuscripts of Ovid,' 46–7.

3   Hyginus, *Myths of Hyginus*, ed. Grant, 5–15; Chance, *Medieval Mythography* (1994), 158–9.

4 Fulgentius's *Mitologiae* is cited by book and fable number from Helm's edition; translations are from Whitbread, *Fulgentius the Mythographer*.

5 Chance, *Medieval Mythography* (1994), 256.

6 Martianus Capella, *De nuptiis*, ed. Dick, 1.6. Citations of *De nuptiis*, by book/section number, are from Dick's edition; translations are from Stahl and Johnson.

7 Barnard, *Myth of Apollo and Daphne*, 65–8; Revard, 'Christ and Apollo.'

8 Barnard, *Myth of Apollo and Daphne*, 65.

9 Blumenfeld-Kosinski, *Reading Myth*, 101.

10 Paris BN MS Lat. 16238, fols 12v, 13r. For a brief description of Bolent's commentary, see Allen, 'Eleven Unpublished Commentaries,' 284.

11 On Ridewall's procedure, see Smalley, *English Friars*, 110–15, and Allen, 'Commentary as Criticism,' 25–47. Ridewall's exposition of Apollo, as well as several other 'portraits,' unfortunately is not included in the only modern edition, by Liebeschütz. The discussion above refers to the text found in Oxford, Bodleian MS 571, fols 101v–6v, the beginning of which is edited in Allen, 'Commentary as Criticism,' 28–9; translations are mine.

12 Berchorius, *De formis* 20 (all citations of this text, by page number, from Engels's 1966 edition); all translations of Bersuire are from Reynolds's dissertation.

13 On this phenomenon, see Wenzel, 'Classics.'

14 Text cited parenthetically by line number from Grisdale, ed., *Three Middle English Sermons*, First Sermon, 'Secundum membrum principale,' 13–14; cf. Wenzel, 'Classics,' 129, 142.

15 Qtd. and translated in Wenzel, 'Classics,' 137–8.

16 That Scylla's delight in Apollo's music betokens a life of lust rather than chastity follows from Ovid's comparison of Minos, the enemy king for whom the infatuated Scylla betrays her father and kingdom, with the handsome figure of Apollo (*Met.* 8.30–1).

17 Collins, *Combat Myth*, 63–7.

18 Kerkeslager, 'Apollo,' 116–21 (at 119). In light of this original polemical intention on the part of the author of Revelation, the personification of Prophetic Revelation in John Ridewall's *Lectura in Apocalypsim* (c. 1331–2) as the laurel-crowned daughter of Apollo is an almost perverse reflex of the friar's classicizing aims. For text and discussion of Ridewall's Apocalypse commentary, see Smalley, *English Friars*, 115–21, 312–14. All quotations of the Latin Bible are from the Vulgate; translations are from the Douay-Rheims edition.

19 Clement, *Exhortation to the Heathen*, chap. 1, p. 171.

20 Ibid., chap. 1, pp. 171–2.

21 Ibid., chap. 1, p. 173; Halton, 'Clement's Lyre,' 182.
22 Clement, *Exhortation to the Heathen*, chap. 11, p. 203.
23 This point is treated fully in Halton, 'Clement's Lyre,' 182–4.
24 Clement, *Exhortation to the Heathen*, chap. 1, p. 172; chap. 11, p. 205.
25 Lactantius, *Divinarum institutionum* 1.7.1 (chapter and section divisions follow Heck and Wlosok's edition up to book four); translations from Fletcher.
26 Freund, 'Christian Use and Valuation,' 273; see further Freund's detailed analysis of the four oracles quoted by Lactantius, 269–84, and Busine, *Paroles d'Apollon*, 385–92.
27 Lactantius, *Divinarum institutionum* 1.7.1, 1.7.9–10; 4.13.11; 7.13 (subsection numbers not available for book seven).
28 Cf. Freund, 'Christian Use and Valuation,' 281–2.
29 Beatrice, 'Monophysite Christology,' 22; cf. 15.
30 Qtd in Fontenrose, *The Delphic Oracle*, Q250, p. 349; cf. Parke and Wormell, *The Delphic Oracle*, vol. 1, p. 289; vol. 2, p. 209, no. 518.
31 *Carmen* ii. 2.7, discussed in Cameron, 'Gregory of Nazianzus,' 240–1, and Busine, *Paroles d'Apollon*, 422–3.
32 Qtd in Fontenrose, *The Delphic Oracle*, Q268, p. 354.
33 Jacobus de Voragine, *The Golden Legend*, vol. 1, no. 6, pp. 38–9; Ross, *Middle English Sermons*, 316.
34 Qtd and translated in Beatrice, 'Monophysite Christology,' 5; see further 8–13.
35 Daley, 'Apollo as a Chalcedonian,' 41–7.
36 The kind of measured comparison between Christian and pagan knowledge attempted in the *Eclogue of Theodulus*, however, is significantly different from the outright censure of paganism in early Christian apology; on this point, see Green, 'Genesis,' 56–7.
37 Chaucer includes 'Pseustis' among the musicians at *HF* 1228, right next to 'Marcia' (Marsyas). Bennett, *Chaucer's Book of Fame*, 123, observes the parallel between the story of Pseustis's defeat by Alithia and Marsyas's defeat by Apollo.
38 This odd rhetorical manoeuvre exemplifies one of the strategies discussed by Pascal in his overview of 'unexpected mediaeval uses of pagan material': namely, 'learned allusion ... to a classical myth or legend for the purpose of illustrating a point ... [w]hen that point is actually the condemnation of the study of pagan literature' ('Mediaeval Uses of Antiquity,' 194, 195). References to the *Eclogue* are from the text included in Huygens's edition of Bernard d'Utrecht's *Commentum in Theodolum*, pp. 9–18, cited by line number; translations are from Thomson and Perraud.
39 Cf. Chance, *Medieval Mythography* (1994), 359–60.

40 See Chance's edition of the *Assembly*, 15, for a general comparison of these two texts. All citations refer to this edition.

41 As Reynolds notes, Bersuire's procedure is the inverse of that associated with the English 'classicizing friars,' who used secular fable to gloss Scripture; in contrast, Bersuire uses biblical citation to support 'the spiritual truth he discovers beneath Ovid's fables' ('Sources,' 90). Hexter observes that Bersuire's use of biblical tags to cap his moralizations risks subverting the expected textual hierarchy by making the Bible seem to 'echo' Ovid rather than vice versa ('*Allegari*,' 65–6).

42 Berchorius, *De formis* 21–2.

43 The label 'demoralized,' referring to Chaucer's procedural difference from texts like Bersuire's *Ovidius moralizatus*, is drawn from Børch, 'Geoffrey Chaucer and the Cosmic Text,' 113.

44 Martin, *Acts*, 230–1.

45 As glossed by Pelagius, in a commentary on Paul's epistles mistakenly attributed during the Middle Ages to St Jerome (!), the partnership of Apollo and Paul in God's labour implicitly recalls the employment of the pagan Apollo and Neptune by the Trojan king Laomedon – an episode routinely mocked by early Christian apologists, as discussed below. According to Pelagius, Apollo and Paul are 'mercennarii' [hired hands] on someone else's farm ['in alieno agro']; 'nihil habemus proprium nisi mercedem nostri laboris' [they (we) have nothing apart from the payment they (we) get for their (our) labor]. Text from Souter, ed., *Pelagius's Expositions of Thirteen Epistles*, 142; translation from Bray, *1–2 Corinthians*, 30.

46 St Jerome, *Commentaria in Epistolam ad Titum Liber Unus*, PL 26, cols 598C–598D.

47 Brown, *An Introduction to the New Testament*, 517; see also Hartin, *Apollos*, 61–3, 90–4.

48 [Marius Victorinus], *De verbis Scripturae*, PL 8, cols 1009A–1009B, 1009D. My translation.

49 Berchorius, *De formis* 20.

50 Qtd from Helm's edition, sec. 48, p. 175; translation from Whitbread, *Fulgentius the Mythographer*, 219.

51 Whitbread, *Fulgentius the Mythographer*, 229 n. 15.

52 Qtd in Beatrice, 'Monophysite Christology,' 5.

53 Bunyan, *The Pilgrim's Progress*, 56–60, 88.

54 See Grether, 'Apollyon,' and Kerkeslager, 'Apollo,' 116–21, esp. 119; cf. Ford, *Revelation*, 152.

55 A non-comprehensive list includes, in addition to Bersuire, Fulgentius, *Mitologiae* 1.12 (where the term is *perdens*); Remi-CMC vol. 1, 19.11; Bern-CMC 6.331; Arnulf of Orléans, *Allegoriae* 1.8; VM III 8.16.

56 On the missal's date and provenance, see Edwards, 'Ritual Excommunication,' 82.
57 Text and translation from Edwards, 'Ritual Excommunication,' 255.
58 Astaroth (also Astarte or Astharte) is a false god of the Old Testament whose name is derived from the ancient fertility goddess Astarte (see 1 Kings 31:10, 3 Kings 11:5, and 4 Kings 23:13; cf. Edwards, 'Ritual Excommunication,' 102). Sama probably refers to Sammael, a fallen angel notorious in Jewish legend as 'chief of the Satans and the angel of death' (Davidson, *A Dictionary of Angels*, s.v. 'Sam[m]ael,' 255). Ama may be a corruption of Asmodeus, a Persian devil sometimes identified with the fallen angel Ashmedai and associated with Sammael (see Tob. 3:8 and Davidson, *A Dictionary of Angels*, s.v. 'Asmoday,' 'Asmodee,' 'Asmodeus').
59 This motif also appears in the Anglo-Norman *Vie de Seint Auban* (13th century), in which the Saracens worship 'Apolin,' Satan, and Belial, presented as a group (line 14), and 'Apolin' is said to reside in hell in the company of Satan and odious beasts (lines 65–7). Although 'Apolin' is mentioned elsewhere in the poem in connection to other classical gods, his absorption of Apollyon's demonic status surely leads the poet to feature him in this infernal grouping. Cf. Daniel, *Heroes and Saracens*, 144–5.
60 Citations of the second chapter of the *Ovidius moralizatus* follow the critical edition of van der Bijl, 'Petrus Berchorius,' cited by page number (here 30); translations are Reynolds's.
61 Van der Bijl, 'Petrus Berchorius,' 31.
62 Ibid., 31, 33.
63 For an overview of the euhemeristic theory and its influence, see Cooke, 'Euhemerism,' and cf. Camille, *Gothic Idol*, 50–2.
64 Clement, *Exhortation to the Heathen*, chap. 2, p. 181; Tertullian, 'Apology' 14.4; Minucius Felix, *Octavius* 24.5 ; Lactantius, *Divinarum institutionum* 1.10.3.
65 For example, Clement, *Exhortation to the Heathen*, chap. 2, p. 181; Lactantius, *Divinarum institutionum* 1.10.3; Arnobius, *Adversus gentes* 4.25.
66 Clement, *Exhortation to the Heathen*, chap. 2, p. 180; cf. Arnobius, *Adversus gentes* 4.26.
67 Origen, *Against Celsus* 7.3–6, pp. 612–13; cf. Chrysostom's Homily 29 on First Corinthians (sec. 2) in *Homilies on the Epistles of Paul to the Corinthians*, 169–70.
68 Minucius Felix, *Octavius* 23.5, echoing an episode related by Cicero in which a thief steals the golden beard from a statue of Aesculapius because 'neque enim convenire barbatum esse filium cum in omnibus fanis pater inberbis esset' [it was not fitting for the son to wear a beard when his

father appeared in all his temples beardless] (*De natura deorum* 3.34.83; text and translation are from Rackham's edition). In the Middle Ages this story was moralized in the *Gesta Romanorum*, the *Fasciculus morum*, and Gower, *Confessio amantis* 5.7105–210.

69 Clement, *Exhortation to the Heathen*, chap. 2, p. 179; Augustine, *De civitate Dei* 18.13. Cf. Cicero, *De natura deorum* 3.23.57.

70 Clement, *Exhortation to the Heathen*, chap. 2, p. 182; cf. Arnobius, *Adversus gentes* 3.33.

71 Arnobius, *Adversus gentes* 1.36. One could, of course, find similarity in the humble circumstances of Christ's birth, much as the Greek philosopher Celsus maintained that worshipping Christ, a so-called deified mortal, was no different from worshipping apotheosized pagan figures. Origen's refutation of Celsus on the grounds of Christ's divine nature and moral character also preempts any particular infelicity in the line of argument taken by Arnobius against Apollo here. On the Celsus controversy, see Gamble, 'Euhemerism.'

72 Lactantius, *Divinarum institutionum* 1.10.1–4.

73 Lactantius, *Epitome divinarum institutionum*, cap. 8.

74 Tertullian, 'Apology,' 46.6.

75 Augustine, *De civitate Dei* 3.2.

76 Clement, *Exhortation to the Heathen*, chap. 3, p. 183.

77 Bernardus, *Commentary on the First Six Books of the* Aeneid 6.9 (p. 35); Boccaccio, *Genealogie* 5.3.

78 Three late fourteenth- and early fifteenth-century MSS of the verse *Ovide moralisé* abridged or eliminated the allegorical interpretations (a trend also exemplified by Chaucer's poetry), and the late fifteenth-century Burgundian prose *Ovide moralisé* suppressed the allegorical in favour of the historical, euhemeristic, and moral (Jung, '*Ovide metamorphose* en prose,' 105–9).

79 Maxentius later attempts to bribe Katherine by proposing a statue in her likeness, so that 'alle maner of men shull worchip geve / Onto that ymage as onto a goddesse,' reinforcing Katherine's diagnosis of idol-worship in euhemeristic terms (4.13.883–4). Compare the especially precise equation of idolatry with euhemerism in Guido delle Colonne's *Historia* 10.107–13 (book and section numbering follow Meek's translation). All citations of Capgrave's poem are from Winstead's edition.

80 Caxton's English translation of *Met.*, based on the Burgundian recension of the prose *Ovide moralisé*, summarizes Apollo's appearance as a shepherd at *Met.* 2.676–85 in terms sufficiently general to pertain either to Phaethon's or Aesculapius's death, attesting to the medieval instinct to telescope the

two episodes: 'The ffable affermeth that Phebus sorowynge the deth of hys sone that Jupiter hade slayn with thonder had slayn many geantis also with the same thonder, ffor why the cause the goddes exilled [sic] and banysshed Phebus out of the hevens and toke from hym hys dygnyte' (Caxton, *The Metamorphoses of Ovid*, Book 2, cap. 18; my transcription and punctuation). The account of the episode in the verse *Ovide moralisé*, from which Caxton's text ultimately derives, specifies that Apollo was shepherd to Admetus at this point (2.3485–6). See also VM I 2.116.

81 On this iconographic trend, see Scott, *Caxton Master*, 14, 74 n. 26.

82 Map, *De nugis curialium*, dist. 4, cap. 3, pp. 292–3.

83 Holcot's text is quoted from Allen, 'Mythology,' 226–7; translations mine. According to Smalley, Holcot's Ecclesiasticus commentary dates from 1343–9 (*English Friars*, 147–8).

84 On this point see Camille, *Gothic Idol*, 53. Cf. Bersuire's interpretation of Apollo *in malo* as an evil ruler or prelate whose sins make him an idol to himself ('ydolum sibi') (*De formis* 19).

85 Allen, 'Mythology,' 226.

86 Cf. Caxton: 'Pheton is to vnderstonde a man that by hys pryde & ouermoche wenyng wil mounte & enhaunce hygher hymself than it ne apparteyneth to him, or to enterpryse & take vpon hym more than he may performe' (Caxton, *The Metamorphoses of Ovid*, Book 2, cap. 6).

87 This litany, much-repeated in medieval treatments of idolatry, lent itself to the grotesque, as in Saint Albon's mockery of insensate idols as '[l]arge-lippid' yet mute, with 'gret eyen,' '[b]oistous hondis,' and 'armys long' yet blind, numb, and defenceless (Lydgate, *Saint Albon and Saint Amphibalus* 2.1463, 1475–7, cited from Reinecke's edition).

88 For an overview of biblical and early Christian perspectives on idolatry, see Kamerick, *Popular Piety and Art*, 15–17, and on medieval anxieties regarding fabrication, Camille, *Gothic Idol*, 27–49. On the mimetic proximity between idol and idolater, see Camille, *Gothic Idol*, 14.

89 Lactantius, *On the Deaths of the Persecutors*, chap. 33. In Augustine's view, events of this kind epitomize the folly of polytheism: see his account of hapless pagans who 'propter aegros medicus uel Apollo uel Aesculapius uel ambo simul, quando esset grande periculum' [call in Apollo or Aesculapius as a physician for their sick – or both at once, in a case of grave danger] (*De civitate dei* 4.21). Citations of *De civitate Dei* are from Dombart and Kalb's edition; translations are by Bettenson.

90 Apollo is portrayed here as a generic medieval idol of the 'Mars' type (defined by Camille, *Gothic Idol*, 103), as opposed to an idol of the kind depicted in the temples of Mars and Apollo in Jean Wauquelin's *Chronique*

de Hainault (Brussels, Bibliotheque Royale MSS 9242–4, fol. 174r; 15th century), which depicts Apollo on a pedestal with multiple individualizing attributes.

91 There is also a sense here in which the depiction of Apollo as idol bespeaks his status as a mental 'image' for those listening to Adrastus's story.

92 *Speculum sacerdotale*, chap. 35, p. 143, cited from Weatherly's edition.

93 Kamerick, *Popular Piety and Art*, 27–8; see, further, 13–42, 61–8. Despite the trend toward defence, not all orthodox theologians were equally comfortable with images; see Watson, '"Et que est huius ydoli materia? Tuipse,"' for the example of Walter Hilton. The complexity of attitudes within late medieval religious communities toward images is paralleled by what medieval optical theorists recognized as the 'double nature of vision' itself: the notion that vision, most prominently among the senses, 'has the greatest capacity to reveal truth, and the greatest capacity to deceive' (Akbari, *Seeing through the Veil*, 7). The intersection of medieval optical theory and discourses of spirituality is treated lucidly in Biernoff, *Sight and Embodiment in the Middle Ages*.

94 Augustine, *De civitate Dei* 4.21.9. Augustine rhetorically augments this multiplicity by denouncing the 'falsorum deorum multitudo noxia relinquatur, quam stultorum hominum multitudo uana sectatur' [pernicious mob of false gods to which the silly mob of fools attach themselves] (*De civitate Dei* 4.23.92–3).

95 On the multiplicity of idols, see Zeeman, 'Idol of the Text,' 45.

96 All citations of the *Troy Book* are from Bergen's edition.

97 Inexplicably, Apollo is not included in this catalogue, although he is mentioned along with Venus, Juno, Pallas, Diana, and Minerva [*sic*] in an adjoining passage that briefly lists the gods to whom Troy looked for protection (4.7020–5). Lydgate may have felt it unnecessary to include Apollo in his catalogue of gods because his was the temple in which the sacrifice that precipitates his poetic outrage has just occurred – but Lydgate does not usually hesitate to reinforce the obvious. Interestingly, Lydgate uses the classicizing name 'Phebus' for the sun in a gratuitous mention, near the end of his catalogue of gods, of the habit of elves to wander at midday, 'whan Phebus is most shene' (4.6985). Lydgate seems unaware of the incongruity of such language in the midst of a condemnation of paganism, typical as it may be of his aureate style elsewhere (on which see below, pp. 122–3). Still, Lydgate's insistence that 'I noon excepte of þe false route' suggests that his conspicuous omission of Apollo may be intentional (4.6950).

98 As MacCormack remarks in her discussion of Augustine's view of pagan worship, memorability is not to be underestimated as a polemical tool:

'[e]ven the demons of Christians, who in themselves were no more than a crowd of faceless malign powers, appear in Augustine's pages in the garb of Vergilian deities whose very weaknesses and passions elicit interest' (*The Shadows of Poetry*, 174).

99 All quotations of Bokenham are from Serjeantson's edition, by line number, hereafter abbreviated *LHW*.

100 Lydgate, *Troy Book* 4.7034.

101 Kamerick, *Popular Piety and Art*, 63.

102 Jacobus de Voragine, *The Golden Legend*, vol. 1, no. 98.

103 See Kamerick, *Popular Piety and Art*, 62.

104 Similarly, Mandeville approves of pagan worship of the sun 'because that he chaungeth the tyme and yeueth hete and norisscheth alle thinges vpon erthe ... and for that skylle God hath youen it more gret vertue in the world' (*Mandeville's Travels*, 121). The sun, for Mandeville, is a pagan *simulacrum*: an object of worship evocative of God's presence in the order of nature but *not* a god in and of itself.

105 For these events and the legends that contain them, see Matzke, 'Contributions to the History of the Legend of Saint George,' and *Speculum sacerdotale*, chap. 32.

106 Matzke, 'Contributions to the History of the Legend of Saint George,' 472–4.

107 Jacobus de Voragine, *The Golden Legend*, vol. 1, no. 19.

108 Ibid., vol. 1, no. 49.

109 Ibid., vol. 2, no. 137; *An Alphabet of Tales*, no. 228.

110 Chance, *Medieval Mythography* (1994), 142.

111 Guido's foregrounding of Apollo in his adaptation of Isidore may be compared with one MS family of Ridewall's *Fulgentius metaforalis* that begins with the figures of Apollo and Phaethon, rather than Idolatry and Saturn (the order followed in Liebeschütz's edition). See Allen, 'Commentary as Criticism,' 31, and Chance, *Medieval Mythography* (2000), 294–5.

112 '*Gest Hystoriale*,' lines 4273–5. Cf. Benson, *History of Troy*, 49; on the poem's date, see ibid., 155–6 n. 1.

113 Scott, *Later Gothic Manuscripts*, no. 93, p. 260. A similar error suggests itself in Dunbar's *Goldyn Targe*; on a possible tradition of a female Apollo, see Bawcutt's note to line 75 in *The Poems of William Dunbar*, vol. 2, p. 416.

114 Benson, *History of Troy*, 106–13 (at 111).

115 Lydgate reads Guido's Apollo through Chaucer here: *Troy Book* 2.5593 recalls *FranT* 1031–2, and 'Apollo Delphicus' (2.5922) echoes Chaucer's allusion to Calkas's consultation of 'Daun Phebus or Appollo Delphicus'

in the scene that corresponds with the one from which Lydgate's digression proceeds (*Tr* 1.70).

116 For treatment of this passage, see above, pp. 108–9.

117 On architectural mnemonics in medieval arts of memory, see Carruthers, *The Book of Memory*, 71–9.

118 On this conflation, see Camille, *Gothic Idol*, 129–64, and Tolan, *Saracens*, 105–34.

119 See Daniel, *Heroes and Saracens*, 135–40.

120 See the list of references to 'Apolon' as 'dieu grec et idole sarrasine' in Flutre, *Table des noms propres*, 17; and to 'Apolin, Apollin, Appolin' as 'dieu sarrasin' in Langlois, *Table des noms propres*, 39. Cf. Langlois's entry on 'Apolin, Apollin, Appolin (la gent)' as 'Les Sarrasins.' Extensive discussion of the various gods associated with Islam in the *chansons de geste* is found in Daniel, *Heroes and Saracens*, 121–78.

121 *Laȝamon's Brut*, lines 6936–46; Bodel, *La Chanson des Saisnes*, lines 3318 ('ses diex Mahon et Apolin') and 2856, 4919, 7075 ('la gent Apolin').

122 *Le Roman de Thèbes*, vol. 2, lines 67–74, p. 107.

123 *The Romaunce of the Sowdone of Babylone*, line 86; *Stanzaic Guy of Warwick*, lines 1322, 3187.

124 *The Towneley Plays* 23.589; cf. Tolan's discussion of the mystery plays' attribution of 'Saracen' idolatry to Jews and Romans (*Saracens*, 130–1).

125 On the *Chanson de Roland*, see below. Bodel, *Le Jeu de Saint Nicolas*, lines 1465–6; *The Romance of Sir Beues of Hamtoun*, lines 1379–80; *Firumbras*, lines 262–8, 1427–9.

126 Lines 8, 416–17, 611, 3627–8, 3490–1; text and translations from *The Song of Roland*, ed. Brault, vol. 2.

127 Compare Mahomet's implicit status as 'Father' of the Saracen gods elsewhere, noted in Camille, *Gothic Idol*, 142.

128 On the identification of Juliana with Saint Juliana of Cumae, see Brault's overview of critical opinion in *The Song of Roland*, vol. 1, pp. 334–5.

129 Fulgentius, *Mitologiae* 1.12, and Bern-CMC 10.328, respectively. These mythographic loci are ubiquitous and cited selectively.

130 VM I 1.37; VM II 2.27; VM III 8.3.

131 'Henry of Huntingdon's Herbal,' ed. Rigg, III Prologue 14–15.

132 Text and translation from Oresme, *Nicole Oresme and the Kinematics of Circular Motion*, qtd at 288–9.

133 John of Garland, *Integumenta Ovidii*, 1.7–8, cited from Ghisalberti's edition; translation from 'Integumenta,' ed. Born, 122.

134 Chance's observation of solar allegory in Macrobius's *Saturnalia* antici- pates the logic behind this claim: 'Apollo the sun god, revealer of truth,'

Chance notes, 'symbolizes the intellectual light provided by the scholar reading his text(s)' (*Medieval Mythography* [1994], 82).

135 *Commentum in Martianum Capellam*, 363.12 (cf. VM III 8.1); Macrobius, *Saturnalia* 1.17.40 (cited from Willis's edition and translated by Davies).

136 Lines 199, 205–7. All citations of Henryson's poetry are from Fox's edition.

137 Ibid., 307. Cf. Spearing, *Medieval to Renaissance*, 175–7, and see n. 55 above.

138 Macrobius, *The Saturnalia*, 1.17.59.

139 Ibid., 1.17.31.

140 Martianus Capella, *De nuptiis* 1.9; Remi-CMC, vol. 1, 9.16; Bern-CMC 8.96–105.

141 John the Scot, *Annotationes in Marcianum* 43.9; Remi-CMC, vol. 1, 43.10; VM III 8.16.

142 Isidore, *Etymologiae* 8.11.54–5.

143 Quotation from Bern-CMC 8.105; my translation. Fulgentius, *Mitologiae* 1.12–13, is the source of these commonplaces regarding the significations of the sun's motions and the raven's voice, much repeated by later mythographers (e.g., VM III 8.5). On Apollo's multiplicity, cf. Striar, '"Manciple's Tale,"' 185–6.

144 Fulgentius, *Mitologiae* 1.12.

145 E.g., John the Scot, *Annotationes in Marcianum* 35.6; VM III 8.4.

146 John the Scot, *Annotationes in Marcianum* 35.8; Remi-CMC, vol. 1, 35.8.

147 Remi-CMC, vol. 2, 448.13; VM II 29.

148 Oresme, *Nicole Oresme and the Kinematics of Circular Motion*, 322–3.

149 Kruger, *Dreaming in the Middle Ages*, 143–4, 145. Cf. Newman's discussion of the delusive potential of visions, rooted variously in demonic influence, human fallibility, and nominalist scepticism, in 'What Did It Mean to Say "I Saw"?' 33–41.

150 Kiser, *Telling Classical Tales*, 28–49, esp. 42–7.

151 Lydgate, *Poems*, ed. Norton-Smith, 194.

152 See Ebin, *Illuminator*, 22–7; cf. Lerer, *Chaucer and His Readers*, 35–8.

153 Dunbar, *The Poems of William Dunbar*, ed. Bawcutt, vol. 1, no. 59, lines 257, 267.

154 Quotation from Ebin, *Illuminator*, 75; cf. Fox, 'Dunbar's *The Golden Targe*,' 331–4.

3 Imperial Apollo

1 A suggestive account of the sun as a 'primal signifier' in the poem's representation of love and vision is given by Kolve, 'Looking at the Sun,' qtd at 50.

2 The paradoxes underlying *Tr*'s conception of 'trouthe' are insightfully surveyed in Newman, '"Feynede Loves,"' and Lynch, *Chaucer's Philosophical Visions*, 151–3.

3 Cassandra's well-known connection with Apollo, source of her futile prophetic powers, is not emphasized by Chaucer. Accordingly, Cassandra's appearance in Book Five will not be considered in this chapter; for treatment of this scene in relation to the *Manciple's Tale*, see pp. 219–21.

4 Cf. Blyth, 'Virgilian Tragedy,' 217; Patterson, *Chaucer and the Subject of History*, 84–164.

5 For Augustine and his contemporaries, as MacCormack observes, Virgil's texts 'became building blocks for new structures, just as the columns and capitals of earlier temples and public edifices were ... being reused in the construction of Christian churches' (*The Shadows of Poetry*, 37). Augustine's assimilation of the *Aeneid* into a distinct Christian argument is treated persuasively in the fifth chapter of MacCormack's study.

6 Compare Federico's reading of Chaucer's Troy as a 'utopian' space in *New Troy*, 65–98. Federico also notes that Chaucer creates 'a literally forward-looking version of history that seeks to justify the events of the past in light of what comes later' (71), thus combining a retrospective stance of belatedness with a prescient historical consciousness of what already has happened. Also relevant to this chapter's exploration of *Tr*'s civic mythology is Nolan's recent study of Chaucer's intercalation of the 'historically readable city of Troy' with its citizens' subjectivized experience of dwelling ('Chaucer's Poetics of Dwelling,' 62).

7 Citations of the *Iliad* are based on Fagles's edition.

8 Dictys, 'A Journal of the Trojan War,' 2.28 (cited by book and section number from Frazer's edition).

9 See Dares, 'The Fall of Troy,' 145–6, 154, 160–1 (cited by page number from Frazer's edition); Benoît, *Roman de Troie*, lines 5776–850, 16642–744, 22097ff.; Guido delle Colonne, *Historia* 10.55–300, 22.35–94, 23.74–127, 27.19–49.

10 Guido delle Colonne, *Historia* 23.74–160.

11 Virgil, *Aen.* 6.57–8; Ovid, *Met.* 12.597–606.

12 Dictys, 'A Journal of the Trojan War,' 4.17, 5.7–8; Benoît, *Roman de Troie*, lines 25593–8; Guido delle Colonne, *Historia* 30.48–77; 'Gest Hystoriale,' lines 11782–824; Lydgate, *Troy Book*, 4.5910–6005, 4.6635–73.

13 Barney, Explanatory Notes to *Tr* 4.50–4 (*Riverside Chaucer*, 1044). A Virgilian precedent exists, incidentally, for Apollo's appearance on the battlefield in human disguise, at *Aen.* 9.646–58.

14 On this point, see Minnis, *Chaucer and Pagan Antiquity*, 78–9.
15 For an overview of various treatments of Calchas's treachery in literary tradition and their implications for the outcome of the war, see Rigg, 'Calchas.'
16 Minnis, *Chaucer and Pagan Antiquity*, 80–1.
17 Cf. Fumo, 'Aurelius' Prayer,' 630–1, and 'John Metham's "Straunge Style,"' 234 n. 50.
18 Criseyde's connected pronouncement that 'Drede fond first goddes, I suppose' (*Tr* 4.1408), meanwhile, links her to the atheism of Statius's Capaneus (who echoes a Petronian commonplace); see Fleming, *Classical Imitation*, 83–7.
19 Joseph of Exeter, *Ylias Daretis Phrygii* 3.67. Somewhat inconsistently, Joseph elsewhere expresses similar scepticism from a position of Christian censure, even though the many prophecies in his poem necessarily emerge as truthful. On these and other irregularities in Joseph's view of paganism, see Rigg, 'Joseph of Exeter's Pagan Gods Again.' On the context of Chaucer's 'amphibologies' in ancient and medieval vocabularies of divination, see Fleming, *Classical Imitation*, 50–6, and cf. Minnis, *Chaucer and Pagan Antiquity*, 137. Citations of Joseph's text are from Gompf's edition, hereafter cited by book and line number in the main text. Translations of passages from Joseph's first three books generally follow Bate's edition (which includes only the first half of the epic), while those from the fourth through sixth books adopt Roberts's translation. Occasionally, as above, I prefer one translator's construal of Joseph's densely rhetorical Latin over the other, and in these cases I substitute silently. My understanding of particular passages in the *Ylias* has also been guided by the French translation executed under the direction of F. Mora and the online verse translation by A.G. Rigg (http://www.chass.utoronto.ca/medieval/web-content/ylias/index.html).
20 Incidentally, we never see Criseyde execute this plan – just the contrary: see *Tr* 5.193–4.
21 Cf. Schibanoff, 'Argus and Argyve,' 651.
22 For example, VM II 30; Bern-CMC 6.754–7; Remi-CMC 10.8; VM III 8.5. Cf. Ransom, 'Apollo's Holy Laurel,' 208–9.
23 Arguably, the narrator could be added to this list: like Ovid's Apollo, he is an unsuccessful lover who cultivates his poetic identity from a position of 'unliklynesse' (*Tr* 1.16). On this point see Fumo, 'Chaucer as *Vates*?' 98–9.
24 A recent, provocative analysis of light/dark imagery in *Tr* is Hill, 'She, This in Blak,' 21–3, 43. See also Stokes, 'The Moon in Leo,' which views Criseyde as a false 'lodesterre' identified with the changeable moon. On

Criseyde's superlative beauty, cf. Donaldson's description of her as 'a woman of almost mythological femininity' (*The Swan at the Well*, 81).

25 *MED* s.v. 'sonnish' (adj.), repeatedly echoed by Lydgate.

26 On this and other precedents for Apollo *auricomus*, see Shannon, *Chaucer and the Roman Poets*, 343–4, and Windeatt, ed., *Troilus and Criseyde*, note to 5.8.

27 As Maggie Kilgour indicates in a personal communication, Virgil's portrayal of the divine flames that set Ascanius's hair ablaze ('crinem ... flagrantem') at *Aen.* 2.679–86 provides an imagistic basis for the *auricomus* motif, particularly in relation to Ovid's reprise of this scene in his account, in another father-son tale, of Phaethon's flaming hair (*Met.* 2.319) as he falls like a comet from the sky. Rays of light also encircle Apollo's head and hair at *Met.* 2.40–1, 124.

28 Compare Mieszkowski, 'Chaucer's Much Loved Criseyde,' which nonetheless goes too far in denying agency to Criseyde; for a more balanced view, see Pearsall, 'Criseyde's Choices,' 20–1.

29 These sources, which could not have been known directly to Chaucer, are discussed in Boitani, 'Antiquity and Beyond,' 4, 17.

30 Isidore, *Etymologiae* 8.11.54.

31 Fleming, *Classical Imitation*, 118–22.

32 Apollo is 'pius Arquitenens' at *Aen.* 3.75, while for Aeneas *pietas* supplies a recurrent epithet.

33 It echoes descriptions of Jason, betrayer of Medea, in Apollonios Rhodios's *Argonautika*, and of Apollo's plague-bearing arrows in *Iliad* 1. See Miller, 'Virgil,' 108, and cf. the Virgilian parallel between Apollo's and Aeneas's eroticized suffering discussed in chapter 1, pp. 63–5.

34 On these warnings as well as the multiple Ovidian contexts in play, see Fleming, *Classical Imitation*, 123; Fumo, '"Little *Troilus*,"' esp. 290–2; and Hagedorn, *Abandoned Women*, 131–6.

35 Cf. Fumo, '"Little *Troilus*,"' 312–14; on *Tr*'s critique of Ovidian remedy more generally, see Calabrese, *Chaucer's Ovidian Arts of Love*, 65–80. Christ is tempted to heal himself at Matt. 27:42; Mark 15:31; and Luke 23:35, 37. See also Arbesmann, 'The Concept of "Christus Medicus."'

36 Barney's and Windeatt's critical editions of *Tr* affirm Root's identification of Joseph as 'Chaucer's Dares' in his article of that title. Chaucer also mentions Dares at *BD* 1070 and *HF* 1467. Joseph's *Ylias*, which was excerpted in several contemporary anthologies, survives in six manuscripts from the thirteenth and fourteenth centuries, two including commentaries; see *Joseph Iscanus*, ed. Gompf, 51–5.

37 Root, 'Chaucer's Dares,' 6–18; Windeatt, *Troilus and Criseyde: Oxford Guides*, 75–7.

38 On Joseph's remarkable classicism, see Sedgwick, 'Bellum Troianum,' esp. 66; Roberts, 'Worthy of Their Envy,' 16; Rigg, A History of Anglo-Latin Literature, 99–102; and the extensive documentation of Joseph's debt to classical and post-classical models in Gärtner, Klassische Vorbilder.

39 Joseph's multivalent treatment of the pagan pantheon is ably examined in Parker, 'Pagan Gods,' and Rigg, 'Joseph of Exeter's Pagan Gods Again'; see also Riddehough, 'A Forgotten Poet,' 255–6.

40 In Filostrato 4.118, Troilo experiences a 'dopplia doglia' when he believes Criseida, who has just fainted from grief at the prospect of her exchange, to have died. It is generally thought that Chaucer, struck by Boccaccio's phrase in this relatively insignificant moment late in the action, was reminded of Virgil's words to Statius in Dante, Purgatorio 22.56 that identify the Thebaid as a poem about the 'doppia trestizia di Giocasta' (referring to the civic rivalry between Jocasta's two sons) – a phrase closer than Boccaccio's to Chaucer's usage, since it encapsulates the theme of an epic. Although the Theban matter encompassed by the Dantean phrase is not directly related to Chaucer's Trojan subject (Schless, Chaucer and Dante, 102), it is potentially appropriate to the Theban prehistory with which Chaucer occasionally underscores his poem's action. See Wetherbee, 'Per Te Poeta Fui,' 155–6, and Chaucer and the Poets, 31–3; Fleming, Classical Imitation, 49–50; and Patterson, Chaucer and the Subject of History, 132–5.

41 See Bate's edition of Joseph, Trojan War I–III, p. 155 n. 1, and Dunkle, 'Satirical Themes.'

42 The pertinence of the logic behind Hecuba's expression of her 'gemino ... planctu' to Tr becomes apparent when we recall that an identification of Troilus as 'the kyng Priamus sone of Troye' follows directly upon mention of his 'double sorwe' (Tr 1.2).

43 Chaucer mentions 'Alete' in conjunction with Thesiphone (and 'Megera,' the third Fury) at Tr 4.24. The appearance of Joseph's Allecto is modelled on the same Fury's provocation of the war between the Trojans and the Latins in Aeneid 7, but Joseph's addition of Thesiphone is not paralleled in Virgil.

44 Dunkle, 'Satirical Themes,' 208.

45 Alan of Lille's reorientation of his text from the inspiration of Apollo to that of the Christian God corresponds with Phronesis's progression from rational to theological education; cf. Kensak, 'Silences of Pilgrimage,' 196. Joseph's rhetoric also follows in the tradition of Clement of Alexandria regarding the superior music of Christ's lyre (see above, pp. 82–3), as well as medieval notions of inspiration derived from the Holy Spirit rather than Apollo or the Muses (on which see Curtius, European Literature,

233–7; Ziolkowski, 'Classical Influences,' 23–9; and Verbaal, 'Invocatio Musae,' 57–63).

46 See Mora's edition of Joseph of Exeter, L'Iliade, 319 n. 146.

47 Derived from Fulgentius, Mitologiae 1.14. Cf. Paris's defence of his dream's veracity at Ylias 2.611–12.

48 The connection between Apollo and Paris as rapists is supported by the fact that Paris hunted wild beasts before reclining beneath Apollo's laurel (just as Apollo's hunt of Python preceded his enamourment with Daphne), as well as by Paris's reference to the whispering sound of the breeze stirring the leaves of the laurel, possibly an allusion to Ovid's final image of Daphne, as the laurel, waving her branches and leafy head in the breeze (Met. 1.566–7). It is significant that Chaucer also allusively connects the Judgment of Paris with Apollo's pursuit of Daphne in Tr; see Fleming, Classical Imitation, 113–24.

49 In Dares and his redactors, in the period after Apollo's and Neptune's mistreatment at Troy Laomedon offends the visiting Argonauts and Hercules later sacks Troy in revenge, abducting Laomedon's daughter Hesione and prompting the Trojan abduction of Helen in requital; in this tradition, the anger of the two gods is not directly linked to either war. Ovid provides a different version of events in Met. 11.196–217: Neptune punishes Laomedon by flooding Troy and demanding the sacrifice of his daughter Hesione; Hercules saves Hesione but is not paid for his service by Laomedon; and Hercules takes revenge by sacking Troy, giving Hesione to Telamon. During the second Trojan War, Neptune opposes and Apollo supports Troy.

50 Tr 2.54–5, 3.1495, 3.1755, 4.31–2, 5.8–14, 5.274–80, 5.1016–22, 5.1107–11.

51 Windeatt, Troilus and Criseyde: Oxford Guides, 206.

52 Interestingly, Joseph's description of Apollo's sympathy derives from Neptune's words to Apollo during the war in Ovid's Met.: 'o mihi de fratris longe gratissime natis, / inrita qui mecum posuisti moenia Troiae, / ecquid, ubi has iamiam casuras aspicis arces, / ingemis?' [O you, by far the most favourite of my brother's sons, / you who vainly built with me the walls of Troy, / when you see this citadel now at last about to fall, do you groan / at all?] (Met. 12.586–90). Neptune, who traditionally supports the Greeks (see, e.g., Virgil, Aen. 5.810–11) but wishes to punish Achilles for having killed his son Cygnus, here goads Apollo to defend his favoured Trojans by guiding Paris's arrow into the body of Achilles. This last detail differs from medieval accounts, where Paris ambushes Achilles in Apollo's temple.

53 Cf. Windeatt, Troilus and Criseyde: Oxford Guides, 205–6.

54 Saville, *The Medieval Erotic Alba*, 213–14; Schibanoff, 'Criseyde's "Impossible" Aubes,' 328; Battles, 'Chaucer,' 331–2.

55 Kolve, 'Looking at the Sun,' 55.

56 Cf. Schibanoff's demonstration of the resonances of Criseyde's *impossibilia* regarding her fidelity with medieval 'lying-songs' whose antifeminist associations create 'an almost certain prediction of the opposite course of behavior on her part' ('Criseyde's "Impossible" Aubes,' 327). Battles finds irony in *Tr* 3.1495–8 for a different reason: the sun *did* fall from its sphere when Phaethon crashed his chariot into the sea ('Chaucer,' 331). The *impossiblia* offered by Criseyde in Book Four as a guarantee of her fidelity while in the Greek camp are even more damningly flawed; see Fumo, '"Little *Troilus*,"' 300–1, and Fleming, 'Criseyde's Poem,' 281.

57 A similar complaint is registered by Pseustis in the *Eclogue of Theodulus*, discussed above, p. 87.

58 Specific textual echoes of the *Aeneid* are surveyed, *inter alia*, in Shannon, *Chaucer and the Roman Poets*, 120–68. Broader assessments of the conceptual overlap between the *Aeneid* and *Tr* include Wetherbee, *Chaucer and the Poets*, 90–2; Fleming, *Classical Imitation*, 172–9; Blyth, 'Virgilian Tragedy'; and Bloomfield, 'Chaucer and the Polis.'

59 A familiar rhyme employed in lines adjoining those quoted above from *HF*, and repeated in the 'Legend of Dido' in *LGW*, further highlights the *Aeneid*'s relevance to *Tr*: Sinon's lie '[m]ade the hors broght into Troye, / Thorgh which Troyens loste al her joye' (*HF* 155–6). Cf. *LGW* 1104–5, 1150–1, 1252–3.

60 On the pertinence to *Tr* of London as Troynovaunt, see Robertson, *Chaucer's London*, 2–3, 169, 221, and Federico, *New Troy*, 67–98.

61 The widespread medieval anti-Virgilian perception of Aeneas as traitor is documented in Baswell, *Virgil in Medieval England*, 17–21, and Hebron, *The Medieval Siege*, 101–5; see also Federico, *New Troy*, 30, 34, and Chaucer's own identification of Aeneas as 'traytour' at *LGW* 1328.

62 Despite their obvious differences, Dares and Virgil can be understood as an intact tradition to the extent that Aeneas's departure from Troy, even when presented as a heroic action, is on some level a betrayal of his country motivated by the instinct to survive. It is not difficult to see how early readers could have supposed that Dares's account of Aeneas's treason was the historical truth and Virgil's account an ahistorical poetic embellishment that exonerates Aeneas, as Petrarch suggested in *De otio religioso* (cited in Kallendorf, *The Other Virgil*, 39). This suspicion of Virgil's veracity seems connected to the early modern subtrend of 'pessimistic' readings of the *Aeneid*, surveyed extensively by Kallendorf, that interrogate rather than affirm the imperial project celebrated by the epic. The

tradition of Aeneas as a traitor, in fact, was considerably more ancient than Dares; it dates 'at least to the fourth century BC,' is alluded to by Livy, refuted by Servius, and even implied by Virgil's own Turnus (*Aen.* 12.15). See Thomas, *Virgil and the Augustan Reception*, 71–3, 79–80 (qtd at 72), which expands upon Casali, 'Altri voci,' 60–1; and Singerman, *Under Clouds of Poesy*, 148–52.

63 For an overview of medieval allegorical (particularly Platonic) approaches to the *Aeneid*, see the introduction by Jones and Jones to their translation of Bernardus Silvestris, *Commentary on the First Six Books of the* Aeneid, xi–xxxii, and Singerman, *Under Clouds of Poesy*, 9–25.

64 Federico sees the foundation of new Troys (Rome and Britain) as implicit in *Tr* but is quick to acknowledge that this restitution lacks reality: 'the poem is far from joyful at the prospect of the rise of new Troy. Instead, the impending fall of old Troy seems here to figure the fall of Britain, not its rise. The text asserts a simultaneity, or equation in both time and space, between old and new Troy rather than a chronologically sequential order to them as separate places' (*New Troy*, 89).

65 On this trend, see Singerman, *Under Clouds of Poesy*, 119–35, and Baswell, *Virgil in Medieval England*, 20.

66 On the tension between tragic and teleological models of civilization in the *Aeneid*, see Rossi, *Contexts of War*, 36–7, 43–4. In the medieval view, the rise and fall of cities like Troy invited understanding in light of Boethius's discussion of Fortune; see Hebron, *The Medieval Siege*, 92–4 (see also 94–6 on Augustine's view of Rome's repetition of Troy's errors). In psychoanalytic terms, the contrapuntal force exerted by the myth of Troy's fall over the rise of later nations is akin to the return of the repressed: as Bellamy asserts, 'the *translatio imperii* as a theory of empire can only be narcissistic – attenuating its proleptic translations of power by relying unwittingly on a repressed Troy to realize its "prophetic moment"' (*Translations of Power*, 36).

67 Bloomfield, 'Chaucer and the Polis,' 304. For an argument that the ethical trajectories of Troilo and Aeneas are contrasted in Boccaccio's *Filostrato*, see McGregor, *Shades of Aeneas*, 15–22. The degree of historical consciousness and intertextual mobility that McGregor discerns in the *Filostrato* has the odd effect of making Boccaccio's poem seem *more* 'Chaucerian' than Chaucerians generally suppose, while raising the possibility that the Virgilianism of Chaucer's poem may to some extent be filtered through Boccaccio's precedent.

68 Aeneas is accused of perpetuating 'Laomedonteae … periuria gentis' [the treason of Laomedon's race] in Dido's Carthage and of instigating another uxorious war in Latium (*Aen.* 4.542, 9.140–5).

69 See Conte, *The Poetry of Pathos*, 150–69, esp. 156–7.

70 Ibid., 156; cf. Blyth, 'Virgilian Tragedy,' 213.

71 Cf. Conte, *The Poetry of Pathos*, 157.

72 The Apollo of the second half of the *Aeneid* is thus more or less consistent with the Apollo of *Georgics* 4, whose paternal relationship to Aristaeus associates him with the transformation of passionate error (Aristaeus's attempted rape of Eurydice) into successful art (the cure of his bees).

73 See Harrison, 'Vergil and the Homeric Tradition,' 214–17, 221–3, and Parke, *Sibyls*, 75–6.

74 Juno reinforces this obliteration of Troy's identity at the very moment that Troy 'becomes' Rome: 'ne vetus indigenas nomen mutare Latinos / neu Troas fieri iubeas Teucrosque vocari / ... occidit, occideritque sinas cum nomine Troia' [command not the native Latins to change their ancient name, nor to become Trojans and be called Teucrians ... fallen is Troy, and fallen let her be, together with her name!] (*Aen.* 12.823–4, 828).

75 Panthus is not the last surrogate of Apollo to suffer in the *Aeneid*: his fate is mirrored by that of Lichas (10.315–17), Haemon's son (10.537–42), and Arruns (11.785–867).

76 Here Virgil may rework an important scene in *Iliad* 20, which Harrison has argued Virgil adapts elsewhere ('Vergil and the Homeric Tradition,' 214–17), in which Apollo rashly pushes Aeneas into battle with Achilles to safeguard Hector, without offering him protection. Poseidon, a supporter of the Greeks, prophesies that Aeneas is fated to preserve Troy's legacy and, for this reason, removes him from battle. The corresponding scene in *Aeneid* 2 also involves Hector, Aeneas, and a prophecy of Aeneas's perpetuation of the Trojan line: Hector plays the role of Neptune, advising Aeneas to stay out of battle and follow his destiny, while Panthus, a priest of Apollo, reenacts his god's endangerment of Aeneas by influencing him to enter the fray.

77 On Troy's 'mythic imperial flavor,' despite its status as a city-state, see Federico, *New Troy*, xv–xvi.

78 See *De civitate Dei* 2.22, 2.25, 3.7, 3.8, 3.14, 3.15. Augustine's view of the gods' role in Troy's fall in connection to *Aeneid* 2 is historically contextualized in MacCormack, *The Shadows of Poetry*, 159–74.

79 *De civitate Dei* 1.3; on Rome as a second Troy, cf. 3.8. Augustine, it could be argued, approached the *Aeneid* as an unfinished epic, one lacking the resolution that the unforgiving engine of history and the new narrative of the Christian dispensation would give it: not the rise but the fall of Rome.

80 *De civitate Dei* 3.2.

81 The convention of Paris's lust as the root of the war, similarly dismissed by Augustine (*De civitate Dei* 3.3), also appears at *Tr* 4.547–8.

82 The notion of a thirteenth book of the *Aeneid*, which I freely adopt here, is of course a pendant to the fifteenth-century *Supplement* to the *Aeneid* composed by the humanist Maffeo Vegio and attached frequently to Virgil's epic in early modern editions. It is an interesting coincidence that Vegio's thirteenth book supplies a resolution for the *Aeneid* somewhat like that of the so-called epilogue of Chaucer's *Tr*: after establishing a peaceful rule in Italy, Aeneas dies and is rewarded for his virtue by means of an apotheosis to the stars. For a description of Vegio's *Supplement* and detailed bibliography, see Kallendorf, *The Other Virgil*, 41–2.

83 *MED* s.v. 'misleden' v. 1(e), 'to blunder, make mistakes,' is the primary sense here, but definition 1(a) ('to lead [sb.] astray; deceive [sb.], betray') could very well be an additional implication.

84 Bloomfield's argument that Troilus should be regarded as an anti-Aeneas because he puts personal desire over civic good is generally consistent with my reading of Troilus in this paragraph ('Chaucer and the Polis').

85 'qua fit ut omnia terrena cacumina temporali mobilitate nutantia non humano usurpata fastu, sed diuina gratia donata celsitudo transcendat' (Augustine, *De civitate Dei* 1 [Praefatio], lines 10–13).

86 Paris and Ulysses both have been seen as allusive alter egos of Criseyde at particular moments; see, Fumo, '"Little *Troilus*,"' 288, 303–4; Hagedorn, *Abandoned Women*, 137; and, on the concurrent feminization of Troilus, McInerney, '"Is this a mannes herte?"' and Hagedorn, *Abandoned Women*, 140–3, 157.

87 On Criseyde as an image of the 'preheroic or subheroic,' see Lambert, '*Troilus*,' 122–5, qtd at 123.

88 See Henryson, *Testament of Cresseid*, line 64.

89 The stanza draws on Dante, *Paradiso* 14.28–30. See *OED* s.v. 'circumscribe' v. 4.

4 Fragmentary Apollo

1 These Foucauldian terms inform Knapp's Bakhtinian reading of *MilT* in *Chaucer and the Social Contest*, 32–44 (esp. 33–4).

2 Quotation from Cook, 'Carnival,' 178. On the Miller and the carnivalesque more generally in *CT*, see also David, *Strumpet Muse*, 92–5; Kendrick, *Chaucerian Play*, 111–12; Ganim, *Chaucerian Theatricality*, 31–6; and Jonassen, 'The Inn.'

3 Quote from Bakhtin, *Rabelais and His World*, 83.

4 Bakhtin, 'Discourse in the Novel,' 342. On the opposition of heterglossic and vatic modes of discourse, see Farrell, 'Introduction,' 3, and, with reference to Chaucer, Ganim, *Chaucerian Theatricality*, 21.

5 Blake acknowledges his adherence to Chaucer's rhetorical order in his
   Descriptive Catalogue: 'The Knight and Squire with the Squire's Yeoman
   lead the procession, as Chaucer has also placed them first in his prologue'
   (Blake, *Complete Writings*, 567). Elsewhere in his illustration of the procession, however, Blake freely departs from Chaucer's order in favour of a
   symbolic arrangement. On principles of order in Blake's *Canterbury
   Pilgrims*, see Kiralis, 'William Blake.'
6 Blake, *Complete Writings*, 568, 571.
7 Stevenson, 'From Canterbury to Jerusalem,' 195.
8 Similarly, the fourteenth illustration of Blake's *Job* depicts the blond
   Apollo/Urizen surrounded by sunlight, inciting his fiery steeds (see
   Blake, *Blake's Job*, 38–9). On the relation of Blake's Urizen to his Squire and
   Apollo, see Allen, 'Blake's Archetypal Criticism,' 176; Bowden,
   'Transportation to Canterbury,' esp. 80–4, and 'Artistic and Interpretive
   Context,' 180 (which claims that Blake viewed the Squire critically).
9 Lerer, *Chaucer and His Readers*, 86. For a critique of Lerer's emphasis on
   fifteenth-century infantilization, see Simpson, *Reform and Cultural
   Revolution*, 48–50.
10 Although the last two lines of *SqT* are missing in several MSS, their
   presence in Ellesmere, Hengwrt, and other important MSS led Skeat to
   declare them genuine, a position that has been accepted. These lines
   clearly circulated in enough MSS for them to be known widely as the
   Squire's last words in the fifteenth century. For summary of the textual
   problems surrounding these lines, see Baker, ed., *The Squire's Tale*, 75–7.
11 Wood, *Chaucer and the Country of the Stars*, 102, overlooks this connection
   in remarking that Chaucer 'never used Apollo [as opposed to Phebus] in
   an astronomical periphrasis' outside *SqT*; while Aurelius's prayer is not an
   astronomical periphrasis, it is consistent with *SqT* in astrological vocabulary. When Chaucer refers to the god without reference to his astrological
   function, he names him either 'Appollo' or 'Phebus,' the former more
   frequently. Chaucer calls the non-astrological figure 'Apollo' twelve times
   and 'Phebus' only five times in his works, exclusive of *MancT* (where
   the god's recurrent designation as 'Phebus' likely owes to Chaucer's
   source). *FranT* 1078 ('Phebus') is not included in these figures, since it
   uniquely slips between the astrological and non-astrological senses, as
   explained above. Chaucer also prefers 'Apollo' when imagining the god in
   his oracular capacity (*Tr* 4.114, distinguished from a nearby use of 'Phebus'
   at 4.120, as at 1.69–70 ['Daun Phebus or Appollo Delphicus']). When used
   in non-astrological situations, the name 'Phebus' seems to be given to

Apollo at his most 'human.' Chaucer uses 'Sol' to refer to the sun only at
CYT 826, 1440 (in its alchemical sense) and 'Titan' only at *Tr* 3.1464.

12 The solar motions of 'the laurer-crowned Phebus' at *Tr* 5.1107 form a rare
    exception to Chaucer's usual practice, as does the conflation of astro-
    logical process and mythological fable in *Mars* (which does not, of course,
    qualify as a periphrasis).

13 Such a review is readily available in Lawton, *Chaucer's Narrators*, 106–29,
    and Baker, ed., *The Squire's Tale*, 59–74.

14 On the Squire as poet-figure, see Cooper, *Structure*, 144–5, and Edwards,
    Ratio and Invention, 132. Lawton argues against an individuating psychol-
    ogy for the Squire as a narrator who simply 'sounds like a poet, or like
    Chaucer when he self-consciously plays the poet' (*Chaucer's Narrators*, 115).

15 *SqT* has been read both as parody, like *Thop*, of the genre of romance
    (Seymour, 'Some Satiric Pointers') and as self-parody on Chaucer's part
    (Wood, *Chaucer and the Country of the Stars*, 98–9; on the biographical
    details shared by Chaucer and his Squire, see DiMarco's explanatory
    headnote to the Squire's portrait, *Riverside Chaucer*, 802). Alternatively, *SqT*
    has been viewed not as outright parody but as a youthful work that
    Chaucer later assigned to a young pilgrim to expose its poetic immaturity
    (Larson, 'The Squires Tale,' 606–7).

16 On Fragment V's preoccupation with rhetoric, see Miller, 'Augustinian
    Wisdom'; on astrology as a unifying rhetorical device, see Wood, *Chaucer
    and the Country of the Stars*, 92–102.

17 Spearing, *Medieval to Renaissance*, 37.

18 Neville, 'The Function of the *Squire's Tale*,' 170–2.

19 Haller, 'Chaucer's *Squire's Tale*.'

20 Peterson, 'Finished Fragment.'

21 Jost, 'Potency and Power,' 64, 68.

22 Miller, 'Chaucer's Rhetorical Rendition of Mind,' 227, and 'Augustinian
    Wisdom,' 246.

23 Spearing, *Medieval to Renaissance*, 37; and Spearing, ed., *The Franklin's
    Prologue and Tale*, 72.

24 Frese, *Ars Legendi*, 173–7.

25 Ibid., 173.

26 Pearsall, 'Squire as Story-Teller,' 87.

27 Haller, 'Chaucer's *Squire's Tale*,' 289.

28 Jost, 'Potency and Power,' 68, 70. Berger, 'F-Fragment,' 101–2, argues that
    the Squire's disclaimer of eloquence forms an excuse for self-display,
    whereas the Franklin's similar disclaimer (*FranT* 36–41) is sincere.

29 Quite possibly, Chaucer's conception of the Squire changed between the composition of his *GP* description and the tale (whichever was written first), or Chaucer simply neglected to iron out their relationship. Also possible is that Chaucer did not originally write the tale with the Squire in mind, and that these lines reflect the familiar Chaucerian persona of humble outsider to love; see Larson, 'The Squires Tale,' 600–1.

30 As suggested in Robinson, *The Works of Geoffrey Chaucer*, note to *SqT* 279.

31 Stillwell, 'Chaucer in Tartary,' 187–8. Edwards studies the same conflict between romance form and scientific realism, characterizing *SqT* as a 'romance of natural wonders' that deliberately resists the romance precedent of linking marvels with the supernatural (*Ratio and Invention*, 131–45; qtd at 140). On *SqT* as an Asiatic 'composite' romance, see Goodman, 'Chaucer's *Squire's Tale*.' For a different view of the Squire's attitude toward rational explanation, see Fyler, 'Domesticating the Exotic.'

32 These terms are taken, respectively, from Coghill, *The Poet Chaucer*, 167 (qtd in Baker, ed., *The Squire's Tale*, 43) and McCall, 'The Squire in Wonderland.'

33 On the political context of *SqT* and its relation to the Knight's Crusades, see DiMarco, 'Historical Basis of Chaucer's Squire's Tale'; on its cultural relativism, see Lynch, 'East Meets West,' 541. On *SqT*'s scientific sophistication, see DiMarco, 'Dialogue,' and his survey of the primary material in 'The Squire's Tale.' Other important analyses of the Squire's scientific interests include Bloomfield, 'Chaucer's *Squire's Tale*,' and Edwards, *Ratio and Invention*, 131–45.

34 Wood, *Chaucer and the Country of the Stars*, 84, affirmed by North, *Chaucer's Universe*, 285. Although he admits the distinction to be fine, Wood believes the astrological periphrases in the tale to be parody, in contrast with the serious use of such devices in *Tr*, largely because these are appropriate to an epic like *Tr* but not a romance like *SqT*. Once again, the assumption that the Squire intends a typical romance impedes recognition of his innovations within the genre.

35 On astrological allegory, see especially North, *Chaucer's Universe*, 263–88. Despite these rational interests, the Squire, on the basis of one misunderstood section of the tale, is often charged with anti-intellectualism and aristocratic snobbery, e.g., by Pearsall, 'Squire as Story-Teller,' 87; Haller, 'Chaucer's *Squire's Tale*,' 290; Peterson, 'Finished Fragment,' 69; Kahrl, 'Chaucer's *Squire's Tale*,' 203; and Miller, 'Chaucer's Rhetorical Rendition of Mind,' 231–33. Concerning the Squire's disdainful dismissal of the opinions of the crowd that wonders aloud about the four gifts (*SqT* 189–262), many conclude that the Squire disapproves of *all* of the crowd's

speculations, but the Squire's criticisms fall specifically upon those who fear the marvels because they are ignorant of their basis in empirical science: 'As lewed peple demeth comunly / Of thynges that been maad moore subtilly / Than they kan in hir lewednesse comprehende; / They demen gladly to the badder ende' (221–4). Far from disparaging the view of those who seek rational causes for the marvels, the Squire follows Boethius, Thomas Aquinas, and Roger Bacon in defending rational explanations for what otherwise seems magical or impossible. On this point see DiMarco, 'Dialogue,' 58–9; on the technological basis of magic in *SqT*, see Lionarons, 'Magic,' 377–80.

36 *Pace* McCall, 'The Squire in Wonderland,' 109.

37 DiMarco, 'Supposed Satiric Pointers,' 330.

38 See Wise, 'Flight Myths,' and cf. Hart, *Prehistory of Flight*, 116–33.

39 Emphases added throughout this section.

40 This rhyme pair has attracted especial scorn, from Pearsall's denunciation of it as an 'egregious pun' ('Squire as Story-Teller,' 86), to Haller's remark that it was 'doubtless as embarrassing in the fourteenth century as it is now' ('Chaucer's *Squire's Tale*,' 290), to Berry's dismissal of it as an 'infelicity' and 'a failed search for a rhyme word' ('Flying Sources,' 288). Such criticisms reveal less about the Squire's device than about modern distaste for *rime riche*, which Chaucer held in high enough esteem to feature at the end of the first sentence of *GP*. The Squire's use of a rhetorical device to illustrate his own distance from rhetorical expertise instead seems consistent with his general emphasis on the rarefied nature of his material and his admiring remoteness from matters of eloquence. Cf. Goodman, 'Chaucer's *Squire's Tale*,' 132–3, for one of the few affirmative readings of the Squire's pun.

41 Berry adduces Virgil's rhetorically deceptive Sinon (allusively introduced by the steed of brass, through its link with the Trojan Horse) as a model of the Squire's tercelet. Less apt is Berry's extension of the implications of the tercelet's Virgilian abuse of rhetoric to the Squire on the basis of the familiar scholarly imprimatur of the 'oft-made criticism of Chaucer's Squire as an out-of-control rhetorician' ('Flying Sources,' 297–300).

42 Cf. Lerer's analysis, *Chaucer and His Readers*, 75–6, of the rhyme pair *mente/ entente* in *SqT*, used both as an image of the 'immediacy of Canacee's knowledge' of the falcon's speech and the tercelet's hypocritical concealment of his true intentions.

43 For the view that these solar associations link the brass steed with the astrolabe, see Osborn, *Time and the Astrolabe*, 34–54.

44 Manly and Rickert, *The Text of the* Canterbury Tales, vol. 4, 483–4; Chaucer, *Complete Works*, ed. Skeat, vol. 5, note to *SqT* 671–2; Baker, ed., *The Squire's Tale*, 75–6; and Partridge, 'Minding the Gaps,' 61–76.

45 Seaman, '"Wordes of the Frankeleyn to the Squier,"' 15–17.

46 Dane, '"Tyl Mercurius House He Flye."'

47 Noted by Kahrl, invoking a private suggestion of Robert E. Kaske's, in 'Chaucer's *Squire's Tale*,' 205 n. 45. Kahrl refers to the fragmentary section of *Thop* as the second, not the third fit; I follow the numbering scheme established by Burrow, '"Sir Thopas."'

48 In Bloomfield's opinion, the summary itself 'seems to indicate that Chaucer deliberately chose to stop, for he normally does not summarize his story before he tells it' ('Chaucer's *Squire's Tale*,' 33). Cooper, *Structure*, 146, similarly views the prolepsis as a signal of intentional incompletion, and argues that its function is to suggest the shape of the tale as a whole – which she believes is interrupted by the Franklin – while sparing Chaucer the labour of having to write it. See also Goodman, 'Chaucer's *Squire's Tale*,' 135.

49 In addition to Clark, '*Does* the Franklin Interrupt the Squire?' 160–1, and Seaman, '"Wordes of the Frankeleyn to the Squier,"' see Lawton, *Chaucer's Narrators*, 115, and Goodman, 'Dorigen and the Falcon,' 74 n. 17. Lawton further argues that the last two lines of the tale may be a scribal addition intended to create the illusion of an interruption (*Chaucer's Narrators*, 126). Clark, on the other hand, seems to believe that an interruption would be more appropriate at the end of Part Two rather than two lines into Part Three ('*Does* the Franklin Interrupt the Squire?' 161). Seaman's formal comparison of the Sq-Fran link with other interruptions and links in the *Tales* reaches the curious conclusion that *SqT is* intentionally incomplete due to its mid-sentence termination, which must signal an interruption, but that it is *not* interrupted by the Franklin. The Franklin's praise, then, either is 'an end comment written before the Squire's Tale, in anticipation of a finished tale [i.e., before Chaucer decided to have the tale interrupted], or it is a comment that is meant to come after an interruption by someone else' ('"Wordes of the Frankeleyn to the Squier,"' 18).

50 Although the Knight's and Host's interruptions of *MkT* and *Thop*, unlike the Franklin's words to the Squire, are dismissive in tone, there is a Chaucerian precedent for a commendatory interruption of a longwinded narrative: the Pardoner's interjection in *WBProl* 164–5, which however differs from the Franklin's in calling for the narrative to be resumed.

51 On the contrast in genre and style between the Squire's and Franklin's tales, see Cooper, *Oxford Guides*, 227, and Lynch, 'East Meets West,' 543–4,

549–50; cf. Osborn's remark that 'the form the Franklin announces for his story, a Breton lay, is in itself almost a rebuke to the Squire, as stories of this kind were typically short and to the point' (*Time and the Astrolabe*, 296 n. 13).

52 Cf. Cooper, *Oxford Guides*, 241.

53 Stevens, 'Chaucer's "Bad Art,"' 133. Cf. Kamowski, 'Trading the "Knotte,"' 399–400.

54 For the view that the Franklin both emulates and critiques aristocratic eloquence, see Brown and Butcher, *The Age of Saturn*, 75–85.

55 Translations of Geoffrey of Vinsauf's *Poetria nova* from Nims's edition (60); cf. Miller, 'Augustinian Wisdom,' 270 n. 15, and Spearing, *The Franklin's Prologue and Tale*, 75. The Franklin's prolific rhetoric was seminally established by Harrison, 'The Rhetorical Inconsistency of Chaucer's Franklin.' Many critics nonetheless find the Franklin's rhetoric more effective or mature than the Squire's, often motivated by ironic interpretations of *SqT*: see, e.g., Berger, 'F-Fragment,' 101–2, 138, and Miller, 'Augustinian Wisdom.' For an argument that the Franklin's rhetoric is 'over-reaching' (implicitly, like the Squire's), see Burlin, 'Art of Chaucer's Franklin,' 62.

56 Cf. Ross's argument that the Franklin's transparent pose lampoons 'conventional aspirations to rhetorical eminence' associated with laureate identity (*The Making of the English Literary Canon*, 41).

57 Haller notes that Aurelius is the Franklin's 'tribute to the Squire' ('Chaucer's *Squire's Tale*,' 294), and Cooper remarks that 'Aurelius is the Squire raised to a higher degree of superlatives' (*Structure*, 148). Miller adduces *Roman de la rose* 61–6, the description of Springtime's robe, as the source for both the Squire's robe in the *GP* and the Franklin's pun on colours ('Augustinian Wisdom,' 269–70 n. 15).

58 Kolve, 'Rocky Shores,' 191. Other important discussions of the sustained connection between art and illusion in *FranT* are Ferster, 'Interpretation and Imitation'; McEntire, 'Illusions and Interpretation'; and Knopp, 'Poetry as Conjuring Act.' Although some critics discern a rational basis for the magic in *FranT* in court entertainment and automata (e.g., Luengo, 'Magic and Illusion'; Braswell, 'Magic of Machinery'; Lionarons, 'Magic,' 380–2; Lightsey, 'Chaucer's Secular Marvels,' 304–9), the illusory power of marvels in the tale as well as its disinterest in the technological causes of marvels warrants against this. On this point, see DiMarco, 'Dialogue,' 56–60; for a detailed critique of Luengo's and Braswell's line of argument, see Kolve, 'Rocky Shores,' 179–87.

59 See Kolve, 'Rocky Shores,' 187–91.

60   Ibid., 187.

61   For discussion of these illustrations, see Jones, *Medieval Medicine*, 73–5, 102. Seznec reproduces and analyses a comparable fifteenth-century image, attributed to Maso Finiguerra, of Apollo Medicus as book-wielding magician; see *Survival of the Pagan Gods*, 28–9.

62   On the moral ambivalence of medical charms in the Middle Ages, see Rawcliffe, *Medicine and Society*, 94–6.

63   'Henry of Huntingdon's Herbal,' ed. Rigg, I Prologue, line 11; see also III Prologue, lines 10–15, and IV Epilogue 2, lines 1–2. Cf. Apollo's remark at *Met.* 1.522 that 'herbarum subiecta potentia nobis' [the power of herbs is subject to me]; see Hoffman, *Ovid and the Canterbury Tales*, 170–1, on the relation of this line to Aurelius's prayer. Elsewhere in the series of miniatures depicting the descent of the medical art in BL Sloane MS 6, Aesculapius's students are portrayed gathering herbs and roots, which are then refined into powders.

64   Here I differ from Kolve, 'Rocky Shores,' who sees Chaucer, not the Franklin as narrator, as the clerk's surrogate, concurring instead with Berger's reading of the Franklin's absorption into the fiction of the clerk's magic, in 'F-Fragment,' 147–8. The hyperbolic detail in the Franklin's *GP* portrait that 'It snewed in his hous of mete and drynke' (345) shares the spirit of wish-fulfilment fantasy (à la utopian narratives like the *Land of Cokayne*) behind the pageant of marvels in the clerk of Orleans' study.

65   Wood, *Chaucer and the Country of the Stars*, 265–6.

66   McEntire, 'Illusions and Interpretation,' 148. On the Franklin as a victim of his tale's illusory optimism, see Eaton, 'Narrative Closure.'

67   Davenport, *Chaucer*, 190.

68   Lydgate imitates these lines in the *Troy Book*, though it is unclear whether he appreciates the parodic quality of this Chaucerian passage whose exaggerated rhetoric so strongly forbodes Lydgate's own poetic style:

>   Til Pheb*us* char lowe gan declyne
>   His golden axtre, þat so cler doth shine,
>   –þis to seyne, þe sonne went[e] dou*n*[.]   (4.627–9)

The passage is also echoed (unironically) in the *Kingis Quair*: 'Till Phebus endit had his bemes bryght / And bad go farewele euery lef and floure; / This is to say, approchen gan the nyght' (stanza 72, qtd from McDiarmid's edition).

69   Osborn suggests that the Franklin's rhetorical self-deflation parodies the 'ineptly artificing' periphrasis with which *SqT* breaks off (*Time and the Astrolabe*, 103).

70 Book 1, sec. 25 (p. 13) in Helm's edition; translated by Whitbread. See
    Hammond, 'Chaucer and Lydgate Notes.'

71 See Fumo, 'Aurelius' Prayer,' 634–5 n. 20, for some prolegomena to this
    discussion.

72 See the lucid analysis of Fulgentius's Prologue in Relihan, *Ancient
    Menippean Satire*, 152–63.

73 Knight's characterization of Aurelius's rhetorical style, particularly in his
    prayer to Apollo, as 'elaborate' and 'circumlocutionary,' reinforces his
    affinity with the Squire ('Rhetoric and Poetry,' 25).

74 See Morgan, *The Franklin's Tale*, notes to lines 347–62 and 393–7, for these
    and other indications that Apollo does not grant Aurelius's prayer. On the
    discrepancy between the prayer and the tale's action, and its relevance to
    how the rocks ultimately 'disappear,' see Wood, *Chaucer and the Country of
    the Stars*, 245–71.

75 For detailed analysis of the relation of these scenes to *FranT*, see Fumo,
    'Aurelius' Prayer,' 624–5, 627–8. Not discussed in my article but also
    plausibly influential upon Aurelius's prayer is Pynoteüs's lengthy appeal
    to the solar Apollo to vivify a statue of his dead lover Neptisphelé, in
    Froissart, *La Prison amoureuse*, lines 1744–918. Like Arcita's prayer,
    Pynoteüs's is successful.

76 Cf. Kahrl's observation that the Franklin, in 'trying to outdo [the Squire]
    in the use of colors of rhetoric' attempts 'to set both the matter of true
    eloquence and also true gentility straight' ('Chaucer's *Squire's Tale*,' 205).

77 I use this phrase in a different sense from Sandra J. McEntire, who
    identifies it with Boccaccio's Tebano, whom she characterizes as 'truly a
    poet, a son of Apollo' because he produces real art, not illusion ('Illusions
    and Interpretation,' 157). As I have argued throughout this book, 'real art'
    is precisely what Apollo does *not* authorize.

78 On the poem as a journey of enlightenment, see Koonce, *Chaucer and the
    Tradition of Fame*, 178–81, and Joyner, 'Parallel Journeys,' 18.

79 Delany, *Chaucer's* House of Fame, 86.

80 I would not go so far as to characterize *HF* as 'intentionally incomplete,'
    as do some critics, but I do regard it as imaginatively intact insofar as
    Chaucer was, on some level, aware that the uncertainty regarding
    'auctorite' in the last surviving line was appropriate ballast for a book that
    began with a wary confrontation with a god identified with the precarious
    construction of authority. See also Ross, *The Making of the English Literary
    Canon*, 319 n. 54.

81 Apollo's portrayal as a temperamental god follows from the reference to
    Marsyas at *HF* 1229–32 as well as various strategies of 'humanization' in

the invocation itself, particularly its subtle reinforcement of the etiology of the laurel as a narrative of loss (evoked in Chaucer's promise to 'kisse' the laurel). See Fumo, 'Chaucer as *Vates*?' 96–8; cf. Boitani, *Chaucer and the Imaginary World of Fame*, 163; Havely, ed., *The House of Fame*, note to 1106–8; and Minnis with Scattergood and Smith, *Oxford Guides to Chaucer*, 177–8.

82 For a different view of the relation between *SqT* and *HF* regarding *auctoritas*, see Berry, 'Flying Sources,' 305.

83 For example, Sharon-Zisser, 'The *Squire's Tale*'; Scala, 'Canacee'; and Kamowski, 'Trading the "Knotte."'

84 One exception is the spurious eight-line continuation of *SqT* found in BL Lansdowne MS 851 and Oxford, Bodleian MS Selden Arch. B.14, which defers the end of the story until a later point in the journey rather than providing it; see Baker, ed., *The Squire's Tale*, 31–2, 76–7, 242–3. On the lack of continuations of the tale before Spenser, see Baker, ed., *The Squire's Tale*, 30–7; Burrow, 'Poems Without Endings'; Partridge, 'Minding the Gaps,' 61–2.

85 Stevens, 'Chaucer's "Bad Art,"' 133. Cf. Kaske, 'The Knight's Interruption,' 249, and on closure in Fragment V more generally, Lee, 'Question of Closure.'

86 Partridge, 'Minding the Gaps,' 61.

87 Lawton's valuable survey of the reception of *SqT*, for example, begins with the Renaissance; his only attention to fifteenth-century views of the tale is given to the 'singular' view of one unsympathetic scribe (*Chaucer's Narrators*, 106–29). An exception to this trend is chapter 2 of Lerer's *Chaucer and His Readers*, which nevertheless overlaps only superficially with the present section's concerns.

88 Berry, '"Sundrie Doubts,"' 107.

89 Spearing's contention that Chaucer, in abandoning *SqT*, rejects medieval aesthetics in favour of a proto-Renaissance romance sensibility exemplified by *FranT* thus espouses an overly narrow model of periodization that elides both the popularity of *SqT* in the Renaissance and, as the following pages demonstrate, the tale's epitomization of Chaucerian authority in the fifteenth century (*Medieval to Renaissance*, 38).

90 My argument in this section is therefore differently oriented from Lawton's observations on the influence of Chaucer's 'high style' voice upon fifteenth-century poetic practice. In my reading, Chaucer's 'high style' is not, as Lawton claims, 'remarkably consistent and stable' (*Chaucer's Narrators*, 131) but is itself the subject of critical examination and contestation, especially within the narratorial context of Fragment V.

91 Lydgate, *Saint Albon and Saint Amphibalus*, ed. Reinecke, lines 8–14, 24–5. A similarly phrased profession of modesty occurs in Lydgate, *Fall of Princes*, ed. Bergen, 9.3401–7.

92 Pearsall, *John Lydgate*, 145–7, notes Lydgate's dependence on the Franklin's modesty topoi but not that of the Squire.

93 On Lydgate's development of a 'mythology of poetry' based on the antithesis of a Chaucerian 'golden age' of poetic fertility with a world of poetic impoverishment associated with patronage, see Lerer, *Chaucer and His Readers*, 34–8.

94 Cf. Lydgate, *Fall of Princes*, ed. Bergen, 3.13–16, and 'A Mumming for the Mercers of London' (in *Minor Poems*, ed. MacCracken, 695–8), lines 11–35. On the attempt of the 'Mumming' to marry a 'foreign – classical or European – tradition of eloquence and a native cultural practice' via such references to classical inspiration, see Nolan, *John Lydgate and the Making of Public Culture*, 99–106.

95 Cited by line number from MacCracken's edition.

96 Lydgate, *Poems*, ed. Norton-Smith, 194 (see further 192–5); on Lydgate's vocabulary of illumination, see also Kean, *Chaucer*, vol. 2, 226–34; and Ebin, *Illuminator*, 19–48. Lydgate's association of aureation with Apollo is overtly classicizing, unlike, for example, Hoccleve's vocabulary of illumination in his praise of Chaucer's 'ornat endytyng, / That is to al þis land enlumynyng' in *Regement of Princes*, lines 1973–4 (in Hoccleve, *Works*, ed. Furnivall). Lydgate's classicization of Chaucer is exemplified by the first long sentence of the *Siege of Thebes*, the attempt of which to outdo *GP* 1–18 is immediately marked by Lydgate's substitution of 'briȝte phebus' for Chaucer's 'yonge sonne' (Lydgate, *Siege of Thebes*, line 1). Cf. Wood's observation of the Squire's own classicization of the first sentence of *GP* at *SqT* 47–57, in which the 'sonne' similarly is personified as 'Phebus' (*Chaucer and the Country of the Stars*, 98–9).

97 On Bokenham's rejection of aureate diction for plain speech, see Hilles, 'Gender,' esp. 202–6. On Bokenham's critique of Chaucer's classicizing poetics, see Delany, *Impolitic Bodies*, 32–69; for a different view, see Wakelin, *Humanism*, 67–70.

98 Scattergood's translation (Skelton, *The Complete English Poems*, 413).

99 Hoccleve, *Regement of Princes*, line 1962.

100 See Spurgeon, *Five Hundred Years of Chaucer Criticism and Allusion 1357–1900*, vol. 1, xciii–xciv. Challenged by Kean, *Chaucer*, vol. 2, 210–39, Spurgeon's view was reasserted by Spearing, *Medieval to Renaissance*, 340 n. 14. Lerer, *Chaucer and His Readers*, 57–84 argues that *SqT* was most important to the next generation of writers as a model of their feelings of adolescent subjection to 'father Chaucer.' Lerer also notes that the reception of Chaucer as eloquent is related to the Squire's own goal of eloquence, but dwells on the Squire's questionable ambition rather than the perspective of the Franklin (90).

101 Quoted from Brewer, *Chaucer*, 78–9; translated by R.G.G. Coleman.

102 See Carlson, 'Chaucer, Humanism, and Printing.'

103 Lerer, *Chaucer and His Readers*, 147–63.

104 Carlson, 'Chaucer, Humanism, and Printing,' 282.

105 On the importance of invocation to Chaucer's poetic practice, see Hardman, 'Chaucer's Muses.'

106 Cf. Hieatt, *Chaucer*, 15–16.

107 Lawton, 'Dullness,' 768. On the political aspects of poetic self-deprecation, see also Ross, *The Making of the English Literary Canon*, 45–6, and Esolen, 'The Disingenuous Poet Laureate.'

108 Lerer, *Chaucer and His Readers*, 70. See also Scanlon, 'Lydgate's Poetics,' 79–80.

109 In another sense, Lydgate's summary of *SqT* attempts to 'grant the Squire's fragment the status of a finished piece'; see Kamowski, 'Trading the "Knotte,"' 400–1; cf. Scanlon, 'Lydgate's Poetics,' 80.

110 Citations of the *Temple of Glas*, by line number, are from Norton-Smith's edition of Lydgate's *Poems*.

111 For a similar conjunction, see Lydgate, *Siege of Thebes*, lines 833–44.

112 For a different account of the influence of the rhetorical style of *SqT* upon Lydgate, see Lee, 'Question of Closure,' 193–4.

113 Quoted from Pearsall's edition (lines 1–2). These lines' debt to *SqT* is noted in Chaucer, *Complete Works*, ed. Skeat, vol. 5, note to *SqT* 671–2.

114 Scattergood, 'Skelton's *Garlande of Laurell*,' 131. See also the discussion of the 'whimsical' character of Occupacioun's list (which, ironically, lacks notice of several of Skelton's major poems) in Kinsman and Yonge, *John Skelton*, xi–xii.

115 This parallel is noted in Chaucer, *Complete Works*, ed. Skeat, vol. 5, note to *SqT* 671–2.

116 On Skelton's literary enemies, see Scattergood, 'Skelton's *Garlande of Laurell*,' 132–3. Skelton's attitude toward his critics was not always hostile, however; he is at least partially responsible, for example, for adding explanatory glosses to certain of his poems with the intent of demystifying their obliquities (although many of these glosses, we shall see, have just the opposite effect). On this point, see Scattergood, 'Early Annotations'; on the glosses' tendency to 'problematize interpretation,' see Griffiths, *John Skelton*, 101–28 (at 111).

117 *The Poetical Works of John Skelton*, ed. Dyce, vol. 1, xlix.

118 On the ironic dimensions of the *Laurel*, see Spearing, *Medieval to Renaissance*, 212.

119 On the glosses' authorship, see Scattergood, 'Early Annotations,' 290; Griffiths, *John Skelton*, 106–11. As Scattergood notes, these glosses, which

mainly surround Occupacioun's list, 'appear to be designed to amplify and extend the poem by adducing, sometimes in a fairly arbitrary fashion, analogous material' ('Early Annotations,' 293). Text and translations of the glosses are from *The Book of the Laurel*, ed. Brownlow; references to line numbering are adjusted to reflect Scattergood's edition, on which all other citations are based.

120 Perhaps for this reason, John Bale's list of Skelton's works in his *Illustrium maioris Britanniae Scriptorum Summarium* (1548, later enlarged and reissued), based on Occupacioun's list and including the same lost works, itemizes Skelton's 'Apollo' not by the title Skelton gives it in the *Laurel* but the otherwise unattested 'Apollinem fatiloquum' [Prophesying Apollo]; see Gordon, *John Skelton*, 209–10. This association among Skelton, Apollo, and (Virgilian) prophetic inspiration may also explain Skelton's cryptic Latin verses at lines 1212–16, framed in oracular language and predicting the birth of a boy 'Deli de sanguine cretus' [descended from the blood of Delos], who will be 'alter Apollo' [another Apollo] (translations from Scattergood, ed., *Complete English Poems*, note to 1212–18). Brownlow suggests that 'the joke, a broad one, is that the boy will be another Apollo because he is born of Delian, i.e., Apollonian, blood,' alluding to Skelton's apparent impregnation of the Margery of the previous stanzas (note to 1205a–9, p. 195). Skelton's 'oracle,' it should be noted, parodies Virgil's fourth Eclogue, which celebrates Apollo's reign and concerns the birth of a *puer* in connection to the return of a Virgin (cf. Skelton's reference in 1215 to the boy's mother as 'meretrix castissima talis' [a most chaste harlot]).

121 Text and translation from Singleton's edition of the *Paradiso*. On the relation between genital penetration and spiritual infusion in early Christian understandings of Apollo's oracle, see Smith, 'Myth of the Vaginal Soul.'

122 Fumo, 'Chaucer as *Vates*?' 95–6.

123 Cf. *The Poetical Works of John Skelton*, ed. Dyce, vol. 1, xxxix. Chaucer in part escapes this bind in the *Retraction* because of his reliance on a faulty memory ('and many another book, if they were in my remembrance' [*Retr* 1087]) rather than a 'boke of remembrauns' (*Laurel* 1149).

124 This assessment of Skelton's caution toward the vatic project should be compared with contextualization of his claim to poetic authority within larger traditions of poetic mastery in Skelton, 'Master Poet,' and Griffiths's study of Skelton's multifarious articulations of the poet's role in *John Skelton and Poetic Authority*.

125 Hieatt, 'Room of One's Own,' 147.

126 Citations of the *Faerie Queene* (abbreviated *FQ*), by book/canto/stanza number, are from Roche's edition.

127 Kennedy, 'Spenser's Squire's Literary History,' 49.

128 Berry, '"Sundrie Doubts,"' 118.

129 In the version of *CT* to which Spenser most likely had access in one of Thynne's four editions, however, the 'Wordes of the Frankeleyn to the Squier' are spoken instead by the Merchant, and the tale following the Squire's is *MerT*. While this difference in arrangement significantly alters the implications of the fragmentary end of *SqT* and the status of *FranT* as a response to it, Hieatt has argued that Spenser nonetheless exploits the latent narrative energy between the two tales, which in Thynne's order bookend the 'marriage group,' by shaping the *SqT* continuation around the marital ideology of the *FranT*. In Cheney's view, this reshaping corrects *SqT*'s unfulfilled celebration of magic through a 'moral allegory figuring human love as the true magic force in society.' See Hieatt, *Chaucer*, 24–5, 77, and 'Room of One's Own,' 158–9; Cheney, 'Spenser's Completion,' 153.

130 Berry, '"Sundrie Doubts,"' 121.

131 Hieatt, *Chaucer*, 77–8, and 'Room of One's Own,' 159–60. Cf. Lawton's account of the Renaissance view of the Chaucer of *SqT* as 'the true father of English epic' (*Chaucer's Narrators*, 119).

132 Berry, '"Sundrie Doubts,"' 122.

133 For a more detailed development of this paragraph's argument, see Fumo, 'Chaucer as *Vates*?' 96, 102–3. On poetic metempsychosis, see *The Works of Edmund Spenser*, ed. Greenlaw et al., vol. 4, p. 180, note to 4.2.34.

134 Lydgate's ambivalent turn to Chaucer in *Life of Our Lady* is a more distant precedent for Spenser's invocation of Chaucer. In what must be called an anti-invocation, Lydgate expresses his 'grete nede' for Chaucer to 'conveye and directe / And with his supporte, amende eke and corecte / The wronge traceȝ, of my rude penne' but regrets that this is impossible now that Chaucer is dead (2.1646–9). Lydgate instead prays for Chaucer's soul and rejects the inspiration of Clio and Calliope in favour of that of the Virgin.

135 See Brownlee, 'Pauline Vision,' esp. 202–10; Hawkins, 'Metamorphosis of Ovid,' esp. 156–9; and Levenstein, 'Re-Formation of Marsyas.' On the essentially intertextual nature of *invocatio* as a poetic trope, see Sharrock, 'An A-musing Tale,' 208.

136 As observed in Wallace, *Chaucerian Polity*, 249, 255.

5 Domestic Apollo

1 For the sake of consistency this chapter hereafter follows Chaucer in referring to the protagonist of *MancT* as 'Phebus.' When the name 'Apollo'

is used, it refers to the god in other contexts, or in general. On ancient references to Delphi as a house (*domos*) and Apollo's Pythia as a wife-figure, see Maurizio, 'Narrrative,' 156.

2   Machaut, *Voir dit*, 8005; hereafter cited parenthetically by line number from the edition of Leech-Wilkinson and Palmer (translations are Palmer's). Only the version in the *Seven Sages of Rome*, which treats the events in straightforward fabliau terms and centres upon the construction of a physical contraption adjacent to the bedroom, is comparable to *MancT* in its emphasis on domestic space. Cf. Wallace's reading of the *MancT* as deconstructive of household rhetoric and exemplary of 'the claustrophobic intensity of domestic drama' (*Chaucerian Polity*, 252).

3   For an argument that *MancT* represents a 'nightmare version of Chaucer's own poetic' as exemplified by *KnT*, see Børch, 'Chaucer's Poetics.'

4   Dean, 'Ending of the *Canterbury Tales*,' 27.

5   Quotation from McCall, *Chaucer among the Gods*, 148. An exhaustive bibliography cannot be provided here, but a sense of the range of sociopolitical readings of *MancT* can be gathered from the diverse approaches of Fradenburg, 'Manciple's Servant Tongue'; Askins, 'The Historical Setting'; and Salisbury, 'Murdering Fiction.' On the other hand, the major syntheses of Chaucer's representations of antiquity by Fyler, McCall, Minnis, and Calabrese devote only nine pages collectively to *MancT*.

6   In this sense, Phebus's house constitutes a false destination for the pilgrims, a monument to the divagation of Christian pilgrimage into the realm of curiosity and disorder; see Zacher, *Curiosity and Pilgrimage*, 87–129, esp. 121–2.

7   In the former view, represented by Delany, 'Slaying Python,' esp. 71–4; Raybin, 'Death of a Silent Woman'; Cox, 'The Jangler's "Bourde"'; and Storm, 'Speech,' the silence of Phebus's wife and the garrulousness of the Manciple's mother converge in the silencing of the crow. The latter view assumes a tiered or antithetical relationship between the Manciple's and Parson's tales; see, for example, Wood, 'Speech'; Allen, 'Penitential Sermons'; and Kensak, 'Silences of Pilgrimage.'

8   Phebus's irresolution regarding 'truth' in connection to sexual fidelity, factual evidence, and accuracy of expression – all of which this chapter explores – highlights the multivalence of *trouthe* as a late medieval cultural concept discussed by Richard Firth Green in *A Crisis of Truth: Literature and Law in Ricardian England*, from which this chapter's title takes its cue. *MancT*'s fraught, internally contradictory demarcation of 'truth' and 'treason' (see *MancT* 271, 298, and Herman, 'Treason') attests to the discord inherent in Green's 'fundamental shift in popular attitudes to the nature of

evidence and proof' in late fourteenth-century England (Green, *A Crisis of Truth*, xiv).

9 Martianus Capella, *De nuptiis* 1.11.

10 See the *De nuptiis* commentaries of John the Scot, 9.15; Remigius of Auxerre 9.15; and Bernard Silvestris, 8.90–6; and cf. Keith, *Play of Fictions*, 89.

11 Virgil, *Aen.* 6.81; Ovid, *Met.* 14.152–3. See Keith, *Play of Fictions*, 82–3 for a discussion of the Sibyl, *vox*, and prophecy.

12 Lines 173–5.

13 This chapter always distinguishes between Chaucer's crow and all other versions' attestations of a raven in the same role (not to be confused with the separate character of Minerva's informing crow [*cornix*], whose advice to Apollo's raven [*corvus*] immediately precedes the events of the Coronis episode in Ovid's *Met.*). For clarification of these discrete but overlapping avian roles in Ovidian tradition, see Fumo, 'Thinking upon the Crow.' A concise overview of Chaucer's adjustments to Ovid's and other versions of the Coronis story is found in Cooper, 'Chaucer and Ovid,' 79.

14 [Pseudo-]Lactantius Placidus, *Narrationes* 2.10; Arnulf, *Allegoriae* 2.10. On the problem of attribution and textual history of the *Narrationes*, see Cameron, *Greek Mythography*, 3–32.

15 Phineus appears in Apollonios Rhodios, *Argonautika*, 2.178–497; Ovid, *Met.* 7.2–4; Virgil, *Aen.* 3.211–13; Statius, *Thebaid* 8.255–8; and Hyginus, *Fabulae* no. 19.

16 Ovid's account of the punishment of the Pierides, whose irreverent challenge of the Muses to a storytelling contest results in their transformation into magpies, is a variation on this motif. Avian metamorphosis preempts the Pierides' attempt to speak, but rather than losing their voices completely, the '[rauca] garrulitas' [raucous chatter] of which they were guilty all along simply is replicated in their new form of song (*Met.* 5.678).

17 On the relevance of the Marsyas narrative as related in *HF* to the crow's predicament in *MancT*, see Wallace, *Chaucerian Polity*, 250–1.

18 Arnulf, *Allegoriae* 7.13.

19 It is interesting to observe, however, that *MancT* and most of its noted medieval vernacular analogues remove the Apollo and Coronis story from the continuum of its Ovidian narrative sequence only to embed it in the different narrative sequences of various story collections and lyrical anthologies. Versions of the myth are contained in Gower's *Confessio amantis*, the *Seven Sages of Rome*, and Machaut's *Voir dit* (which includes the crow's warning of the raven but ends with the birth of Aesculapius) as well as the *Canterbury Tales*. All treat the Coronis narrative not as a free-standing exemplum – to be sure, *MancT* satirizes and problematizes

its status as such – but as a promiscuous participant, apropos of its subject matter, in other narratives.

20 See Fumo, 'Thinking upon the Crow.'

21 For examples of these interpretive techniques on the part of commentators as they involve the association between crow and raven, and crow and Coronis, see ibid., 360–5.

22 Keith, *Play of Fictions*, 63–93, qtd at 48.

23 On Ovid's continuation of the theme of *usus vocis* in the Aglauros episode, see ibid., 131–3.

24 For opposing views on the characterization of Chaucer's crow, see Scattergood, 'Manciple's Manner,' 134–5, and McGavin, 'How Nasty.'

25 For example, in Hyginus, *Poetica astrononmica* 2.40 (in Grant, *Myths of Hyginus*); VM I 2.114; and Thomas of Walsingham, *Archana deorum* 2.3.50–8. On the tensions between these two versions within Ovid's oeuvre, see Newlands, 'Ovid's Ravenous Raven,' and cf. Keith, *Play of Fictions*, 50–2.

26 In a related Islamic version, 'When Mohammed was hiding in a cave from his enemies, the crow, at that time a light-plumaged bird, spotted him and screamed "ghar! ghar!" (cave! cave!) to indicate the place of concealment. Mohammed's enemies, however, did not understand the bird, and passed on. When the Prophet came out of the cave, he turned the crow's feathers completely black and ordered it to cry "ghar" as long as crows should live' (Rowland, *Birds with Human Souls*, 38).

27 The *Epic of Gilgamesh* and the Jewish *Sibylline Oracles* contain analogues of the Old Testament Flood narrative that reverse the order of the birds' departure in the biblical account, taking the raven's failure to return to the ark as evidence that, unlike the dove, it has found dry land on which to settle; for discussion, see Schwartz, *Noah's Ark*, 38, and Lewis, *A Study of the Interpretation of Noah and the Flood*, 33. In these versions, therefore, the raven is the champion rather than the delinquent of the providential order. This positive view of Noah's raven survives in the Deluge pageant in the BL Harley MS 2214 version of the Chester mystery cycle printed by Deimling, which follows the biblical sequence but nonetheless interprets the raven's failure to return as a sign that 'drye it is on hill or playne, / and god hath done some grace ('De Deluvio Noe,' *The Chester Plays*, lines 263–4).

28 Ginzberg, *The Legends of the Jews*, vol. 1, 163–4.

29 Hugh of Fouilloy, *The Medieval Book of Birds*, 176–7.

30 Rowland, *Birds with Human Souls*, 146–7.

31 Guillaume de Deguileville, *Pèlerinage*, lines 24011–72; cf. Sloth's affiliation with the raven, lines 13802–20. Citations of Deguileville's poem refer to Lydgate's translation.

32 'The Flood,' *The York Plays,* lines 228, 231.

33 'Processus Noe cum filiis,' *The Wakefield Pageants,* lines 479–506.

34 Rowland refers the legend of Noah's punishment of the raven to Hebrew folklore (*Birds with Human Souls,* 145–6), but according to Korotayev et al., its circulation was confined to the East and did not infiltrate Judaeo-Christian tradition ('Return of the White Raven'). It is, however, conceivable that a miniature in the fourteenth-century Queen Mary's Psalter (BL MS Royal 2B.VII), which draws substantially on apocryphal and legendary material, attests to Western awareness of this legend. On fol. 7r, raven and dove are both portrayed as white when Noah releases them from the ark; in one compartment of the scene, the white raven feeds on carrion, while in another, a dark, long-beaked bird in a pose of death floats in the water among drowning creatures and the devil. If the dark bird is intended to represent the raven, the scene most likely portrays a temporal sequence in which the white raven, released from the ark, succumbs to fleshly desires and is darkened either as punishment for failing to return or because physically defiled with sin.

35 Neckam, *De naturis rerum,* 1.61.

36 Neckam, *De laudibus,* 529, 533, in Wright's edition of *De naturis rerum.*

37 In one strand of the legend's transmission, the problem is averted through the raven's punishment for failing to guard Coronis from would-be lovers rather than exposing her adultery: see Hyginus, *Fabulae* no. 102; [Pseudo-] Lactantius Placidus, *In Statii Thebaida commentum,* 3.506; and VM II 32.

38 Evrart de Conty, *Le livre des eschez amoureux moralisés,* 2.15.2; translations mine.

39 In Ovid's version, Coronis acknowledges her guilt: 'potui poenas tibi, Phoebe, dedisse, / sed peperisse prius; duo nunc moriemur in una' [Phoebus, I could have paid the penalty to you, / but given birth first] (*Met.* 2.608–9).

40 Chaucer's Wife of Bath shows familiarity with this story-type when she quips, 'A wys wyf, if that she kan hir good, / Shal beren hym on honde the cow [i.e., chough] is wood' (*WBProl* 231–2). Cf. Storm, 'Speech,' 120.

41 Quoted from the twelfth-century prose version 'The Merchant and His Magpie,' ed. Benson and Andersson, 366, and the fourteenth-century Middle English poetic version in *Seven Sages,* ed. Brunner, lines 2209–10.

42 Notably, in both the twelfth-century French prose version quoted above and the thirteenth-century French verse version (printed by Clouston, 'The Tell-Tale Bird,' 442–7), but not in the fourteenth-century Middle English version, the magpie is female, and talks in a feminine manner. Uniquely in the French verse version, the husband kills both magpie and wife.

43 Hazelton, 'Manciple's Tale,' 16, and Wallace, Chaucerian Polity, 254. For similar views, see Harwood, 'Language and the Real,' 270–1, and Børch, 'Chaucer's Poetics,' 289–90.

44 Apollo's failure as a self-reader in Ovid's version, discussed in chapter 1 (pp. 42–5), supplies a fitting precedent.

45 In effect, the crow – who does not adopt his familiar caw until after his metamorphosis – shifts here from an elevated vocal affiliation with the nightingale, to whose song his is compared at line 136, to a less noble kinship with the cuckoo, whose vocalization traditionally correlates with its name (MED s.v. 'cokkou' n. 2). Such a shift, of course, invites context-ualization in a long medieval tradition of avian debates contrasting the two birds, a topic beyond the scope of this chapter. In light of fourteenth-century musical theory, the crow's demotion in courtly register from association with the melodious nightingale to the monotonous cuckoo prepares for his later adoption of a recognizably corvid identity. Italian music theorist Marchetto of Padua's Lucidarium (1317/1318) paired the sounds of the crow and the cuckoo as examples of 'inarticulate but literate vox … which cannot be understood and yet can be written down' (Leach, Sung Birds, 36; on musical juxtapositions of the nightingale's and cuckoo's songs, see Leach 122–8).

46 Børch, 'Chaucer's Poetics,' 289.

47 Wood, Road to Delphi, 46, 99. Cf. Maurizio's account of the 'superabun-dance of meaning' in oracles that 'suspend[s] narration' and fills it with 'the interpretative gesture of the oracle-seeker' ('Narrative,' 139).

48 For broad context, see Craun, Lies, Slander, and Obscenity, 187–230.

49 See Wenzel, Explanatory Notes to ParsT 603–7 (Riverside Chaucer, 961).

50 The term augur was held to derive from avis + garrio (to chatter); see Isidore, Etymologiae, 8.9.19–20, and Remi-CMC, vol. 1, 10.3. The association between augury and speech also emerges from Hyginus's etiology of the alphabet, which by one account Mercury invented by tracing the flight formation of birds; Apollo added to this ur-alphabet by playing his lyre (Fabulae no. 277).

51 Boccaccio, Genealogie 5.19.

52 Fumo, 'Thinking upon the Crow.'

53 For ancient bibliography on the crow's prophetic nature in particular, see Keith, Play of Fictions, 12 n. 12. On the raven's prophetic capacities, see Fulgentius, Mitologiae 1.13 (the voice of Apollo's raven bears sixty-four interpretations); [Pseudo-]Lactantius Placidus, In Statii Thebaida commen-tum 3.506 (the raven as 'comes obscurus tripodum'); and various

commentaries on the raven that accompanies Rhetoric in Book 5 of
Martianus Capella's *De nuptiis*.

54 This commonplace ultimately derives from Virgil, *Georgics* 1.388 and is
echoed in Chaucer, *PF* 363.

55 Isidore, *Etymologiae* 12.7.44.

56 Line 18772; further, lines 18520–4, 18771–4. By extension, the raven's cry,
'*cras! cras!*' (tomorrow! tomorrow!), associated earlier in the poem with
procrastination, may also evoke prophetic vision. On the moral significance traditionally attached to '*cras! cras!*' see Rowland, *Birds with Human
Souls*, 36–7, and Bitterling, 'Middle English *Cras*.'

57 Plutarch, 'The Oracles at Delphi,' in *Moralia*, 333; Vernant, 'Parole,' 23. On
the protective tactic of ambiguity in medieval prophecy, see Yandell,
'Prophetic Authority,' 83.

58 As demonstrated by Fleming, *Classical Imitation*, 53–5.

59 Oresme, *Livre de divinacions* 50–1; text and translations from Coopland's
edition, cited by page number.

60 Ibid., 99, citing Seneca, *De beneficiis* 6.30.3.

61 Ibid., 99.

62 Cf. Scattergood's discussion of this social issue in relation to *MancT*
without reference to prophecy ('Manciple's Manner,' 126–7).

63 Steinberg, 'Poetry and Prophecy,' 151.

64 Oresme, *Livre de divinacions* 97.

65 Edgar Allen Poe's 'The Raven,' whose *dramatis personae* consist of a
scholar, a deceased wife, and a speaking raven, can be read as a kind of
sequel to the Coronis narrative (cf. Adams, 'Classical Raven Lore,' 53), and
as such provides support for this section's reading of *MancT*. What comes
to obsess Poe's narrator is the raven's prophetic reputation as a messenger
of tidings from the beyond: '"Prophet! said I, thing of evil! – prophet still,
if bird or devil!"' (85). This obsession leads the narrator to treat the raven
as an oracle, masochistically shaping his inquiries around the one word
that the raven is capable of enigmatically reciting, 'Nevermore.' When the
narrator's interrogation of the raven leads to a point of despair over
Lenore's memory and his own prospect of salvation, he accuses the bird of
lying, and identifies his deception with the blackness of the raven's
feathers: 'Leave no black plume as a token of that lie thy soul hath
spoken!' (99). Quoted by line number from Mabbot's edition.

66 Ross is right to point out that Chaucer 're-invest[s] Cassandra with the
voice of narrative and interpretive authority' in his reworking of
Boccaccio's shrewish and relatively unprophetic Cassandra ('Believing
Cassandra,' 346). The authority of Chaucer's Cassandra, however, is

ineffective, and this aspect of her curse is linked in *Tr* to her unsympathetic affect, which makes her, in Troilus's eyes, less an educator than a
jangler. If Cassandra 'reclaims our attention from the morally shallow and
self-centered privatism of the lovers,' standing out among her fellow
Trojans as a 'pagan capable of truth' (Fleming, *Classical Imitation*, 225–6),
her sense of moral and intellectual superiority compromises her communication of truth, making her an unsuccessful rhetor lacking the power of
emotional persuasion.

67 On this projection, cf. Ross, 'Believing Cassandra,' 347.

68 Cassandra's unladylike manner is implied in Boccaccio's *Filostrato* when
her rebuke by Troilo is welcomed by Hecuba, Helen, and the other ladies
with whom she is initially introduced (*Fil.* 7.102; cf. 7.84). In a rather funny
moment in Joseph of Exeter's *Ylias* (3.362–98), Cassandra, speaking in a
prophetic rage, calls Helen a cow (*iuvenca*) upon her glamorous debut
appearance in Troy. An embarrassed Priam apologizes to the regal Helen
for the rantings of his insane daughter and orders Cassandra put in chains.

69 As Scattergood, 'Manciple's Manner,' 135, observes; for a different
interpretation, see McGavin, 'How Nasty,' 451.

70 Some scribes smoothed out this ambiguity by rephrasing: 'I sey him thy
wif swyue' (Cambridge, University Library MS Ii.iii.26); 'he dud here
swyue' (McCormick MS, University of Chicago Library 564). See Manly
and Rickert, *The Text of the Canterbury Tales*, vol. 8, 165.

71 *Pace* McGavin, 'How Nasty,' 451; cf. Wallace, *Chaucerian Polity*, 253.

72 Tissol, *The Face of Nature*, 32; cf. Tissol's discussion of an Ovidian example
in which a god (Mercury) treats a human utterance as kledonomantic (34).
On the pertinence of complex aspects of semiotic linguistics to oracular
discourse, see Maurizio, 'Narrative,' 136–44.

73 Cicero, *De divinatione* 2.40.84; discussed by Tissol, *The Face of Nature*, 31–2.

74 As McGavin argues, 'How Nasty,' 448–9. Quotation from Leach, *Sung
Birds*, 20.

75 Askins, 'Historical Setting,' 93. Viewed from a slightly different angle, the
scene integrates semiotic problems raised by birdsong with those surrounding prophetic revelation and modes of truth-telling. As Leach
demonstrates, birdsong in the Middle Ages was considered 'prelinguistic'
utterance that was semiotically untrustworthy, likely to deceive especially
in the case of birds – like the magpie and, here, Phebus's crow (*MancT* 134)
– that 'countrefete' human speech (cf. the Summoner's jay-like declama-
tion, *GP* 642–6). Medieval theorists held that birds, as non-rational
animals, cannot 'mean' in their own right; only humans can bring rational
meaning to birdsong, for example by transforming it, according to

established 'symbolic and generic' procedures, into musical forms like the *caccia* (Leach, *Sung Birds*, 40–2, 160). Similarly, in the *Manciple's Tale*, meaning gets attached to the crow's 'Cokkow!' only when Phebus transmutes it into a rational idea: an announcement of cuckoldry. On the rhetorical dimensions of the disjunction between the crow's utterance and its effect, see Wallace, *Chaucerian Polity*, 252.

76 See Minnis, *Chaucer and Pagan Antiquity*, 136–7.

77 Wood, *The Road to Delphi*, 43.

78 Ibid., 108.

79 Fleming, *Classical Imitation*, 217.

80 For discussion of this oracle in the context of Chaucer, see ibid., 52, and Minnis, *Chaucer and Pagan Antiquity*, 34–5.

81 An interesting comparison could be drawn with *Met.* 1, in which Apollo's desire for Daphne, despite their fate not to unite, becomes a kind of false hope that jars with his status as god of prophecy: 'suaque illum oracula fallunt' [his oracles deceived him] (*Met.* 1.491).

82 Barchiesi, *Speaking Volumes*, 133.

83 Certain textual inconsistencies connected to the unfinished state of the *Canterbury Tales* have traditionally kept *MancT* separated from Fragment X, but these tales regularly appear in sequence in the manuscripts and have increasingly been regarded by critics as tightly connected thematically. For an overview of the textual problem and a defence of the *MancT-ParsT* sequence, see Powell, 'Game Over.'

84 Boccaccio, *Genealogie*, 5.19; my translation.

Bibliography

Primary Sources

An Alphabet of Tales. Ed. Mary Macleod Banks. EETS os 126–7. 1904–5. Millwood, NY: Kraus Reprint, 1987.

Apollodorus. *Library*. In *Apollodorus' Library and Hyginus' Fabulae: Two Handbooks of Greek Mythology*. Trans. R. Scott Smith and Stephen M. Trzaskoma. 1–94. Indianapolis: Hackett, 2007.

Apollonios Rhodios. *The Argonautika*. Trans. Peter Green. Berkeley: University of California Press, 1997.

Arnobius. *The Seven Books of Arnobius Against the Heathen (Adversus gentes)*. In *Fathers of the Third Century: Gregory Thaumaturgus, Dionysius the Great, Julius Africanus, Anatolius and Minor Writers, Methodius, Arnobius*. In *The Ante-Nicene Fathers*. Ed. A. Cleveland Coxe. Gen. eds Alexander Roberts and James Donaldson. American repr. of the Edinburgh ed. Vol. 6, 413–540. Grand Rapids, MI: Eerdmans, 1986.

Arnulf of Orléans. *Allegoriae super Ovidii Metamorphosin*. In 'Arnolfo d'Orléans, Un Cultore di Ovidio nel Seculo XII.' Ed. Fausto Ghisalberti. *Memorie del reale istituto Lombardo di scienze e lettere* 24 (1932): 157–234.

The Assembly of Gods: Le Assemble de Dyeus, or Banquet of Gods and Goddesses, with the Discourse of Reason and Sensuality. Ed. Jane Chance. Kalamazoo, MI: Medieval Institute, 1999.

Augustine, St. *Concerning the City of God against the Pagans*. Trans. Henry Bettenson. 1972. London: Penguin, 1984.

– *De civitate Dei*. In *Avrelii Avgvstini opera*. Part 14, 1–2. [Ed. Bernard Dombart and Alfons Kalb.] CCSL 47–8. Turnholt: Brepols, 1955.

Benoît de Sainte-Maure. *Le roman de Troie*. Ed. Léopold Constans. 6 vols. Paris: Librairie de Firmin Didot, 1904–12.

[Berchorius, Petrus.] *De formis figurisque deorum. Reductorium morale, liber XV: Ovidius moralizatus, cap. i.* Ed. J. Engels. Utrecht: Institut voor Laat Latijn der Rijksuniversiteit, 1966.

– 'The *Ovidius Moralizatus* of Petrus Berchorius: An Introduction and Translation.' Trans. William Donald Reynolds. PhD diss. University of Illinois at Urbana Champaign, 1971.

– 'Petrus Berchorius, Reductorium morale, liber XV: *Ovidius moralizatus,* cap. ii.' Ed. Maria S. van der Bijl. *Vivarium* 9.1 (1971): 25–48.

– *Reductorium morale, liber XV, cap. Ii–xv: Ovidius moralizatus.* Ed. J. Engels. Utrecht: Institut voor Laat Latijn der Rijksuniversiteit, 1962.

Bernardus Silvestris (attr.). *The Commentary on the First Six Books of the* Aeneid *of Vergil Commonly Attributed to Bernardus Silvestris.* Ed. Julian Ward Jones and Elizabeth Frances Jones. Lincoln: University of Nebraska Press, 1977.

– *The Commentary on Martianus Capella's* De Nuptiis Philologiae et Mercurii *Attributed to Bernardus Silvestris.* Ed. Haijo Jan Westra. Toronto: Pontifical Institute of Mediaeval Studies, 1986.

Bernard d'Utrecht. *Commentum in Theodolum (1076–1099).* Ed. R.B.C. Huygens. Biblioteca degli 'Studi Medievali' 8. Spoleto: Centro Italiano di Studi sull'Alto Medioevo, 1977.

Biblia sacra iuxta vulgatam clementinam. Ed. Alberto Colunga and Laurentio Turrado. 8th ed. Madrid: Biblioteca de Autores Cristianos, 1991.

Blake, William. *Blake's* Job: *William Blake's* Illustrations of the Book of Job: *With an Introduction and Commentary by S. Foster Damon.* Providence, RI: Brown University Press, 1966.

– *Complete Writings: With Variant Readings.* Ed. Geoffrey Keynes. London: Oxford University Press, 1966.

Boccaccio, Giovanni. *Il Filostrato.* Ed. Vincenzo Pernicone. Trans. Robert P. apRoberts and Anna Bruni Seldis. New York: Garland Publishing, 1986.

– *Genealogie deorum gentilium libri.* Ed. Vincenzo Romano. *Opera* 10–11. Scrittori d'Italia 200–1. Bari: Giuseppe Laterza and Figli, 1951.

Bodel, Je[h]an. *La Chanson des Saisnes.* Ed. Annette Brasseur. Geneva: Librairie Droz S.A., 1989.

– *Le Jeu de Saint Nicolas.* Ed. F.J. Warne. Oxford: Basil Blackwell, 1968.

Boethius. *The Consolation of Philosophy.* In *The Theological Tractates; The Consolation of Philosophy.* Trans. H.F. Stewart, E.K. Rand, and S.J. Tester. Loeb Classical Library. Rev. ed. Cambridge, MA: Harvard University Press; London: William Heinemann, 1973.

Bokenham, Osbern. *Legendys of Hooly Wummen.* Ed. Mary S. Serjeantson. EETS os 206. London: Oxford University Press, 1938 (for 1936).

Bunyan, John. *The Pilgrim's Progress, from this World to that which is to come.* Ed. James Blanton Wharey. Rev. Roger Sharrock. 2nd ed. Oxford: Clarendon Press, 1960.

Capgrave, John. *The Life of St. Katherine.* Ed. Karen A. Winstead. Kalamazoo, MI: Medieval Institute, 1999.

Caxton, William, trans. *The Metamorphoses of Ovid.* 2 vols. New York: George Braziller, in association with Magdalene College, Cambridge, 1968.

Chaucer, Geoffrey. *The Complete Works of Geoffrey Chaucer.* Ed. Walter W. Skeat. 6 vols. Oxford: Clarendon Press, 1894.

– *The Riverside Chaucer.* Gen ed. Larry D. Benson. 3rd ed. Boston: Houghton Mifflin, 1987.

– *Troilus and Criseyde: A New Edition of 'The Book of Troilus.'* Ed. B.A. Windeatt. 1984. London: Longman, 1990.

– *The Works of Geoffrey Chaucer.* Ed. F.N. Robinson. 2nd ed. Boston: Houghton Mifflin, 1961.

The Chester Plays. Ed. Hermann Deimling. EETS es 62, 115. 1892. London: Oxford University Press, 1968.

Chrysostom, St John. *Homilies on the Epistles of Paul to the Corinthians.* In *The Nicene and Post-Nicene Fathers.* The Oxford Translation rev. by Talbot W. Chambers. Gen. ed. Philip Schaff. Vol. 12. Grand Rapids, MI: Eerdmans, 1983.

Cicero, Marcus Tullius. *De divinatione.* In *De senectute; De amicitia; De divinatione.* Trans. William Armistead Falconer. Loeb Classical Library. London: William Heinemann; New York: G.P. Putnam's Sons, 1927.

– *De natura deorum; Academica.* Trans. H. Rackham. Loeb Classical Library. Cambridge, MA: Harvard University Press; London: William Heinemann, 1979.

– *Tusculan Disputations.* Trans. J.E. King. Loeb Classical Library. Cambridge, MA: Harvard University Press; London: William Heinemann, 1971.

Clement of Alexandria. *Exhortation to the Heathen.* In *The Ante-Nicene Fathers.* Ed. A. Cleveland Coxe. Gen eds. Rev. Alexander Roberts and James Donaldson. American repr. of the Edinburgh ed. Vol. 2, 171–206. Edinburgh: T and T Clark; Grand Rapids, MI: Eerdmans, 1986.

Cornford, Frances. *Collected Poems.* London: Cresset Press, 1954.

Dante Alighieri. *Paradiso.* Trans. Charles S. Singleton. Bollingen Series 80. 1975. Princeton: Princeton University Press, 1977.

– *Purgatorio.* Trans. Charles S. Singleton. Bollingen Series 80. 1973. Princeton: Princeton University Press, 1977.

Dares the Phrygian. 'The Fall of Troy: A History.' In *The Trojan War*, trans. Frazer, 133–68.

De deorum imaginibus libellus. In *Fulgentius Metaforalis: Ein Beitrag zur Geschichte der antiken Mythologie im Mittelalter*. Ed. Hans Liebeschütz, 117–28. Leipzig: B.G. Teubner, 1926.

Dictys of Crete. 'A Journal of the Trojan War.' In *The Trojan War,* trans. Frazer, 19–130.

Dunbar, William. *The Poems of William Dunbar*. Ed. Priscilla Bawcutt. 2 vols. Glasgow: Association for Scottish Literary Studies, 1998.

Eclogue of Theodulus. In *Ten Latin Schooltexts of the Later Middle Ages*. Trans. Ian Thomson and Louis Perraud, 110–57. Mediaeval Studies 6. Lewiston: Edward Mellen, 1990.

Eneas: Roman du xiie siècle. Ed. J.-J. Salverda de Grave. 2 vols. Paris: E. Champion, 1925–9.

Eneas: A Twelfth-Century French Romance. Trans. John A. Yunck. New York: Columbia University Press, 1974.

Evrart de Conty. *Le livre des eschez amoureux moralisés*. Ed. Françoise Guichard-Tesson and Bruno Roy. Montreal: Éditions CERES, 1993.

Fasciculus Morum: A Fourteenth-Century Preacher's Handbook. Ed. and trans. Siegfried Wenzel. University Park, PA: Pennsylvania State University Press, 1989.

'Firumbras.' In *Firumbras and Otuel and Roland*. Ed. Mary Isabelle O'Sullivan, 3–58. EETS os 198. London: pub. for the EETS by Humphrey Milford, Oxford University Press, 1935 (for 1934).

The Floure and the Leafe; The Assembly of Ladies; The Isle of Ladies. Ed. Derek Pearsall. Kalamazoo, MI: Western Michigan University Press, 1990.

Frazer, R.M., Jr, trans. *The Trojan War: The Chronicles of Dictys of Crete and Dares the Phrygian*. Bloomington: Indiana University Press, 1966.

Froissart, Jean. *La prison amoureuse/The Prison of Love*. Ed. and trans. Laurence de Looze. New York: Garland, 1994.

Fulgentius. *Fabii Planciadis Fulgentii v.c. Opera*. Ed. Rudolfus Helm. 1898. Stuttgart: B.G. Teubner, 1970.

– *Fulgentius the Mythographer*. Trans. Leslie George Whitbread. Columbus: Ohio State University Press, 1971.

Gesta Romanorum. Trans. Charles Swan. New York: Dover, [1959].

The 'Gest Hystoriale' of the Destruction of Troy. Ed. George A. Panton and David Donaldson. EETS os 39, 56. 1869; London: N. Trübner, 1874.

Giovanni del Virgilio. *Allegorie librorum Ovidii metamorphoseos*. In 'Giovanni del Virgilio espositore delle "Metamorfosi."' Ed. Fausto Ghisalberti. *Il Giornale Dantesco* 34, ns 4 (1933): 43–110.

Gower, John. *Confessio amantis*. In *The English Works of John Gower*. Ed. G.C. Macaulay. 2 vols. EETS es 81–2. 1900–1. London: Oxford University Press, 1969.

Greenlaw, Edwin, et al., ed. *The Works of Edmund Spenser: A Variorum Edition.*
11 vols. Baltimore: Johns Hopkins Press, 1932–57.

Grisdale, D.M., ed. *Three Middle English Sermons from the Worcester Chapter Manuscript F.10.* Leeds School of English Language Texts and Monographs 5. Kendal, England: T. Wilson, for Members of the School of English Language in the University of Leeds, 1939.

Guido delle Colonne. *Historia destructionis Troiae.* Trans. Mary Elizabeth Meek. Bloomington: Indiana University Press, 1974.

Guillaume de Deguileville. *Pèlerinage de vie humaine / The Pilgrimage of the Life of Man.* Trans. John Lydgate. Ed. F.J. Furnivall and Katharine B. Locock. EETS es 77, 83, 92. 3 vols in 1. Millwood, NY: Kraus Reprint, 1978.

Henryson, Robert. *The Poems of Robert Henryson.* Ed. Denton Fox. Oxford: Clarendon Press; New York: Oxford University Press, 1981.

Hoccleve, Thomas. *Works: The Regement of Princes and Fourteen Minor Poems.* Ed. Frederick J. Furnivall. EETS es 72. London: Kegan Paul, Trench, and Trübner, 1897.

The Holy Bible: Translated from the Latin Vulgate. [Douay-Rheims Edition.] New York: P.J. Kenedy and Sons, 1914.

Homer. *The Iliad.* Trans. Robert Fagles. New York: Penguin, 1990.

The Homeric Hymns. Ed. and trans. Apostolos N. Athanassakis. Baltimore: Johns Hopkins University Press, 1976.

Horace. *The Odes and Epodes.* Trans. C.E. Bennett. Loeb Classical Library. Rev. ed. Cambridge, MA: Harvard University Press; London: William Heinemann, 1927.

Hugh of Fouilloy. *The Medieval Book of Birds: Hugh of Fouilloy's Aviarium.* Ed. and trans. Willene B. Clark. Binghamton, NY: Medieval and Renaissance Texts and Studies, 1992.

Huntingdon, Henry of. 'Henry of Huntingdon's Herbal.' Ed. and trans. A.G. Rigg. *Mediaeval Studies* 65 (2003): 213–92.

Hyginus. *The Myths of Hyginus.* Trans. and ed. Mary Grant. Humanistic Studies 34. Lawrence, KS: University of Kansas Publications, 1960.

Isidore of Seville. *The Etymologies of Isidore of Seville.* Ed. Stephen A. Barney et al. Cambridge: Cambridge University Press, 2006.

– *Isidori Hispalensis episcopi etymologiarvm sive originvm libri XXI.* Ed. W. M. Lindsay. 2 vols. Oxford: Oxford University Press, 1911.

Jacobus de Voragine. *The Golden Legend: Readings on the Saints.* Trans. William Granger Ryan. 2 vols. Princeton: Princeton University Press, 1993.

John of Garland. 'The Integumenta on the Metamorphoses of Ovid by John of Garland – First Edited with Introduction and Translation.' Ed. Lester Kruger Born. PhD diss. University of Chicago, 1929.

– *Integumenta Ovidii: Poemetto inedito del secolo XIII*. Ed. Fausto Ghisalberti. *Testi e documenti inediti o rari* 2. Messina: Giuseppe Principato, 1933.

Iohannis Scotti [John the Scot]. *Annotationes in Marcianum*. Ed. Cora E. Lutz. Cambridge, MA: The Mediaeval Academy of America, 1939.

Joseph of Exeter [Joseph Iscanus]. *The Iliad of Dares Phrygius*. Trans. Gildas Roberts. Cape Town: A.A.Balkema, 1970.

– *L'Iliade: Épopée du xiie siècle sur la guerre de Troie*. Trans. under the direction of Francine Mora. Turnhout: Brepols, 2003.

– *Joseph Iscanus: Werke und Briefe*. Ed. Ludwig Gompf. Leiden: Brill, 1970.

– *Trojan War I–III*. Ed. and trans. A.K. Bate. N.p.: Bolchazy-Carducci; Warminster: Aris and Phillips, 1986.

Keats, John. *The Complete Poems*. Ed. John Barnard. 3rd ed. New York: Penguin, 1988.

– *The Letters of John Keats*. Ed. Maurice Buxton Forman. 4th ed. London: Oxford University Press, 1952.

The Kingis Quair of James Stewart. Ed. Matthew P. McDiarmid. Totowa, NJ: Rowman and Littlefield, 1973.

Lactantius. *On the Deaths of the Persecutors* (*De mortibus persecutorum*). In *Lactantius: The Minor Works*. Trans. Sister Mary Francis McDonald. The Fathers of the Church 54, 117–203. Washington, DC: Catholic University of America Press, 1965.

– *Divinarum institutionum libri septem*. Ed. Eberhard Heck and Antonie Wlosok. Bibliotheca Scriptorum Graecorum et Romanorum Teubneriana. 2 vols (of 4). München: K.G. Saur Verlag, 2005–.

– *The Divine Institutes*. Trans. William Fletcher. In *The Ante-Nicene Fathers*. Ed. A. Cleveland Coxe, vol. 7, 9–223. Gen. eds Alexander Roberts and James Donaldson. American repr. of the Edinburgh ed. Grand Rapids, MI: Eerdmans, 1985.

– *Epitome divinarum institutionum*. Ed. Eberhard Heck and Antonie Wlosok. Bibliotheca Scriptorum Graecorum et Romanorum Teubneriana. Stuttgart: B.G. Teubner, 1994.

– *The Epitome of the Divine Institutes*. Trans. William Fletcher. In *The Ante-Nicene Fathers*. Ed. A. Cleveland Coxe, vol. 7, 224–55. Gen. eds. Alexander Roberts and James Donaldson. American repr. of the Edinburgh ed. Grand Rapids, MI: Eerdmans, 1985.

[Pseudo-] Lactantius Placidus. *Narrationes fabvlarvm Ovidianarvm*. In *P. Ovidi Nasonis Metamorphoseon libri XV*. Ed. Hugo Magnus, 625–721. Berlin: Weidmann, 1914.

– *In Statii Thebaida commentum*. Ed. R.D. Sweeney. Vol. 1. Stuttgart: B.G. Teubner, 1997.

Laȝamon. *Laȝamon's Brut*. Ed. G.L. Brook and R.F. Leslie. EETS os 250, 277. London: Oxford University Press, 1963 (for 1961).

Lydgate, John. *A Critical Edition of John Lydgate's Life of Our Lady*. Ed. Joseph A. Lauritis et al. Duquesne Studies, Philological Series 2. Pittsburgh: Duquesne University Press, 1961.

– *Fall of Princes*. Ed. Henry Bergen. EETS es 121–4. London: Oxford University Press, 1924.

– *The Minor Poems of John Lydgate*. Vol. 2. Ed. Henry Noble MacCracken. EETS os 192. London: Oxford University Press, 1934.

– *Poems*. Ed. John Norton-Smith. 1966. Oxford: Clarendon Press, 1968.

– *Reson and Sensuallyte*. Ed. Ernst Sieper. 2 vols. EETS es 84, 89. London: Oxford University Press, 1901, 1903.

– *Saint Albon and Saint Amphibalus*. Ed. George F. Reinecke. New York: Garland, 1985.

– *Siege of Thebes*. Ed. Axel Erdmann. EETS es 108, 125. 1911, 1930. London: Oxford University Press, 1960.

– *Troy Book*. Ed. Henry Bergen. EETS es 97, 103, 106, 126. London: Kegan Paul, Trench, and Trübner, 1906–35.

Machaut, Guillaume de. *Le livre dou voir dit*. Trans. R. Barton Palmer. Ed. Daniel Leech-Wilkinson. New York: Garland, 1998.

Macrobius, [Ambrosius Theodosius]. *The Saturnalia*. Trans. Percival Vaughan Davies. New York: Columbia University Press, 1969.

– *Saturnalia*. Ed. Jacobus Willis. 2 vols. Leipzig: B.G. Teubner, 1970.

Mandeville's Travels. Ed. M.C. Seymour. Oxford: Clarendon Press, 1967.

Map, Walter. *De nugis curialium / Courtiers' Trifles*. Ed. and trans. M.R. James. Rev. C.N.L. Brooke, and R.A.B. Mynors. Oxford: Clarendon Press, 1983.

Martianus Capella. *De nuptiis Philologiae et Mercurii*. In *Martianus Capella*. Ed. Adolfus Dick. Rev. Jean Préaux. 1925. Stuttgart: Teubner, 1969.

– *The Marriage of Mercury and Philology*. In *Martianus Capella and the Seven Liberal Arts*. Trans. William Harris Stahl and Richard Johnson with E.L. Burge. Vol. 2. New York: Columbia University Press, 1977.

'The Merchant and His Magpie.' In *The Literary Context of Chaucer's Fabliaux: Texts and Translations*. Ed. Larry D. Benson and Theodore M. Andersson, 366-71. Indianapolis: Bobbs-Merrill, 1971.

Milton, John. *Complete Poems and Major Prose*. Ed. Merritt Y. Hughes. Indianapolis: Bobbs-Merrill, 1957.

Minucius Felix. 'Octavius.' In *Tertullian and Minucius Felix*, trans. Glover, 314–437.

Neckam, Alexander. *De naturis rerum, libri duo, with the Poem of the Same Author, De laudibus divinae sapientiae*. Rolls Series 34. Ed. Thomas Wright. London: Longman, Green, Longman, Roberts, and Green, 1863.

Nietzsche, Friedrich. *The Birth of Tragedy and Other Writings*. Ed. Raymond Geuss and Ronald Speirs. Trans. Ronald Speirs. Cambridge: Cambridge University Press, 1999.

Oresme, Nicole. *Livre de divinacions*. In *Nicole Oresme and the Astrologers: A Study of His Livre de Divinacions*. Ed. and trans. G.W. Coopland. Liverpool: University Press of Liverpool, 1952.

– *Nicole Oresme and the Kinematics of Circular Motion: Tractatus de commensurabilitate vel incommensurabilitate motuum celi*. Ed. and trans. Edward Grant. Madison: University of Wisconsin Press, 1971.

Origen. *Origen against Celsus*. In *The Ante-Nicene Fathers*. Trans. Frederick Crombie. Ed. A. Cleveland Coxe, vol. 4, 395–669. Gen. eds Alexander Roberts and James Donaldson. American repr. of the Edinburgh ed. Edinburgh: T and T Clark; Grand Rapids, MI: Eerdmans, [n.d.].

Ovid. *The Art of Love, and Other Poems*. Trans. J.H. Mozley. Rev. G.P. Goold. Loeb Classical Library. 2nd ed. Cambridge, MA: Harvard University Press, 1979.

– *Fasti*. Trans. James George Frazer. Rev. G.P. Goold. Loeb Classical Library. 2nd ed. 1989. Cambridge, MA: Harvard University Press, 1996.

– *Heroides and Amores*. Trans. Grant Showerman. Loeb Classical Library. 1921. London: William Heinemann; New York: G.P. Putnam's Sons, 1925.

– *Metamorphoses I–IV*. Ed. and trans. D.E. Hill. Warminster, Wiltshire: Aris and Phillips, 1985.

– *Metamorphoses V–VIII*. Ed. and trans. D.E. Hill. Warminster, Wiltshire: Aris and Phillips, 1992.

– *Metamorphoses IX–XII*. Ed. and trans. D.E. Hill. Warminster, Wiltshire: Aris and Phillips, 1999.

– *Metamorphoses XIII–XV*. Ed. and trans. D.E. Hill. Warminster, Wiltshire: Aris and Phillips, 2000.

– *P. Ovidi Nasonis Metamorphoses*. Ed. R.J. Tarrant. Oxford: Oxford University Press, 2004.

– *Tristia; Ex Ponto*. Trans. Arthur Leslie Wheeler. Rev. G.P. Goold. Loeb Classical Library. 2nd ed. 1988. Cambridge, MA: Harvard University Press, 1996.

Ovide moralisé: Poème du commencement du quatorzième siècle. Ed. C. de Boer. Vol. 1. *Verhandelingen der Koninklijke Akademie van Wetenschappen te Amsterdam, Afdeeling Letterkunde, Nieuwe Reeks* 15 (1915): 1–374.

Pliny. *Natural History*. Trans. W.H.S. Jones; rev. A.C. Andrews. Vol. 7. 1956. Cambridge, MA: Harvard University Press, 1980.

Plutarch. *Moralia*. Trans. Frank Cole Babbitt. Loeb Classical Library. Vol. 5. 1936. London: William Heinemann; Cambridge, MA: Harvard University Press, 1957.

Poe, Edgar Allen. *Collected Works of Edgar Allen Poe*. Ed. Thomas Ollive Mabbot. 3 vols. Cambridge: Belknap Press-Harvard University Press, 1969–78.

Propertius. *Elegies.* Ed. and trans. G.P. Goold. Loeb Classical Library. Cambridge, MA: Harvard University Press, 1990.

Remigius Autissiodorensis [Remigius of Auxerre]. *Commentum in Martianum Capellam.* Ed. Cora E. Lutz. 2 vols. Leiden: Brill, 1962–5.

Robbins, Rossell Hope, ed. *Secular Lyrics of the XIVth and XVth Centuries.* Oxford: Clarendon Press, 1952.

The Romance of Sir Beues of Hamtoun. Ed. Eugen Kölbing. EETS es 46, 48, 65. 1885–94. Repr. as one volume. Millwood, NY: Kraus Reprint, 1978.

Le Roman de Thèbes. Ed. Léopold Constans. 2 vols. New York: Johnson Reprint, 1968.

The Romaunce of the Sowdone of Babylone and of Ferumbras his Sone who Conquerede Rome. Ed. Emil Hausknecht. EETS es 38. 1881. London: pub. for the EETS by Oxford University Press, 1969.

Ross, Woodburn O., ed. *Middle English Sermons.* EETS os 209. 1940 (for 1938), repr. 1960. Millwood, NY: Kraus Reprint, 1987.

Seneca. *Moral Essays: De beneficiis.* Trans. John W. Basore. Vol. 3. Cambridge, MA: Harvard University Press, 1935.

Servius Grammaticus. *Servii grammatici qui feruntur in Vergilii carmina commentarii.* Ed. Georgius Thilo and Hermannus Hagen. 3 vols. Leipzig, 1881–7.

The Seven Sages of Rome: Southern Version. Ed. Karl Brunner. EETS os 191. London: pub. for the EETS by H. Milford, Oxford University Press, 1933.

Shelley, Percy Bysshe. *The Complete Poetical Works of Shelley Including Materials Never Before Printed in Any Edition of the Poems.* Ed. Thomas Hutchinson. Oxford: Clarendon Press, 1904.

Skelton, John. *The Book of the Laurel.* Ed. F.W. Brownlow. Newark, DE: University of Delaware Press; London: Associated University Presses, 1990.

– *The Complete English Poems.* Ed. John Scattergood. Harmondsworth: Penguin, 1983.

– *The Poetical Works of John Skelton.* Ed. Alexander Dyce. 2 vols. 1843. New York: AMS Press, 1965.

The Song of Roland: An Analytical Edition. Ed. Gerard J. Brault. 2 vols. University Park, PA: The Pennsylvania State University Press, 1978.

Souter, Alexander, ed. *Pelagius's Expositions of Thirteen Epistles of St. Paul.* Part 2: Text and Apparatus Criticus. Texts and Studies 9. Cambridge: Cambridge University Press, 1926.

Speculum sacerdotale. Ed. Edward H. Weatherly. EETS os 200. London: Early English Text Society, 1936 (for 1935).

Spenser, Edmund. *The Faerie Queene.* Ed. Thomas P. Roche, Jr, with C. Patrick O'Donnell Jr. 1978. Harmondsworth: Penguin, 1987.

Stanzaic Guy of Warwick. Ed. Alison Wiggins. Kalamazoo, MI: Medieval Institute Publications, 2004.

Statius. *Statius*. Trans. J.H. Mozley. 2 vols. Cambridge, MA: Harvard University Press; London: William Heinemann, 1967.

Tertullian. 'Apology.' In *Tertullian and Minucius Felix*, trans. Glover, 2–227.

– *Tertullian and Minucius Felix*. Trans. T.R. Glover. Loeb Classical Library. Cambridge, MA: Harvard University Press; London: William Heinemann, 1977.

Tibullus. *Catullus, Tibullus, and Pervigilium Veneris*. Trans. F.W. Cornish et al. Loeb Classical Library. Rev. ed. Cambridge, MA: Harvard University Press; London: William Heinemann, 1962.

The Towneley Plays. Ed. Martin Stevens and A.C. Cawley. EETS ss 13–14. Oxford: Oxford University Press, 1994.

[Trevisa, John.] *On the Properties of Things: John Trevisa's Translation of* Bartholomaeus Anglicus De proprietatibus rerum. [Ed. M.C. Seymour et al.] 3 vols. Oxford: Clarendon Press, 1975–88.

Vatican Mythographers. *Mythographi Vaticani I et II*. Ed. Péter Kulscár. CCSL 91c. Turnholt: Brepols, 1987.

– *Scriptores rerum mythicarum Latini tres Romae nuper reperti*. Ed. Georgius Henricus Bode. Cellis: E.H.C. Schulze, 1834.

La Vie de Seint Auban: An Anglo-Norman Poem of the Thirteenth Century. Ed. Arthur Robert Harden. Oxford: Basil Blackwell, for the Anglo-Norman Text Society, 1968.

Vinsauf, Geoffrey of. *Poetria nova*. Trans. Margaret F. Nims. Wetteren, Belgium: Universa Press, 1967.

Virgil. *Virgil*. Trans. H. Rushton Fairclough. Loeb Classical Library. 2 vols. Rev. ed. 1935. Cambridge, MA: Harvard University Press; London: William Heinemann, 1967.

Wace. *Wace's Roman de Brut: A History of the British*. Trans. Judith Weiss. Rev. ed. Exeter: University of Exeter Press, 2002.

The Wakefield Pageants in the Towneley Cycle. Ed. A.C. Cawley. Manchester: Manchester University Press, 1958.

Walsingham, Thomas. *De archana deorum*. Ed. Robert A. van Kluyve. Durham: Duke University Press, 1968.

The York Plays. Ed. Richard Beadle. London: Edward Arnold, 1982.

Secondary Sources

Adams, John F. 'Classical Raven Lore and Poe's Raven.' *Poe Studies* 5.2 (1972): 53.

Aers, David, ed. *Medieval Literature: Criticism, Ideology and History*. New York: St Martin's Press, 1986.

Ahern, Charles F., Jr. 'Ovid as *Vates* in the Proem to the *Ars Amatoria*.' *CP* 85.1 (1990): 44–8.

Ahl, Frederick. 'Apollo: Cult and Prophesy in Ovid, Lucan, and Statius.' In *Apollo*, ed. Solomon, 113–34.

Akbari, Suzanne Conklin. *Seeing through the Veil: Optical Theory and Medieval Allegory*. Toronto: University of Toronto Press, 2004.

Allen, Judson Boyce. 'Commentary as Criticism: The Text, Influence, and Literary Theory of the Fulgentius Metaphored of John Ridewall.' In *Acta Conventus Neo-Latini Amstelodamensis: Proceedings of the Second International Congress of Neo-Latin Studies, Amsterdam 19–24 August 1973*. Ed. P. Tuynman et al., 25–47. München: Wilhelm Fink Verlag, 1979.

– 'Eleven Unpublished Commentaries on Ovid's *Metamoprhoses* and Two Other Texts of Mythographic Interest: Some Comments on a Bibliography.' In *The Mythographic Art*, ed. Chance, 281–9.

– 'Mythology in the Bible Commentaries and *Moralitates* of Robert Holkot.' PhD diss. Johns Hopkins University, 1963.

Allen, Mark. 'Penitential Sermons, the Manciple, and the End of *The Canterbury Tales*.' *SAC* 9 (1987): 77–96.

Allen, Orphia Jane. 'Blake's Archetypal Criticism: *The Canterbury Pilgrims*.' *Genre* 11 (1978): 173–89.

Allen, Peter L. *The Art of Love: Amatory Fiction from Ovid to the* Romance of the Rose. Philadelphia: University of Pennsylvania Press, 1992.

Anderson, William S. 'Multiple Change in the *Metamorphoses*.' *TPAPA* 94 (1963): 6–8.

Anderson, William S., ed. *Ovid's* Metamorphoses: *Books 1–5*. Norman, OK: University of Oklahoma Press, 1997.

– *Ovid's* Metamorphoses: *Books 6–10*. Norman, OK: University of Oklahoma Press, 1972.

Arbesmann, Rudolph. 'The Concept of "Christus Medicus" in St. Augustine.' *Traditio* 10 (1954): 1–28.

Armstrong, Rebecca. 'Retiring Apollo: Ovid on the Politics and Poetics of Self- Sufficiency.' *CQ* 54.2 (2004): 528–50.

Arn, Mary-Jo. 'Three Ovidian Women in Chaucer's *Troilus*: Medea, Helen, Oenone.' *ChR* 15.1 (1980): 1–10.

Askins, William. 'The Historical Setting of *The Manciple's Tale*.' *SAC* 7 (1985): 87–105.

Astell, Ann W. 'Nietzsche, Chaucer, and the Sacrifice of Art.' *ChR* 39.3 (2005): 323–40.

Baker, Donald C., ed. *The Squire's Tale*. In *Variorum Edition of the Works of Geoffrey Chaucer: The Canterbury Tales*. Vol. 12, part 1. Norman, OK: University of Oklahoma Press, 1990.

Bakhtin, M[ikhail] M. 'Discourse in the Novel.' In *The Dialogic Imagination*, ed. Michael Holquist and trans. Caryl Emerson and Michael Holquist, 259–422. Austin: University of Texas Press, 1981.

– *Rabelais and His World*. Trans. Helene Iswolsky. Bloomington, IN: Indiana University Press, 1984.

Barchiesi, Alessandro. 'Narrative Technique and Narratology in the *Metamorphoses*.' In *Cambridge Companion to Ovid*, ed. Hardie, 180–99.

– *Speaking Volumes: Narrative and Intertext in Ovid and Other Latin Poets*. Ed. and trans. Matt Fox and Simone Marchesi. London: Duckworth, 2001.

– 'Venus' Masterplot: Ovid and the Homeric Hymns.' In *Ovidian Transformations*, ed. Hardie et al., 112–26.

Barnard, Mary E. *The Myth of Apollo and Daphne from Ovid to Quevedo: Love, Agon, and the Grotesque*. Duke Monographs in Medieval and Renaissance Studies 8. Durham: Duke University Press, 1987.

– 'Ovid's Apollo and Daphne: A Foolish God and a Virgin Tree.' *Anales de historia antigua y medieval* 18–19 (1975–6): 353–62.

Baswell, Christopher. *Virgil in Medieval England: Figuring the* Aeneid *from the Twelfth Century to Chaucer*. Cambridge: Cambridge University Press, 1995.

Battles, Paul. 'Chaucer and the Traditions of Dawn-Song.' *ChR* 31.4 (1997): 317–38.

Beatrice, Pier Franco. 'Monophysite Christology in an Oracle of Apollo.' *IJCT* 4.1 (1997): 3–22.

Bellamy, Elizabeth J. *Translations of Power: Narcissism and the Unconscious in Epic History*. Ithaca: Cornell University Press, 1992.

Bennett, J.A.W. *Chaucer's Book of Fame: An Exposition of 'The House of Fame.'* Oxford: Clarendon Press, 1968.

Benson, C. David. *The History of Troy in Middle English Literature: Guido delle Colonne's* Historia Destructionis Troiae *in Medieval England*. Suffolk: D.S. Brewer, 1980.

Berger, Harry Jr. 'The F-Fragment of the *Canterbury Tales*.' *ChR* 1.2–1.3 (1966): 88–102, 135–56.

Bernstein, Carol L. 'Subjectivity as Critique and the Critique of Subjectivity in Keats's *Hyperion*.' In *After the Future: Postmodern Times and Places*, ed. Gary Shapiro, 41–52. Albany: State University of New York Press, 1990.

Berry, Craig A. 'Flying Sources: Classical Authority in Chaucer's *Squire's Tale*.' *ELH* 68 (2001): 287–313.

– '"Sundrie Doubts": Vulnerable Understanding and Dubious Origins in Spenser's Continuation of the Squire's Tale.' In *Refiguring Chaucer*, ed. Krier, 106–27.

Bierl, Anton. 'Apollo in Greek Tragedy: Orestes and the God of Initiation.' In Solomon, *Apollo*, 81–96.

Biernoff, Suzannah. *Sight and Embodiment in the Middle Ages*. New York: Palgrave Macmillan, 2002.

Bitterling, Klaus. 'Middle English *Cras*.' *ES* 5 (1993): 437–40.

Bloomfield, Josephine. 'Chaucer and the Polis: Piety and Desire in the *Troilus and Criseyde*.' *MP* 94.3 (1997): 291–304.

Bloomfield, Morton W. 'Chaucer's *Squire's Tale* and the Renaissance.' *Poetica* 8 (1981): 28–35.

Blumenfeld-Kosinski, Renate. *Reading Myth: Classical Mythology and Its Interpretations in Medieval French Literature*. Stanford: Stanford University Press, 1997.

Blyth, Charles. 'Virgilian Tragedy and *Troilus*.' *ChR* 24.3 (1990): 211–22.

Bode, Christoph. 'Hyperion, *The Fall of Hyperion*, and Keats's Poetics.' *Wordsworth Circle* 31.1 (2000): 31–7.

Boitani, Piero. 'Antiquity and Beyond: The Death of Troilus.' In *The European Tragedy of Troilus*, ed. Piero Boitani, 1–19. Oxford: Clarendon, 1989.

– *Chaucer and the Imaginary World of Fame*. Cambridge: D.S. Brewer, 1984.

Børch, Marianne. 'Chaucer's Poetics and the *Manciple's Tale*.' *SAC* 25 (2003): 287–97.

– 'Geoffrey Chaucer and the Cosmic Text: Rejecting Analogy.' In *Text and Voice*, ed. Børch, 97–120.

Børch, Marianne, ed. *Text and Voice: The Rhetoric of Authority in the Middle Ages*. Odense, Denmark: University Press of Southern Denmark, 2004.

Bowden, Betsy. 'The Artistic and Interpretive Context of Blake's "Canterbury Pilgrims."' *Blake: An Illustrated Quarterly* 13.4 (1980): 164–90.

– 'Transportation to Canterbury: The Rival Envisionings by Stothard and Blake.' In *Appropriating the Middle Ages: Scholarship, Politics, Fraud*, ed. Tom Shippey with Martin Arnold, 73–111. Studies in Medievalism 11. Cambridge: D.S. Brewer, 2001.

Boyd, Barbara Weiden, ed. *Brill's Companion to Ovid*. Leiden: Brill, 2002.

Bradley, Edward M. 'Ovid *Heroides* 5: Reality and Illusion.' *CJ* 64.4 (1969): 158–62.

Braswell, Mary Flowers. 'The Magic of Machinery: A Context for Chaucer's *Franklin's Tale*.' *Mosaic* 18.2 (1985): 101–10.

Bray, Gerald. *1–2 Corinthians*. Ancient Christian Commentary on Scripture: New Testament 7. Gen. ed. Thomas C. Oden. Downers Grove, IL: InterVarsity Press, 1999.

Brewer, Derek, ed. *Chaucer: The Critical Heritage*. Vol. 1. London: Routledge and Kegan Paul, 1978.

Brown, Peter, and Andrew Butcher. *The Age of Saturn: Literature and History in the* Canterbury Tales. Oxford: Basil Blackwell, 1991.

Brown, Raymond E. *An Introduction to the New Testament*. The Anchor Bible Reference Library. New York: Doubleday, 1997.

Brownlee, Kevin. 'Pauline Vision and Ovidian Speech in *Paradiso* 1.' In *The Poetry of Allusion: Virgil and Ovid in Dante's* Commedia, ed. Rachel Jacoff and Jeffrey T. Schnapp, 202–13. Stanford: Stanford University Press, 1991.

– *Poetic Identity in Guillaume de Machaut*. Madison: University of Wisconsin Press, 1984.

Brownlee, Kevin, et al. 'Vernacular Literary Consciousness *c*.1100–*c*.1500: French, German and English Evidence.' In *Cambridge History of Literary Criticism*, ed. Minnis and Johnson, 422–71.

Burlin, Robert B. 'The Art of Chaucer's Franklin.' *Neophilologus* 51 (1967): 55–73.

Burrow, J[ohn]. A. 'Poems Without Endings.' *SAC* 13 (1991): 17–37.

– 'The Portrayal of Amans in *Confessio Amantis*.' In *Gower's 'Confessio Amantis': Responses and Reassessments*, ed. A.J. Minnis, 5–24. Cambridge: D.S. Brewer, 1983.

– '"Sir Thopas": An Agony in Three Fits.' *RES* ns 22, no. 85 (1971): 54–8.

Busine, Aude. *Paroles d'Apollon: Pratiques et traditions oraculaires dans l'antiquité tardive (IIe–VIe siècles)*. Leiden: Brill, 2005.

Cairns, Francis, ed. *Papers of the Liverpool Latin Seminar, Third Volume*. Liverpool: Francis Cairns, 1981.

Calabrese, Michael A. *Chaucer's Ovidian Arts of Love*. Gainesville: University Press of Florida, 1994.

Calvino, Italo. 'Ovid and Universal Contiguity.' In *The Uses of Literature: Essays*, trans. Patrick Creagh, 146–61. San Diego: Harcourt Brace, 1986.

Cameron, Alan. *Greek Mythography in the Roman World*. Oxford: Oxford University Press, 2004.

– 'Gregory of Nazianzus and Apollo.' *Journal of Theological Studies* 20.1 (1969): 240–1.

Camille, Michael. *The Gothic Idol: Ideology and Image-Making in Medieval Art*. Cambridge: Cambridge University Press, 1989.

Cannon, Christopher. *The Making of Chaucer's English: A Study of Words*. Cambridge: Cambridge University Press, 1998.

Carlson, David R. 'Chaucer, Humanism, and Printing: Conditions of Authorship in Fifteenth-Century England.' *UTQ* 64.2 (1995): 274–88.

– *Chaucer's Jobs.* New York: Palgrave Macmillan, 2004.

Carruthers, Mary. *The Book of Memory: A Study of Memory in Medieval Culture.* Cambridge: Cambridge University Press, 1990.

Casali, Sergio. 'Altri voci nell' "Eneide" di Ovidio.' *Materiali e discussioni per l'analisi dei testi classici* 35 (1995): 59–76.

– 'Apollo, Ovid, and the Foreknowledge of Criticism (*Ars* 2.493–512).' *CJ* 93.1 (1997): 19–27.

– 'Enone, Apollo pastore e l'amore immedicabile: Giochi ovidiani su di un topos elegiaco.' *Materiali e discussioni per l'analisi dei testi classici* 28 (1992): 85–100.

Chance, Jane. *Medieval Mythography: From Roman North Africa to the School of Chartres, A.D. 433–1177.* Gainesville: University Press of Florida, 1994.

– *Medieval Mythography: From the School of Chartres to the Court at Avignon, 1177–1350.* Gainesville: University Press of Florida, 2000.

Chance, Jane, ed. *The Mythographic Art: Classical Fable and the Rise of the Vernacular in Early France and England.* Gainesville: University of Florida Press, 1990.

Cheney, Patrick. 'Spenser's Completion of *The Squire's Tale*: Love, Magic, and Heroic Action in the Legend of Cambell and Triamond.' *Journal of Medieval and Renaissance Studies* 15 (1985): 135–55.

Claasen, Jo-Marie. *Displaced Persons: The Literature of Exile from Cicero to Boethius.* Madison: University of Wisconsin Press, 1999.

Clark, John W. '*Does* the Franklin Interrupt the Squire?' *ChR* 7.2 (1972): 160–1.

Clauss, James J. 'The Episode of the Lycian Farmers in Ovid's *Metamorphoses*.' *Harvard Studies in Classical Philology* 92 (1989): 297–314.

Clouston, W.A. 'The Tell-Tale Bird: Latin Source, Other European Versions and Asiatic Analogues of the *Manciple's Tale*.' In *Originals and Analogues of Some of Chaucer's Canterbury Tales*, ed. F.J. Furnivall et al., 437–80. Chaucer Society, 2nd series 7, 10, 15, 20, 22. London: Oxford University Press, 1872–87.

Coghill, Neville. *The Poet Chaucer.* 2nd ed. Oxford: Oxford University Press, 1967.

Collins, Adela Yarbro. *The Combat Myth in the Book of Revelation.* Harvard Dissertations in Religion 9. Missoula, MT: Scholars Press, 1976.

Conte, Gian Biagio. *The Poetry of Pathos: Studies in Virgilian Epic.* Ed. S.J. Harrison. Oxford: Oxford University Press, 2007.

Cook, Jon. 'Carnival and *The Canterbury Tales*: "Only equals may laugh" (Herzen).' In *Medieval Literature*, ed. Aers, 169–91.

Cooke, John Daniel. 'Euhemerism: A Mediaeval Interpretation of Classical Paganism.' *Speculum* 2.4 (1927): 396–410.

Cooper, Helen. 'Chaucer and Ovid: A Question of Authority.' In *Ovid Renewed: Ovidian Influences on Literature and Art from the Middle Ages to the Twentieth Century,* ed. Charles Martindale, 71–81. Cambridge: Cambridge University Press, 1988.

– 'The Classical Background.' In *Chaucer: An Oxford Guide,* ed. Steve Ellis, 255–71. Oxford: Oxford University Press, 2005.

– *Oxford Guides to Chaucer:* The Canterbury Tales. 2nd ed. Oxford: Oxford University Press, 1996.

– *The Structure of the Canterbury Tales.* London: Duckworth, 1983.

Copeland, Rita. 'Lydgate, Hawes, and the Science of Rhetoric in the Late Middle Ages.' In *John Lydgate,* ed. Scanlon and Simpson, 232–57.

– *Rhetoric, Hermeneutics, and Translation in the Middle Ages: Academic Traditions and Vernacular Texts.* Cambridge: Cambridge University Press, 1991.

Copley, Frank Olin. '*Servitium amoris* in the Roman Elegists.' *TPAPA* 78 (1947): 285–300.

Cosgrove, Denis. *Apollo's Eye: A Cartographic Genealogy of the Earth in the Western Imagination.* Baltimore: Johns Hopkins University Press, 2001.

Cottino-Jones, Marga. 'The Myth of Apollo and Daphne in Petrarch's *Canzoniere*: The Dynamics and Literary Function of Transformation.' In *Francis Petrarch, Six Centuries Later: A Symposium,* ed. Aldo Scaglione, 152–76. Chapel Hill: Department of Romance Languages, University of North Carolina; Chicago: The Newberry Library, 1975.

Courcelle, Pierre. *Connais-toi toi-même: De Socrate à Saint Bernard.* 3 vols. Paris: Études Augustiniennes, 1974.

Cox, Catherine S. 'The Jangler's "Bourde": Gender, Renunciation, and Chaucer's Manciple.' *South Atlantic Review* 61.4 (1996): 1–21.

Crabbe, Anna. 'Literary Design in the *De Consolatione Philosophiae*.' In *Boethius: His Life, Thought and Influence,* ed. Margaret Gibson, 237–74. Oxford: Basil Blackwell, 1981.

Craun, Edwin D. *Lies, Slander, and Obscenity in Medieval English Literature: Pastoral Rhetoric and the Deviant Speaker.* Cambridge: Cambridge University Press, 1997.

Curtius, Ernst Robert. *European Literature and the Latin Middle Ages.* Trans. Willard R. Trask. 1953. New York: Harper and Row, 1963.

Daley, Brian E. 'Apollo as a Chalcedonian: A New Fragment of a Controversial Work from Early Sixth-Century Constantinople.' *Traditio* 50 (1995): 31–54.

Dane, Joseph A. '"Tyl Mercurius House He Flye": Early Printed Texts and Critical Readings of the *Squire's Tale*.' *ChR* 34.3 (2000): 309–16.

Daniel, Norman. *Heroes and Saracens: An Interpretation of the* Chansons de Geste. Edinburgh: Edinburgh University Press, 1984.

Davenport, W.A. *Chaucer: Complaint and Narrative*. Cambridge: D.S. Brewer, 1988.

David, Alfred. *The Strumpet Muse: Art and Morals in Chaucer's Poetry*. Bloomington, IN: Indiana University Press, 1976.

Davis, Gregson. *The Death of Procris: 'Amor' and the Hunt in Ovid's Metamorphoses*. Rome: Edizioni dell'Ateneo, 1983.

Davidson, Gustav. *A Dictionary of Angels, Including the Fallen Angels*. New York: The Free Press, 1967.

Dean, James. 'The Ending of the *Canterbury Tales*, 1952–1976.' *Texas Studies in Literature and Language* 21.1 (1979): 17–33.

Delany, Sheila. *Chaucer's House of Fame: The Poetics of Skeptical Fideism*. 1972. Gainesville: University Press of Florida, 1994.

– *Impolitic Bodies: Poetry, Saints, and Society in Fifteenth-Century England*. New York: Oxford University Press, 1998.

– 'Slaying Python: Marriage and Misogyny in a Chaucerian Text.' In *Writing Woman: Women Writers and Women in Literature, Medieval to Modern*, ed. Sheila Delany, 47–75. New York: Schocken Books, 1983.

Desmond, Marilynn, and Pamela Sheingorn. *Myth, Montage, and Visuality in Late Medieval Manuscript Culture: Christine de Pizan's* Epistre Othea. Ann Arbor: University of Michigan Press, 2003.

Detienne, Marcel. *Apollon le couteau à la main: Une approche expérimentale du polythéisme grec*. Paris: Éditions Gallimard, 1998.

– 'Apollo's Slaughterhouse.' Trans. Anne Doueihi. *Diacritics* 16.2 (1986): 46–53.

– 'Forgetting Delphi between Apollo and Dionysus.' *CP* 96.2 (2001): 147–58.

DiMarco, Vincent [J.] 'The Dialogue of Science and Magic in Chaucer's *Squire's Tale*.' In *Dialogische Strukturen / Dialogic Structures: Festschrift für Willi Erzgräber*, ed. Thomas Kühn and Ursula Schaefer, 50–68. Tübingen: Gunter Narr Verlag, 1996.

– 'The Historical Basis of Chaucer's Squire's Tale.' In *Chaucer's Cultural Geography*, ed. Kathryn L. Lynch, 56–75. New York: Routledge, 2002.

– 'The Squire's Tale.' In *Sources and Analogues of the Canterbury Tales*, ed. Robert M. Correale and Mary Hamel, vol. 1, 169–209. Cambridge: D.S. Brewer, 2002.

– 'Supposed Satiric Pointers in Chaucer's *Squire's Tale*.' *ES* 78.4 (1997): 330–3.

Dimmick, Jeremy, et al., eds. *Images, Idolatry, and Iconoclasm in Late Medieval England: Textuality and the Visual Image*. Oxford: Oxford University Press, 2002.

Donaldson, E. Talbot. *The Swan at the Well: Shakespeare Reading Chaucer*. New Haven: Yale University Press, 1985.

Dunkle, J. Roger. 'Satirical Themes in Joseph of Exeter's *De Bello Troiano.'* *Classica et Mediaevalia* 38 (1987): 203–13.

Durling, Robert M. 'Ovid as *Praeceptor Amoris.' CJ* 53.4 (1958): 157–67.

Eaton, R.D. 'Narrative Closure in Chaucer's Franklin's Tale.' *Neophilologus* 84 (2000): 309–21.

Ebin, Lois A. *Illuminator, Makar, Vates: Visions of Poetry in the Fifteenth Century.* Lincoln: University of Nebraska Press, 1988.

Edwards, Genevieve Steele. 'Ritual Excommunication in Medieval France and England, 900–1200.' PhD diss. Stanford University, 1997.

Edwards, Robert R. *Ratio and Invention: A Study of Medieval Lyric and Narrative.* Nashville: Vanderbilt University Press, 1989.

Esolen, Anthony M. 'The Disingenuous Poet Laureate: Spenser's Adoption of Chaucer.' *SP* 87 (1990): 285–311.

Evert, Walter H. *Aesthetic and Myth in the Poetry of Keats.* Princeton: Princeton University Press, 1965.

Farrell, Thomas J. 'Introduction: Bakhtin, Liminality, and Medieval Literature.' In *Bakhtin and Medieval Voices,* 169–209. Gainesville: University Press of Florida, 1995.

Federico, Sylvia. *New Troy: Fantasies of Empire in the Late Middle Ages.* Minneapolis: University of Minnesota Press, 2003.

Feldherr, Andrew. 'Metamorphosis in the *Metamorphoses.'* In *Cambridge Companion to Ovid,* ed. Hardie, 163–79.

– 'Reconciling Niobe.' In *Aetas Ovidiana,* ed. Nelis, 125–45.

Ferster, Judith. 'Interpretation and Imitation in Chaucer's Franklin's Tale.' In *Medieval Literature,* ed. Aers, 148–68.

Fish, Jeffrey. 'Physician, Heal Thyself: The Intertextuality of Ovid's Exile Poetry and the *Remedia Amoris.' Latomus* 63.4 (2004): 864–72.

Fisher, John H. 'A Language Policy for Lancastrian England.' *PMLA* 107.5 (1992): 1168–80.

Fleming, John V. *Classical Imitation and Interpretation in Chaucer's* Troilus. Lincoln: University of Nebraska Press, 1990.

– 'Criseyde's Poem: The Anxieties of the Classical Tradition.' In *New Perspectives on Criseyde,* ed. Cindy L. Vitto and Marcia Smith Marzec, 277–98. Asheville, NC: Pegasus Press, 2004.

Flutre, Louis-Fernand. *Table des noms propres avec toutes leurs variantes figurant dans les romans du Moyen Age.* Poitiers: Centre d'Études Supérieures de Civilisation Médiévale, 1962.

Fontenrose, Joseph [E.] 'Apollo and the Sun-God in Ovid.' *AJP* 61.4 (1940): 429–44.

– *The Delphic Oracle: Its Responses and Operations with a Catalogue of Responses.* Berkeley: University of California Press, 1978.

– *Python: A Study of Delphic Myth and Its Origins.* 1959. Berkeley: University of California Press, 1980.

Ford, J. Massyngberde. *Revelation: Introduction, Translation and Commentary.* Anchor Bible 38. Garden City, NY: Doubleday, 1975.

Foucault, Michel. 'Truth and Power.' In *Power/Knowledge: Selected Interviews and Other Writings 1972–1977*, ed. Colin Gordon, trans. Colin Gordon et al., 109–33. New York: Pantheon Books, 1972.

Fox, Denton. 'Dunbar's *The Golden Targe.'* *ELH* 26.3 (1959): 311–34.

Fradenburg, Louise. 'The Manciple's Servant Tongue: Politics and Poetry in *The Canterbury Tales.'* *ELH* 52.1 (1985): 85–118.

Frécaut, Jean Marc. 'La Métamorphose de Niobé chez Ovide.' *Latomus: Revue D'Études Latines* 39 (1980): 129–43.

Fredericks, B.R. 'Divine Wit vs. Divine Folly: Mercury and Apollo in *Metamorphoses* 1–2.' *CJ* 72.3 (1977): 244–9.

Frese, Dolores Warwick. *An* Ars Legendi *for Chaucer's* Canterbury Tales. Gainesville: University of Florida Press, 1991.

Freund, Stefan. 'Christian Use and Valuation of Theological Oracles: The Case of Lactantius' *Divine Institutes.'* *VC* 60 (2006): 269–84.

Fulkerson, Laurel. 'Apollo, *Paenitentia*, and Ovid's *Metamorphoses.'* *Mnemosyne* 59.3 (2006): 388–402.

– '*Omnia vincit amor*: Why the *Remedia* Fail.' *CQ* 54.1 (2004): 211–23.

Fumo, Jamie C. 'Aurelius' Prayer, *Franklin's Tale* 1031–79: Sources and Analogues.' *Neophilologus* 88 (2004): 623–35.

– 'Chaucer as *Vates*? Reading Ovid through Dante in the *House of Fame*, Book 3.' In *Writers Reading Writers: Intertextual Studies in Medieval and Early Modern Literature in Honor of Robert Hollander*, ed. Janet Levarie Smarr, 89–108. Newark: University of Delaware Press, 2007.

– 'The God of Love and Love of God: Palinodic Exchange in The Prologue of the *Legend of Good Women* and the "Retraction."' In *The Legend of Good Women: Context and Reception*, ed. Carolyn Collette, 157–75. Cambridge: D.S. Brewer, 2006.

– 'John Metham's "Straunge Style": *Amoryus and Cleopes* as Chaucerian Fragment.' *ChR* 43.2 (2008): 213–35.

– '"Little *Troilus*": Heroides 5 and Its Ovidian Contexts in Chaucer's *Troilus and Criseyde.'* *SP* 100.3 (2003): 278–314.

– 'Thinking upon the Crow: The *Manciple's Tale* and Ovidian Mythography.' *ChR* 38.4 (2004): 355–75.

Fyler, John M. *Chaucer and Ovid.* New Haven: Yale University Press, 1979.

– 'Domesticating the Exotic in the *Squire's Tale.'* *ELH* 5.1 (1988): 1–26.

– '*Omnia vincit amor*: Incongruity and the Limitations of Structure in Ovid's Elegiac Poetry.' *CJ* 66.3 (1971): 196–203.

Gagé, Jean. *Apollon Romain: Essai sur le culte d'Apollon et le développement du 'ritus Graecus' à Rome des origines à Auguste*. Paris: E. De Boccard, 1955.

Galloway, Andrew. 'Authority.' In *A Companion to Chaucer*, ed. Peter Brown, 23–39. Oxford: Basil Blackwell, 2000.

Gamble, Harry Y. 'Euhemerism and Christology in Origen: Contra Celsum III 22–43.' *VC* 33 (1979): 12–29.

Ganim, John M. *Chaucerian Theatricality*. Princeton: Princeton University Press, 1990.

Gärtner, Thomas. *Klassische Vorbilder mittelalterlicher Trojaepen*. Stuttgart: B.G. Teubner, 1999.

Gershenson, Daniel E. *Apollo the Wolf-God*. McLean, VA: Institute for the Study of Man, 1991.

Gibert, John. 'Apollo's Sacrifice: The Limits of a Metaphor in Greek Tragedy.' *Harvard Studies in Classical Philology* 101 (2003): 159–206.

Gibson, Roy K., ed. *Ovid: Ars Amatoria Book 3*. Cambridge: Cambridge University Press, 2003.

Gibson, Roy [K.], et al., eds. *The Art of Love: Bimillenial Essays on Ovid's Ars Amatoria and Remedia Amoris*. Oxford: Oxford University Press, 2006.

Gillis, Daniel. *Eros and Death in the Aeneid*. Rome: 'L'Erma' di Bretschneider, 1983.

Ginsberg, Warren. '*Ovidius ethicus*? Ovid and the Medieval Commentary Tradition.' In *Desiring Discourse: The Literature of Love, Ovid through Chaucer*, ed. James J. Paxson and Cynthia A. Gravlee, 62–71. Selinsgrove, PA: Susquehanna University Press; London: Associated University Presses, 1998.

Ginzberg, Louis. *The Legends of the Jews*. Trans. Henrietta Szold. 7 vols. Philadelphia: Jewish Publication Society of America, 1909–38.

Goodman, Jennifer R. 'Chaucer's *Squire's Tale* and the Rise of Chivalry.' *SAC* 5 (1983): 127–36.

– 'Dorigen and the Falcon: The Element of Despair in Chaucer's *Squire's* and *Franklin's Tales*.' In *Representations of the Feminine in the Middle Ages*, ed. Bonnie Wheeler, 69–89. Feminea Medievalia 1. Dallas: Academia, 1993.

Gordon, Ian A. *John Skelton, Poet Laureate*. Melbourne: Melbourne University Press in assoc. with Oxford University Press, 1943.

Gosling, A[nne]. 'Augustan Apollo: The Conflation of Literary Tradition and Augustan Propaganda.' *Pegasus* 28 (1985): 1–6.

– 'Political Apollo: From Callimachus to the Augustans.' *Mnemosyne*, 4th series, 45.4 (1992): 501–12.

Green, Richard Firth. *A Crisis of Truth: Literature and Law in Ricardian England*. Philadelphia: University of Pennsylvania Press, 1999.

– *Poets and Princepleasers: Literature and the English Court in the Late Middle Ages*. Toronto: University of Toronto Press, 1980.

Green, R.P.H. 'The Genesis of a Medieval Textbook: The Models and Sources of the Ecloga Theoduli.' *Viator* 13 (1982): 49–106.

Grether, Herbert G. 'Apollyon.' In *The Anchor Bible Dictionary*, ed. David Noel Freedman, vol. 1, 301–2. New York: Doubleday, 1992.

Griffiths, Jane. *John Skelton and Poetic Authority: Defining the Liberty to Speak.* Oxford: Clarendon Press, 2006.

Gross, Nicholas P. 'Rhetorical Wit and Amatory Persuasion in Ovid.' *CJ* 74.4 (1979): 305–18.

Gruber, Joachim. *Kommentar zu Boethius* De Consolatione Philosophiae. Berlin: Walter de Gruyter, 1978.

Hagedorn, Suzanne C. *Abandoned Women: Rewriting the Classics in Dante, Boccaccio, and Chaucer.* Ann Arbor: University of Michigan Press, 2004.

Haight, Elizabeth Hazelton. 'An "Inspired Message" in the Augustan Poets.' *AJP* 39.4, whole no. 156 (1918): 341–66.

Hainsworth, P.R.J. 'The Myth of Daphne in the *Rerum Vulgarium Fragmenta*.' *Italian Studies* 34 (1979): 28–44.

Haller, Robert S. 'Chaucer's *Squire's Tale* and the Uses of Rhetoric.' *MP* 62.4 (1965): 285–95.

Halton, Thomas. 'Clement's Lyre: A Broken String, a New Song.' *The Second Century: A Journal of Early Christian Studies* 3.4 (1983): 177–99.

Hammond, Eleanor Prescott. 'Chaucer and Lydgate Notes.' *MLN* 27.3 (1912): 91–2.

Hanna, Ralph, et al. 'Latin Commentary Tradition and Vernacular Literature.' In *Cambridge History of Literary Criticism*, ed. Minnis and Johnson, 363–421.

Hardie, Philip. 'Approximative Similes in Ovid: Incest and Doubling.' *Dictynna* 1 (2004): 83–112.

– '*Lethaeus Amor*: The Art of Forgetting.' In *The Art of Love*, ed. Gibson et al., 166–90.

– 'Ovid into Laura: Absent Presences in the *Metamorphoses* and Petrarch's *Rime Sparse*.' In *Ovidian Transformations*, ed. Hardie et al., 254–70.

– *Ovid's Poetics of Illusion.* Cambridge: Cambridge University Press, 2002.

Hardie, Philip, ed. *The Cambridge Companion to Ovid.* Cambridge: Cambridge University Press, 2002.

Hardie, Philip, et al., eds. *Ovidian Transformations: Essays on the 'Metamorphoses' and Its Reception.* Cambridge: Cambridge Philological Society, 1999.

Hardman, Phillipa. 'Chaucer's Muses and His "Art Poetical."' *RES* 37.148 (1986): 478–94.

Harrison, Benjamin S. 'The Rhetorical Inconsistency of Chaucer's Franklin.' *SP* 32.1 (1935): 55–61.

Harrison, E.L. 'Vergil and the Homeric Tradition.' In *Papers*, ed. Cairns, 209–25.

Hart, Clive. *The Prehistory of Flight*. Berkeley: University of California Press, 1985.

Hartin, Patrick J. *Apollos: Paul's Partner or Rival?* Collegeville, MN: Liturgical Press, 2009.

Harwood, Britton J. 'Language and the Real: Chaucer's Manciple.' *ChR* 6.4 (1972): 268–79.

Havely, Nicholas R., ed. *The House of Fame*. Durham: Durham Medieval Texts, 1994.

Havsteen, Sven Rune, et al., eds. *Creations: Medieval Rituals, the Arts, and the Concept of Creation*. Turnhout, Belgium: Brepols, 2007.

Hawkins, Peter S. 'The Metamorphosis of Ovid.' In *Dante's Testaments: Essays in Scriptural Imagination*, ed. Peter S. Hawkins, 145–58. Stanford: Stanford University Press, 1999.

Hazelton, Richard. 'The *Manciple's Tale*: Parody and Critique.' *JEGP* 62.1 (1963): 1–31.

Hebron, Malcolm. *The Medieval Siege: Theme and Image in Middle English Romance*. Oxford: Clarendon Press, 1997.

Heinrichs, Katherine. *The Myths of Love: Classical Lovers in Medieval Literature*. University Park, PA: Pennsylvania State University Press, 1990.

Herman, Peter C. 'Treason in the *Manciple's Tale*.' *ChR* 25.4 (1991): 318–28.

Hexter, Ralph. 'The *Allegari* of Pierre Bersuire: Interpretation and the *Reductorium Morale*.' *Allegorica* 10 (1989): 51–84.

– 'Ovid in the Middle Ages: Exile, Mythographer, and Lover.' In *Brill's Companion to Ovid*, ed. Boyd, 413–42.

Hieatt, A. Kent. *Chaucer, Spenser, Milton: Mythopoeic Continuities and Transformations*. Montreal: McGill-Queen's University Press, 1975.

– 'Room of One's Own for Decisions: Chaucer and *The Faerie Queene*.' In *Refiguring Chaucer*, ed Krier, 147–64.

Hill, T.E. *'She, This in Blak': Vision, Truth, and Will in Geoffrey Chaucer's Troilus and Criseyde*. New York: Routledge, 2006.

Hilles, Carroll. 'Gender and Politics in Osbern Bokenham's *Legendary*.' *New Medieval Literatures* 4 (2001): 189–212.

Hinds, Stephen. *Allusion and Intertext: Dynamics of Appropriation in Roman Poetry*. Cambridge: Cambridge University Press, 1998.

– 'Booking the Return Trip: Ovid and *Tristia* 1.' *Proceedings of the Cambridge Philological Society* 31 (1985) 13–32.

Hoffman, Richard L. *Ovid and the Canterbury Tales*. London: Oxford University Press, 1966.

Huot, Sylvia. 'The Daisy and the Laurel: Myths of Desire and Creativity in the Poetry of Jean Froissart.' In *Contexts: Style and Values in Medieval Art and*

Literature, ed. Daniel Poirion and Nancy Freeman Regalado. Spec. issue of
   Yale French Studies 80 (1991): 240–51.
– *From Song to Book: The Poetics of Writing in Old French Lyric and Lyrical
   Narrative Poetry*. Ithaca: Cornell University Press, 1987.
– *The* Romance of the Rose *and Its Medieval Readers: Interpretation, Reception,
   Manuscript Transmission*. Cambridge: Cambridge University Press, 1993.
Jackson, Stanley W. 'The Wounded Healer.' *BHM* 75 (2001): 1–36.
Jacobsen, Garrett A. 'Apollo and Tereus: Parallel Motifs in Ovid's *Meta-
   morphoses*.' *CJ* 80.1 (1984): 45–52.
Jacobson, Howard. *Ovid's* Heroides. Princeton: Princeton University Press, 1974.
Janan, Micaela. 'The Book of Good Love? Design versus Desire in
   Metamorphoses 10.' *Ramus* 17.2 (1988): 110–37.
Javitch, Daniel. 'Rescuing Ovid from the Allegorizers.' *Comparative Literature*
   30.2 (1978): 97–107.
Jonassen, Frederick B. 'The Inn, the Cathedral, and the Pilgrimage of *The
   Canterbury Tales*.' In *Rebels and Rivals: The Contestive Spirit in* The Canterbury
   Tales, ed. Susana Greer Fein et al., 1–35. Kalamazoo, MI: Medieval Institute
   Publications, 1991.
Jones, Peter Murray. *Medieval Medicine in Illuminated Manuscripts*. Rev. ed.
   London: British Library, 1998.
Jordan, Robert M. *Chaucer's Poetics and the Modern Reader*. Berkeley: University
   of California Press, 1987.
Jost, Jean E. 'Potency and Power: Chaucer's Aristocrats and Their Linguistic
   Superiority.' In *The Rusted Hauberk: Feudal Ideals of Order and Their Decline*,
   ed. Liam O. Purdon and Cindy L. Vitto, 49–76. Gainesville: University Press
   of Florida, 1994.
Joyner, William. 'Parallel Journeys in Chaucer's *House of Fame*.' *Papers on
   Language and Literature* 12.1 (1976): 3–19.
Jung, Marc-René. '*Ovide metamorphose* en prose (Bruges, vers 1475).' In '*A
   L'heure encore de mon escrire': Aspects de la littérature de Bourgogne sous Philippe
   le Bon et Charles le Téméraire*, ed. Claude Thiry, 99–115. Louvain-la-Neuve,
   Belgium: Les Lettres Romanes, 1997.
Kahrl, Stanley J. 'Chaucer's *Squire's Tale* and the Decline of Chivalry.' *ChR* 7.3
   (1973): 194–209.
Kallendorf, Craig. *The Other Virgil: 'Pessimistic' Readings of the* Aeneid *in Early
   Modern Culture*. Oxford: Oxford University Press, 2007.
Kamerick, Kathleen. *Popular Piety and Art in the Late Middle Ages: Image
   Worship and Idolatry in England 1350–1500*. New York: Palgrave, 2002.
Kamowski, William. 'Trading the "Knotte" for Loose Ends: The *Squire's Tale*
   and the Poetics of Chaucerian Fragments.' *Style* 31.3 (1997): 391–412.

Kaske, R.E. 'The Knight's Interruption of the *Monk's Tale*.' *ELH* 24.4 (1957): 249–68.

Kean, P.M. *Chaucer and the Making of English Poetry*. 2 vols. London: Routledge and Kegan Paul, 1972.

Keith, A.M. *The Play of Fictions: Studies in Ovid's* Metamorphoses *Book 2*. Ann Arbor: University of Michigan Press, 1992.

Kendrick, Laura. *Chaucerian Play: Comedy and Control in the* Canterbury Tales. Berkeley: University of California Press, 1988.

Kennedy, William J. 'Spenser's Squire's Literary History.' In *Worldmaking Spenser: Explorations in the Early Modern Age*, ed. Patrick Cheney and Lauren Silberman, 45–62. Lexington: University Press of Kentucky, 2000.

Kensak, Michael. 'Apollo *exterminans*: The God of Poetry in Chaucer's *Manciple's Tale*.' *SP* 98.2 (2001): 143–57.

– 'The Silences of Pilgrimage: *Manciple's Tale, Paradiso, Anticlaudianus*.' *ChR* 34.2 (1999): 190–206.

Kerényi, Karl. *Apollo: The Wind, the Spirit, and the God*. Trans. Jon Solomon. Dallas: Spring, 1983.

Kerkeslager, Allen. 'Apollo, Greco-Roman Prophecy, and the Rider on the White Horse in Rev. 6:2.' *Journal of Biblical Literature* 112.1 (1993): 116–21.

Kinsman, Robert S., and Theodore Yonge. *John Skelton: Canon and Census*. [New York: for the] Renaissance Society of America, 1967.

Kiralis, Karl. 'William Blake as an Intellectual and Spiritual Guide to Chaucer's *Canterbury Pilgrims*.' *Blake Studies* 1 (1968–9): 139–90.

Kiser, Lisa J. *Telling Classical Tales: Chaucer and the* Legend of Good Women. Ithaca: Cornell University Press, 1983.

– *Truth and Textuality in Chaucer's Poetry*. Hanover, NH: University Press of New England, 1991.

Knapp, Peggy. *Chaucer and the Social Contest*. New York: Routledge, 1990.

Knight, Stephen. 'Rhetoric and Poetry in the *Franklin's Tale*.' *ChR* 4 (1970): 14–30.

Knopp, Sherron. 'Poetry as Conjuring Act: The *Franklin's Tale* and *The Tempest*.' *ChR* 38.4 (2004): 337–54.

Knox, Peter E. 'In Pursuit of Daphne.' *Transactions of the American Philological Association* 120 (1990): 183–93.

– *Ovid's* Metamorphoses *and the Traditions of Augustan Poetry*. Cambridge: Cambridge Philological Society, 1986.

Knox, Peter E, ed. *Ovid's Heroides: Select Epistles*. Cambridge: Cambridge University Press, 1995.

Kolve, V.A. 'Looking at the Sun in Chaucer's *Troilus and Criseyde*.' In *Chaucer and the Challenges of Medievalism: Studies in Honor of H.A. Kelly*, ed. Donka Minkova and Theresa Tinkle, 31–71. Frankfurt am Main: Peter Lang, 2003.

– 'Rocky Shores and Pleasure Gardens: Poetry vs. Magic in Chaucer's *Franklin's Tale.*' In *Poetics: Theory and Practice in Medieval English Literature,* ed. Piero Boitani and Anna Torti, 165–95. Cambridge: D.S. Brewer, 1991.

Koonce, B.G. *Chaucer and the Tradition of Fame: Symbolism in* The House of Fame. Princeton: Princeton University Press, 1966.

Korotayev, Andrey, et al. 'Return of the White Raven: Postdiluvial Reconnaissance Motif A2234.1.1 Reconsidered.' *Journal of American Folklore* 119.472 (2006): 203–35.

Krier, Theresa M., ed. *Refiguring Chaucer in the Renaissance.* Gainesville: University Press of Florida, 1998.

Kruger, Stephen F. *Dreaming in the Middle Ages.* Cambridge: Cambridge University Press, 1992.

Lambert, Mark. '*Troilus,* Books I–III: A Criseydan Reading.' In *Essays on 'Troilus and Criseyde,'* ed. Mary Salu, 105–25. Cambridge: D.S. Brewer, 1980.

Langlois, Ernest. *Table des noms propres de toute nature compris dans les chansons de geste.* Paris: Librairie Émile Bouillon, 1904.

Larson, Charles. '*The Squires Tale*: Chaucer's Evolution from the Dream Vision.' *Revue des Langues Vivantes* 43 (1977): 598–607.

Lateiner, Donald. 'Mythic and Non-Mythic Artists in Ovid's Metamorphoses.' *Ramus* 13.1 (1984): 1–30.

Lawton, David. *Chaucer's Narrators.* Cambridge: D.S. Brewer, 1985.

– 'Dullness and the Fifteenth Century.' *ELH* 54.4 (1987): 761–99.

Leach, Eleanor Winsor. 'Ekphrasis and the Theme of Artistic Failure in Ovid's Metamorphoses.' *Ramus* 3.2 (1974): 102–42.

Leach, Elizabeth Eva. *Sung Birds: Music, Nature, and Poetry in the Later Middle Ages.* Ithaca: Cornell University Press, 2007.

Leavitt, John. 'Poetics, Prophetics, Inspiration.' In *Poetry and Prophecy: The Anthropology of Inspiration,* ed. John Leavitt, 1–60. Ann Arbor: University of Michigan Press, 1997.

Le Bonniec, H[enri]. 'Apollon dans les *Métamorphoses* d'Ovide.' In *Journées Ovidiennes de Parménie: Actes du colloque sur Ovide (24–26 juin 1983),* ed. Jean Marc Frécaut and Danielle Porte, 145–74. Collection Latomus 189. Brussels: Revue d'Études Latines, 1985.

Lee, Brian S. 'The Question of Closure in Fragment V of *The Canterbury Tales.*' *Yearbook of English Studies* 22 (1992): 190–200.

Lerer, Seth. *Chaucer and His Readers: Imagining the Author in Late-Medieval England.* Princeton: Princeton University Press, 1993.

Levenstein, Jessica. 'The Re-Formation of Marsyas in *Paradiso* 1.' In *Dante for The New Millenium,* ed. Teodolinda Barolini and H. Wayne Storey, 408–21. New York: Fordham University Press, 2003.

Lewis, Jack P. *A Study of the Interpretation of Noah and the Flood in Jewish and Christian Literature*. Leiden: Brill, 1968.

Lightsey, Scott. 'Chaucer's Secular Marvels and the Medieval Economy of Wonder.' *SAC* 23 (2001): 289–316.

Lionarons, Joyce Tally. 'Magic, Machines, and Deception: Technology in the *Canterbury Tales*.' *ChR* 27.4 (1993): 377–86.

Luengo, Anthony. 'Magic and Illusion in *The Franklin's Tale*.' *JEGP* 77 (1978): 1–16.

Lynch, Kathryn L. *Chaucer's Philosophical Visions*. Cambridge: D.S. Brewer, 2000.

– 'East Meets West in Chaucer's Squire's and Franklin's Tales.' *Speculum* 70 (1995): 530–51.

MacCormack, Sabine. *The Shadows of Poetry: Vergil in the Mind of Augustine*. Berkeley: University of California Press, 1998.

Machan, Tim William. *Textual Criticism and Middle English Texts*. Charlottesville: University Press of Virginia, 1994.

MacKinney, Loren M. 'Medical Ethics and Etiquette in the Middle Ages: The Persistence of Hippocratic Ideals.' *BHM* 26.1 (1952): 1–31.

Manly, John M., and Edith Rickert. *The Text of the* Canterbury Tales: *Studied on the Basis of All Known Manuscripts*. 8 vols. Chicago: University of Chicago Press, 1940.

Martin, Francis, ed. *Acts*. Ancient Christian Commentary on Scripture: New Testament 5. Gen. ed. Thomas C. Oden. Downers Grove, IL: InterVarsity Press, 2006.

Martindale, Charles. *Redeeming the Text: Latin Poetry and the Hermeneutics of Reception*. Cambridge: Cambridge University Press, 1993.

Martindale, Charles, and Richard F. Thomas, eds. *Classics and the Uses of Reception*. Maldon, MA: Blackwell, 2006.

Matzke, John E. 'Contributions to the History of the Legend of Saint George, with Special Reference to the Sources of the French, German and Anglo-Saxon Metrical Versions.' *PMLA* 17, ns 10 (1902): 464–535.

Maurizio, Lisa. 'Narrative, Biographical and Ritual Conventions at Delphi.' In *Sibille e linguaggi oracolari: Mito, storia, tradizione: Atti del convegno, Macerata-Norcia, settembre 1994*, ed. Ileana Chirassi Colombo and Tullio Seppilli, 133–58. Pisa: Istituti editoriali e poligrafici internazionali, 1998.

McCall, John P. *Chaucer among the Gods: The Poetics of Classical Myth*. University Park, PA: The Pennsylvania State University Press, 1979.

– 'The Squire in Wonderland.' *ChR* 1.2 (1966): 103–9.

McEntire, Sandra J. 'Illusions and Interpretation in the *Franklin's Tale*.' *ChR* 31.2 (1996): 145–63.

McGavin, John J. 'How Nasty is Phoebus's Crow?' *ChR* 21.4 (1987): 444–58.

McGregor, James H. *The Shades of Aeneas: The Imitation of Virgil and the History of Paganism in Boccaccio's* Filostrato, Filocolo, *and* Teseida. Athens, GA and London: University of Georgia Press, 1991.

McInerney, Maud Burnett. '"Is this a mannes herte?" Unmanning Troilus through Ovidian Allusion.' In *Masculinities in Chaucer: Approaches to Maleness in the* Canterbury Tales *and* Troilus and Criseyde, ed. Peter G. Beidler, 221–35. Cambridge: D.S. Brewer, 1998.

McKay, K.J. 'Solar Motifs or, Something New under the Sun.' *Antichthon* 10 (1976): 35–43.

McKeown, J.C. *Ovid: Amores.* Vol. 2. Leeds: Francis Cairns, 1989.

McKinley, Kathryn L. 'Manuscripts of Ovid in England 1100–1500.' *English Manuscript Studies 1100–1700* 7 (1998): 41–85.

– *Reading the Ovidian Heroine: 'Metamorphoses' Commentaries 1100–1618.* Leiden: Brill, 2001.

Mieszkowski, Gretchen. 'Chaucer's Much Loved Criseyde.' *ChR* 26.2 (1991): 109–32.

Miller, Andrew M. *From Delos to Delphi: A Literary Study of the Homeric Hymn to Apollo.* Leiden: Brill, 1986.

Miller, John [F.] 'Callimachus and the *Ars Amatoria*.' *CP* 78.1 (1983): 26–34.

– 'Disclaiming Divine Inspiration: A Programmatic Pattern.' *Wiener Studien* 20 (1986): 151–64.

– 'The Lamentations of Apollo in Ovid's *Metamorphoses*.' In *Ovid: Werk und Wirkung: Festgabe fur Michael von Albrecht zum 65*, ed. Werner Schubert, vol. 1, 413–21. Studien zur klassischen Philologie 100. Frankfurt am Main: Peter Lang, 1999.

– 'Ovid and Augustan Apollo.' In *Aetas Ovidiana*, ed. Nelis, 165–80.

– 'Virgil, Apollo, and Augustus.' In *Apollo*, ed. Solomon, 99–112.

Miller, Robert Daniel. 'The Origin and Original Nature of Apollo.' PhD diss. University of Pennsylvania, 1939.

Miller, Robert P. 'Augustinian Wisdom and Eloquence in the F-Fragment of the *Canterbury Tales*.' *Mediaevalia* 4 (1978): 244–75.

– 'Chaucer's Rhetorical Rendition of Mind: The Squire's Tale.' In *Chaucer and the Craft of Fiction*, ed. Leigh A. Arrathoon, 219–40. Rochester, MI: Solaris Press, 1986.

Minnis, A[lastair] [J.] *Chaucer and Pagan Antiquity.* Cambridge: D.S. Brewer, 1982.

– '*De vulgari auctoritate*: Chaucer, Gower and the Men of Great Authority.' In *Chaucer and Gower: Difference, Mutuality, Exchange*, ed. R.F. Yeager, 36–74. *ELS* Monograph Series 51. Victoria: University of Victoria, 1991.

– *Medieval Theory of Authorship: Scholastic Literary Attitudes in the Later Middle Ages*. London: Scolar Press, 1984.

Minnis, A[lastair] [J.], and Ian Johnson, eds. *The Cambridge History of Literary Criticism*. Vol. 2, *The Middle Ages*. Cambridge: Cambridge University Press, 2005.

Minnis, A[lastair] [J.], with V.J. Scattergood and J.J. Smith. *Oxford Guides to Chaucer: The Shorter Poems*. Oxford: Clarendon Press, 1995.

Morgan, Gareth. 'Dido the Wounded Deer.' *Vergilius* 40 (1994): 67–8.

Morgan, Gerald, ed. *The Franklin's Tale from The Canterbury Tales*. By Geoffrey Chaucer. London: Hodder and Stoughton, 1980.

Myerowitz, Molly. *Ovid's Games of Love*. Detroit: Wayne State University Press, 1985.

Nagle, Betty Rose. 'Erotic Pursuit and Narrative Seduction in Ovid's Metamorphoses.' *Ramus* 17.1 (1988): 32–51.

– *The Poetics of Exile: Program and Polemic in the* Tristia *and* Epistulae ex Ponto *of Ovid*. Collection Latomus 170. Brussels: Revue D'Études Latines, 1980.

Nelis, Damien, ed. *Aetas Ovidiana?* Spec. issue of *Hermathena* 177–8 (2004–5): 5–307.

Neville, Marie. 'The Function of the *Squire's Tale* in the Canterbury Scheme.' *JEGP* 50.2 (1951): 167–79.

Newlands, Carole E. 'Ovid's Ravenous Raven.' *CJ* 86.3 (1991): 244–55.

Newman, Barbara. '"Feynede Loves," Feigned Lore, and Faith in Trouthe.' In *Chaucer's 'Troilus': Essays in Criticism*, ed. Stephen A. Barney, 257–75. Hamden, CT: Archon Books, 1980.

– 'What Did It Mean to Say "I Saw"? The Clash between Theory and Practice in Medieval Visionary Culture.' *Speculum* 80.1 (2005): 1–43.

Newman, J.K. *Augustus and the New Poetry*. Collection Latomus 88. Brussels-Berchem: Revue D'Études Latines, 1967.

Nicoll, W.S.M. 'Cupid, Apollo, and Daphne (Ovid, *Met.* 1.452ff.).' *CQ* ns 30 (1980): 174–82.

Nolan, Barbara. 'Chaucer's Poetics of Dwelling in *Troilus and Criseyde*.' In *Chaucer and the City*, ed. Ardis Butterfield, 57–75. Cambridge: D.S. Brewer, 2006.

Nolan, Maura. *John Lydgate and the Making of Public Culture*. Cambridge: Cambridge University Press, 2005.

North, J.D. *Chaucer's Universe*. Oxford: Clarendon Press, 1988.

O'Daly, Gerard. *The Poetry of Boethius*. Chapel Hill: University of North Carolina Press, 1991.

Osborn, Marijane. *Time and the Astrolabe in the* Canterbury Tales. Norman: University of Oklahoma Press, 2002.

Otto, Walter F. *The Homeric Gods: The Spiritual Significance of Greek Religion.* Trans. Moses Hadas. 1954. Boston: Beacon Press, 1964.

Parke, H.W. *Sibyls and Sibylline Prophecy in Classical Antiquity.* Ed. B.C. McGing. London: Routledge, 1988.

Parke, H.W., and D.E.W. Wormell. *The Delphic Oracle.* 2 vols. Oxford: Basil Blackwell, 1956.

Parker, Hugh C. 'The Pagan Gods in Joseph of Exeter's *De Bello Troiano*.' *MAe* 64 (1995): 273–8.

Partridge, Stephen. 'Minding the Gaps: Interpreting the Manuscript Evidence of the *Cook's Tale* and the *Squire's Tale*.' In *The English Medieval Book: Studies in Memory of Jeremy Griffiths*, ed. A.S.G. Edwards et al., 51–85. London: British Library, 2000.

Pascal, Paul. 'Mediaeval Uses of Antiquity.' *CJ* 61.5 (1966): 193–7.

Patterson, Lee. *Chaucer and the Subject of History.* Madison: University of Wisconsin Press, 1991.

Pearsall, D[erek] A. 'Criseyde's Choices.' In *SAC* Proceedings, No. 2, 1986, ed. John V. Fleming and Thomas J. Heffernan, 17–29. Knoxville: New Chaucer Society, 1987.

– *John Lydgate.* London: Routledge and Kegan Paul, 1970.

– 'The Squire as Story-Teller.' *UTQ* 34.1 (1964): 82–92.

Percival, Florence. *Chaucer's Legendary Good Women.* Cambridge: Cambridge University Press, 1998.

Peterson, Joyce E. 'The Finished Fragment: A Reassessment of the *Squire's Tale*.' *ChR* 5.1 (1970): 62–74.

Powell, Stephen D. 'Game Over: Defragmenting the End of the *Canterbury Tales*.' *ChR* 37.1 (2002): 40–58.

Putnam, Michael C.J. 'Daphne's Roots.' In *Aetas Ovidiana*, ed. Nelis, 71–89.

Ransom, Daniel J. 'Apollo's Holy Laurel: *Troilus and Criseyde* III, 542–43.' *ChR* 41.2 (2006): 206–12.

Rawcliffe, Carole. *Medicine and Society in Later Medieval England.* 1995. London: Sandpiper Books, 1999.

Raybin, David. 'The Death of a Silent Woman: Voice and Power in Chaucer's *Manciple's Tale*.' *JEGP* 95.1 (1996): 19–37.

Relihan, Joel C. *Ancient Menippean Satire.* Baltimore: Johns Hopkins University Press, 1993.

Revard, Stella P. 'Christ and Apollo in the Seventeenth-Century Religious Lyric.' In *New Perspectives on the Seventeenth-Century English Religious Lyric*, ed. John R. Roberts, 143–67. Columbia: University of Missouri Press, 1994.

Reynolds, Suzanne. *Medieval Reading: Grammar, Rhetoric and the Classical Text.* Cambridge: Cambridge University Press, 1996.

Reynolds, William D. 'Sources, Nature, and Influence of the *Ovidius Moralizatus* of Pierre Bersuire.' In *The Mythographic Art*, ed. Chance, 83–99.

Riddehough, Geoffrey B. 'A Forgotten Poet: Joseph of Exeter.' *JEGP* 46 (1947): 254–9.

Rigg, A.G. 'Calchas, Renegade and Traitor: Dares and Joseph of Exeter.' *Notes and Queries* 45.2 (1998): 176–8.

– *A History of Anglo-Latin Literature 1066–1422*. Cambridge: Cambridge University Press, 1992.

– 'Joseph of Exeter's Pagan Gods Again.' *MAe* 70.1 (2001): 19–28.

Risden, E.L., et al., eds. *Prophet Margins: The Medieval Vatic Impulse and Social Stability*. New York: Peter Lang, 2004.

Roberts, Gildas. 'Worthy of Their Envy: The Literary Merits of Joseph of Exeter's Trojan Epic.' *University of Cape Town Studies in English* 2 (1971): 13–23.

Robertson, D.W., Jr. *Chaucer's London*. New York: John Wiley and Sons, 1968.

Root, Robert Kilburn. 'Chaucer's Dares.' *MP* 15.1 (1917): 1–22.

Rosati, Gianpiero. 'The Art of *Remedia Amoris*: Unlearning to Love?' In *The Art of Love*, ed. Gibson et al., 143–65.

– 'Narrative Techniques and Narrative Structures in the *Metamorphoses*.' In *Brill's Companion to Ovid*, ed. Boyd, 271–304.

Ross, Trevor. *The Making of the English Literary Canon: From the Middle Ages to the Late Eighteenth Century*. Montreal: McGill-Queen's University Press, 1998.

Ross, Valerie A. 'Believing Cassandra: Intertextual Politics and the Interpretation of Dreams in *Troilus and Criseyde*.' *ChR* 31.4 (1997): 339–56.

Rossi, Andreola. *Contexts of War: Manipulation of Genre in Virgilian Battle Narrative*. Ann Arbor: University of Michigan Press, 2004.

Rowland, Beryl. *Birds with Human Souls*. Knoxville: University of Tennessee Press, 1978.

Salisbury, Eve. 'Murdering Fiction: The Case of *The Manciple's Tale*.' *SAC* 25 (2003): 309–16.

Sallis, John. *Crossings: Nietzsche and the Space of Tragedy*. Chicago: University of Chicago Press, 1991.

Saville, Jonathan. *The Medieval Erotic Alba: Structure as Meaning*. New York: Columbia University Press, 1972.

Scala, Elizabeth. 'Canacee and the Chaucer Canon: Incest and Other Unnarratables.' *ChR* 30.1 (1995): 15–39.

Scanlon, Larry. 'Lydgate's Poetics: Laureation and Domesticity in the *Temple of Glass*.' In *John Lydgate*, ed. Scanlon and Simpson, 61–97.

Scanlon, Larry, and James Simpson, eds. *John Lydgate: Poetry, Culture, and Lancastrian England*. Notre Dame: University of Notre Dame Press, 2006.

Scattergood, V.J. [John]. 'The Early Annotations to John Skelton's Poems.'
  In *Reading the Past: Essays on Medieval and Renaissance Literature*, ed. John
  Scattergood, 288–97. Dublin: Four Courts Press, 1996.
– 'The Manciple's Manner of Speaking.' *Essays in Criticism* 24.2 (1974): 124–46.
– 'Skelton's *Garlande of Laurell* and the Chaucerian Tradition.' In *Chaucer
  Traditions: Studies in Honour of Derek Brewer*, ed. Ruth Morse and Barry
  Windeatt, 122–38. Cambridge: Cambridge University Press, 1990.
Schibanoff, Susan. 'Argus and Argyve: Etymology and Characterization in
  Chaucer's *Troilus*.' *Speculum* 51.4 (1976): 647–58.
– 'Criseyde's "Impossible" *Aubes*.' *JEGP* 76 (1977): 326–33.
Schless, Howard H. *Chaucer and Dante: A Revaluation*. Norman, OK: Pilgrim
  Books, 1984.
Schwartz, Donald Ray. *Noah's Ark: An Annotated Encyclopedia of Every Animal
  Species in the Hebrew Bible*. Northvale, NJ: Jason Aronson, 2000.
Scott, Kathleen L. *The Caxton Master and His Patrons*. Cambridge: Cambridge
  Bibliographical Society, 1976.
– *Later Gothic Manuscripts, 1390–1490*. Vol. 6. London: H. Miller, 1996.
Seaman, David M. '"The Wordes of the Frankeleyn to the Squier": An
  Interruption?' *ELN* 24.1 (1986): 12–18.
Sedgwick, Walter Bradbury. 'The *Bellum Troianum* of Joseph of Exeter.'
  Speculum 5.1 (1930): 49–76.
Seymour, M.C. 'Some Satiric Pointers in the *Squire's Tale*.' *ES* 70.4 (1989):
  311–14.
Seznec, Jean. *The Survival of the Pagan Gods: The Mythological Tradition and Its
  Place in Renaissance Humanism and Art*. Trans. Barbara F. Sessions. New
  York: Bollingen Foundation, 1953.
Shannon, Edgar Finley. *Chaucer and the Roman Poets*. Cambridge, MA: Harvard
  University Press, 1929.
Sharon-Zisser, Shirley. 'The *Squire's Tale* and the Limits of Non-Mimetic
  Fiction.' *ChR* 26.4 (1992): 377–94.
Sharrock, Alison. 'An A-musing Tale: Gender, Genre, and Ovid's Battles with
  Inspiration in the *Metamorphoses*.' In *Cultivating the Muse*, ed. Spentzou and
  Fowler, 207–27.
– *Seduction and Repetition in Ovid's* Ars Amatoria 2. Oxford: Clarendon Press,
  1994.
Simpson, James. *Reform and Cultural Revolution*. Oxford English Literary
  History 2, 1350–1547. Oxford: Oxford University Press, 2002.
Singerman, Jerome E. *Under Clouds of Poesy: Poetry and Truth in French and
  English Reworkings of the* Aeneid, 1160–1513. New York: Garland, 1986.

Skelton, Robin. 'The Master Poet: John Skelton as Conscious Craftsman.'
    Mosaic 6.3 (1973): 67–92.
Smalley, Beryl. *English Friars and Antiquity in the Early Fourteenth Century.*
    Oxford: Basil Blackwell, 1960.
Smith, Gregory A. 'The Myth of the Vaginal Soul.' *Greek, Roman, and Byzantine
    Studies* 44 (2004): 199–225.
Solodow, Joseph B. *The World of Ovid's* Metamorphoses. Chapel Hill:
    University of North Carolina Press, 1988.
Solomon, Jon, ed. *Apollo: Origins and Influences.* Tucson: The University of
    Arizona Press, 1994.
Sourvinou-Inwood, Christiane. *'Reading' Greek Culture: Texts and Images,
    Rituals and Myths.* Oxford: Clarendon Press, 1991.
Spearing, A.C. *Medieval to Renaissance in English Poetry.* Cambridge: Cam-
    bridge University Press, 1985.
– 'Textual Performance: Chaucerian Prologues and the French *Dit*.' In *Text and
    Voice*, ed. Børch, 21–45.
Spearing, A.C., ed. *The Franklin's Prologue and Tale.* By Geoffrey Chaucer. Rev.
    ed. Cambridge: Cambridge University Press, 1994.
Spentzou, Efrossini. 'Introduction: Secularizing the Muse.' In *Cultivating the
    Muse*, ed. Spentzou and Fowler, 1–28.
– *Readers and Writers in Ovid's* Heroides: *Transgressions of Genre and Gender.*
    Oxford: Oxford University Press, 2003.
Spentzou, Efrossini, and Don Fowler, eds. *Cultivating the Muse: Struggles for Power
    and Inspiration in Classical Literature.* Oxford: Oxford University Press, 2002.
Spurgeon, Caroline F.E. *Five Hundred Years of Chaucer Criticism and Allusion
    1357–1900.* 3 vols. New York: Russell and Russell, 1960.
Steinberg, Theodore L. 'Poetry and Prophecy: A Skelton Key.' In *Prophet
    Margins*, ed. Risden et al., 149–65.
Stevens, Martin. 'Chaucer's "Bad Art": The Interrupted Tales.' In *The
    Rhetorical Poetics of the Middle Ages: Reconstructive Polyphony, Essays in Honor
    of Robert O. Payne*, ed. John M. Hill and Deborah M. Sinnreich-Levi, 130–48.
    Madison, NJ: Fairleigh Dickinson University Press; London: Associated
    University Presses, 2000.
Stevenson, Warren. 'From Canterbury to Jerusalem: Interpreting Blake's
    Canterbury Pilgrims.' In *Chaucer Illustrated: Five Hundred Years of The
    Canterbury Tales in Pictures*, ed. William K. Finley and Joseph Rosenblum,
    191–209. New Castle, DE: Oak Knoll Press; London: The British Library,
    2003.
Stillinger, Thomas C. *The Song of Troilus: Lyric Authority in the Medieval Book.*
    Philadelphia: University of Pennsylvania Press, 1992.

Stillwell, Gardiner. 'Chaucer in Tartary.' *RES* 24, no. 95 (1948): 177–88.

Stinton, T.C.W. *Euripides and the Judgement of Paris*. London: Society for the Promotion of Hellenic Studies, 1965.

Stokes, M. 'The Moon in Leo in Book V of *Troilus and Criseyde*.' *ChR* 17.2 (1982): 116–29.

Storm, Mel. 'Speech, Circumspection, and Orthodontics in the *Manciple's Prologue* and *Tale* and the Wife of Bath's Portrait.' *SP* 96.2 (1999): 109–26.

Striar, Brian. 'The "Manciple's Tale" and Chaucer's Apolline Poetics.' *Criticism* 33.2 (1991): 173–204.

Sturm-Maddox, Sara. *Petrarch's Laurels*. University Park, PA: Pennsylvania State University Press, 1992.

Taylor, Karla. *Chaucer Reads 'The Divine Comedy.'* Stanford: Stanford University Press, 1989.

Thomas, Richard F. *Virgil and the Augustan Reception*. Cambridge: Cambridge University Press, 2001.

Tinkle, Theresa. *Medieval Venuses and Cupids: Sexuality, Hermeneutics, and English Poetry*. Stanford: Stanford University Press, 1996.

Tissol, Garth. *The Face of Nature: Wit, Narrative, and Cosmic Origins in Ovid's Metamorphoses*. Princeton: Princeton University Press, 1997.

Tolan, John V. *Saracens: Islam in the Medieval European Imagination*. New York: Columbia University Press, 2002.

Tournoy, Gilbert. 'Apollo and Admetus: The Forms of a Classical Myth through the Middle Ages and the Renaissance.' In *Forms of the 'Medieval' in the 'Renaissance': A Multidisciplinary Exploration of a Cultural Continuum*, ed. George Hugo Tucker, 175–203. Charlottesville, VA: Rookwood Press, 2000.

Utz, Richard. 'Writing Alternative Worlds: Rituals of Authorship and Authority in Late Medieval Theological and Literary Discourse.' In *Creations*, ed. Havsteen et al., 121–38.

Van Tress, Heather. *Poetic Memory: Allusion in the Poetry of Callimachus and the Metamorphoses of Ovid*. Leiden: Brill, 2004.

Verbaal, Wim. 'Invocatio Musae: Inspired by the Muse, the Inescapable Reality.' In *Creations*, ed. Havsteen et al., 49–64.

Vernant, Jean-Pierre. 'Parole et signes muets.' In *Divination et rationalité*, ed. Jean-Pierre Vernant et al., 9–25. Paris: Éditions du Seuil, 1974.

Voigts, Linda Ehrsam. 'The Significance of the Name Apuleius to the *Herbarium Apulei*.' *BHM* 52 (1978): 214–27.

Wakelin, Daniel. *Humanism, Reading, and English Literature 1430–1530*. Oxford: Oxford University Press, 2007.

Wallace, David. *Chaucerian Polity: Absolutist Lineages and Associational Forms in England and Italy*. Stanford: Stanford University Press, 1997.

Watson, Nicholas. '"Et que est huius ydoli materia? Tuipse": Idols and Images in Walter Hilton.' In *Images*, ed. Dimmick et al., 95–111.
– 'The Politics of Middle English Writing.' In *The Idea of the Vernacular: An Anthology of Middle English Literary Theory 1280–1520*, ed. Jocelyn Wogan-Browne et al., 331–52. Exeter: University of Exeter Press, 1999.
Wenzel, Siegfried. 'The Classics in Late-Medieval Preaching.' In *Mediaeval Antiquity*, ed. Andries Welkenhuysen et al., 127–43. Leuven, Belgium: Leuven University Press, 1995.
Wetherbee, Winthrop. *Chaucer and the Poets: An Essay on* Troilus and Criseyde. Ithaca: Cornell University Press, 1984.
– '"*Per te poeta fui, per te cristiano*": Dante, Statius, and the Narrator of Chaucer's *Troilus*.' In *Vernacular Poetics in the Middle Ages*, ed. Lois Ebin, 154–76. Kalamazoo: Medieval Institute Publications, 1984.
Wheeler, Stephen M. *A Discourse of Wonders: Audience and Performance in Ovid's 'Metamorphoses.'* Philadelphia: University of Pennsylvania Press, 1999.
White, Keith D. *John Keats and the Loss of Romantic Innocence*. Amsterdam: Rodopi, 1996.
Williams, Frederick. 'Augustus and Daphne: Ovid *Metamorphoses* 1,560–63 and Phylarchus *FGrH* 81 F 32 (b).' In *Papers*, ed. Cairns, 249–57.
Williams, Gareth D. *Banished Voices: Readings in Ovid's Exile Poetry*. Cambridge: Cambridge University Press, 1994.
Wills, Jeffrey. 'Callimachean Models for Ovid's "Apollo-Daphne."' *Materiali e discussioni per l'analisi dei testi classici* 24 (1990): 143–56.
Wimsatt, James I. *Chaucer and His French Contemporaries: Natural Music in the Fourteenth Century*. Toronto: University of Toronto Press, 1991.
Windeatt, Barry. *Troilus and Criseyde: Oxford Guides to Chaucer*. Oxford: Clarendon Press, 1992.
Winkler, Martin M. 'Neo-Mythologism: Apollo and the Muses on the Screen.' *IJCT* 11.3 (2005): 383–423.
Wise, Valerie Merriam. 'Flight Myths in Ovid's Metamorphoses: An Interpretation of Phaethon and Daedalus.' *Ramus* 6.1 (1977): 44–59.
Wood, Chauncey. *Chaucer and the Country of the Stars: Poetic Uses of Astrological Imagery*. Princeton: Princeton University Press, 1970.
– 'Speech, the Principle of Contraries, and Chaucer's Tales of the Manciple and the Parson.' *Mediaevalia* 6 (1980): 209–29.
Wood, Michael. *The Road to Delphi: The Life and Afterlife of Oracles*. New York: Farrar, Straus and Giroux, 2003.
Yandell, Stephen. 'Prophetic Authority in Adam of Usk's *Chronicle*.' In *Prophet Margins*, ed. Risden et al., 79–100.

Zacher, Christian K. *Curiosity and Pilgrimage: The Literature of Discovery in Fourteenth-Century England*. Baltimore: Johns Hopkins University Press, 1976.

Zanker, Paul. *The Power of Images in the Age of Augustus*. Trans. Alan Shapiro. 1988. Ann Arbor: University of Michigan Press, 1990.

Zeeman, Nicolette. 'The Idol of the Text.' In *Images*, ed. Dimmick et al., 43–62.

Ziolkowski, Jan M. 'Classical Influences on Medieval Latin Views of Poetic Inspiration.' In *Latin Poetry and the Classical Tradition: Essays in Medieval and Renaissance Literature*, ed. Peter Godman and Oswyn Murray, 15–38. Oxford: Clarendon Press, 1990.

Index

Page numbers in italics refer to figures.

338 Index